QUESTIONS & ANSWERS

TO HELP YOU PASS THE REAL ESTATE EXAM

Fourth Edition

John W. Reilly

Paige Bovee Vitousek

Real Estate
Education Company
a division of Dearborn Financial Publishing, Inc.

This book is dedicated to Kristine, Sean and Jennifer,
from Paige and Dad.

92 93 94 10 9 8 7 6 5 4 3 2

Library of Congress Cataloging-in-Publication Data

Reilly, John W.
    Questions and answers to help you pass the real estate exam / John W. Reilly, Paige Bovee Vitousek.
—4th ed.

p. cm.
ISBN 0-7931-0418-1

    1. Real estate business—United States—Examinations, questions, etc. 2. Real property—United States—Examinations, questions, etc.
I. Vitousek, Paige Bovee. II. Title. III. Title: Questions and answers to help you pass the real estate exam.

HD1375.R44 1992   92–10
333.33'076—dc20   CIP

Publisher: Carol Luitjens
Acquisition Editor: Margaret M. Maloney
Development Editor: Diana Faulhaber
Cover Design: Mary Kushmir
Project Editor: Betty T. Moore

CUYAHOGA COMMUNITY COLLEGE

COURSE: REAL 171, Real Estate Financing
                 B & A Bldg., Room 209, Thurs., 7:00-10:00PM

TEXTBOOK: Essentials of Real Estate Finance
                 David Sirota, 6th Edition

INSTRUCTOR: Richard Siegel, 446-0578

GRADES:

1) Students must attend a minimum of 60% of the classes to avoid a Final Grade of F.

2) There will be a total of Three Exams. Each exam is worth 1/3 of your Final Grade.

3) A = 90-100%
   B = 80- 89%
   C = 70- 79%
   D = 60- 69%
   F = Below 60%

4) Attendance & Class Participation will be used by the Instructor in determining a borderline Final Grade (e.g. 89 = A?).

5) There are no make-up exams. If you miss an exam, regardless of the reason, the Instructor will subjectively determine your Final Grade.

SCHEDULE - FALL QUARTER, 1993

Sep. 23	Introduction
30	Chap. 1
	Chap. 2
Oct. 7	Chap. 3
14	Chap. 4
	EXAM # 1
21	Chap. 5
28	Chap. 6
	Chap. 7
Nov. 4	Chap. 8
	EXAM # 2
11	NO CLASS
18	Chap. 11
25	NO CLASS
Dec. 2	Chap. 12
9	Chap. 14
	EXAM # 3

Contents

Introduction

WHO SHOULD USE THIS BOOK

This book was designed specifically for the real estate student who wants to pass the licensing exam on the first try. We hope that person is you!

You can acquire all the necessary knowledge of basic real estate principles through the classroom, the textbook and the guidance of a skillful teacher. Even so, you may be like many examinees who still lack confidence that they are "testwise" and that they can "ace" the exam on the first attempt. *Questions and Answers* is a book of similar tests that can be used for practice, building confidence, discovering weak areas, learning how to avoid mechanical errors, and improving test-taking time.

This workbook is ideally used:

- as a supplement to the text in a basic real estate course
- by one who has completed the course yet wants to review while waiting to take the state exam
- by one not enrolled in any formal class but who needs to refresh those ideas and concepts

Whatever the reason, *Questions and Answers* enables you to approach the exam with complete confidence in your ability to pass.

Not all states use the same examination. Applied Measurement Professionals (AMP) and Psychological System, Inc. (PSI) are used in some states, while in other states exams are developed and administered under state-approved testing programs. Assessment Systems Inc. (ASI) (which purchased the entire real estate testing division of Educational Testing Service [ETS]), is used by a majority of states. The questions in this book will be equally helpful to students preparing for any type of state or school exam, since the explanatory answers give the needed information to handle any type question on any topic. These explanatory answers are the key to the effectiveness of this book.

WHY WE WROTE THIS BOOK

When one of the authors, John Reilly, a lawyer, was first entering real estate years ago, he took a real estate course from a school that also offered practice exams. He thought that he would pass these practice exams easily because he had passed two bar exams previously. He was surprised when he failed some of the school's practice exams; however, his exam techniques began to improve as he developed a feel for the exam and started to anticipate the test writer's objectives.

He then realized the vast difference between real estate knowledge and examination application. Again, the appropriate knowledge can be acquired through the classroom and books, but the best way to be test-wise is through the experience of taking similar tests.

The authors are opposed to the strict memorization of questions and answers. Therefore, do not expect to see the questions in this book repeated verbatim on any state exam; yet, chances are the exam will contain questions similar to those included in this book. For example, once you understand that a quitclaim deed gives the grantor the least exposure to liability for a title defect, you won't miss the three or four variations that could be found among different questions on a quitclaim deed.

In the course of developing this material, the authors have subjected these questions and answers to the battlefield of classroom sessions, and their validity has survived. The authors noted inadequate coverage of the question and answer approach among the many fine real estate principles textbooks. Even books that have a great many questions typically fail to give any explanation as to why the suggested answer is correct.

There is a time for theory and a time for practical application. This book will simulate the real thing.

WHAT SUBJECTS ARE COVERED

This book consists of multiple-choice questions and answers, divided into topics consistent with those subjects covered on most real estate licensing examinations. Each main topic has a series of questions followed by explanatory answers. In addition, there are appendices that cover typical state-specific licensing laws, mathematics, review exams and sample final examinations.

Testing agencies continue to make substantial changes in the format of the broker and salesperson examinations. New areas, or revisions, have been made in Real Estate Settlement Procedures Act (RESPA), federal fair housing amendments, timesharing, agency relationships and disclosure, appraisal, financing, and taxation. All of these, plus more, have been incorporated into this edition of the book.

HOW TO USE THIS BOOK

There are two approaches that you can use for the most effective study and learning. It is really a matter of individual preference as to which method is most effective.

One technique is to answer only five questions at a time. After each five questions, look up the answers, then do five more, etc. This method will build your confidence as you go along. It also gives you immediate feedback. Sometimes, if you answer large numbers of questions at a time without looking up the answers until later, you can't remember why you made the answer choice you did.

The other technique supports answering the entire exam before looking at the answers, allowing one minute per question. Many people feel this not only builds reading speed, but also allows you to compare the percentage correct with the test goal (70 to 75 percent) and dramatically increases your confidence in testing skills.

In our own experience, preparing over 20,000 students for the exam, we prefer the first method. Although it may take longer, it is "tried and true," and seems to work best for most. We all know, however, that what works for one is not necessarily the magic answer for all. We would therefore recommend using your own judgement or relying on the expertise and wisdom of your teacher.

Whichever method is used, however, we feel you should not circle your answers in the book, but rather put them on a separate piece of paper so that when you want to re-study the material, you can't see the previous answers. Likewise, if you save this paper, you can compare the results the second time around.

When you have mastered all of the chapters and appendix material, go ahead and complete the practice final examinations. Reserve enough uninterrupted time to take the final and review exams under simulated testing conditions.

For Those in a Hurry

If you find yourself with this book in hand and relatively little time in which to prepare, or if you feel you already are prepared, we suggest you first take the review quizzes and practice final examinations in the back of the book. If you miss questions on a specific topic, concentrate your remaining time on those particular areas of the book.

We have also included "speed questions" (designated ❖), which are specific questions for those in a hurry that convey the essential points in each chapter. Do these as a minimum. If you have the time later, go back and complete the remaining questions that expand on an essential point.

TEST-TAKING TIPS

Here are some test-taking techniques to keep in mind when taking the practice final.

1. Take the test in a quiet place, with no telephones or outside distractions. Allow yourself three hours for test and review.
2. Never leave a question blank; after narrowing down your choices, take an educated guess.
3. Choose the best answer; there may be more than one alternative that is partially correct.
4. First impressions are generally correct if the question is read carefully. Therefore, as a general rule, *don't change your answers.* If, however, you discover you have misread the question, or that a later question has "triggered-off" your memory so that you now understand what is being sought, only then should an answer be changed.

5. Don't look for trick questions; you may out-smart yourself. If the question is concerned with the exception to a general rule, then specific data will be keyed to that exception. When in doubt, remember the exam tests for only the minimal level of competency to enter the field of real estate.

6. After taking a test, check your results. Don't just evaluate those questions answered incorrectly, but go over *all* answers. Understanding *why* an answer was correct, and *why* the other choices were *not* correct is the key to mastery and success.

By using this book in the preceding manner, you will acquire an instinct for the actual examination. You will gain confidence by experiencing similar problems. You will have learned how to take the test and how to pass it.

For the actual exam, we offer a few final suggestions.

1. Do not eat a heavy meal either the night before or the morning of the exam.

2. Don't pay attention to other test candidates, as they may be nervous, anxious or unprepared. Have confidence that your knowledge is unique and that you are prepared and will pass.

3. Take occasional short breaks. Look up from your paper, stretch your arms and legs, take a few deep breaths and rest for a minute.

4. As you work through the exam, answer the easy questions first. You may find clues in later questions helping you with the more difficult ones. Be sure, however, you mark in the exam booklet the question you have skipped.

5. Many people prefer working out all the math questions at the same time, thus keeping their mind focused on numerical terms and concepts. If using a calculator, be sure to take extra batteries.

ACKNOWLEDGMENTS

The authors express their gratitude to all those who contributed to the development of this edition of *Questions and Answers*.

In particular, we wish to thank:
Mark Barker, DREI, Career Education Systems, Prairie Village, Kansas; Marta Saint-James, Western Wayne Oakland County Association of REALTORS®, Farmington, Michigan; Robert L. Borkowicz, Wright College, Chicago, Illinois; Ben Simon, Berks Real Estate Institute, Reading, Pennsylvania; Mary Coveny, CareerMatch Consultants, Inc., Schaumburg, Illinois; and Diane F. McDonald, DREI, Real Estate Career Trainers, Williamantic, Connecticut.

ABOUT THE AUTHORS

Paige Bovee Vitousek, DREI, is an author, lecturer, and instructor of real estate principles and practices, and president/owner for over 21 years of Hawaii's largest real estate school. She is an active real estate broker, and a Graduate, REALTORS® Institute. She is the first educator in Hawaii to receive the prestigious Designated Real Estate Instructor (DREI) award from the Real Estate Educators Association. She has also authored *Principles and Practices of Hawaiian Real Estate,* a textbook geared to practice in her home state.

John W. Reilly, DREI, is a real estate educator and an attorney currently practicing in Honolulu. He is a member of the New York, California, Hawaii, and federal bars as well as a REALTOR®. He is a law school professor, a lecturer, and a licensed real estate instructor for both salesperson and broker prelicense courses. He is past president of the Real Estate Educators Association and recipient of their 1988 Real Estate Educator of the Year Award. He is a nationally recognized expert in the techniques of preparing students for the real estate licensing examination. Mr. Reilly is also the author of several leading reference works, most notably, *The Language of Real Estate* and *Agency Relationships in Real Estate.*

PART A Real Property and Laws Relating to Ownership

This part contains questions on the topics of

- The legal concepts of real property
- Ways title to property may be held
- Methods to legally describe property
- The role of encumbrances, easements and restrictions on property ownership
- The government's rights and restrictive powers
- Aspects of condominium and cooperative ownership

Expect about 20 percent of the general portion of the examination to contain questions on the topics covered in Part A.

Chapter 1 Forms of Ownership

Questions in this chapter will test your comprehension of the following topics:

- Differences between the various ways to hold title to real property (e.g., tenancy in common, joint tenancy, tenancy by the entirety, severalty)
- Other forms of ownership: corporate, time share, limited partnership
- Ways in which a tenancy can be terminated
- Who should advise the buyer on how to hold title

The "Methods of Ownership" chart summarizes the differences in tenancy types that you studied in your prelicense course.

METHODS OF OWNERSHIP

	Tenancy in Severalty	Tenancy in Common	Joint Tenancy	Tenancy by Entireties
DEFINITION	Property held by one person, severed from all others.	Property held by 2 or more persons with no right of survivorship.	Property held by 2 or more individuals (not corporation), with right of survivorship.	Property held by husband and wife with right of survivorship.
CREATION	Any transfer to one person.	By express act; also by failure to express the tenancy.	Express intention plus 4 unities of time, title, interest and possession (with statutory exception).	Express intention, only husband & wife. Divorce automatically results in tenancy in common.
POSSESSION	Total.	Equal right of possession.	Equal right of possession.	Equal right of possession.
TITLE	One title in one person.	Each co-owner has a separate legal title to his undivided interest; will be equal interests unless expressly made unequal.	One title to the whole property since each tenant is theoretically deemed owner of whole; must be equal undivided interests.	One title in the marital unit.
CONVEYANCE	No restrictions (check release of marital rights if any).	Each co-owner's interest may be conveyed separately by its owner; purchaser becomes tenant in common.	Conveyance of 1 co-owner's interest breaks his tenancy; purchaser becomes tenant in common.	Cannot convey without consent of spouse.
EFFECT OF DEATH	Entire property subject to probate & included in gross estate for federal & state death taxes.	Decedent's fractional interest subject to probate & included in gross estate for federal & state death taxes. The property passes by will to devisees or heirs, who take as tenants in common. No survivorship rights.	No probate & can't be disposed of by will; property automatically belongs to surviving co-tenants (last one holds in severalty). Entire property included in decedent's gross estate for federal estate tax purposes, minus % attributable to survivor's contribution, i.e., the net value.	Right of survivorship so no probate. Same death taxes as joint tenancy.
CREDITOR'S RIGHTS	Subject to creditor claims.	Co-owner's fractional interest may be sold to satisfy his creditor. Buyer becomes tenant in common.	Joint tenant's interest also subject to execution sale, joint tenancy is broken & purchaser becomes tenant in common. Creditor gets nothing if debtor tenant dies before sale.	Only a creditor of both spouses can execute on property.
PRESUMED BY LAW	None.	Favored in doubtful cases; presumed to be equal interests.	Not favored so must be expressly stated.	Must be expressly stated.

QUESTIONS

1. Only a husband and wife may hold title to real property as:
   (A) joint tenants.
   (B) tenants by the entirety.
   (C) tenants in common.
   (D) tenants by the severalty.

❖ 2. One of the advantages of a joint tenancy is that:
   (A) it cannot be terminated without the consent of each tenant.
   (B) it can be held in different fractional shares.
   (C) it avoids the delays and expenses of probate.
   (D) it can only exist between husband and wife.

3. Which of the following events would create a tenancy in common?
   (A) Transfer of one joint tenant's interest to a third party
   (B) Death of one of two joint tenants
   (C) Transfer of one joint tenant's interest to the other joint tenant
   (D) Death of one of four joint tenants

4. A tenant in common may transfer his or her interest under which of the following circumstances?
   (A) Only with the permission and approval of the other tenants in common
   (B) At any time, without permission or approval, even under protest
   (C) Only at the expiration of the lease
   (D) Only for a valuable consideration

❖ 5. A woman and her brother hold property in joint tenancy. What results if the woman deeded her part to herself and her husband?
   (A) The deed to the husband is invalid.
   (B) The joint tenancy is severed.
   (C) All three now hold title in joint tenancy.
   (D) The joint tenancy remains the same.

6. A property is purchased by a brother and sister with equal shares. This could be:
   (A) a tenancy by the entirety.
   (B) a joint tenancy.
   (C) a tenancy in community.
   (D) a tenancy in severalty.

7. Two sisters, F and M, inherit real property from their mother with no stipulation except that one-third is to go to F and two-thirds to M. Which of the following is true?
   (A) F and M are joint tenants of the property.
   (B) M may not mortgage her interest in the property without F's consent.
   (C) Upon F's death, her part of the property reverts to M.
   (D) Upon M's death, her share passes to her heirs or devisees.

8. If title to a farm is held in tenancy by the entirety, which of the following is true?
   (A) A specifically enforceable contract to sell the farm must be signed by husband and wife.
   (B) A creditor of one spouse can assert a valid lien on the farm.
   (C) Either husband or wife may partition the property.
   (D) The shares may be unequal.

❖ 9. When purchasing real estate, the form or method of ownership (severalty, tenants in common, joint tenants) should **BEST** be determined by:
   (A) a broker.
   (B) a buyer and attorney.
   (C) a seller and CPA.
   (D) a salesperson.

10. T and S take title to a farm as joint tenants. Assuming S dies, which of the following is true?
   (A) T holds title with S's heirs.
   (B) T holds title to the whole farm subject to the marital interest of S's surviving husband.
   (C) The farm may be sold to satisfy S's creditors.
   (D) T is the sole owner of the property.

11. In a joint tenancy among five people, all of the following are true **EXCEPT**:
   (A) Shares must be equal.
   (B) Any party may convey his or her share without consent of the others.
   (C) Any of the five parties may will away their share.
   (D) One of the owners may sell to another, who now owns a one-fifth tenancy in common.

12. A joint tenancy may accomplish all of the following **EXCEPT:**
    (A) sell the interest.
    (B) give away the interest.
    (C) encumber the interest.
    (D) devise the interest.

13. Tenancy in common is most directly related to which of the following?
    (A) Survivorship
    (B) Ownership
    (C) Probate
    (D) Partition

❖ 14. An action brought by a co-owner of property to compel the severance of respective interests is an action for:
    (A) foreclosure.
    (B) quiet title.
    (C) forfeiture.
    (D) partition.

15. A tenancy in common must have the unity of:
    (A) time.
    (B) title.
    (C) interest.
    (D) possession.

❖ 16. When someone owns property to the exclusion of all other persons, this person is said to hold the property in:
    (A) personalty.
    (B) common.
    (C) severalty.
    (D) secret.

17. In the case of three tenants in common owning a property, which of the following is true?
    (A) A tenant's estate ends upon his or her death.
    (B) There is just one title to the property representing the undivided interests of all cotenants.
    (C) Each tenant has a separate and distinct interest.
    (D) The last surviving tenant would hold title in severalty.

18. A tenant in common can do which of the following?
    (A) Encumber the whole property
    (B) Convey any part of the property so as to bind the interest of another tenant in common.
    (C) Sell the entire property
    (D) Own two-thirds of the property

19. A husband and wife contact a broker about selling their home. The wife has a number of outstanding debts. Which is true of this property held as tenancy by the entirety?
    (A) The listing broker should get both husband and wife to sign the listing.
    (B) The wife's creditors have a right to take one-half of the property in settlement of the debts.
    (C) The property should not be sold until the debts have been paid.
    (D) The debts of both spouses are of no importance to the broker listing the property.

20. Which of the following statements apply equally to two joint tenants and to tenants by the entirety?
    (A) There can be no right to file a partition suit.
    (B) The last living tenant becomes sole owner.
    (C) A deed signed by one party will convey a fractional interest.
    (D) A deed will not convey any interest unless signed by both spouses.

21. Where two cousins hold title to property, one having one-third interest and the other having two-thirds interest, title would be held in:
    (A) joint tenancy.
    (B) tenancy by the entirety.
    (C) tenancy in common.
    (D) tenancy in severalty.

22. A conveys property to B and C who are unrelated and not joint tenants. When B dies, what most likely happens to ownership of the property?
    (A) C is the sole owner.
    (B) B's share goes to his heirs.
    (C) Property reverts back to A.
    (D) B's share escheats to the state.

❖ 23. All of the following tenancies would permit partition if the husband and wife cannot agree on the sale of the property **EXCEPT:**
    (A) joint tenancy.
    (B) tenancy by the entirety.
    (C) tenancy in common.
    (D) tenancy in partnership.

24. Which is true regarding the liability of a limited partner?
    (A) Liability is to the extent of his or her investment.
    (B) Liability is without limits.
    (C) Liability is limited to short-term debts of the partnership.
    (D) Personal liability is limited to a stated percentage of partnership debts.

25. When two or more owners have concurrent, unequal interests in the same property, they hold title as:
    (A) joint tenants.
    (B) tenants in common.
    (C) tenants by the entirety.
    (D) tenants for years.

26. The four unities of title, time, interest and possession normally would be found in which of the following?
    (A) Tenancy in common
    (B) Partnership
    (C) Mortgage or trust deed
    (D) Joint tenancy

27. A corporation cannot hold title to real property with an individual as joint tenants because:
    (A) it is in violation of the securities act.
    (B) a corporation has perpetual existence.
    (C) it is difficult to list all stockholders in the deed.
    (D) a corporation cannot convey title to real property.

28. A, B and C own property as joint tenants. C dies, then B sells his interest in the property to D. The property is now owned:
    (A) by A, D, and C's widow and E (his sole heir) as joint tenants.
    (B) by A and D as joint tenants.
    (C) by A and D as tenants in common, each with one-half interest.
    (D) by A, D and B's wife.

29. The **BEST** term that describes a group of investors who pool their financial resources to acquire real property is:
    (A) rental pool.   (C) consolidation.
    (B) syndication.   (D) assemblage.

❖ 30. Which is usually true under commonly accepted principles of tenancy law?
    (A) Unless otherwise specified, a conveyance of property to a man and woman is automatically construed as a "tenancy by the entirety."
    (B) Tenancy by the entirety is characterized by a right of survivorship, which may be severed only by divorce or by joint conveyance of the husband and wife.
    (C) A joint tenancy may be created by operation of law rather than by intent of the parties.
    (D) Tenants by the entirety may will away their separate halves of the property.

❖ 31. C, B and S are tenants in common. If B dies:
    (A) C's share in the property is unaffected.
    (B) B's interest goes to C.
    (C) B's interest goes to C and S.
    (D) B's interest automatically goes to her surviving spouse.

32. The right of survivorship is a feature of which of the following types of tenancy?
    (A) Joint tenancy
    (B) Tenancy in common
    (C) Tenancy in severalty
    (D) Tenancy for years

33. One of the distinguishing characteristics of joint tenancy is that:
    (A) tenants possess separate estates.
    (B) tenants may possess unequal interests in a single estate.
    (C) interests of a deceased tenant pass to the remaining tenants.
    (D) interests of a deceased tenant pass to heirs rather than to the other tenants.

❖ 34. Which of the following methods of ownership could result in a double-income taxation?
    (A) Joint tenancy   (C) Corporation
    (B) Common tenancy   (D) Partnership

❖ 35. A joint tenant in real property who wishes to dispose of the interest:
    (A) may not file for partition.
    (B) has no recourse except to sell the interest to other joint tenants.
    (C) may convey to a nontenant who becomes a tenant in common.
    (D) has no recourse except to buy out the other joint tenants.

❖ **36.** When owners of a tenancy by the entirety are divorced, they:
- (A) become tenants in common.
- (B) become tenants at sufferance.
- (C) remain tenants by entireties.
- (D) automatically become joint tenants with right of survivorship.

37. All of the following are in harmony with joint tenancy ownership **EXCEPT**:
- (A) probate.
- (B) survivorship.
- (C) undivided interest.
- (D) equal shares.

❖ **38.** A buyer is thinking of purchasing an interest in a resort condominium that would guarantee possession of a specific two-bedroom unit for March of every year. Which of the following forms of ownership might a broker recommend?
- (A) Time-sharing
- (B) Corporate
- (C) Cooperative
- (D) Syndication

39. If *B* and *C* are partners in a business and invested in a parcel of real estate as tenants in common, which of the following would be true about the investment?
- (A) They must have equal interests.
- (B) They must have unity of time.
- (C) They would have to sell at the same time.
- (D) They both have equal rights of possession.

40. Which of the following **BEST** describes a tenancy in severalty?
- (A) Property held by several people with right of survivorship
- (B) Property held by a corporation and a partnership together
- (C) Property held by several people whose interest passes to their respective heirs
- (D) Property held by one person, whose ownership rights are severed from all others

41. Broker helped the *M*'s prepare an offer to purchase a three-bedroom home. The *M*'s asked broker whether they should hold title as joint tenants. Broker should advise them to:
- (A) take title as tenants by the entirety.
- (B) consult a title company.
- (C) take title as tenants in common.
- (D) consult an attorney.

42. In a will, *A* left a farm to a daughter and a brother—the daughter to take three-quarters interest and the brother one-quarter interest. *A* stated that there would be "a right of survivorship between them." How will they hold title?
- (A) As joint tenants
- (B) As tenants in common
- (C) As tenants by the entirety
- (D) As tenants in severalty

43. A testator prepared a will leaving his farm to his wife and daughter, the wife to have a two-thirds interest and the daughter a one-third. Title would be held as:
- (A) tenants by the entirety.
- (B) joint tenants.
- (C) tenants in severalty.
- (D) tenants in common.

44. A mother and son could hold property in which manner?
- (A) Tenants by the entirety
- (B) Community property
- (C) Joint tenants
- (D) Tenancy in severalty

❖ **45.** *C* and *S* own a farm as joint tenants. Which of the following statements is true?
- (A) *S*'s wife has a dower interest in the property.
- (B) *C* can transfer his interest in the property by will.
- (C) Upon *S*'s death his interest will pass to his widow.
- (D) *C* can sell his half interest in the farm without *S*'s consent.

❖ **46.** Your client plans to get divorced shortly before closing of a property she and her boyfriend just purchased and asks you about how to hold title to the property. You should suggest she:
- (A) get divorced first.
- (B) conceal the pending divorce.
- (C) consult an attorney.
- (D) choose joint tenancy.

47. When a person who owns real estate in severalty dies testate, the property:
- (A) goes entirely to the surviving joint tenant.
- (B) is probated and distributed according to the will.
- (C) is solely vested in the remaining tenant in common.
- (D) reverts to the county be escheat.

48. Assume a real estate broker incorporates his or her real estate firm. Which is true?
    (A) The firm is a separate legal entity, distinct from the broker.
    (B) The broker is liable for the debts of the corporation.
    (C) The broker can advertise solely in his or her individual name.
    (D) The shareholders must have real estate licenses.

49. In what way is tenancy by the entirety different from joint tenancy for a husband and wife?
    (A) Right of survivorship
    (B) Equal undivided interest
    (C) Creditors of both can claim the property
    (D) One spouse can sell only with the other's consent.

ANSWERS

1. **B** The marital unit actually owns the property. Husband and wife could also hold title as (A), (C) or (D) in severalty if each holds different property separately. Tenancy by the entirety exists in a minority of states.

2. **C** There is no interest left in the deceased joint tenant's estate, so there is nothing to probate. A joint tenancy can be severed by transfer of one tenant's interest. Shares must be equal, and anyone but a corporation can be a joint tenant. Consent from all is needed to sell the property, not an interest.

3. **A** The third party would be a tenant in common with the remaining joint tenants. The original tenancy would be severed. In (D), the three remaining owners would still be joint tenants as to each other.

4. **B** To avoid this result, some cotenants enter into a right of first refusal agreement whereby any sale would have to be offered first to the other cotenants. Choice (D) is wrong because there could be a gift of a tenancy in common interest as well as a sale.

5. **B** The joint tenancy is severed upon the transfer, with the brother owning one-half undivided interest and the husband and wife owning the other half, which could be held as tenancy by the entirety, joint tenancy or tenancy in common. They are tenants in common as to their respective half interests.

6. **B** Only husband and wife can be tenants by the entirety. It could also be a tenancy in common, but this is not one of the choices.

7. **D** There is no right of survivorship with tenancy in common. In a joint tenancy, the shares must be equal. Just as tenants in common can transfer their interest, they can also mortgage it, although most lenders do not prefer to hold a joint tenancy type of security.

8. **A** If only one spouse had signed such a contract, then the buyer could not obtain specific performance against the nonsigning spouse. The creditor must be a creditor of the "marital unit," which explains why lenders often insist on both spouses signing loan agreements or mortgages.

9. **B** Such a determination would involve the practice of law, especially because there are important estate tax ramifications. A broker should be able to describe the difference among the various types of tenancies; however, he or she should not make a recommendation or the ultimate decision.

10. **D** Joint tenants hold the property free from claims of dower or curtesy of spouses, free from claims of creditors or heirs of a deceased joint tenant and free from the laws of descent.

11. **C** As to choice (D), if No. 1 conveyed a one-fifth share to No. 6, then Nos. 2, 3, 4 and 5 would be joint tenants as to each other, with a total four-fifths undivided interest, while No. 6 would be a tenant in common with a one-fifth undivided interest. A will is ineffective to transfer a joint tenant's interest because the interest ceases at death of the joint tenant and passes to the surviving joint tenants.

12. **D** There is no property left to transfer by will (devise) because the remaining joint tenant(s) have survived to the decedent's interest.

13. **B** Tenancy in common is a popular form of ownership. It is joint tenancy that deals with survivorship.

14. **D** If the cotenants cannot reach an agreement on splitting the property, then any one tenant can petition the court to partition the property. They can try to physically divide the property (partition in kind) or else sell it and split the net proceeds. Most courts first attempt a partition in kind, but this is sometimes impossible—for example, in the case of a studio condominium property.

15. **D** Although a joint tenancy traditionally requires all of these four unities, each tenant in common has only an undivided interest to possess the whole. Thus, in a tenancy in common involving two people, each person would own a 50 percent interest in 100 percent of the property.

16. **C** This person's ownership is severed from that of anyone else. Personalty (A) is another word for personal property.

17. **C** Unlike joint tenancy, each cotenant has an undivided interest. There is no right, however, to possess any specific portion of the property. (A), (B), and (D) refer to joint tenancy.

18. **D** Choices (A), (B) and (C) require the consent of all cotenants.

19. **A** Many courts would still enforce a listing against the sole signing spouse (meaning the one signing could be liable for a commission), but it is best to get both to sign. Both spouses must owe the creditor for the possibility of executing against the home to exist (there may be a different result if they are joint tenants).

20. **B** (A) and (D) are true in a tenancy by the entirety. (D) is false as it relates to joint tenancy. (C) is true as it relates to a joint tenancy. (A) is false regarding joint tenancy.

21. **C** The key to this question is the unequal shares.

22. **B** *B* and *C* are tenants in common. The interest of the deceased tenant in common passes to his heirs.

23. **B** The marital unit owns the property in tenancy by the entirety, so one spouse cannot seek partition.

24. **A** A general partner usually is liable for all the debts of the partnership. A limited partner loses limited liability if he or she participates in the management of the partnership.

25. **B** The unequal interests indicate there is a tenancy in common.

26. **D** Many state statutes have relaxed the traditional rules of these four unities and thus allow one person to transfer title to oneself and another as joint tenants or to use a nominee.

27. **B** Corporations have perpetual existence unless dissolved, so the corporation would always be the surviving joint tenant.

28. **C** *A* and *D* are not joint tenants because they have separate titles created at different times. *A* and *B* were fifty-fifty joint tenants after *C*'s death and then *D* bought *B*'s interest; this severed the joint tenancy.

29. **B** The word *syndication* refers to a group of people united for the purpose of making and operating an investment. It may take the form of a limited partnership or a general partnership. A rental pool (A) refers to an arrangement whereby participating owners of rental apartments agree to make their apartments available for rental and share in the profits and losses according to an agreed-upon formula.

30. **B** In most states, a tenancy involving survivorship must be created by clear and definite words. Otherwise, it will be construed as a tenancy in common. In a few states, however, the mere conveyance to husband and wife is automatically a tenancy by the entirety.

31. **A** *B*'s interest goes to her heirs.

32. **A**   Tenant-in-common interests pass to the heirs or will beneficiaries rather than to the surviving tenant in common.

33. **C**   This is the right of survivorship.

34. **C**   A corporation is subject to tax on its profits, and the stockholders will be taxed again on any dividends.

35. **C**   Joint tenancies may be severed by transfer of one's interest in the property. In some cases, the parties agree to give their cotenants a right of first refusal.

36. **A**   Since the marital unit is ended, the tenancy by entirety also ends. Often there is a property settlement agreement resolving who gets the property, or the owners may elect to form a joint tenancy or a tenancy in common. Otherwise, by operation of law, it is held in tenancy in common.

37. **A**   An attractive feature of joint tenancy ownership is that it avoids the delay and expense of probate. Contrary to popular belief, however, it does not avoid the payment of death taxes by the estate of the deceased joint tenant.

38. **A**   Time-sharing is a recent development in communal living. Different people purchase the right to use a piece of real property (typically a condominium unit) for a set period each year for a definite or indefinite period of years. The different owners could be tenants in common (called time-interval ownership), members of a special club or lessees under a vacation lease plan.

39. **D**   Tenants in common can have different interests and need not acquire the property at the same time or from the same deed. The only unity required is that of possession—an undivided interest to possess the entire parcel.

40. **D**   Tenancy in severalty is ownership of property severed from anyone else's ownership. Choice (B) would describe a tenancy in common. (Corporations can't hold title as joint tenants.)

41. **D**   Brokers should not determine the best tenancy for those with whom they deal. Because of the important tax and estate implications of such a selection, and attorney should be consulted. Title companies insure good title; they don't advise how to select the method of holding title.

42. **B**   A may have wanted to create a joint tenancy, but joint tenants must have equal shares. The law favors tenancy in common, so the courts in this case would keep the shares at three-quarters and one-quarter, but eliminate the right of survivorship.

43. **D**   Devisees under a will frequently obtain title to the deceased's real property as tenants in common. Because the interests are unequal, they cannot be joint tenants. Only husband and wife can be tenants by the entirety.

44. **C**   Choices (A) and (B) are forms of ownership requiring the parties to be husband and wife.

45. **D**   Dower does not apply to joint-tenancy property. There is no property left in the estate to pass by will since the remaining joint tenants survive to the interest of the deceased joint tenant.

46. **C**   The client can be best served by having an experienced real estate attorney discuss the best type of tenancy based on the pending divorce.

47. **B**   A tenant in severalty is the sole owner of the property; and if he or she dies leaving a will (testate), the property passes according to the terms of the probated will.

48. **A**   The corporation is a separate legal entity under state law. Usually, only the principal broker needs a broker license.

49. **D**   One joint tenant spouse can sever the joint tenancy, whereas only the marriage can sell tenancy by entirety property.

Chapter 2   Interests in Real Property

Questions in this chapter will test your comprehension of the following topics:

- Estates and interests in real property such as fee simple and life estates
- The difference between fixtures and personal property
- The effect of riparian rights on ownership
- The creation of interests in real property under a last will and testament

Although a row of houses in a neighborhood might all look the same, each property is unique. The real estate agent needs to understand what bundle of rights attach to the property. A title report will often provide helpful information on the interests involved.

False Friends

The following words are often confused with one another. Note the difference in meaning of these false friends.

Remainder/Reversion: At the termination of the life estate, the property may revert back to the grantor or remain away from the grantor if a remainderman is designated.

Executor/Testator: A Testator writes a will, whereas the Executor (also called a personal representative) carries out the terms of the will.

Devise/Demise: A devise is a transfer of real property by will; a demise is a transfer by lease of the (demised) premises.

Testate/Intestate: To die with a will is to die testate; without one is to die intestate (in which case the state writes the will).

QUESTIONS

1. When a deed does not specify the estate being conveyed, it is presumed to transfer:
   (A) a defeasible fee.
   (B) a fee simple absolute.
   (C) an estate for years.
   (D) a life estate.

❖ 2. One is seized of property when he or she is:
   (A) the lawful owner.
   (B) a trespasser.
   (C) in possession of property under a lease.
   (D) fulfilling the required period for adverse possession.

3. If A deeds property to B and her heirs, with the stipulation that if B leaves no heirs the property will then go to C, then C now holds which type of estate?
   (A) Contingent life estate
   (B) Contingent reversion fee
   (C) Contingent remainder fee
   (D) Reversionary interest

4. In a deed that states "to A for his life," the grantor has what type of interest?
   (A) Life estate   (C) Reversion
   (B) Remainder   (D) Right of reentry

5. A life estate may be granted:
   (A) only when it is for the duration of the grantee's life.
   (B) for the duration of the life of someone other than the grantee.
   (C) for a definite term.
   (D) only to a grantee over the age of majority.

6. A freehold could be any of the following EXCEPT:
   (A) a life estate.
   (B) a fee simple estate.
   (C) an estate for years.
   (D) a defeasible fee estate.

7. Fee simple is all of the following EXCEPT:
   (A) an estate of inheritance.
   (B) a freehold estate.
   (C) a less than freehold estate.
   (D) indefinite as to its duration.

❖ 8. A hospital receives a gift of real property from an elderly couple who reserve to themselves a life estate. The hospital is which of the following?
   (A) Grantor
   (B) Remainderman
   (C) Reversionary party
   (D) Donor

9. An owner of a life estate can do all of the following EXCEPT:
   (A) sell.   (C) devise.
   (B) mortgage.   (D) lease.

10. A widow who is willed the use of the family home for the rest of her natural life, with provision that title shall to the children upon her death, holds:
   (A) a fee simple estate.   (C) an easement.
   (B) a leasehold.   (D) a life estate.

11. Which of the following is correct regarding a life estate?
   (A) It must be measured by the life of one person only.
   (B) Because it is based on life, it may not be encumbered by the holder.
   (C) It may be created by will or deed.
   (D) It requires that the holder make principal payments on any encumbrances.

12. The degree, quantity or nature of a person's interest in real property is known as his or her:
   (A) estate.   (C) curtesy,
   (B) dower.   (D) possession.

❖ 13. The return of land to the grantor or grantor's heirs when the grant is over is BEST described as:
   (A) remainder.   (C) kickback.
   (B) reversion.   (D) surrender.

14. An estate in land vested in a grantee "until he or she marries" is properly classifiable as:
   (A) an estate in equity.
   (B) a defeasible fee.
   (C) less than a freehold estate.
   (D) a life estate.

❖ 15. An example of a less-than-freehold estate is:
   (A) a life estate.
   (B) a leasehold estate.
   (C) an estate on condition subsequent.
   (D) a mortgaged estate.

16. With respect to real property, the term "estate" is **BEST** described as:
    (A) all property left by the deceased.
    (B) a bequest of a specific property in a will
    (C) fee simple ownership of property
    (D) the nature and degree of an interest in real property

❖ 17. Which of the following provides the greatest assurance that you are getting fee simple ownership?
    (A) The owner will give a general warranty deed.
    (B) The owner can furnish title insurance.
    (C) The deed contains the covenant of seisin.
    (D) The habendum clause states that a fee estate is what is being conveyed.

❖ 18. The interest in real property with the **LEAST** bundle of rights is:
    (A) tenancy at will.
    (B) fee simple absolute.
    (C) fee simple subject to condition subsequent.
    (D) tenancy at sufferance.

19. All of the following are characteristics of a fee simple estate **EXCEPT**:
    (A) freely transferable.
    (B) freely inheritable.
    (C) definite duration.
    (D) unlimited duration.

20. An estate for life that a husband takes at the death of his wife in one-third of those lands of which she was seized at the time of her death is called:
    (A) fee simple estate.
    (B) dower.
    (C) curtesy.
    (D) estate in remainder.

21. If *H* possessed a fee simple estate, he could do any of the following to the property **EXCEPT**:
    (A) sell it.
    (B) subdivide it.
    (C) use it contrary to zoning regulations.
    (D) will it.

22. An estate for years in real estate can also be called:
    (A) a leasehold.
    (B) a fee simple conditional.
    (C) a fee.
    (D) a joint tenancy.

❖ 23. Of the following, the largest estate or ownership in real property is:
    (A) estate at sufferance.
    (B) estate at will.
    (C) life estate.
    (D) fee simple estate.

24. The holder of all of the following would be a "freeholder" **EXCEPT**:
    (A) life estate.
    (B) defeasible fee.
    (C) unrecorded vendor's deed.
    (D) estate for years.

25. The grantor of a life estate can do all of the following **EXCEPT**:
    (A) grant title using an assumed name.
    (B) receive the title upon the death of the life tenant.
    (C) take back fee title at any time.
    (D) create a life estate for the life of more than one person.

❖ 26. A licensee is concerned about a construction project going on next to a property he or she is selling. Where would he or she be best advised to go to clarify any question about an encroachment?
    (A) City attorney
    (B) Planning department
    (C) Licensed surveyor
    (D) Tax office records

27. With what type of estate is the phrase "of indefinite duration" **MOST** usually associated?
    (A) Estate of inheritance
    (B) Tenancy at sufferance
    (C) Leasehold estate
    (D) Estate for years

28. The phrase "chattel real" refers specifically to:
    (A) a leasehold interest.
    (B) secured property.
    (C) the sovereign's personal property.
    (D) the mortgagor's interest in realty.

❖ 29. An example of personal property is:
    (A) household furnishings.
    (B) wall-to-wall carpeting.
    (C) built-in dishwasher.
    (D) garbage disposal.

30. All of the following terms apply to real property **EXCEPT**:
    (A) chattel mortgage.   (C) fixture.
    (B) fee simple.   (D) appurtenances.

❖ 31. Which of the following is typically personal property?
    (A) Gas and mineral rights
    (B) Water rights
    (C) A beneficiary's rights under a real property trust
    (D) Trees on a farm

❖ 32. Personal property is usually defined as "all property **NOT** classified as real property." Which of the following best defines real property?
    (A) Land and the air above it
    (B) Land and the area below and above the surface to infinity and all the improvements thereon
    (C) The land, buildings thereon and anything permanently affixed to the land and/or buildings
    (D) Land and the mineral rights in the land

33. Gas stoves and electric refrigerators are generally:
    (A) not considered fixtures in the sale of rental apartment buildings.
    (B) considered fixtures in private homes and would go automatically to the buyer.
    (C) included in the sale of an apartment rental building.
    (D) deemed to be real property.

34. Generally, things or objects of a temporary or easily movable nature are:
    (A) realty.   (C) personalty.
    (B) devises.   (D) appurtenances.

❖ 35. Assume the contract for the sale of real property includes the sale of certain removable items, such as paintings and furniture. Upon delivery of the deed, the seller should also deliver a(n):
    (A) bill of sale.
    (B) estoppel certificate.
    (C) chattel mortgage.
    (D) satisfaction piece.

36. Each of the following is an appurtenance **EXCEPT**:
    (A) barn.   (C) fence.
    (B) orchard.   (D) trade fixture.

❖ 37. The most important factor in determining whether something is a fixture is:
    (A) the method of its attachment.
    (B) its size.
    (C) its weight.
    (D) the intention of the party who attached it.

38. All of the following are required for a valid bill of sale **EXCEPT**:
    (A) signature of the seller.
    (B) description of the items.
    (C) date of transaction.
    (D) name of buyer.

39. Which of the following **BEST** describes personal property?
    (A) Chattel   (C) Fixture
    (B) Appurtenance   (D) Improvement

40. "Littoral" property is located:
    (A) on a hillside.
    (B) on the seashore.
    (C) on the boundary line.
    (D) on a stream.

41. All of the following are synonymous with land and improvements and rights therein **EXCEPT**:
    (A) real estate.   (C) Realtist.
    (B) real property.   (D) realty.

42. In real estate, the term "improvements" most nearly means:
    (A) fences, wells, drains and roadways.
    (B) additions to the original structure.
    (C) everything artificial or constructed except the land.
    (D) upgrades to the interior.

43. The rights of ownership, including the right to use, possess, enjoy and dispose of a thing in any legal way as to exclude everyone else without rights from interfering, is called:
    (A) corporeal ownership.
    (B) incorporeal ownership.
    (C) bundle of rights.
    (D) survivorship.

❖ 44. An appropriation of land for some public use made by the owner and accepted for such use by or on behalf of the public, such as streets in a platted subdivision, is called:
    (A) easement.   (C) public grant.
    (B) dedication.   (D) condemnation.

45. An owner of real property is in doubt whether or not riparian rights are included. This can best be determined by reviewing:
    (A) the water department records of the county recorder.
    (B) the title policy.
    (C) the grant deed.
    (D) the appropriate state law.

46. The boundary of your property line is changed by:
    (A) accretion.
    (B) avulsion.
    (C) encroachments.
    (D) construction of a fence.

❖ 47. A riparian owner is one who owns land bounding on:
    (A) municipal property.
    (B) a waterway.
    (C) a national forest.
    (D) unsurveyed public lands.

48. In a physical sense, real estate may be said to include everything **EXCEPT**:
    (A) the surface of the earth.
    (B) the air above the surface.
    (C) personal property.
    (D) the subsurfaces.

49. A trait that distinguishes real property from personal property is that real property:
    (A) can be mortgaged.
    (B) is considered permanent, fixed and immovable.
    (C) can be freely transferred.
    (D) is always taxed at a higher rate.

50. Riparian rights are those rights possessed by:
    (A) an owner living in a townhouse sub-division.
    (B) an owner living on a waterway.
    (C) an owner entitled to ripened fruit from crops.
    (D) owners of land granting easements for city water pipes.

51. The removal of land when a stream suddenly changes its channel is:
    (A) adverse possession.
    (B) breach.
    (C) avulsion.
    (D) accretion.

❖ 52. When a landowner sells his or her one-acre farm, he or she must:
    (A) specifically reserve the mineral rights therein, or they will automatically pass to the buyer.
    (B) specifically describe the air rights in the deed for the buyer to gain title thereto.
    (C) sign a quitclaim deed to release air rights.
    (D) release any riparian rights.

53. Father deeds a life estate in the farm to his son G. G sells this interest to H. What happens to the farm when H dies?
    (A) It goes back to G.
    (B) It goes to the father.
    (C) It goes to H's heirs.
    (D) It goes to the state.

54. The loss of one's real estate by the gradual wearing away of soil through the operation of natural causes is:
    (A) erosion.   (C) curtilage.
    (B) escheat.   (D) obsolescence.

55. An important characteristic of land is that it may be modified or improved. Such improvements tend to increase the value of real estate. All of the following are improvements **EXCEPT**:
    (A) a new access road. (C) a new house.
    (B) utilities.   (D) planted crops.

56. All of the following types of property are normally real property **EXCEPT**:
    (A) water rights.   (C) air space rights.
    (B) appurtenances.   (D) furniture.

57. Riparian rights are best described as those rights:
    (A) specifically granted for a specified source of water.
    (B) found in the records of the county recorder's office.
    (C) an owner has from a natural watercourse abutting or crossing the land.
    (D) obtained by the purchase of fixtures.

❖ 58. An example of a right, privilege or improvement that belongs to and passes with a property is described as:
    (A) an emblement.   (C) a restriction.
    (B) an appurtenance.   (D) an encroachment.

59. The word "fee" used in connection with real property means:
    (A) the money charged by a broker for services rendered.
    (B) an estate of inheritance.
    (C) the charge made for searching title.
    (D) leased land.

60. The rights to the space above the ground within vertical planes are **BEST** described as:
    (A) air rights.   (C) solar rights.
    (B) bundle of rights.   (D) riparian rights.

61. Crops that grow on land and require annual planting and cultivation are called:
    (A) emblements.   (C) real property.
    (B) fructus naturales.   (D) fixtures.

62. All rights in the land that happen to pass with the conveyance of the land are **BEST** described as:
    (A) reversion interests.
    (B) warranties.
    (C) tenements.
    (D) reservation interests.

❖ 63. Items that are affixed as appurtenances to land are usually real property. All of the following are real property **EXCEPT**:
    (A) growing trees.
    (B) trade fixtures.
    (C) buried water tanks.
    (D) buildings.

64. A man dies testate, leaving a wife and minor son. He leaves all of his property to his son. His wife claims her elective share under the Uniform Probate Code. His property would be distributed as follows:
    (A) all to the wife.
    (B) all to the son.
    (C) part to the wife and part to the son.
    (D) none to the wife.

65. A man who makes a will is called:
    (A) a testator.   (C) a testatrix.
    (B) an executor.   (D) an administrator.

66. A woman who acquires real property under the terms of a will is known as:
    (A) a personal representative.
    (B) an executrix.
    (C) a devisee.
    (D) a testatrix.

67. A devisee
    (A) receives real property by will.
    (B) receives personal property under a bill of sale.
    (C) receives property by escheat.
    (D) receives property through foreclosure.

❖ 68. The word "intestate" **MOST** nearly means:
    (A) to die leaving a will.
    (B) to die without leaving a will.
    (C) to die without leaving an heir.
    (D) to die leaving property to the state.

69. Real property conveyed by a codicil to a will is conveyed by:
    (A) demise.   (C) decree.
    (B) devise.   (D) degree.

70. Probate means an action to:
    (A) cure a defect by a quitclaim deed.
    (B) prove title by adverse possession.
    (C) process a will establishing its validity.
    (D) process a partition of property.

71. A devise is:
    (A) a gift of real estate.
    (B) a trust in perpetuity.
    (C) a real estate gift by last testament.
    (D) a plan or scheme of development.

72. The property of a person who dies intestate passes by:
    (A) succession.   (C) acquisition.
    (B) accretion.   (D) prescription.

73. When a person dies intestate and no heirs can be found for intestate succession, the real property will revert to the government through a process known as:
    (A) reconveyance.   (C) escheat.
    (B) reversion.   (D) succession.

74. When a person dies testate, the real property:
    (A) escheats and is sold at an auction by the state.
    (B) goes to the next of kin.
    (C) passes to the devisee.
    (D) goes to the administrator.

75. Personal property bestowed in a will would be all of the following **EXCEPT**:
    (A) a codicil.   (C) a bequest.
    (B) a gift.   (D) a legacy.

76. Title to the owner's real estate can be transferred at the death of the owner by which of the following?
    - (A) Warranty deed
    - (B) Special warranty deed
    - (C) Trustee's deed
    - (D) Last will and testament

77. The word "escheat" refers to:
    - (A) the feudal custom of the king's seizure of land.
    - (B) the right of the government to take private property for a public purpose upon payment.
    - (C) the acquisition of title by adverse possession.
    - (D) the right of the government to acquire title where the owner dies without a will and without heirs.

78. When a person dies intestate and without heirs, the property:
    - (A) escheats to the government.
    - (B) is immediately disposed of by sale at public auction.
    - (C) passes to the devisees.
    - (D) passes to those named in the will.

❖ 79. In probating an estate, which of the following is the last to receive payment, if any?
    - (A) Holder of the second mortgage
    - (B) Creditors
    - (C) Heirs
    - (D) The government for taxes

80. When a person dies without a will, he or she is said to have died:
    - (A) testate.
    - (B) intestate.
    - (C) in escheat.
    - (D) without heirs.

81. Which of the following words would be **LEAST** associated with the others in this group?
    - (A) Testator
    - (B) Devise
    - (C) Intestate
    - (D) Will

❖ 82. What document is prepared to evidence that personal property is pledged to secure a loan?
    - (A) Bill of sale
    - (B) Chattel mortgage
    - (C) Bargain and sale deed
    - (D) Partial release

83. Which one of the following instruments does **NOT** transfer an interest in real property?
    - (A) Option
    - (B) Lease
    - (C) Bill of sale
    - (D) Agreement of sale

84. *H* executed a will. After his death, the probate court declared the will invalid because it did not meet the state law requirements. Which of the following will receive title to *H*'s real estate?
    - (A) The devisees named in the will.
    - (B) Those entitled under the state laws of intestate succession.
    - (C) The property escheats to the state.
    - (D) The previous owners of the property.

85. Who usually selects the executor of an estate?
    - (A) Probate court
    - (B) Administrator
    - (C) Testator
    - (D) Heirs

❖ 86. If a property owner dies without a will, his or her real property will go to which of the following?
    - (A) The government by escheat
    - (B) The heirs by descent
    - (C) Whomever was living on the property at the time
    - (D) Back to the original grantor

87. Under which of the following conditions would a property owner have riparian rights?
    - (A) When minerals are discovered under the land
    - (B) When the land is contiguous to a stream
    - (C) When the property is in a geothermal area
    - (D) When the property borders on the ocean

88. When a person dies testate, his or her real property would:
    - (A) escheat to the government.
    - (B) pass to the next of kin.
    - (C) descend to the survivors.
    - (D) pass to the devisees.

89. All of the following can be said about a party wall built on the property line between two lots **EXCEPT**:
  (A) Each owner is responsible for one-half of the maintenance fees.
  (B) Each owns the half of the wall on his or her side and has an easement on the other half.
  (C) Only one owner is responsible for the maintenance on the wall.
  (D) Neither owner may destroy the wall without the other's permission.

90. The main purpose of the Uniform Commercial Code is which of the following?
  (A) To prevent fraud in the proof of fictitious oral sales contracts
  (B) To regulate personal property items pledged in a sale contract
  (C) To make real property transactions more uniform
  (D) To regulate commercial leasing

ANSWERS

1. **B** While a defeasible fee (one subject to a condition) and a life estate can be transferred by deed, they must be clearly specified. An estate for years is transferred (demised) by lease. A fee simple absolute is one that is not qualified (or conditional).

2. **A** Seisin (sometimes spelled "seizin") was the ancient equivalent of ownership; it required some possession coupled with a freehold interest. Seisin had to be delivered to the new owner ("livery of seisin").

3. **C** A reversionary interest under choice (D) is when the property will return to the grantor or the grantor's heirs. Here the property will "remain" away from the grantor and C will be the fee owner provided that (contingent upon) B dies leaving no heirs. Remainders are either vested (owned now) or contingent.

4. **C** When A dies, his life estate ends, and the property will revert back to the grantor. Rights of reentry are found in leases and also in a fee simple subject to a condition subsequent in which the condition is broken or violated.

5. **B** The measuring life for a life estate can be that of someone other than the grantee—A to B for the life of C. Thus, upon C's death the property will revert back to A. If B were to predecease C, B's heirs would have an interest in the property until C dies. This is called an "estate pur autre vie."

6. **C** An estate for years is a leasehold. Next to the fee simple absolute and the defeasible fee, the life estate is the most common freehold estate today. While it is not an estate of inheritance, it is an estate for an indefinite, or unpredictable, duration.

7. **C** One of the key features of a fee simple is that the property can continue in the same family line through inheritance. The two most popular forms of freehold estates are fee simple (including absolute and conditional fees) and life estates.

8. **B** After the death of both spouses the life estate will end and ownership will *remain* away from the grantor's estate. The hospital's remainder interest will then ripen into a fee simple absolute estate. Here is another way to remember what a remainder estate is—it is the estate that remains after the existing life estate terminates.

9. **C** A devise is a transfer by will (do not confuse with demise, which is a transfer by lease), but there is no estate left for heirs after the owner of the life estate (life tenant) dies. The buyer, lender and lessee take their interest with knowledge, subject to the life estate, so their interests cease when the life estate ceases. Lenders rarely lend on a life estate; and, if so, they may require a term life insurance policy or an agreement with the remainderman as further security. Incidentally, any buyer of a life estate would then own a "life estate pur autre vie."

10. **D** During her life she has ownership of a life estate. Her children have a remainder interest. Despite having ownership rights in the property, the widow can't commit "waste," such as tearing the structure down or converting it into a triplex rental.

11. **C**   Life estates are frequently created by will—the husband leaves the home to his wife for life and then to their kids. There could be several "life tenants, or the survivor of them." The owner of the fee (grantor of life estate) is responsible for any mortgage principal payments, but the life tenant is responsible for carrying charges, such as interest, taxes and maintenance.

12. **A**   This is the classic definition of estate (Latin for "status")—it ranges from absolute ownership to mere possession.

13. **B**   A reversion occurs when the land returns to the grantor or heirs of the grantor. A remainder occurs when the land will remain away from the grantor or heirs.

14. **B**   This is a freehold estate in fee simple, which can be terminated upon the happening of an event such as marriage. It is also called a determinable fee or qualified fee.

15. **B**   Leaseholds are less than freehold based on ancient feudal classifications in which only "freemen" had protection of the courts and the serfs had no interest in land although they had possession under leases.

16. **D**   (A) and (B) could include personal property, and (C) is just one example of an estate.

17. **B**   Under (A) and (B) you would have a claim for money damages if it turned out the grantor did not have the title as promised. There is more assurance of recovering money from the title company than a grantor. For example, perhaps the title, due to some off-record risk (such as forgery in the chain of title), prevented clear ownership of title. Title insurance companies only insure the title subject to stated exceptions; they cannot correct the actual defects that may be found in the title. Also, a deed could be used to transfer a life estate, which is not fee simple ownership.

18. **D**   This involves a tenant who stays in possession after lease termination without the consent of the lessor. A trespasser might try to claim title by way of adverse possession—the tenant cannot because his or her claim is not hostile.

19. **C**   It is indefinite in time; unless conveyed to another, it will come to an end only in the event the owner dies without having left heirs or a valid will (in which case escheat occurs).

20. **C**   Dower is the wife's interest upon the husband's death. The technical rules of dower and curtesy vary greatly from state to state. Many states, usually community property states, have abolished these ancient marital estates and replaced them with the "spouse's right of election"—the right to receive a certain percentage of the deceased spouse's estate.

21. **C**   All but (C) are within the "bundle of rights." *H* has a fee simple owner. He may not violate the governmental limitation.

22. **A**   It is a leasehold interest for a definite period of time, whether it is one year, ten years or even ten days.

23. **D**   The largest bundle of rights attaches to a fee simple estate.

24. **D**   An estate for years is the only "less than freehold" estate to choose here. An unrecorded vendor's (seller) deed would transfer a freehold estate provided the grantor owned one and there was valid delivery (recording is advised but not required).

25. **C**   Grantors *should* grant title using the same name in which they acquired title. If they don't, this may cause title search problems. However, all that is required for a valid transfer is delivery, and that involves the *intention* of the grantor to relinquish all control to the grantee. Under choice (B) the grantor can structure the transfer so he or she keeps a reversionary interest. A life estate can be for the life of more than one person.

26. C   While public records may contain maps of the proper boundaries, these records do not usually reveal any encroachments, such as a fence two feet over a line. The licensee should retain a surveyor to verify the boundaries and reveal any encroachments.

27. A   An example is the freehold estate called a fee simple.

28. A   This reflects the feudal distinction between freehold interests in real property and nonfreehold interests, which were treated as personal property (chattels personal).

29. A   (B), (C) and (D) are generally treated as being fixtures (chattels real), and thus title passes with the land upon sale. Unless the contract of sale provides otherwise, the seller can remove personal property prior to closing.

30. A   A chattel mortgage is a security interest in personal property. It has been replaced under the Uniform Commercial Code with the security agreement and financing statement.

31. C   The beneficiary does not own the real property, only an interest in the trust. All contracts involving the sale or transfer of property should be executed by the trustee, not the beneficiary only.

32. B   Real property includes rights in the land, air rights, subsurface rights and improvements.

33. C   While homeowners may tend to want to keep their favorite appliances with them, investors in apartment buildings usually intend to make these appliances become an integral part of the property.

34. C   (A), (B) and (D) involve real property. Personalty is another word for chattel or personal property.

35. A   A bill of sale is especially useful to investors for purposes of allocating values to personal property that can depreciate at faster rates than real property for income tax purposes.

36. D   A trade fixture such as a merchant's display case does not become a part of the landlord's property during the term of the lease. Trade fixtures are removable by the tenant.

37. D   While (A), (B) and (C) are factors, most courts emphasize the intention test.

38. C   While the date is frequently given, it is not as essential a these other items. Nevertheless, anyone preparing a bill of sale should insert a date.

39. A   Chattel is derived from the word cattle, one of early man's most prized possessions. A synonym is personalty.

40. B   Littoral property borders on the ocean or sea. Riparian property is located on a watercourse or over an underground nonnavigable stream.

41. C   "Realtist" is a registered trade name, which is owned by the National Association of Real Estate Brokers, founded by black real estate brokers.

42. C   The definitions of (A), (B) and (D) are not quite as broad as (C), thus C is more comprehensive.

43. C   Real property is a collection of all one's rights in a certain parcel.

44. B   A dedication is, in effect, a grant *to* the public, which may be either a fee simple or an easement. Condemnation is the government's taking private property for a public use with just compensation.

45. D   Riparian rights are those rights an owner has to the adjoining nonnavigable water such as rights to swim, boat, or irrigate. These rights are created by operation of state law. If in doubt, an owner should check with a local real estate attorney.

46. A   Accretion is the gradual addition of soil (alluvion) to the shoreline (littoral accretion) or to the land bordering a stream (riparian accretion), which then becomes the property of the shoreline or the streamside owner. Avulsion is the tearing away of land caused by a sudden natural occurrence, but the original property line stays intact.

47. **B** A littoral owner has land that bounds on the ocean. If the land borders on a navigable waterway, then there are no riparian rights because the government would have the control over this property.

48. **C** This is the vertical concept of ownership, which includes subsurface and air rights, as opposed to horizontal ownership as found in condominiums.

49. **B** Personal property can be mortgaged (chattel mortgage), taxed at a higher rate and transferred easily by delivery of possession or a bill of sale.

50. **B** Such riparian owner would be the beneficiary of any increased land due to accretion and could take some of the water for personal use.

51. **C** The key word here is "suddenly"; no change in ownership results.

52. **A** Mineral rights and air rights are typically part of the real estate being sold and, unless reserved to the grantor, will automatically pass to the grantee. Some states, and sometimes a previous grantor, however, may have already reserved the mineral rights before the owner obtains title. Therefore, it is important to check state law and the status of the owner's title before taking title.

53. **C** The life estate is valid until *G* dies, and thus it passes to *H*'s heirs upon *H*'s death. It is an estate for the life of another (an estate *pur autre vie*).

54. **A** Erosion will result in a loss of one's property. Curtilage describes the enclosed space of ground and buildings immediately surrounding a dwelling-house, such as a courtyard or fenced-in area.

55. **D** Improvements refer to man-made, constructed additions or developments, such as roads, buildings or fences, which are usually part of the real estate. Planted crops are usually personal property, technically known as "fructus industriales."

56. **D** Furniture is personalty unless it is a built-in fixture.

57. **C** These riparian rights arise by operation of law, and attach to property bordering on a non-navigable stream.

58. **B** Appurtenances are rights in land that pass to the new owner. Emblements are annual crops produced by cultivation and are treated as personal property.

59. **B** Fee refers to a fee simple, which is a freehold estate of inheritance. The broker typically earns a "commission."

60. **A** The air rights are just one of many of the bundle of rights that go with ownership. Many skyrise office buildings and condominiums are built after the developer purchases the air rights. Solar rights involve easements to give access to light and air.

61. **A** Note that trees and shrubs *not* requiring annual cultivation would be real property called "fructus naturales."

62. **C** "Tenement" is a broad term covering rights to buildings, fences, easements and rents. Reversion interests return to the grantor in the future and reservation interests remain with the grantor. Warranties may be expressed in the deed.

63. **B** Trade fixtures can be removed by the tenant upon expiration of the lease. They are considered personal property, such as display cabinets, storage systems or barber chars. Growing trees are classified as *fructus naturales.*

64. **C** In those states adopting the Uniform Probate Code, she would be entitled to one-third absolute interest in all his property (i.e., she could elect to renounce the will).

65. **A** A testatrix is a female. Executors (those named in a will) and administrators (those named by the court) handle the settlement of the deceased's estate—a more popular name today is that of "personal representative."

66. C   Real property conveyed by will is called a devise, and the recipient is called a devisee.

67. A   A bequest is a gift of personal property, and a legacy is a gift of money to a legatee.

68. B   In the case of intestacy, the state will, in effect, write a will under its laws of intestate succession (or laws of descent).

69. B   A codicil is an addition to a will that must be executed with the same formality as the original will. A demise is a transfer of a real property interest by lease.

70. C   When a testator dies, it is necessary to prove the validity of the will and give notice to any creditors that they may file claims. This is all part of the process of transferring title out of the name of the deceased owner.

71. C   The devisee must wait for the probate process to settle the decedent's estate and pay the just debts before the devisee will obtain marketable title.

72. A   Each state has its own rules as to who will succeed to the intestate's property. In effect, the state writes the will.

73. C   Most state laws allow a long period between death and title passing to the government so that next of kin have sufficient time to file claims.

74. C   Testate means to die with a valid will in which real property is passed by way of a devise.

75. A   A codicil is an addition to a will and could transfer real property as well as personal property. Bequest is the transfer of personal property, and a legacy is money.

76. D   A will differs from a transfer by deed in that a provision in a will is effective only after death and probate. A deed is effective upon delivery during the grantor's lifetime. A will can be rewritten anytime prior to the death of the testator.

77. D   Escheat also applies to abandonment of real property. Choice (B) refers to eminent domain.

78. A   While the property escheats to the government, it is not usually disposed of until ample time has gone by for any possible next of kin to make their claim known.

79. C   Secured creditors, the government, and unsecured creditors all receive payment before the heirs. Sometimes a devisee finds out that the real property he or she was to receive had to be sold to pay all of the debts of the deceased.

80. B   If a person dies without a will and leaves no heirs (or next or kin), then the property escheats to the government.

81. C   Intestate means there is no will, while the rest involve a will prepared by a testator. A devise is real property passing by will.

82. B   In those states that have adopted the Uniform Commercial Code, the chattel mortgage is called a security agreement; and it is the financing statement that is recorded.

83. C   A bill of sale is used to transfer title to personal property and is sometimes used in real estate transactions, so the seller will warrant that there are no unpaid liens on the title. (A), (B) and (D) all transfer an equitable interest in real property.

84. B   In the event of the death of a person who did not leave a valid will, state law will specify which relatives are entitled to succeed to the real and personal property. This is sometimes referred to as the *state laws of intestate succession* or *laws of descent*.

85. C   The deceased person has designated the executor in the will. If one was not designated or the one designated does not qualify, then the probate court will appoint an administrator. In some states, the executor and administrator are referred to as "personal representatives."

86. **B** Each state has its own set of rules (of descent) for the method by which property will pass upon intestacy. Escheat would occur only if there were no surviving relatives as well as no will.

87. **B** Riparian rights belong to owners on a watercourse. They are rights to acquire title to accreted land, and rights to boating, swimming and so forth.

88. **D** When a person dies testate, the real property will be devised to those people named in the will. If the person has died intestate, then state law would determine to whom the property would descend.

89. **C** Party walls are more frequently used in large city tenements. They involve reciprocal easements of support.

90. **B** Where personal property is used as security in a land sales contract, the creditor-seller should, under the U.C.C., perfect the lien by filing a financing statement, which describes the particular personal property.

Chapter 3   Condominiums and Cooperatives

Questions in this chapter test your comprehension of the following topics:

- The difference between owning a condominium and a cooperative
- Documents involved with condominiums, including bylaws, declaration, and master deed
- Condominium conversions

Condominiums are created under specific state statutes. Only general questions on the condominium and cooperative forms of ownership will appear on the general portion of the exam. Specific state law matters may appear in the State portion of the test.

False Friends

The following words are often confused with one another. Note the difference in meaning of these false friends:

Proprietary Lease/Apartment Deed: The seller conveys a cooperative apartment by way of a proprietary lease, and a condominium apartment by way of an apartment deed.

Common Interest/Common Element: Each condominium apartment is assigned a percentage of undivided interest in the project's common elements described in the Declaration (e.g., elevators, roofs, land, foundations, etc.).

QUESTIONS

1. The purchaser of all of the following apartment units could have a fee simple interest **EXCEPT:**
   (A) condominium apartment.
   (B) cooperative apartment.
   (C) town house apartment.
   (D) timeshare apartment.

2. Under the condominium law all of the following are true about apartments **EXCEPT:**
   (A) Individual apartments may be mortgaged.
   (B) Title insurance may be issued on individual apartments.
   (C) Taxes are assessed on individual apartments.
   (D) Rents are paid on the common elements.

❖ 3. Common elements in a residential condominium usually include all of the following **EXCEPT:**
   (A) girders and stairways.
   (B) parking stalls assigned to particular apartments.
   (C) elevators.
   (D) roofs.

4. *A* purchased a two-bedroom condominium. He now holds:
   (A) a freehold interest in his unit.
   (B) a proprietary lease.
   (C) a reversionary interest.
   (D) a leasehold estate.

5. All of the following are true concerning properties registered under the condominium law **EXCEPT:**
   (A) Each apartment has its own deed.
   (B) Each apartment may be conveyed or encumbered as if it were separate and distinct from all other apartments.
   (C) Each apartment is assessed its own maintenance fee.
   (D) Each apartment has its own proprietary lease.

6. How can a condo apartment owner avoid payment of the apportioned share of common expenses?
   (A) By not using certain common elements
   (B) By abandoning his or her apartment
   (C) By leasing his or her apartment
   (D) Payment is required.

7. The owners of an apartment in a condominium can do all of the following **EXCEPT:**
   (A) convey a freehold title to a grantee.
   (B) hypothecate the apartment as security for a mortgage.
   (C) lease their unit.
   (D) partition the common elements.

❖ 8. Which is true about apartment ownership?
   (A) In a condominium, each owner is responsible for his or her own mortgage payments, as well as those of his or her fellow apartment owners.
   (B) In a cooperative association, if one or more members fail to pay their share of the mortgage, the other owners must make payments for the defaulting members or risk foreclosure on the entire property.
   (C) In a condominium, each unit owner is a voting member of the association of owners.
   (D) In a cooperative association, taxes are collected twice a year.

9. Each owner of a condominium unit has all of the following **EXCEPT:**
   (A) own real estate tax bill on his or her unit.
   (B) own deed to his or her unit.
   (C) own maintenance dues on his or her unit.
   (D) own deed to the common elements.

10. The swimming pool in a condominium project is usually:
    (A) a common interest.
    (B) a common element.
    (C) a common profit.
    (D) a common tenancy.

11. The owner of a condominium apartment holds which of the following?
    (A) A proprietary lease
    (B) A proprietary estate
    (C) A separately taxable freehold estate
    (D) A tenancy by entirety estate

12. Under the condominium form of ownership, common elements typically include all of the following **EXCEPT:**
    (A) exits, girders and storage for janitors.
    (B) guest parking stalls.
    (C) recreational areas.
    (D) apartment interiors.

❖ 13. What condominium fees are **LEAST** likely to be paid by a condominium owner?
   (A) Recreation fees
   (B) Maintenance fees
   (C) Stock transfer fees
   (D) Hazard insurance

❖ 14. All of the following are true concerning apartment ownership **EXCEPT**:
   (A) Ownership in a cooperative usually requires purchase of shares of stock in the cooperative corporation or association.
   (B) Individual apartments in a condominium are conveyed and are financed as if they were single-family dwellings on separate pieces of land.
   (C) Cooperative owners can usually sell their units only with prior board of director approval.
   (D) Cooperative owners receive a deed.

15. Which of the following is true concerning the difference between owning a condominium or owning a cooperative?
   (A) A buyer can be deeded fee simple title of a condominium unit.
   (B) The owner of a co-op apartment unit owns an undivided tenancy in common interest in his or her unit.
   (C) Only the condominium owner is entitled to exclusive possession.
   (D) Only the cooperative owner is entitled to property tax deductions.

16. Which of the following is true about condominium ownership?
   (A) Included in the definition of common elements would be any basements, gardens, lodging for janitors, recreational facilities and interiors of apartments.
   (B) The Declaration of Horizontal Property Regime, also called the Condominium Declaration, need not include a description of the limited common elements because property is restricted to use by a certain limited group.
   (C) It only applies to residential buildings.
   (D) Owners have the same tax benefits as do owners of single-family homes.

17. Which of the following is true concerning condominium ownership?
   (A) If the bylaws require the board of directors to secure property insurance, the insurance premiums shall be common expenses to be apportioned among the owners according to their percentage of common interest.
   (B) If a mortgagee forecloses on A's apartment and B purchases the apartment at the foreclosure sale, B is liable for all the unpaid common expenses that existed prior to the sale.
   (C) The board of directors of the association consists of community leaders who have no ownership interest.
   (D) No unit can be sold without the prior approval of all owners.

18. An individual owner in a condominium can normally do which of the following?
   (A) File a suit for partition of the common elements
   (B) Be exempt from paying part of the common expenses by waiving or abandoning the use or enjoyment of the common elements
   (C) Sell the limited common elements separate from the apartment
   (D) Cast a vote at association meetings

19. The bylaws governing a property that is subject to the condominium law generally would include all of the following **EXCEPT**:
   (A) provisions for election of a board of directors of the association of apartment owners.
   (B) the method in which each apartment owner's share of the common expenses will be collected.
   (C) provisions for conduction association meetings.
   (D) the percentage of common interest for each apartment.

❖ 20. If the board of directors of a condominium project obtains insurance coverage:
   (A) the premiums are common expenses.
   (B) individual apartment owners cannot insure their own apartment contents.
   (C) the premiums are refundable.
   (D) the insurance covers theft losses in individual units.

21. An owner or lessee may submit his or her property to the Horizontal Property Act, and it will become a condominium by terms of the act when:
    (A) the certificate of completion is issued by the appropriate county official.
    (B) all the units have been sold.
    (C) the final report is issued.
    (D) the declaration is recorded.

❖ 22. Which of the following terms **BEST** describes a modern form of real property ownership that involves the guaranteed right of occupancy and use of a specific property for a specific portion of each year for either a fixed number of years or forever?
    (A) Time-sharing　　(C) Periodic tenancy
    (B) Recreation lease　(D) Life estate

23. Which of the following is true concerning condominium conversion?
    (A) An owner might favorably consider converting an apartment building to a condominium in an area with strict rent controls.
    (B) Condominium conversions receive universal support from city managers and governments.
    (C) Condominium conversions are illegal and fraudulent.
    (D) Tenants have no right to buy their converted unit.

24. All of the following practices are generally true in a conversion of an apartment building to a condominium **EXCEPT**:
    (A) The existing tenants on month-to-month leases are given longer than 30-day notices to relocate.
    (B) The existing tenants are given the first right to purchase their units.
    (C) Renovations are made to individual apartments.
    (D) The tenants can extend their leases for five years.

25. What can the taxing agency do when a condominium apartment owner defaults in paying his or her real property tax?
    (A) Seek to foreclose against the apartment owner
    (B) Seek to recover from the condominium association
    (C) Put locks on the front door
    (D) Collect from the lender

26. A owns Apt. 22 in the Blueridge condominium development. What part of the condominium does A own?
    (A) The entire floors, walls and ceilings of his unit
    (B) An equal share of each unit in the Blueridge
    (C) The air space within Apt. 22
    (D) The parking stall and swimming pool

27. Which of the following statements comparing condominium with cooperative ownership is true?
    (A) The financing arrangements in a cooperative situation make it a more attractive purchase than a condominium.
    (B) Cooperative associations generally exercise much more rigid control regarding the qualifications of new buyers and tenants of buyers than do condominiums.
    (C) Cooperative ownership is less expensive.
    (D) Cooperative ownership offers greater tax benefits.

28. Traditionally, one of the principal advantages of a condominium over a cooperative has been:
    (A) lower maintenance.
    (B) greater security.
    (C) better location.
    (D) easier financing.

❖ 29. All of the following documents would be used in the typical condominium project **EXCEPT**:
    (A) association bylaws.　(C) proprietary lease.
    (B) master deed.　　　　(D) declaration.

❖ 30. In a residential condominium project, which of the following events would require an amendment to the condominium declaration?
    (A) Purchase and installation of a new air-conditioning unit
    (B) Negotiation of a new property management agreement
    (C) Relocation of the boundaries of several units
    (D) Renegotiation of the building's master insurance policy

31. Which of the following is true regarding ownership of a cooperative apartment unit?
    (A) Each unit is taxed separately.
    (B) Each unit can receive title insurance for its fee simple interest.
    (C) Each unit is owner-occupied.
    (D) Each unit is conveyed by a proprietary lease.

❖ 32. In recent times, the time-share condominium has become a very important influence in marketing real estate in resort area. It has generally caused a reduction in the:
    (A) cost of ownership.
    (B) number of occupants.
    (C) real property taxes.
    (D) maintenance fees.

ANSWERS

1. **B**   A co-op purchaser would obtain a proprietary lease plus stock in the corporation or association that owned the entire building. The condo purchaser could own a fee interest in the air space, even if the land on which the condo was constructed was a long-term leasehold estate.

2. **D**   Since individual apartments (fee ownership) are considered as "homes in the sky," an owner has most of the bundle of rights as for a single-family home. The purchaser can obtain separate financing, and a title company will insure his or her interest. Owners pay a prorata share of common expenses, not rent.

3. **B**   Common elements consist of those areas used in common by all owners and include elevators, lobbies, recreation areas and laundry room. Areas assigned for the exclusive use of individual owners are called limited common elements (such as storage closets and reserved parking stalls). Different rules apply to limited common elements that relate to maintenance responsibility and permission to make additions or alterations.

4. **A**   Note that this freehold interest is a recent creation of state condominium legislation. Choice (B) involves a cooperative apartment in which there can be no separate fee ownership.

5. **D**   Condominium apartments have separate and distinct ownership qualities. Each is subject to the liens and encumbrances of its individual owner.

6. **D**   If owners were allowed to reduce their monthly maintenance expenses (association dues) by electing not to use the swimming pool, for example, there would be much chaos in managing the condominium. Likewise, until title to the abandoned apartment is transferred, the owner is still liable for common expenses.

7. **D**   The owners can convey, mortgage, lease and encumber, just as if they owned a single-family home. However, they generally cannot partition the common elements.

8. **B**   In a condo, the owners are not responsible for the mortgage payments of other owners. But in a co-op, there is usually one blanket mortgage, so all owners must make up the defaults of other unit owners to avoid foreclosure of the one mortgage. Of course, they would place a lien on the defaulting owner's interest to the extent of their cash advances. If ten people own one unit, they are not all voting members; usually it is one member per unit.

9. **D**   Taxes and special assessments are levied against each individual apartment and not on the building as a whole. Title to common elements is held in common.

10. **B**   The common interest is the percentage of ownership in the common elements. Each owner is responsible for a share of maintaining the common elements, such as the swimming pool. A common profit would be some venture, such as coin-operated vending machines that generate money for the association. This profit would then be shared among each owner according to his or her common interest.

11. **C**   The owner may hold an apartment in severalty or joint tenancy. The owner does, however, have a percentage undivided interest in the common elements, which is like a tenancy-in-common estate.

12. **D** While guest parking stalls are typically common elements, reserved parking stalls are limited common elements appurtenant to specific apartments.

13. **C** Stock-transfer fees are paid in connection with the transfer of a cooperative apartment.

14. **D** In addition to stock purchase, the co-op purchaser would become a lessee under a proprietary lease to the specific apartment unit, not a grantee under a deed.

15. **A** The co-op owner does have an undivided interest in the common areas, although it stems from the individually held stock and lease ownership and not from any deed as in a condominium.

16. **D** Common elements do not include apartment interiors. The limited common elements must be specifically described in the declaration and it must be noted to which units they are appurtenant. Condos may include commercial or industrial land uses.

17. **A** Apartment owners should still obtain insurance for damages caused within their respective units. The unpaid expenses are generally made part of the association's overall common expenses and apportioned among all owners including the purchaser at the foreclosure sale.

18. **D** The common elements are not usually the subject of an action for partition. Payment of expenses for common elements is not based on how much they are used by each owner.

19. **D** The board is a powerful voice in managing the operations of the condominium project. The owner's proportionate responsibility for the common expenses is usually fixed according to his or her percentage of common interest. The board, however, generally determines the most efficient method to collect and disburse these funds.

20. **A** Failure of the board to obtain such coverage could be a basis for liability for negligence. Each person should obtain coverage for apartment contents.

21. **D** The declaration is the critical document in creating the condominium. In order to sell the condominium, many other steps must be taken to acquire the necessary government approval.

22. **A** Many time-sharing projects are structured as vacation leases, club memberships, or time interval ownership. For example, each unit may have several tenant-in-common owners who have agreed upon the time when each is entitled to occupancy during the year.

23. **A** If an owner is subject to rent controls that prohibit or make it difficult to raise rents to achieve the return desired, the owner probably would want to convert. City managers and governments are considering laws to limit conversion because it removes rentals from the market and increases the housing shortage for people not financially secure enough to buy.

24. **D** Most states require a minimum of 90 days' notice and generally require the developer to give the tenant the first right to purchase his or her unit. There is a growing trend of governmental regulation in the area of condominium conversion due to the housing problems created by frequent relocation of tenants and the reduction in the number of available rental units. Long lease extensions are not granted.

25. **A** Most state laws require that state real property taxes be assessed against individual units and not against the property as a whole. Thus, the association is not liable.

26. **C** Condominium ownership is ownership of air space in a horizontal plane. The floors, walls and ceilings are typically common elements.

27. **B**   Until recently, individual financing for cooperative units was impossible because no lender could be subject to the blanket mortgage on the building. The 1980s show a trend in state laws toward easing this financing restraint. While some condominium associations require prior approval of buyers and tenants, this practice is much more prevalent in cooperative associations.

28. **D**   Until recently, buyers of co-op units were unable to obtain individual financing because of the problem that there already was a blanket mortgage on the co-op. Some states are legislating to remove this financing obstacle.

29. **C**   The proprietary lease along with a stock or trust certificate is typically used in a cooperative housing project.

30. **C**   While the board of directors is empowered to handle operational decisions as in (A), (B) and (D), any major changes in the established boundaries would usually require unanimous owner approval (along with all mortgagees' consent as well).

31. **D**   The basic cooperative concept is that the corporation (or trust) owns the building and the cooperative unit owner owns a proprietary lease to the unit. The fee simple interest is in the corporation and taxes are assessed against the property as a whole, with each unit owner being assessed by the corporation for his or her respective share. Some co-ops require owner occupancy.

32. **A**   Under time-sharing, a person is concerned with ownership rather than renting. Because the total cost of the unit is divided up among the various time-share owners, a person can acquire an interest in a unit at a relatively low cost. The trade-off is that use is limited to select periods.

Chapter 4   Encumbrances: Easements, Restrictions and Liens

The questions in this chapter test your comprehension of the following topics:

- Various types of easements, including easements appurtenant, in gross, and prescriptive
- The creation and termination of easements
- Easements and license distinguished
- Restrictive covenants in deeds and leases
- Liens affecting the title to real property

Note that all liens are encumbrances but that not all encumbrances are liens. There are two general classifications of encumbrances: (1) those that affect the title, such as judgments, mechanic's liens, mortgages, to secure a debt or obligation; and (2) those that affect the physical condition of the property such as restrictions, easements, and encroachments.

False Friends

The following words are often confused with one another. Note the difference in meaning of these false friends:

Lienor/Lienee: The creditor (lienor) has a lien on the property of the debtor (lienee) to satisfy a claim or debt.

Encroachment/Encumbrance: An encroachment is an unauthorized intrusion of one property onto another property; it is an encumbrance on both properties until the liability is resolved by court action or agreement.

Appurtenant/In Gross: An easement appurtenant benefits and runs with the land whereas an easement in gross does not benefit any land. It is personal to the owner (there is no dominant estate).

Easement/License: An easement is a permanent right in property whereas a license may be revoked.

QUESTIONS

1. All the following statements about deed restrictions, are true **EXCEPT**:
   (A) They are frequently encountered in residential subdivisions.
   (B) They are called restrictive covenants.
   (C) They terminate upon the death of the grantor.
   (D) Once established, they run with the land and are limitations on the use of future grantees.

2. An easement appurtenant:
   (A) is the usual type of easement granted to utility companies to permit them to run electric lines across the property.
   (B) runs with the land.
   (C) has only a dominant estate.
   (D) benefits the servient estate.

3. Restrictions in a deed that benefit only the grantor:
   (A) cannot be removed by the grantor.
   (B) must be more lenient than current zoning laws.
   (C) may be removed by the grantor issuing a quitclaim deed.
   (D) may be changed by a subsequent grantee.

❖ 4. An easement created by adverse use is said to have been created by:
   (A) express grant.   (C) reservation.
   (B) implication of law. (D) prescription.

❖ 5. Restrictive covenants in a deed:
   (A) must be consistent and not at variance with the zoning.
   (B) cannot be more strict than the current zoning use.
   (C) are the same as conditions in a deed.
   (D) are an encumbrance on the property.

6. All the following events would terminate an easement **EXCEPT**:
   (A) when dominant and servient tenements merge.
   (B) when the particular purpose for which the easement was created ceases.
   (C) absence or nonuse of the easement for several years.
   (D) when the dominant tenement abandons the easement.

7. When an easement appurtenant exists between two parcels of land that are separately owned:
   (A) the dominant tenement has use of this easement only for ingress and egress.
   (B) the servient tenement must have created the easement in writing.
   (C) the dominant tenement is benefited by the easement.
   (D) the servient tenement may revoke the use of easement by giving proper notice.

8. Which of the following creates deed restrictions?
   (A) Local building inspector
   (B) Authorized authorities
   (C) Planning commission
   (D) Grantor

9. All of the following restrictions are government restrictions **EXCEPT**:
   (A) police power.   (C) escheat.
   (B) covenant.   (D) eminent domain.

10. A restriction is considered to be which one of the following?
   (A) Lien   (C) Encumbrance
   (B) Color of title   (D) Abstract

11. To the holder of the dominant tenement, an easement is:
   (A) an encumbrance.   (C) a restriction.
   (B) an appurtenance.   (D) an encroachment.

12. A deed subject to a restrictive covenant involves which one of the following?
   (A) Zoning restriction
   (B) Encumbrance
   (C) Life estate
   (D) Defective title

❖ 13. The right of a water company to lay and maintain water mains along the rear of a lot is called:
   (A) an appurtenance.
   (B) a riparian right.
   (C) an easement in gross.
   (D) a right of encroachment.

14. Which of the following is true?
    (A) The owner of the servient tenement generally has rights to subsurface profits.
    (B) The owner of the dominant tenement has the right to drill an oil well on the servient property.
    (C) The servient estate benefits from an easement.
    (D) The servient estate can terminate an easement by abandonment.

15. A recorded easement may be removed from the records by:
    (A) recording a quitclaim deed signed by the owner of the easement (the dominant tenement).
    (B) instituting a lis pendens action.
    (C) filing a marginal release.
    (D) giving a three-day notice followed by an Unlawful Detainer Action.

16. Which of the following is true?
    (A) When an easement has been created, it remains in effect even after the dominant and servient properties are merged into one.
    (B) The mere nonuse of an easement right is sufficient evidence to bring about abandonment.
    (C) An easement is created for the benefit of the servient tenement.
    (D) Easements are encumbrances affecting the physical use of land.

17. A property owner, by use of a deed restriction, may do all of the following **EXCEPT**:
    (A) prohibit a use of property that would be allowed under existing zoning laws.
    (B) limit the size and shape of the buildings.
    (C) change the zoning of the property.
    (D) limit the placement of a dwelling on a lot.

❖ 18. A party wall would be found:
    (A) along a property line.
    (B) between the dining and living rooms.
    (C) facing the direction from which bad weather usually comes.
    (D) between the upper and lower stories of a structure.

19. An easement would **MOST** likely be involved with which of the following?
    (A) Right-of-way   (C) Defeasance
    (B) Subordination   (D) Estoppel

❖ 20. When one has permission to use land, but has no other rights, one has a:
    (A) tenancy in common.
    (B) leasehold estate.
    (C) tenancy at sufferance.
    (D) license.

21. An easement is most commonly terminated by:
    (A) abandonment.
    (B) quitclaim deed.
    (C) the owner of the servient tenement.
    (D) operation of law.

22. The most practical method of imposing restrictions on all lots in a large new subdivision is:
    (A) by publishing the restrictions in a newspaper of general circulation.
    (B) by including the restrictions as covenants in all deeds.
    (C) by recording the restrictions, prior to any sales, in the manner provided by law.
    (D) by posting the restrictions on the property.

23. Which of the following deed restrictions is valid?
    (A) Limitations on materials used or the type of architecture
    (B) That the property cannot be sold to persons of a certain race
    (C) Property must not be used for religious purposes
    (D) The restriction must always be the same as the existing zoning

24. If, after *C* purchases a property, he has a survey made and finds that his neighbor, through error, has recently built an ornamental fence two fee over *C's* land, this would be a basic example of:
    (A) a party wall.
    (B) an encroachment.
    (C) an appurtenance.
    (D) adverse possession.

25. A person owning beachfront property sells the two lots between his or her lot and the public road. This person would be best advised to reserve from the transfer which type of right-of-way?
    (A) Easement in gross
    (B) Easement of necessity
    (C) Easement appurtenant
    (D) License

26. What type of easement exists in which there is a dominant estate and a servient estate?
    (A) Easement in gross
    (B) Easement appurtenant
    (C) Easement for profit
    (D) Easement by license

27. The right to enter upon the property of another and to fish in the pond on the property is called:
    (A) a trespass.   (C) a riparian right.
    (B) a license.   (D) an encroachment.

28. Which of the following does **NOT** create an easement?
    (A) Express grant   (C) Assignment
    (B) Prescription   (D) Implied grant

29. Which of the following statements is true about restrictive covenants found in deeds?
    (A) They are encumbrances.
    (B) They automatically expire upon violation.
    (C) If the restriction violates another law, the entire deed is void.
    (D) They must be the same as local zoning laws.

❖ 30. A landowner wants to give his neighbor the right to cross over his property but the land-owner does not wish to make this a perma-nent, irrevocable right. The broker should advise the owner to consider granting what type of right?
    (A) Easement in gross
    (B) Right-of-way
    (C) License
    (D) Easement appurtenant

31. Encumbrances that are considered liens on real estate can be created by:
    (A) special assessments and improvement taxes.
    (B) covenants that restrict the use of the property.
    (C) easements.
    (D) personal restrictions.

32. All of the following statements regarding restrictive covenants on real property are true **EXCEPT**:
    (A) They run with the land.
    (B) They are enforceable in court unless contrary to public policy.
    (C) They are limited to a specific time period.
    (D) They may be removed from the record without legal action.

❖ 33. Of the following liens, which normally takes priority over all other liens?
    (A) Judgment liens
    (B) Mortgage liens
    (C) Mechanics' liens
    (D) Real property tax liens

34. The priority of a mechanic's lien depends on the:
    (A) date of recordation.
    (B) date of the contract.
    (C) date of completion.
    (D) date on which work commenced.

35. A materialman's lien takes precedence over which of the following?
    (A) A first mortgage recorded prior to the time of the visible commencement of work
    (B) A lien for delinquent real property taxes
    (C) Mechanic's lien for broker's commission
    (D) Previously recorded judgment liens

36. The lender wants to insure the first priority of his or her lien. The lender should make sure of which of the following?
    (A) That all other liens are removed from title or subordinated from the property being used as collateral.
    (B) The borrower has an unconditional fee simple estate with no liens.
    (C) The borrower's father cosigns the note.
    (D) The loan is insured.

37. Of the following, which usually must be recorded to become effective?
    (A) Judgment   (C) Mechanic's lien
    (B) Warranty deed (D) Easement

38. All of these professionals may file a mechanic's lien after completing work and not being paid **EXCEPT**:
    (A) carpenter.
    (B) real estate broker.
    (C) electrician.
    (D) engineer.

❖ 39. Which of the following is an encumbrance, but **NOT** a lien?
    (A) Mortgage   (C) Trust deed
    (B) Restriction   (D) Taxes

40. Encumbrances that are considered liens on real estate can be created by:
    (A) special assessments and improvement taxes.
    (B) covenants that restrict the use of the property.
    (C) zoning regulations.
    (D) easements.

❖ 41. A recorded notice of a current lawsuit involving title to real property is termed:
    (A) a lis pendens.
    (B) a writ of execution.
    (C) an attachment.
    (D) an order to show cause.

42. In distinguishing between an attachment lien and a judgment lien:
    (A) an attachment is made after judgment.
    (B) an attachment lien applies to all property of the debtor.
    (C) a judgment lien is a general lien.
    (D) a judgment lien can be obtained prior to court decision.

43. The discharge of certain property from the lien of a judgment, mortgage or claim is:
    (A) a release of lien.
    (B) a lien binder.
    (C) a lien statement.
    (D) a tax.

44. A valid, outstanding claim or encumbrance that would affect or impair an owner's title to real property is all of the following **EXCEPT**:
    (A) color of title.
    (B) cloud on the title.
    (C) judgment.
    (D) federal estate taxes.

45. A chattel mortgage is a lien on:
    (A) real property.
    (B) personal property.
    (C) encumbrances.
    (D) land.

46. A court-issued order to sell property to satisfy a judgment is known as:
    (A) an easement.
    (B) an encumbrance.
    (C) an attachment.
    (D) a writ of execution.

❖ 47. Which of the following statements is true?
    (A) All liens are encumbrances.
    (B) All encumbrances are liens.
    (C) Specific liens affect all property of the debtor located in the state.
    (D) Judgments are specific liens.

48. A legal right of a creditor to have a debt or charge satisfied from the personal property of the debtor is:
    (A) a mortgage.   (C) a right of way.
    (B) a lien.   (D) an escheat.

49. Which of the following encumbrances would constitute a lien on real property?
    (A) Easement   (C) Restriction
    (B) Encroachment   (D) Mortgage

50. Usually a mechanic's lien is removed from public record by:
    (A) court order.
    (B) payment in full.
    (C) recording a release.
    (D) satisfaction of the judgment.

51. A mechanic's lien filed for record today for work commenced two weeks ago usually has priority over all **BUT** which one of the following?
    (A) A mortgage filed five days ago
    (B) A second mortgage recorded three days ago
    (C) An unrecorded mortgage that was given a month ago
    (D) A three-week-old judgment lien

52. Which of the following liens would have top priority in the event of foreclosure of the subject property?
    (A) State income tax lien recorded first
    (B) Federal estate tax lien recorded second
    (C) Mechanic's lien for work commenced before any other lien was recorded
    (D) Real property tax lien recorded last

❖ 53. Which of the following is true regarding an encumbrance on real property?
    (A) An encumbrance effectively prevents the passing of title from grantor to grantee.
    (B) An encumbrance may indicate a lien.
    (C) Encumbrances are liens that restrict use of the property.
    (D) Encumbrances are restrictions that transfer title to property.

54. A laborer on a parcel of real property can do which of the following if he is not paid for his work?
    (A) Post a bond
    (B) File a lien
    (C) Start foreclosure proceedings
    (D) Remove his improvements

ANSWERS

1. **C** Restrictive covenants run with the land, are not terminated by death but may expire at the end of a stated time or upon release by all benefiting owners.

2. **B** One of the features of an easement appurtenant is that it runs with the land. Also, it is granted in writing. It has both a dominant and a servient estate. Choice (A) refers to an easement in gross that doesn't benefit any adjacent parcel of real estate.

3. **C** For example, assume a grantor of Lot 1 reserved an easement to benefit neighboring Lot 2. At any time, easement interest in Lot 1 could be released by way of a quitclaim deed. While a more lenient deed restriction may limit a building to three stories, it would not, however, have priority over a zoning law that permits only two stories, for example.

4. **D** Prescriptive easements usually require open, notorious and hostile use for the same statutory period as adverse possession.

5. **D** Restrictive covenants and zoning regulations are often at variance with each other; the one that is more strict or severe will control the use of the affected property, except in certain situations where a deed restriction is against public policy or in violation of law.

6. **C** Regarding choice (A), if the owner of Lot 1 buys Lot 2, any easements over Lot 2 that benefit Lot 1 would cease because an easement is an interest in another's land. An easement to cross the pasture to fish in the lake would cease when the lake was filled in and converted to a shopping center. Regarding choice (C), this requires complete abandonment in order to terminate.

7. **C** The dominant tenement is the benefiting property that is served by the other. Easements appurtenant are generally irrevocable and the stated purpose may be for more than ingress and egress.

8. **D** (A), (B) and (C) involve public restrictions, such as zoning and building code regulations.

9. **B** Covenants (promises) involve private restrictions. Police power is the general governmental power to pass rules to protect the health, welfare and safety of the community—for example, zoning, licensing laws and building codes.

10. **C** A lien is a charge against a property for a debt, whereas an encumbrance is anything that limits the value or use of the property. All liens are encumbrances, but not all encumbrances are liens.

11. **B** To the servient tenement, the easement is an encumbrance. To the dominant tenement, it is something that attaches to the land and benefits it.

12. **B** Restrictive covenants are private restrictions found in deeds and leases that encumber the property.

13. **C**   Easements in gross are rights in the land of another person that benefit someone else (legal or natural), but there is no dominant estate as with an easement appurtenant. Appurtenances are property rights that attach to and benefit a parcel of land; riparian rights are water rights.

14. **A**   The owner of the servient tenement owns the land and has all the bundle of rights except the easement created for the benefit of the dominant tenement. This easement is limited to the created purpose (i.e., if it is a right-of-way, then there is no right to drill).

15. **A**   A quitclaim deed is effective to release the easement interest of the grantor. Lis pendens gives notice of a pending lawsuit; it is not an actual lawsuit. Marginal releases involve the satisfaction of mortgages.

16. **D**   Upon merger, there is no longer any land of *another,* an essential element of an easement. To terminate an easement by nonuse, there must be clear acts of abandonment, such as building a cement wall across the former easement right-of-way.

17. **C**   Whichever is the more strict—a restriction or a zoning regulation—will control the use of the property. A popular restriction is to limit the height of buildings and sometimes even the minimum cost or size of the structures.

18. **A**   A party wall is a shared wall between two adjoining buildings. Each party owns one half and has an easement of support in the other half. Party wall agreements should be in writing because they involve an interest in real property, according to the statute of frauds.

19. **A**   A right-of-way is a right to cross over someone's property, usually to gain ingress and egress to a neighboring property. Subordination, defeasance and estoppel are terms used in financing.

20. **D**   Such permission is revocable, unlike an easement. For example, the right to enter a movie theater is a revocable license. In addition to a use right, a lessee may have the right to make improvements.

21. **B**   An easement can be terminated by abandonment or operation of law (merger), but is normally terminated by the owner of the dominant tenement quitclaiming his or her interest in the servient tenement.

22. **C**   Because a declaration of restrictions ("CC & Rs" or Covenants, Conditions and Restrictions, as they are sometimes called) can be quite lengthy, it is easier to record one set in the public record office and then, by incorporation by reference, make each deed subject to that prior recorded declaration of restrictions.

23. **A**   Racial and religious restrictions are barred under federal and most state antidiscrimination laws.

24. **B**   *C* could bring a lawsuit to seek removal of the fence. Failure to do so for a long enough time might result in the neighbor obtaining title to the disputed land by adverse possession. This would be an encumbrance on *C's* land, not an appurtenance. A party wall is located on or adjacent to the property line and is usually created by agreement and is for the support of each party's structure.

25. **C**   To maintain access to the road, the owner should clearly reserve in the deed an easement appurtenant that will benefit the beachfront lot and "run with the land" to bind successive owners of the two lots permanently. An easement in gross would personally benefit the beachfront owner but may not be transferable to future grantees. This could reduce the marketability of the beachfront lot.

26. **B**   In most situations of easements appurtenant, the two properties involved are adjacent or contiguous. With an easement in gross, there is no dominant estate.

27. **B** A license is a right or privilege to use another's property. Unlike an easement, it is revocable. A riparian right is the right of the owner of land bordering on a nonnavigable water to the use of the water.

28. **C** Grants are used to create rights, while assignments are used to transfer rights.

29. **A** Because restrictions control the use of property, it is important for a potential buyer (or the buyer's broker) to ascertain the extent of these encumbrances on the free use of the property *before* the buyer commits himself or herself to buy.

30. **C** A license is a mere right or privilege to use another's property. This right can be revoked at any time. An easement appurtenant is irrevocable; an easement in gross often is irrevocable; and a right-of-way is a specific type of easement (it may be appurtenant or in gross).

31. **A** Not all encumbrances are liens, although all liens are encumbrances. Liens are specific charges on real property for payment of a debt. They include mortgages, tax liens or mechanics' liens. Restrictions are merely encumbrances.

32. **C** Restrictive covenants found in deeds may have a specific time limit but this is not a requirement. One method of removal is a quitclaim deed from all the beneficiaries of the restriction.

33. **D** Real property tax liens even have priority over prior recorded special and general liens. Do not confuse with income tax or estate tax liens, whose priority is set by the date of recordation.

34. **D** The lien, once recorded, usually relates back to the date of visible commencement of work. Thus, buyers of property that shows evidence of recent construction should either obtain waivers from laborers or rely on an extended title insurance policy.

35. **C** Brokers can't file mechanics' liens. Real property tax liens have priority; other liens usually have priority based on date of recordation.

36. **A** Prior liens should be removed or placed junior through subordination. The lender usually would not want to lend on a *conditional* fee simple estate without further assurances against loss.

37. **C** Most state statutes require public notice of the mechanic's lien. An unrecorded deed is effective between the grantor and grantee. Judgments have legal effect on entry, but they do not become liens until recordation.

38. **B** Most states do not treat a broker as a laborer, mechanic or materialman, because he or she seldom does anything to enhance the property's value. The broker's legal remedy then is to file a lawsuit if attempts to negotiate a settlement are futile.

39. **B** A restriction is not a charge on property for the payment of a debt; it is a physical encumbrance.

40. **A** Failure to pay assessments or taxes can result in liens being placed on the property. Restrictive covenants and easements are popular physical encumbrances on land but are not liens.

41. **A** The lis pendens is the notice of suit, whereas an attachment is the actual seizure of specific property by a court pending the outcome of the lawsuit. The writ of execution is an order for the sale of property to satisfy the judgment.

42. **C** Judgment liens usually apply against all the property of the judgment debtor.

43. **A** Most releases are recorded.

44. **A** Color of title refers to claiming adverse possession, often under a defective deed. An unreleased dower interest and a possible claim of heirs are examples of clouds on title.

45. **B**   The chattel mortgage has been replaced in some states by the security agreement and financing statement under the Uniform Commercial Code.

46. **D**   If a judgment is not paid or satisfied, then the creditor can ask the court to execute on the property of the defendant.

47. **A**   Judgments (D) are general liens. Easements (B) are encumbrances but not liens.

48. **B**   Judgment liens could be satisfied from proceeds of sale of debtors' personal property.

49. **D**   Choices (A), (B) and (C) are encumbrances but not liens.

50. **C**   To clear the records, it is necessary to record a release.

51. **D**   The mechanic's lien relates back to the visible commencement of work.

52. **D**   Priority typically depends on date of recordation except in cases of governmental (state and county) real property tax liens and special assessments. The correct order of priority is (D), (C), (A), (B) because mechanics' liens relate to the date when work started.

53. **B**   Many grantees agree to accept title subject to certain disclosed encumbrances. All liens (mortgages, judgments or taxes) are encumbrances, but not all encumbrances (easements, restrictions or encroachments) are liens.

54. **B**   The laborer's most immediate remedy is to follow appropriate state law procedures for filing a mechanic's lien. If the mechanic obtains a judgment and the owner still refuses to pay the debt, then the property can be sold at a foreclosure sale with the mechanic getting enough of the proceeds to pay the debt and the owner getting the balance. Choice (D) is an example of self-help and would be a trespass.

Chapter 5 Governmental Restrictions: Zoning and Eminent Domain

The questions in this chapter test your comprehension of the following topics:

- The difference between a variance and a nonconforming use
- Eminent domain and the police power
- Zoning ordinances and building codes

Even a landowner with a fee simple absolute title may find that the use of the real property is often subject to governmental restrictions. Under the constitutional right of eminent domain, the government can take property for a public use if it pays just compensation. Under the police power, the government can pass reasonable rules such as zoning and building codes to protect the health, welfare and safety of society. In addition to these public restrictions, the property may also be subject to private deed restrictions.

False Friends

The following words are often confused with one another. Note the difference in meaning of these false friends:

Variance/Nonconforming Use: A variance is an exception to the existing zoning, whereas a nonconforming use arises when there is a change to the zoning while an existing use is permitted to continue.

Police Power/Eminent Domain: When property is taken under eminent domain, there must be payment of just compensation; a taking under the police power does not require compensation.

QUESTIONS

1. A landowner is advised by the government that a public utilities company plans to cross his or her property with a power line. If the landowner refuses, the utilities company can seek to acquire this right through the use of:
   (A) police action. (C) accretion.
   (B) eminent domain. (D) partition action.

❖ 2. Which of the following is a variance?
   (A) A large, new supermarket located in an area zoned for small retail shops
   (B) An old grocery store located in an area recently rezoned residential
   (C) Several choices of similar homes at the same price
   (D) A restriction in a deed that differs from the zoning

3. All of the following are examples of public restrictions **EXCEPT**:
   (A) police power. (C) eminent domain.
   (B) encroachment. (D) taxation.

4. When property represents a nonconforming use with regard to current zoning regulations, all of the following are true **EXCEPT**:
   (A) The use is legal and permissible as long as the building exists with no major structural changes.
   (B) If the building is destroyed, no new structure may be erected on the land that is not in conformity with existing zoning.
   (C) The use may continue even though it is in conflict with zoning.
   (D) The use must stop.

❖ 5. The right of the government to place reasonable restrictions on the use of privately held land is known as:
   (A) restrictive covenant.
   (B) police power.
   (C) subordination.
   (D) eminent domain.

❖ 6. If an area is rezoned industrial and a commercial establishment is given permission to continue its operation in that area, this is an example of which of the following?
   (A) Variance
   (B) Nonconforming use
   (C) Variable zoning
   (D) Restrictive zoning

7. Building codes have the ability to do all the following **EXCEPT**:
   (A) influence architectural style of buildings.
   (B) establish acceptable material and construction standards for buildings.
   (C) regulate safety of buildings in certain areas.
   (D) require an attorney review each transaction.

8. When the owner of property suffers financial loss from the exercise of police power, such as through the application of zoning laws:
   (A) the owner must be justly compensated for the loss.
   (B) there is a condemnation proceeding.
   (C) the owners will never be allowed to continue their use under the former zoning.
   (D) the owner can appeal to the zoning commission.

9. All of the following are used in municipal planning **EXCEPT**:
   (A) building codes.
   (B) housing codes.
   (C) subdivision regulations.
   (D) subdivision covenants.

10. All of the following are limitations or regulations of property exercised by government **EXCEPT**:
   (A) police power. (C) subordination.
   (B) taxation. (D) escheat.

❖ 11. *C* wants to extend the side of his house beyond the setback boundary. Which must *C* obtain?
   (A) Variance
   (B) Nonconforming use
   (C) Subordination agreement
   (D) Reservation

❖ 12. A governmental agency may acquire a certain property for public use by utilizing:
   (A) an attachment.
   (B) the right of eminent domain.
   (C) a suit to quiet title.
   (D) a claim of adverse possession.

13. Eminent domain **MOST** nearly means:
    (A) sale to a public corporation.
    (B) private use with consideration.
    (C) public use without compensation.
    (D) public use with compensation.

14. What is the greatest power the government has to affect the value of real property?
    (A) FHA minimum housing standards
    (B) Ad valorem taxes
    (C) Zoning
    (D) Declassification

15. A grandfather clause in a zoning ordinance may permit an owner to:
    (A) remodel the exterior of a building that is a nonconforming use.
    (B) enlarge a building that is a nonconforming use.
    (C) collect damages from the government.
    (D) sue for specific performance.

16. Zoning ordinances control the use of privately owned land by establishing land-use districts. All of the following are usual zoning districts **EXCEPT**:
    (A) residential.   (C) rental.
    (B) commercial.   (D) industrial.

17. Regulations established by local governments setting forth the construction requirements of structures are **BEST** described by which term?
    (A) Conveyance   (C) Common law
    (B) Devise   (D) Building code

18. Eminent domain, taxation, police power and escheat are:
    (A) restrictions on the ownership of any property.
    (B) benefits belonging to the owner of real property.
    (C) private restrictions on personal property.
    (D) factors that only affect owners of land abutting government owned property.

19. Zoning is done by authority of:
    (A) the mayor.
    (B) law of eminent domain.
    (C) police power.
    (D) petition.

❖ 20. *A*, a landowner, builds a small factory in the city. After the factory is built, the city adopts a zoning ordinance in which the area in question is designated a residential area. Which of the following statements about *A*'s alternatives is true?
    (A) *A* must move his plant to a portion of the city zoned for industrial purposes.
    (B) *A* may continue to operate as a nonconforming use.
    (C) *A* should abandon the plant and sue the city for damages.
    (D) *A* is entitled to a variance.

21. The provisions of county building codes are designed to establish minimum:
    (A) sideline and setback lines for buildings.
    (B) construction standards for buildings within the county.
    (C) standards for flood control.
    (D) licensing requirements for contractors.

22. When a zoning regulation permits a specific use of a property, but a private restriction contained in the deed limits that use of the property, the one that would prevail is the:
    (A) deed restriction.
    (B) zoning law.
    (C) master plan.
    (D) building restriction.

❖ 23. Which of the following is the **BEST** description of the purpose of a building permit?
    (A) Municipal control of the volume of building
    (B) Evidence of compliance with municipal regulations
    (C) Regulation of area and bulk of buildings
    (D) Evidence that construction fees have been paid

24. There are several ways in which land use is regulated or controlled. All of the following are means **EXCEPT**:
    (A) resolutions passed by local REALTOR® boards.
    (B) zoning ordinances.
    (C) public ownership.
    (D) restrictions contained in sellers' deeds.

25. Zoning ordinances usually cover such matters as:
    (A) base lines.   (C) deed restrictions.
    (B) setback lines.   (D) prescription.

26. Government restrictions on land include all of the following **EXCEPT**:
    (A) title settlement.   (C) eminent domain.
    (B) taxation.   (D) zoning.

❖ 27. The difference between police power and eminent domain can **BEST** be determined by:
    (A) whether or not the action was by sovereign power or by statute.
    (B) whether or not any compensation was paid to the owner.
    (C) whether or not the owner's use was affected.
    (D) whether or not the improvements are to be destroyed.

28. The right of eminent domain refers to:
    (A) the right of every American citizen to own property.
    (B) an organization's right to condemn property pending an improvement that is for the good of the community.
    (C) an institution or individual acquiring land by grant from the government.
    (D) the government's right to acquire or authorize others to acquire title to property for public use.

29. All of the following are true about the power of eminent domain **EXCEPT**:
    (A) may be exercised by a district school board seeking to obtain property for a public school.
    (B) requires that just compensation be paid the landowner when exercised.
    (C) may be used when a city wants to take an owner's yard to widen the highway.
    (D) may be used if a neighbor needs more access.

30. Compensation often follows a court action relating to which of the following?
    (A) Trustee's sale   (C) Condemnation
    (B) Police power   (D) Quiet title

❖ 31. The taking of private property for public use without compensation is authorized under the principles of:
    (A) escheat.   (C) eminent domain.
    (B) police power.   (D) zoning.

32. An action brought by a landowner against the government in which the landowner claims money damages because his or her property value has been lessened due to government action is best called:
    (A) subrogation.
    (B) attachment.
    (C) inverse condemnation.
    (D) lis pendens.

33. One owner wishes to develop a beauty shop on his or her property in an area zoned for single-family residences. What type of legal process should be requested?
    (A) Nonconforming use
    (B) Downzoning
    (C) Building permit
    (D) Variance

❖ 34. As defined in local zoning ordinances, the distance between lot lines and improvements is known as:
    (A) frontage.   (C) buffer zone.
    (B) setback.   (D) depth.

35. All of the following are effective tools for the municipal planner **EXCEPT**:
    (A) subdivision regulations.
    (B) building codes.
    (C) subdivision covenants.
    (D) zoning ordinances.

36. A zoning ordinance could validly affect all of the following **EXCEPT**:
    (A) height of a building.
    (B) proportion of building area to land area.
    (C) the use of a building.
    (D) the amount of rent charged tenants.

37. A flood-plain control regulation is an example of which type of governmental power?
    (A) Eminent domain   (C) Subdivision
    (B) Police power   (D) Attachment

ANSWERS

1. **B** The powers of eminent domain to take private property (including an air space easement) with just compensation for a public purpose often extend to quasi-public agencies such as public utilities.

2. **A**   Choice (B) is a nonconforming use.

3. **B**   Encroachments are physical encumbrances such as overextending eaves, trees, driveways or buildings.

4. **D**   As long as the nonconforming structure remains unchanged, the use is "grandfathered." However, the property will have to conform eventually to the new zoning.

5. **B**   The police power is given to the government by the constitution and enables the government to pass rules and regulations to protect the health, safety and welfare of the community. Restrictive covenants are private restrictions found in deeds or recorded declarations.

6. **B**   A nonconforming use is the continuation of a use that was permissible prior to the recent zoning change. A variance would be the introduction of a new use that varies from the current zoning.

7. **D**   Building codes directly regulate building materials and indirectly influence some architectural styles, especially in historic and preservation districts. There is no requirement for attorney review.

8. **D**   When property is taken by condemnation under eminent domain, just compensation is awarded, but generally not when property is regulated under police power, such as with a downzoning (e.g. from commercial to residential). Appeals are permitted within stated deadline.

9. **D**   Subdivision covenants are private, not public restrictions.

10. **C**   A fourth limitation by the government would be eminent domain.

11. **A**   *C* usually has to prove some hardship in order to justify a variance from the setback rule. A variance is an exception to a zoning regulation.

12. **B**   The government must pay "just compensation" to the condemnee for the taking. It pays less for acquiring an easement than for the fee simple title. If the government abandons the easement, clear title reverts to the condemnee.

13. **D**   Answer (C) would be a taking by police power. An example of (C) would be the destructive taking of a building to protect some other buildings from a spreading fire.

14. **C**   A government decision to downzone a business district to residential could seriously affect property values.

15. **A**   The owner of a nonconforming use is grandfathered under the old law and can generally do cosmetic remodeling, but can't make major structural changes.

16. **C**   Rental units are permitted in certain residential and commercial categories.

17. **D**   Building codes often are combined with plumbing and electrical codes.

18. **A**   Escheat would have the least frequent impact on real estate ownership in practice.

19. **C**   Police power is a constitutional power given to the government to pass rules and regulations to protect the health, welfare and safety of the community.

20. **B**   Because *A*'s use was permitted under the prior zoning, it will be allowed to continue.

21. **B**   Sideline and setback lines are established typically by zoning regulations.

22. **A**   Whichever rule is more strict—a government regulation or a private restriction—will control.

23. **B**   Building permits not only indicate compliance with building code requirements, but also check conformity with the zoning regulations.

24. **A**   REALTORS® are active in monitoring local land uses but do not make actual regulations.

25. **B**   Base lines (A) are used in government survey descriptions. Choice (D) involves easements.

26. **A**   Title settlement refers to the closing of a real estate transaction.

27. **B** If the value of property is lessened by government regulation under the police power as opposed to a taking under eminent domain, there is no just compensation paid.

28. **D** The government or a quasi-government agency (like a school district) can acquire property for public use upon paying just compensation, which is often determined in a condemnation proceeding with the government bringing suit against the condemnee.

29. **D** A school board would be a "quasi" (in the form of) governmental body authorized to exercise eminent domain powers. It is not a private neighbor (needs to be for a public purpose).

30. **C** Condemnation is the legal proceeding brought under the constitutional right of eminent domain when the government and the landowner cannot agree on an appropriate amount of just compensation.

31. **B** In emergency cases, such as a spreading fire, the government under the police power could destroy a person's property and not be liable for any compensation. Zoning (D) is the regulation, not the taking, of private property.

32. **C** Inverse condemnation is, in effect, an action by the landowner demanding the government complete a taking of the property and pay just compensation (for example if the state is constructing a highway and excavates part of the adjacent landowners' property).

33. **D** A variance is a request for a change to the existing zoning, usually based on some hardship. Downzoning is an action by the local government to change the zoning to a lower classification, such as from commercial to residential. A nonconforming use is a use that is allowed to continue after the area has been rezoned; eventually, the use will have to conform to the new zoning.

34. **B** Setback and sideline (or sideyard) requirements are helpful in keeping some open areas around contiguous properties.

35. **C** Subdivision covenants are private-use restrictions found in deeds and thus not directly available for public planning purposes.

36. **D** Zoning ordinances frequently control building size, height and density.

37. **B** Under the police power, the government can pass regulations to protect the health, welfare and safety of the general public, such as rules regarding types of structures in areas that are accessible to floods and requirements for special flood insurance, before lenders can loan on property located in flood-prone regions.

Chapter 6   Land Description

In the salesperson examination, there may be a few questions involving legal descriptions. In those states where the government survey system is used, these types of questions would be found in the unique state law section. Most probably, however, the problems will involve the metes and bounds description system. Brokers can expect to be tested on both systems.

GOVERNMENT SURVEY SYSTEM

A method of land description used in most states west of the Ohio River is the Government or Rectangular Survey System. It is based on a system of lines of longitude and latitude forming a checkerboard pattern of this portion of the United States. The north-south lines are called *principal* (or *prime*) *meridians* (of which there are 36 in the U.S.), and the east-west lines are called *parallel* or *base lines*. (See Figure 1.)

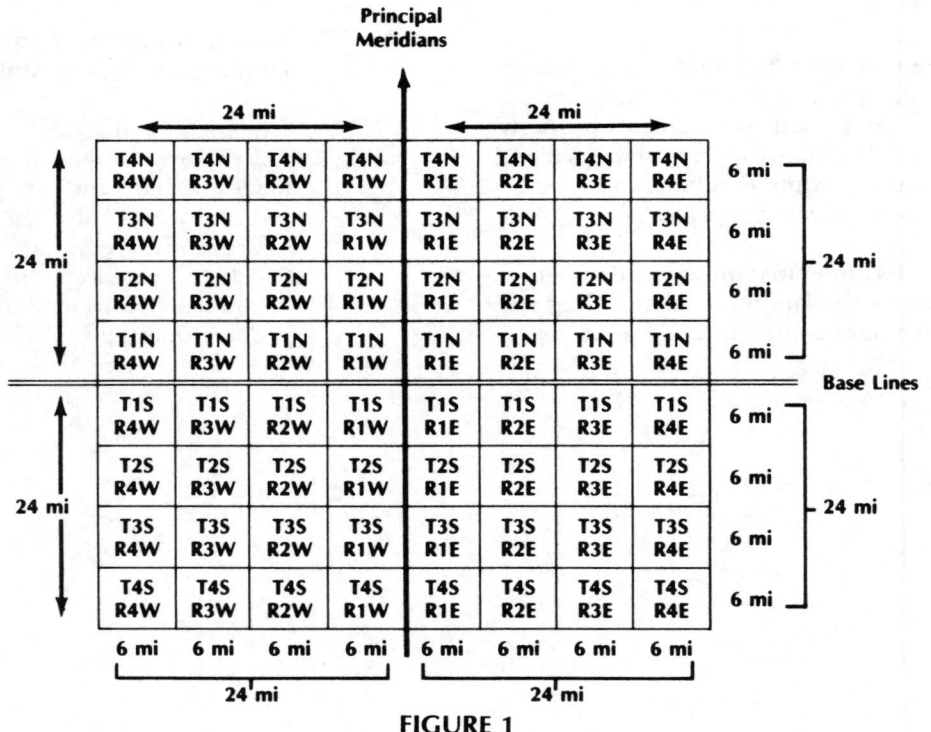

FIGURE 1

To the east and west of each meridian are strips of land six miles wide running in a north-south direction and parallel to each meridian. These north-south strips (columns) are called *ranges* and are identified by consecutive numbers to the east or west of each meridian. To the north or south of each base line are also strips of land six miles wide running in an east-west direction parallel to each base line, and these are identified by consecutive numbers to the north or south of the base line. These east-west strips (rows) are called *tiers*. To keep ranges and tiers straight you might try to remember the word "CARRAT":

Columns
Are
Ranges
Rows
Are
Tiers

Thus, ranges and tiers form squares six miles by six miles called *townships*. Each six mile by six mile township is further broken down into squares of one mile each, called *sections*, thus making 36 sections per township. Each section in a township is identified numerically, starting in the upper right corner running from right to left for six sections, then dropping down to the next row and running left to right for six sections, etc., until each of the 36 sections is numbered. (See Figure 2.)

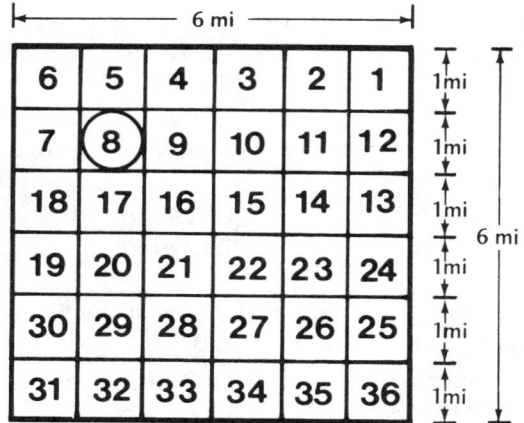

FIGURE 2 (Township)

To further divide a section of 640 acres into smaller areas, it is broken down into ½ section (320 acres), ¼ section (160 acres), etc., as seen on this page. (See Figure 3.)

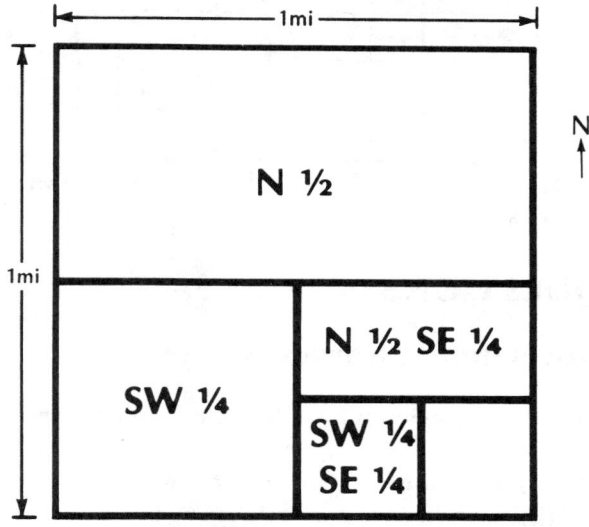

FIGURE 3 (Section)

When *locating* or *identifying* parcels from rectangular descriptions, one reads backwards from the general part of the description to the specific part at the beginning, or more specifically, from the meridian, range, and township to the section or part of a section. Thus, a tract of land in the Southwest one-quarter of the Southeast one-quarter, Section 8, Township 3 South, Range 3 West of the 9th principal meridian (ordinarily abbreviated as SW ¼, SE ¼, S8, T3S, R3W 9th P.M.), would be identified by reading from right to left, first identifying the 9th P.M., then Range 3 West, then Township 3 South, then Section 8, then the Southeast ¼ of Section 8, then the Southwest ¼ of that quarter-section. (See Figure 4.)

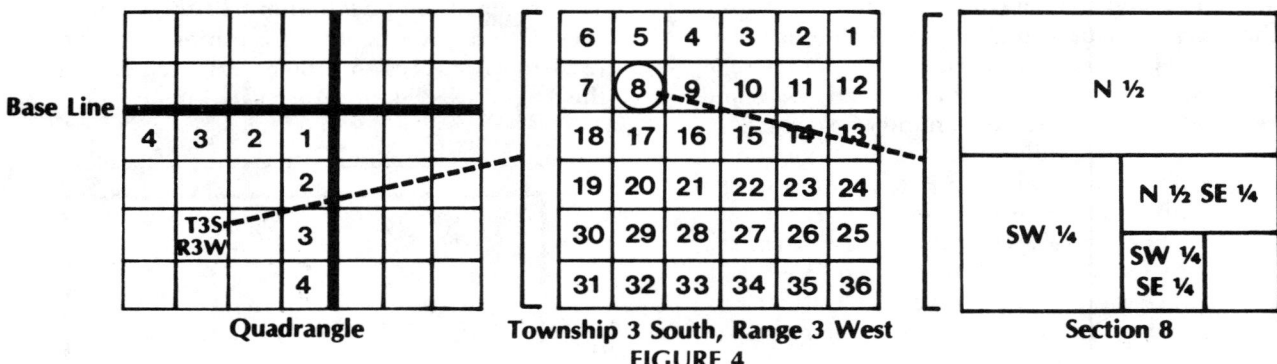

Base Line

T3S R3W

Quadrangle

Township 3 South, Range 3 West

FIGURE 4

N ½

N ½ SE ¼

SW ¼

SW ¼ SE ¼

Section 8

QUESTIONS

Government Survey System

1. The North-South lines that are 24 miles apart are called:
   (A) base lines.   (C) columns.
   (B) meridians.   (D) ranges.

2. A range is numbered to the:
   (A) east or west of a principal meridian.
   (B) north or south of a base line.
   (C) north or south of a principal meridian.
   (D) east or north of a base line.

3. A township contains:
   (A) 6 sections.   (C) 24 sections.
   (B) 16 sections.   (D) 36 sections.

4. A tier is numbered to the:
   (A) east or west of a principal meridian.
   (B) north or south of a base line.
   (C) east or west of a base line.
   (D) north or south of a principal meridian.

❖ 5. The NW ¼ of the NE ¼ of the SW ¼ of Section 12 contains how many acres?
   (A) 10   (C) 30
   (B) 20   (D) 40

6. The horizontal distance between two township boundaries is:
   (A) 6 miles.   (C) 23 miles.
   (B) 18 miles.   (D) 24 miles.

7. Which of the following contains the smallest parcel of land?
   (A) 640 acres   (C) ½ of a township
   (B) 9 square miles   (D) 36 square miles

8. Which of the following contains the largest parcel of land?
   (A) 2 miles square
   (B) 2 sections
   (C) 10 percent of a township
   (D) 43,560 ft. by 43,560 ft.

❖ 9. Section 11 in a township is:
   (A) north of Section 14 and south of Section 2.
   (B) north of Section 17 and south of Section 5.
   (C) north of Section 19 and south of Section 17.
   (D) north of Section 22 and south of Section 10.

10. Section 2 in a township is directly south of what Section of the township directly to its north?
   (A) 2   (C) 32
   (B) 5   (D) 35

11. Each side of a square acre contains approximately:
   (A) 208 ft.   (C) 230 ft.
   (B) 215 ft.   (D) 320 ft.

12. How many acres are in the N ½ of the SE ¼ of the SE ¼ of a section of land?
   (A) 8 acres   (C) 32 acres
   (B) 20 acres   (D) 64 acres

13. How many townships are there in a piece of land 24 miles square?
   (A) 8   (C) 24
   (B) 16   (D) 32

14. The NE ¼ of SW ¼ of Section 8 contains:
   (A) 40 acres.   (C) 120 acres.
   (B) 80 acres.   (D) 160 acres.

❖ 15. In a standard township, which of the following sections would be contiguous to Section 30?

(A) 19, 20, 31 and 32

(B) 29 only

(C) 19, 20, 21, 31 and 32

(D) 19, 29 and 33

❖ 16. What is the shortest distance between the closest borders of Section 2 and Section 35 of the same township?

(A) 2 miles   (C) 6 miles

(B) 4 miles   (D) 12 miles

17. Which of the following is larger than a standard section?

(A) 16 parcels, 40 acres each

(B) 5,000 ft. by 6,000 ft.

(C) 1/36 of a township

(D) 5,280 ft. by 5,280 ft.

METES AND BOUNDS

Metes and bounds descriptions are used often when it is not possible to locate a parcel of land by rectangular survey or by lot and block on a recorded plat map. The first part of a metes and bounds description is used to locate the "point of beginning" of the parcel to be described. To do this, we start from a known monument or other known location, called the point of beginning, and proceed around the boundaries of the property by reference to the linear measurement, direction and course, ending back at the point of beginning. A metes and bounds description may use the Azimuth System or the Bearing System in establishing direction between points along the perimeter of a parcel. In the Azimuth System, all directions are expressed in terms of the angle from North, moving clockwise, through 360 degrees.

Thus, a complete circle is divided into 360 degrees, each degree is further broken down into 60 minutes, and each minute is broken down into 60 seconds. In most metes and bounds descriptions, azimuths are measured clockwise from true north. (See Figure 5.) Example: an azimuth of 120 degrees, 48 minutes, 17 seconds would be written 120° 48' 17".

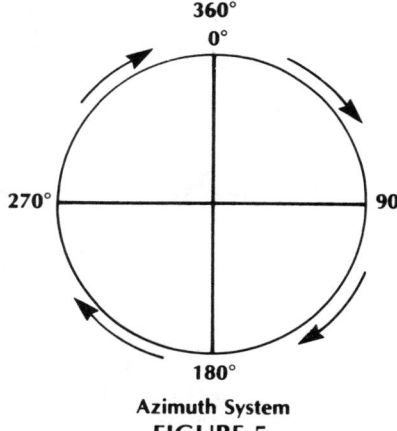

Azimuth System
FIGURE 5

In the Bearing System, the complete circle is divided into four quadrants. The quadrants then are identified North-East, South-East, South-West and North-West. Each contains only 90 degrees, measured from the North-South line toward the east or west. (See Figure 6.) Example: a bearing of North 36 degrees, 18 minutes, 51 seconds West would be written N 36° 18' 51" W.

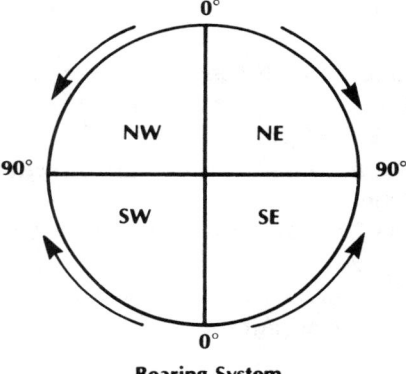

Bearing System

FIGURE 6

Thus a Bearing of S 45° E is equal to 135° Azimuth. (See Figure 7.)

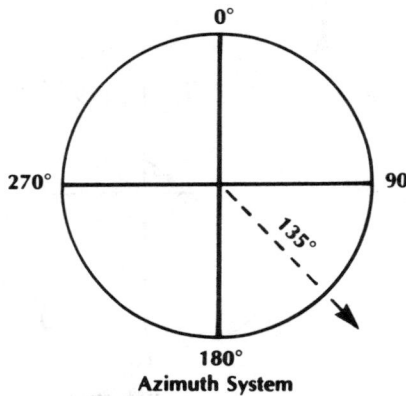

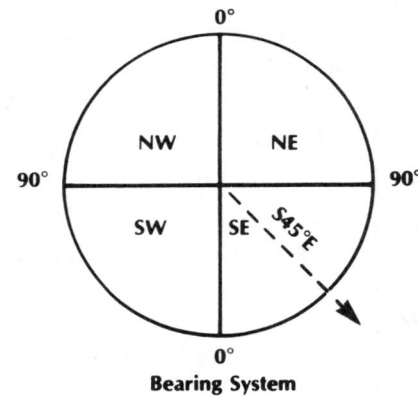

FIGURE 7

QUESTIONS

Metes and Bounds

❖ 1. An azimuth direction of 185° 30' (185 degrees, 30 minutes) from north would read on a Bearing System:
   (A) S 5° 30' W.   (C) W 5° 30' S.
   (B) S 5° 30' E.   (D) E 5° 30' W.

2. In showing the direction of a property line using the Bearing System, all of the following is true **EXCEPT**:
   (A) the letter prefix shows the direction to point.
   (B) the letter suffix shows the direction to swing.
   (C) the system uses 180° quadrants.
   (D) each quadrant has 90°.

❖ 3. The bearing direction of N 80° 50' W is the same as:
   (A) 190° 10'.   (C) 100° 10'.
   (B) 279° 10'.   (D) 350° 10'.

4. The bearing of N 25° 30' W is the same as the Azimuth System direction of:
   (A) 91° 30'.   (C) 179° 30'.
   (B) 341° 30'.   (D) 334° 30'.

5. Which of the following is most nearly due South?
   (A) S 89° 30' E   (C) S 0° 30' W
   (B) S 0° 45' E   (D) S 1° 15' W

6. In a metes and bounds legal description, the "bounds" refers to which of the following?
   (A) Measures   (C) Monuments
   (B) Distances   (D) Compass direction

ANSWERS

Government Survey System

1. **B**   Meridians are the lines 24 miles apart running in a north-south direction that form the east-west sides of a quadrangle (since range lines are 6 miles apart, every 4th range line forms the side of a quadrangle).

2. **A**   Ranges are the land strips running in a north-south direction that lie to the east or west of the meridian. They are thus numbered starting at the meridian, with the numbers getting larger as they move to the east or west of that meridian.

3. **D**   There are 16 townships in a quadrangle, and 36 sections in a township.

4. **B**   Tiers are the strips of land running in an east-west direction that lie to the north or south of a base line. they are thus numbered starting at the base line, with the numbers getting larger as they move to the north or south.

5. **A**   A section contains 640 acres. A fourth (10) of a fourth (40) of a fourth (160); or 640 acres × ¼ = 160 acres × ¼ = 40 acres × ¼ = 10 acres.

6. **A**   Each township is 6 horizontal miles across, or 24 miles across a quadrangle.

7. **A**   640 acres = 1 square mile (1 section), and ½ of a township = 18 square miles.

8. **A**   2 miles square is equal to 4 square miles.

9. **A**   See Figure 2.

10. **D**   See Figure 4.

11. **A**   208 × 208 = 43,264. An acre equals 43,560 sq. ft.

12. **B**   See Figure 3.

13. **B**   See Figure 1.

14. **A**   ¼ × ¼ × 640 = 40. See Figure 3.

15. **A**   See Figure 2.

16. **B**   See Figure 2.

17. **B**   All the other three choices equal one section.

Metes and Bounds

1. **A**   See Figure 7. Azimuth 185° 30' would be the same direction, but written as S 5° 30' W in the Bearing System.

2. **C**   The first letter indicates north or south of the middle horizontal line, and the second letter tells you to swing to the west or east of the center vertical line. (See Figure 6.)

3. **B**   Using Figure 7, an azimuth of 279° 10' is the same direction as a bearing of N 80° 50' W.

4. **D**   Using Figure 7, N 25° 30' W is at the same position (in the same direction) as an Azimuth of 334° 30'.

5. **C**   Choice (C) is only one-half degree to the west of due south.

6. **C**   A metes and bounds description starts at a well-marked point of beginning and follows the boundaries of the land by courses and metes (measures, distances and compass direction) and bounds (landmarks, monuments) and returns to the true point of beginning.

PART B   Valuation of Real Estate

This part contains questions on the topics of the

- Principles of value
- Commonly accepted approaches to value
- Effect of depreciation on value
- Assessment of real property for tax purposes
- Basic principles of federal income taxation of real property

Expect about 15 percent of the general portion of the examination to contain questions on the topics covered in Part B. Brokers can expect another 5 percent on federal income tax aspects.

Chapter 7   Appraisal

Questions in this chapter will test your comprehension of the following topics:

- Use and reconciliation of the three methods of appraisal
- The different types of depreciation, including functional and external obsolescence
- The four elements of value
- The different types of value
- The capitalization of income to arrive at value
- Replacement cost and reproduction cost
- The gross income multiplier technique

False Friends

The following words are often confused with one another. Note the difference in meaning of these false friends:

Functional/External Obsolescence: A loss in value resulting from some internal factor (e.g., poor design, outdated equipment) as opposed to an external factor (e.g., neighborhood change, highway relocation).

Reproduction/Replacement Cost: The cost to construct an exact replica as opposed to the cost to construct a building with similar material and use.

Assemblage/Plottage: Assemblage is the process of joining several parcels to form a larger parcel; the resulting increase in value is called plottage.

Capitalization Rate/Recapture Rate: The cap rate is the rate of return the investor wants on a property; it consists on the return on the investment plus the recapture (through depreciation) of the investment.

With the 1993 requirement that only licensed or certified appraisers can be used to appraise collateral for federally related loans, real estate licensees need to be careful not to represent that their opinions of value are appraisals. Brokers are still able to recommend listing and sales prices, but are prohibited from charging a separate fee for such recommendations. You can expect that some of the appraisal questions will involve math calculations as well.

QUESTIONS

❖ 1. Of the three methods of appraising properties, the replacement cost approach is particularly appropriate and would give the **MOST** accurate value in the appraisal of:
   - (A) a new home
   - (B) a multiple dwelling.
   - (C) an old home.
   - (D) a medium-age home.

2. An appraiser measuring the area of a house would use the:
   - (A) net rentable area.
   - (B) exterior dimensions.
   - (C) room sizes.
   - (D) interior dimensions, excluding partitions.

3. The capitalization rate for improvements is the:
   - (A) recapture rate only.
   - (B) interest rate only.
   - (C) overall rate.
   - (D) interest rate plus recapture rate.

4. The economic life of a building has come to an end when:
   - (A) the building ceases to represent the highest and best use of the land.
   - (B) the value of the land and the building equals the value of the land only.
   - (C) the rent produced is valued at less than a similar amount of money invested elsewhere could produce.
   - (D) the reserve for depreciation equals the cost to replace the building.

5. The market comparison approach to value is an indication of:
   - (A) the lowest value.
   - (B) the highest value.
   - (C) the future value.
   - (D) the range of probable value.

❖ 6. What type of reduction in value is present when a hydrogen gas storage tank is located next to a property?
   - (A) Physical deterioration
   - (B) External obsolescence
   - (C) Functional obsolescence
   - (D) Negligible obsolescence

7. All of the following are characteristic of value **EXCEPT:**
   - (A) utility.
   - (B) scarcity.
   - (C) transferability.
   - (D) cost.

8. Physical deterioration **MOST** closely means:
   - (A) obsolescence.
   - (B) wear and tear.
   - (C) reversion.
   - (D) recapture.

9. The market comparison appraisal approach would be **BEST** used for:
   - (A) estimating the price for new homes in a new subdivision.
   - (B) valuing vacant land.
   - (C) establishing a price on a nonprofit hospital.
   - (D) determining the best price for a small private school.

10. When capitalization is sought, a person is particularly interested in:
   - (A) potential future value.
   - (B) cost value.
   - (C) total capital invested.
   - (D) evaluating income.

11. A capitalization rate incorporates:
   - (A) return on land and building and recapture of building.
   - (B) return on land and building and recapture of land.
   - (C) return on land and recapture of land and building.
   - (D) return on building and recapture of land and building.

12. The purchase and putting together of several pieces of land is **BEST** called:
   - (A) annexation.
   - (B) appreciation.
   - (C) assemblage.
   - (D) integration.

13. Concerning the valuation of residential property, which of the following is true?
    (A) The value of the ordinary single-family residential property should be based on the income it is capable of producing if rented.
    (B) In valuing a residence, functional accessories such as built-in teak cabinets are seldom taken into consideration.
    (C) An older home in a neighborhood of newer homes would retain its value and not be affected by the value of the other homes.
    (D) Recently sold homes in the neighborhood would give a fair indication of the value of similar homes.

14. When the landlord makes improvements to the property, the investment should be recovered over a set period of time. The landlord would use:
    (A) an amortization rate.
    (B) a discount rate.
    (C) a recapture rate.
    (D) a reformation rate.

15. If the replacement cost shows a higher value than the appraised value, which of the following **MOST** probably has occurred?
    (A) Accrued depreciation
    (B) Excessive appraisal
    (C) External obsolescence
    (D) Capitalization

16. In making an appraisal, the before-and-after method is used **MOST** often with:
    (A) condemnation.
    (B) exchange.
    (C) cost of reproduction.
    (D) option.

17. An appraiser often makes a distinction between the physical life and economic life of an improvement. Regarding these two ways to measure "life," which is generally true?
    (A) Economic life lasts longer.
    (B) Economic life and physical age are usually parallel.
    (C) Physical life is shorter.
    (D) Economic life ceases first.

❖ 18. Which of the following facts might be classified as functional obsolescence?
    (A) Exterior needs painting.
    (B) Property fronts on a busy expressway.
    (C) Property has a single-car garage.
    (D) Neighborhood is 50 years old.

19. Assume that the trend in architectural design is toward more contemporary-styled homes. Because of this trend, a conservatively designed home will tend to:
    (A) decrease in value more rapidly.
    (B) decrease in value less rapidly.
    (C) stay the same.
    (D) stay the same and then appreciate.

20. The useful life of a building, or period of time after which the income provided by it is **NOT** sufficient to warrant its maintenance, is called:
    (A) recapture limit.
    (B) economic life.
    (C) reversion limit.
    (D) investment duration.

21. All of the following statements are true **EXCEPT:**
    (A) Functional obsolescence is the result of factors within the property.
    (B) External obsolescence is caused by factors outside the property.
    (C) External obsolescence is the result of one's personal financial condition.
    (D) Deterioration is wear and tear.

22. The **MOST** widely used approach to the appraisal of residential real property is the:
    (A) income approach.
    (B) direct sales comparison approach.
    (C) cost approach.
    (D) gross income multiplier.

23. A broker usually appraises to determine:
    (A) assessed value.   (C) market value.
    (B) book value.   (D) insurance value.

❖ 24. Market value could be determined best by considering which of the following?
    (A) Acquisition cost, market data, replacement
    (B) Comparison, income, replacement
    (C) Purchase price, summation cost
    (D) Income stream, acquisition cost

25. The value of a leased fee property is equal to:
    (A) rent to the landlord.
    (B) rent plus leasehold interest.
    (C) rent plus reversionary right
    (D) commission to broker.

26. The period of time through which a property gives benefits to its owner is **BEST** described as:
    (A) investment duration.
    (B) physical life.
    (C) value duration.
    (D) economic life.

27. Real estate values are **MOST** affected by:
    (A) location.
    (B) availability of money.
    (C) appraisal.
    (D) national trends.

28. A house with four bedrooms and one bath is an example of:
    (A) external obsolescence.
    (B) functional obsolescence.
    (C) over-built obsolescence.
    (D) residual physical depreciation.

29. Which of the following is true of real estate appraisers of property secured by federally related loans?
    (A) They need a master's degree.
    (B) They usually base their fees on a percentage of the appraised value.
    (C) They must hold a state appraiser's license or certification.
    (D) They usually do not inspect the property.

30. An official valuation of property for ad valorem tax purposes is **BEST** described as:
    (A) a capitalization.
    (B) an assessment appraisal.
    (C) tax depreciation.
    (D) tax equalization.

31. Using the income approach to valuation, which of the following is not a proper deduction from effective gross income to determine net income?
    (A) Reserve for replacement
    (B) Interest payments on loans
    (C) Maintenance expenses
    (D) Management costs

32. Capitalization is a process used to:
    (A) determine the value of most residential property.
    (B) convert income into value.
    (C) determine the total remaining capital.
    (D) save money on an investment.

❖ 33. The difference between the cost of replacement and current valuation of a single-family residence is equal to:
    (A) accrued depreciation.
    (B) assessed valuation.
    (C) investment limitation.
    (D) economic replacement.

34. In estimating the value lost by a structure due to physical deterioration, the appraiser places greatest emphasis on:
    (A) the age of the building.
    (B) the condition of the surrounding buildings.
    (C) the observed condition of the subject building.
    (D) the zoning of the neighborhood.

❖ 35. A residence located in an area where there are factories and plants, and where there is much smoke and dust, is suffering from:
    (A) physical depreciation.
    (B) external obsolescence.
    (C) residential regression.
    (D) accrued depreciation.

❖ 36. A post office of unique design and construction is **BEST** appraised by which of the following approaches?
    (A) Income
    (B) Market comparison
    (C) Land residual
    (D) Cost

37. All of the following are true about loss in value due to obsolescence **EXCEPT:**
    (A) Extra-large load-bearing columns in a 30-year-old commercial building would represent incurable functional obsolescence.
    (B) An unattractive storefront window would represent curable functional obsolescence.
    (C) A chemical plant being located across the street from a private residence would represent external obsolescence.
    (D) A larger property next door sold for 20 percent below the listed price.

❖ 38. All of the following are examples of external obsolescence **EXCEPT:**
(A) population density.
(B) direct effect of the elements.
(C) zoning.
(D) nearby highway realignment.

39. In using the direct sales comparison approach to value, the appraiser considers:
(A) the sales price of comparable properties.
(B) the acquisition cost to the present owner.
(C) the income stream.
(D) the vacancy and bad debt factor.

40. Of the following, which type of value would equal the actual market value?
(A) Assessed value   (C) Book value
(B) Insurance value   (D) Comparable value

❖ 41. Market value is most closely related to:
(A) comparable price.
(B) replacement price.
(C) income analysis.
(D) reproduction price.

42. In regard to the capitalization rate:
(A) value of property increases as it increases.
(B) value of property decreases as it decreases.
(C) value of property decreases as it increases.
(D) a changing capitalization rate has no effect on value of the property.

43. The capitalization rate of a property is the ratio between:
(A) the equity of the owner and the selling price.
(B) the net income and the market value.
(C) the sales price and the mortgaged value.
(D) the recapture rate and the land residual.

44. The gross income (rent) multiplier is calculated by dividing the sales price by the:
(A) Monthly net income
(B) Monthly gross income
(C) Annual net income
(D) Annual gross income

45. All of the following are used to estimate value **EXCEPT:**
(A) improvements.   (C) owner's livelihood.
(B) deterioration.   (D) economic life.

❖ 46. A factor by which the appraiser multiplies the total rental income from a property as an estimate of its value is the:
(A) gross income multiplier.
(B) land residual process.
(C) building residual process.
(D) capitalization rate.

47. The cost of constructing a new building, having utility equivalent to the property under appraisal but built with modern materials according to current standards, design and layout, is an appropriate definition of:
(A) reproduction cost.
(B) replacement cost.
(C) residual technique
(D) economic replacement

48. A homogeneous community typically has what effect on real estate values?
(A) Stabilizes them
(B) Causes the value to increase
(C) Causes the value to decrease
(D) Does not have any effect

❖ 49. When an appraiser adjusts the estimate of the value because of a poor floor plan, this is called:
(A) physical depreciation.
(B) functional obsolescence.
(C) cost-adjustment ratio.
(D) structural depreciation.

❖ 50. Highest and best use is concerned with all of the following **EXCEPT:**
(A) net yield to owner.
(B) utility of surrounding area.
(C) relationship to regional development.
(D) interest rate on investment loans.

51. If a building has an estimated remaining economic life of 50 years, the appropriate recapture rate will **MOST** likely be:
(A) 2 percent.   (C) 6 percent.
(B) 3 percent.   (D) 18 percent.

52. An appraiser's fee is typically based on which of the following?
(A) Value of property
(B) Time and expense
(C) Percentage of value plus a flat fee
(D) State regulated fees

53. An appraisal of real estate does which of the following?
    - (A) Determines value
    - (B) Estimates value
    - (C) Guarantees value
    - (D) Assures value

54. Which one of the following **BEST** describes the concept of highest and best use?
    - (A) Gross return
    - (B) Natural and legal use
    - (C) Greatest net return over a given period
    - (D) Homogeneous use

❖ 55. The collection of data and the analysis of different approaches to value is known as:
    - (A) depreciation.
    - (B) amortization.
    - (C) reconciliation.
    - (D) accrual.

❖ 56. The formula used in direct capitalization of income property valuation is:
    - (A) value equals cap rate divided by income.
    - (B) value equals income divided by cap rate.
    - (C) value equals income multiplied by cap rate.
    - (D) value equals income divided by net assets.

57. Replacement cost is **BEST** described as the:
    - (A) original cost adjusted for inflation.
    - (B) cost of building a property of equivalent utility with modern materials.
    - (C) cost of purchasing an equally desirable property.
    - (D) cost of building an exact replica of the subject.

58. An appraisal is needed to make all of the following **EXCEPT:**
    - (A) market value.
    - (B) replacement value.
    - (C) loan value.
    - (D) book value.

❖ 59. In appraising investment property what does the owner deduct to arrive at the net effective income?
    - (A) Federal income taxes
    - (B) Capital improvements
    - (C) Vacancy and bad debt losses
    - (D) All ordinary expenses to the property

60. *C* bought into a new subdivision located near the airport. The airport got federal and state approval to redirect the flight path of incoming planes over the new subdivision. The effect of change is known as:
    - (A) physical obsolescence.
    - (B) functional obsolescence.
    - (C) external obsolescence.
    - (D) nominal obsolescence.

61. Lots are valued at $30,000. Reproduction cost of the dwelling is $170,000. If properties are now selling for $140,000, the accrued depreciation is:
    - (A) $30,000.
    - (B) $50,000.
    - (C) $60,000.
    - (D) $80,000.

62. Assume there are two similar buildings, one of which is leased for much greater rent as a warehouse, the other as a library. What can be said about the capitalization rate used for the library?
    - (A) It would be the same as the warehouse.
    - (B) It would be lower than the warehouse.
    - (C) It would be higher than the warehouse.
    - (D) It has no capitalization rate.

63. The actual price of a piece of real property is **BEST** described as the:
    - (A) book value.
    - (B) replacement value.
    - (C) selling price.
    - (D) market value.

64. An appraiser preparing a market analysis of a parcel of real property would be **MOST** sensitive to the recent market tendencies of:
    - (A) buyers.
    - (B) lenders.
    - (C) brokers.
    - (D) appraisers.

65. Which of the following tends to lower property values?
    - (A) Neighborhood conformity
    - (B) Excessive demand
    - (C) Transferability
    - (D) Deferred maintenance

❖ 66. When a property has suffered a reduction in value due to dry rot and termite damage, appraisers will refer to such reduction as:
    - (A) functional obsolescence.
    - (B) external obsolescence.
    - (C) physical deterioration.
    - (D) residual loss.

67. The period of time necessary to recover an investment in a commercial building is **BEST** described as:
    (A) residual.   (C) recapture.
    (B) reversion.   (D) recovery.

68. Which of the following conditions is an indication of functional obsolescence?
    (A) Cracked foundation
    (B) Neighborhood airport expanded to land jumbo jets
    (C) Ceiling lower than customary
    (D) Increase in special assessments

69. Which of the following **BEST** describes the function of a real estate appraiser?
    (A) Estimates price   (C) Estimates value
    (B) Determines value   (D) Determines price

70. All of the following could be considered functional obsolescence in evaluating a commercial building **EXCEPT:**
    (A) architectural design.
    (B) volume or capacity in relation to site.
    (C) parking plan.
    (D) supply and demand.

71. An appraiser who is evaluating an urban commercial warehouse would look for all of the following factors **EXCEPT:**
    (A) potential income from the property.
    (B) the replacement cost and accrued depreciation.
    (C) economic life of building.
    (D) original cost of the building.

72. Which is the most appropriate appraisal method to use in evaluating a property for fire insurance purposes?
    (A) Market date   (C) Replacement cost
    (B) Capitalization   (D) Comparison

73. All of these facts are important for an appraiser of a commercial shopping center to discover **EXCEPT:**
    (A) the person(s) entitled to possession and ownership.
    (B) the rents and operating expenses.
    (C) all existing encumbrances.
    (D) the current rate for commercial loans.

❖ 74. Which of the following **BEST** describes the highest and best use for a particular property?
    (A) The use that the owner wants
    (B) Whatever is the present use
    (C) The use that produces the greatest net return
    (D) Whatever use produces the highest density zoning

❖ 75. *S* inherited a residence from her father. The value at the date of his death five years ago was $117,000. An appraiser hired to recommend a listing price would be primarily concerned with which of the following?
    (A) The $117,000 figure and the average rate of appreciation of residences the past five years
    (B) The value of similar residences recently sold in the community
    (C) The book value of the dwelling
    (D) The equity at the time of the father's death

76. All of the following would be considered in the cost approach appraisal method **EXCEPT:**
    (A) operating expenses.
    (B) depreciation.
    (C) land value.
    (D) replacement cost

77. Assume you just obtained a listing on a residence located adjacent to a new hamburger drive-in chain store. An appraiser of the residence would give which of the following?
    (A) Careful concern with external obsolescence
    (B) Minimal concern with highest and best use
    (C) Primary attention to the projected income stream
    (D) Maximum concern to the earning potential of the hamburger stand

❖ 78. A broker, in making an informal appraisal for listing purposes, finds comparable residences that have sold recently for $92,000, $82,000 and $102,000. The broker should advise the seller the residence should be listed at which amount?
    (A) Highest
    (B) Lowest
    (C) Average of the three
    (D) Price of the most similar property

79. Which of the following would be the appropriate method of selecting a capitalization rate for an income producing property?
    (A) Gross income divided by value
    (B) Net income divided by value
    (C) Value divided by net income
    (D) Gross expenses divided by net income

❖ 80. Assume that three rental buildings had sales prices and rents as follows: $107,250 and $16,500; $105,625 and $16,250; $112,125 and $17,250. What value would most likely be indicated on a similar building if rents are $16,750?
    (A) $107,250   (C) $108,875
    (B) $108,300   (D) $112,125

81. All of the following are economic characteristics of value **EXCEPT**:
    (A) demand.   (C) utility.
    (B) transferability. (D) expansion.

❖ 82. When evaluating an income property, an appraiser must take into consideration all of the following **EXCEPT**:
    (A) the correct capitalization rate.
    (B) the cost of the building next door.
    (C) net operating income of property.
    (D) the vacancy and bad debt rates.

❖ 83. In using the gross rent multiplier, Comparable A has a value of $88,000 with monthly net income of $880; Comparable B is $90,000 with $900; Comparable C is $95,000 with $950. If you receive $930 a month net income, what is your comparable value
    (A) $91,500   (C) $94,000
    (B) $93,000   (D) $97,500

84. All of the following is true about the direct sales comparison approach **EXCEPT**:
    (A) Offers to sell are helpful to set the lower limits.
    (B) The type of financing for comparable sales is relevant.
    (C) Listing prices of comparable homes are relevant.
    (D) Net operating income figures are not relevant.

85. The capitalization approach to valuation does not consider:
    (A) real property tax.   (C) lot size.
    (B) vacancy rate.   (D) insurance costs.

86. The value of the land plus the reproduction cost less depreciation is the formula for which appraisal approach?
    (A) Direct sales comparison
    (B) Cost
    (C) Income
    (D) Gross rent multiplier

87. Where properties of dissimilar value are placed together, the value of the more expensive property will be affected adversely. This principle of change is called:
    (A) regression.
    (B) progression.
    (C) substitution.
    (D) decreasing return.

88. A new office building constructed in an old neighborhood is for sale. What is the best method of appraisal to use?
    (A) Direct sales comparison
    (B) Cost of construction plus land
    (C) Income
    (D) Replacement method

89. What factors of a building determine the capitalization rate?
    (A) Rent
    (B) Expenses
    (C) Interest and recapture of investment
    (D) Mortgage

ANSWERS

1. **A** The older a building, the more difficult it becomes to accurately adjust for depreciation. The approach based on the principle of substitution—a buyer will not pay more than it costs to duplicate.

2. **B** The appraiser is concerned with exterior dimensions.

3. **D** In vacant land, the capitalization rate is the interest rate alone; however, since a building is a wasting asset, the investor must also "recapture" (or get a return of) the cost of the building.

4. **B** Economic life is the period over which a building can be profitably utilized; it is often shorter than the physical life of the building.

5. **D**   Market comparison approach, also called direct sales comparison approach, indicates probable range due to the principle of substitution; a property's value tends to be set by the cost of obtaining an equally desirable substitute property.

6. **B**   External obsolescence is loss in value due to external causes outside of the property itself, such as a change in zoning.

7. **D**   The elements of value are utility, scarcity, transferability and demand.

8. **B**   Loss in value due to wear and tear is physical deterioration, such as damage from the elements (storms or snow).

9. **B**   Market comparison is used most effectively in the appraisal of properties that are frequently sold in the marketplace. Choices (A), (C) and (D) would be the cost approach.

10. **D**   Capitalization is sought when one wants to determine the present value of a projected income stream, or, in other words, what a person would pay for the right to receive certain monies over a given period.

11. **A**   An investor would get a return *on* the investment in the land and building (similar to receiving interest) and a return *of* his or her investment in the building through recapture (similar to depreciation rate).

12. **C**   Assemblage is the formation of a parcel from two or more lots, to be distinguished from plottage, which is the end result.

13. **D**   In comparing properties, appropriate consideration is given to different amenities, and monetary adjustments are made for each feature. The income approach is not appropriate for residential properties.

14. **C**   Through depreciation, the landlord will recapture the investment in the building and improvements before the building reaches the end of its productive life.

15. **A**   If it costs $100,000 to reproduce a five-year-old building valued at $92,000, there has been an adjustment made for $8,000 of depreciation over the five years.

16. **A**   When there is a condemnation or partial taking of a property, it necessitates determining the value before and after the condemnation. For example, if a ten-acre parcel is worth $1,000 per acre before an eight-acre section is condemned, and the remaining two acres are only worth $500 each after the condemnation, then the condemnee will receive $8,000 for the eight acres plus $1,000 for the loss in value to the two remaining acres.

17. **D**   The value of the building typically ceases before it becomes structurally useless.

18. **C**   Lack of desirability in terms of design or layout as compared with that of a new property serving the same function is functional obsolescence. Usually double garages are functionally more acceptable.

19. **A**   This is an example of loss in value due to functional obsolescence.

20. **B**   Economic life is the period over which a building may be profitably utilized.

21. **C**   Choices (A) and (B) are correct definitions of obsolescence and together with physical deterioration they result in depreciation or loss in value.

22. **B**   The market comparison approach (using comparables) is the approach most commonly used by real estate brokers and salespeople in their every day estimation of market values.

23. **C**   A broker is most concerned with knowing market value to assist a customer in buying, selling or determining loan value. Assessed value is used for tax purposes, and book value for accounting purposes.

24. **B**   All three are appraisal approaches to value. Under choices (A), (C) and (D) acquisition cost is generally not relevant to present value.

25. **C** The purchasers of the fee will pay a price that relates to the receipt of rental income over the term of the lease, as well as the right to receive the property at the termination of the lease (the reversion).

26. **D** Economic life is the period over which a building is profitably utilized.

27. **A** A shack on Waikiki Beach would be far more valuable than a mansion in the middle of the Mojave Desert. The three most important factors affecting value are location, location and location.

28. **B** Lack of desirability due to function, layout or design is an indication of functional obsolescence. One bathroom with four bedrooms is a poor design by modern standards.

29. **D** Effective in 1993, states passed laws requiring appraisers to be licensed or certified, with certification being the higher requirement. It would be unethical to have a contingent appraisal fee.

30. **B** In order to tax property, the taxing body must first evaluate (appraise) the property. It will then be assessed at a certain percentage of its market value. For example, if the assessed rate is 60 percent and the fair market value is $100,000, then the assessed value is $60,000.

31. **B** Neither principal nor interest payments on existing mortgages are deductible as operating expenses, nor is building depreciation.

32. **B** Capitalization determines the present worth of future benefits. In other words, it is the evaluation of a projected income stream.

33. **A** The value of a property under the cost approach is the cost to replace less the accrued depreciation. For this reason, the replacement cost approach is best suited to new properties because they have not accrued any depreciation.

34. **C** Effective age, not actual age, is sought in a determination of depreciation through physical deterioration.

35. **B** External obsolescence is loss in value due to conditions of the surrounding neighborhood. The question does not present any facts indicating this house suffered physical damage caused by the dust and smoke.

36. **D** The cost approach (also called summation approach) is the best way to appraise a property where there is no rental income and no comparables recently bought or sold.

37. **D** Replacing the wide columns would be economically unfeasible. A storefront window most likely could be made attractive at little cost to the owner.

38. **B** Population changes, changes in zoning or highway realignment might cause external obsolescence of the property. Direct effect of the elements (such as wind or snow) could result in physical deterioration.

39. **A** Since the market comparison approach uses prices of recently sold comparables, the acquisition cost of the property is irrelevant.

40. **D** Assessed value is usually based on a percentage of market value. Insurance value is based on replacement cost, less accrued depreciation, and would not consider values of comparable properties.

41. **A** Market value is the most probable price a ready, willing and able buyer, not forced to buy, will pay to a ready, willing and able seller, not forced to sell, allowing a reasonable time for exposure in the open market.

42. **C** For example: $5,000 capitalized at 5 percent is $100,000 ($5,000 divided by .05 =$100,000); $5,000 at 6 percent is $83,333; and at 4 percent it is $125,000.

43. **B** This is usually expressed as a percentage. Capitalization rate is also the rate of yield that the investor expects on the investment.

44. **D**   The gross income multiplier, used to compare investment property in the market data appraisal method, is the ratio between gross income and sales price.

45. **C**   The livelihood of an owner (how one earns one's living) has little to do with property value, except as it relates to the homogeneity of a neighborhood.

46. **A**   A gross income multiplier is obtained by dividing the sales price by the annual gross income of comparable properties recently sold. Choice (B) is used in the income approach.

47. **B**   Reproduction cost is the present cost of reproducing the improvement with an exact replica, not one with just similar utility, as in the more frequently used replacement cost.

48. **A**   Similarity of homes, social patterns and livelihoods in an area tends to stabilize values.

49. **B**   Functional obsolescence is a loss in value due to lack of home's desirability because of poor design, layout or style.

50. **D**   Highest and best use is that use, at the time of the appraisal, most likely to produce the greatest net return over a given period of time.

51. **A**   Using straight-line depreciation, a factor of two percent per year would result in a return of 100 percent of the investment over this building's 50-year useful life.

52. **B**   Appraiser's fees are never based on a percentage of value, as one might then conclude that an appraiser would arrive at a higher value in order to obtain a higher fee. By charging according to time, expenses and reputation, the appraiser assures the integrity of his or her efforts toward a correct evaluation.

53. **B**   An appraisal neither assures nor guarantees value, and the actual sale of the subject property is the best determination of value. Therefore, an appraisal is always considered to be only an estimate of value.

54. **C**   Highest and best use is one of the economic principles of value. Today's highest and best use for a property may be a parking lot, whereas next year it could be a shopping center.

55. **C**   Reconciliation (also called correlation) is more than just averaging the three approaches to value, it weighs many factors.

56. **B**   Conversely, if the rate is unknown, it may be determined by dividing income by value, and if income is unknown, it is determined by multiplying value times rate. If in doubt on a question like this, make up a practical example to see what amount is divided by what.

57. **B**   While replacement cost is the cost of an item of similar utility, reproduction cost is the cost of an exact replica.

58. **D**   The book value of a property can be determined by an accountant sitting in an office and computing the cost of the property plus improvements less depreciation. The other types of value require an inspection and appraisal of the property.

59. **D**   Expenses are deducted to arrive at net effective income. Vacancy and bad debt losses reflect the gross effective income.

60. **C**   The reduction in value to the property was caused by external factors (government action) outside C's control.

61. **C** $140,000 less $30,000 = $110,000 from $170,000 = $60,000.

62. **B**   The library would provide a lower return *on* the investment, although it would provide similar recapture rates (return *of* the investment).

63. **D**   Market value would be the price paid by a willing buyer to a willing seller. The selling price paid to a seller under financial stress may not reflect the actual worth.

64. **A**   Buyers' desires as to types of construction, location, amenities and so on, will have a direct bearing on a property's evaluation.

65. **D** Deferred maintenance would indicate possible physical deterioration.

66. **C** Physical deterioration refers to loss in value due to wear and tear, direct effects of the elements or other physical damage.

67. **C** The recapture rate is based on the theory that the building will be worthless at the end of its economic life, so a factor must be made to recover this "loss" beforehand.

68. **C** Lower than usual ceilings illustrate conditions within the property itself that will cause a reduction in value. Choices (B) and (D) indicate external obsolescence, and (A) is physical.

69. **C** Based on experience and skill, the appraiser estimates as closely as possible the value of the property. Negotiations between buyer and seller will actually determine the price paid for the property.

70. **D** Supply and demand is an element of value. A poor parking plan could reduce the value of an otherwise excellent building.

71. **D** In addition to income and replacement cost (less accrued depreciation), an appraiser might also look for comparable sales of similar warehouses.

72. **C** The fire insurer is interested in the cost of replacing one structure with another structure of similar materials.

73. **D** Title information is needed to identify properly the property and interest being appraised, especially in situations involving transfers of sandwich leases where several people have interests. It is also necessary to know the type of ownership (deed, lease, land contract) and existing encumbrances and restrictions on use. Choice (B) information is needed for the capitalization or income approach to value. Current loan rates are irrelevant to the value of this property.

74. **C** The highest and best use for a parcel could be a parking lot today but an office building three years from now. It depends on the greatest net return, not necessarily the maximum number of units that can be built in a given space.

75. **B** The appraiser would be most concerned with market comparison information. In appraising the residence, neither original cost nor valuation for death tax purposes would have much relevance to the question of what a ready, willing and able buyer would pay *today* for the residence.

76. **A** Operating expenses are more relevant to the income approach to valuation. The cost approach looks more toward what it would cost for a substitute property.

77. **A** While the appraiser would take a look at the impact on value of the adjacent store with the possible increase in noise and traffic, such a store would certainly not have the drastic reduction in value of, say, a chemical plant. The market comparison approach is still the most reliable gauge of the value of a residence. The appraiser should also consider whether the residence was on land zoned for commercial use. If so, then consideration should be given as to what would be the highest and best use of the property.

78. **D** The important aspect of the market comparison approach is to make necessary adjustments in the differences among the comparable properties so as to arrive at the most similar property. More is involved than just averaging sales prices.

79. **B** The income approach utilized *net* income and capitalization rate to arrive at value. Value times the capitalization rate equals net income: i.e., $100,000 × 10 percent = $10,000; so $10,000 divided by $100,000 would equal the capitalization rate of 10 percent.

80. **C** Based on the three properties, the gross rent multiplier is 6.5; or, in other words, the sales prices were 6.5 times the annual rent.

81. **D** The four characteristics are demand, utility, scarcity and transferability (i.e., D.U.S.T.).

82. **B** If the cap rate is off by just ½ percent the difference in valuation can be drastic. One percentage point difference in the cap rate can make a 12½ percent difference in the value estimate. There are

several methods to select the appropriate cap rate: (1) by evaluating net income figures and sales prices of comparable properties, (2) by analyzing the two component parts of the cap rate, i.e., the return *on* the investment (interest) and the return *of* the investment (recapture). The interest rate can be selected using the summation method or the band of investment method. The cap rate is applied to the net operating income after deducting for bad debt and vacancy.

83.   B   The GRM is based on a 10 to 1 ratio.

84.   C   Listing or asking prices reflect what the seller wants, not what the market is willing to pay.

85.   C   The net operating income after deducting expenses is important regardless of the size of the lot.

86.   B   The cost approach adds up the separate parts to total the whole.

87.   A   Progression is the opposite.

88.   D   The cost approach using the replacement method is most accurate, since there is yet little depreciation.

89.   C   Capitalization involves the return *on* and the return *of* the investment money.

Chapter 8 Taxes and Assessments

Questions in this chapter test your comprehension of the following topics:

- Tax-deferred Section 1031 Exchanges
- The process of levying special assessments
- The types of deductions allowed on real property
- The tax aspects of home ownership

Because the tax laws change so frequently, the questions on tax tend to be general. In practice, however, it is essential to keep up to date with the latest changes and to refer clients to competent tax advisers to meet their specific requirements.

QUESTIONS

1. What is the usual way to finance a new sewer line installation in a neighborhood?
   (A) Excise tax
   (B) Special assessment
   (C) Real property tax
   (D) Utility charge

❖ 2. The term "boot" would probably be considered in connection with:
   (A) exchange.   (C) depreciation.
   (B) legal description. (D) leasehold title.

❖ 3. No depreciation for tax purposes is allowed for:
   (A) improvements over 30 years of age.
   (B) land.
   (C) buildings.
   (D) leaseholds.

4. Unpaid real property taxes are usually considered to be:
   (A) promissory notes. (C) solvent credits.
   (B) restrictions.   (D) liens.

❖ 5. *L* is preparing her federal income tax return. She could claim depreciation on all of the following **EXCEPT**:
   (A) a vacant duplex.
   (B) a home rented to a friend.
   (C) vacant land held for investment.
   (D) a rented single-family dwelling.

❖ 6. The compulsory charge the government imposes against benefiting property owners for street improvements or road repairs is called:
   (A) general tax.
   (B) special excise tax.
   (C) property use tax.
   (D) special assessment.

7. If you sell your home and reinvest the proceeds in the purchase of a new and more expensive home, within what period of time must you buy the new home to defer the payment of taxes on any profits realized in the sale of your old home?
   (A) Six months
   (B) One year
   (C) Twenty-four months
   (D) Five years

8. In order to defer payment of a portion of federal income tax on realized gain, principal payments in the year of the sale on an installment sale must remain under what percent of the total price?
   (A) 29 percent   (C) 35 percent
   (B) 30 percent   (D) No limit

9. The federal income tax allows an investor to gradually write off his or her original investment. Which of the following methods is used?
   (A) Exchanges   (C) Depreciation
   (B) Installment   (D) Acceleration

10. An investor who is retired would be interested in:
    (A) adjusted gross income.
    (B) gross income.
    (C) rental income.
    (D) net spendable income.

11. Which of the following is used as a basis for real property tax assessment?
    (A) Land only
    (B) Building only
    (C) Both land and building
    (D) Neither land nor building

❖ 12. *S* sells his home for $80,000. He owned this house for nine years and made a profit of $15,000. Eight months later, he bought a new home for $150,000. What taxable gain will he have in the year of the purchase?
    (A) None
    (B) $6,000
    (C) $10,000 (tax deferred over a three-year period)
    (D) $15,000

13. Real property taxes are determined by which of the following ways?
    (A) On an ad valorem basis
    (B) According to the number of occupants
    (C) Loan-to-value ratio
    (D) Duration of ownership

14. A seller sold his or her principal residence and reinvested the sales proceeds in a more expensive residence the same day. At the end of the year when he or she pays income taxes, what will be the minimum he or she will have to pay on the profits?
    - (A) Capital gains tax
    - (B) Ordinary income tax
    - (C) No tax
    - (D) Gross excise tax

15. *S* owns an investment apartment hotel on three acres of land. For tax purposes, which of the following can *S* depreciate?
    - (A) The land
    - (B) The improvements
    - (C) Rental income
    - (D) Net operating expenses

16. Examples of deductible expenses on an owner's tax return for a vacation home are all of the following **EXCEPT:**
    - (A) mortgage interest.
    - (B) property taxes.
    - (C) mortgage principal.
    - (D) casualty losses.

17. Assume you pay $5,000 in interest on your home. If you are in the top tax bracket, you can deduct how much against taxable income?
    - (A) 0
    - (B) $1,500
    - (C) $4,500
    - (D) $5,000

18. Before calculating the gain on the sale of your home, you can do all of the following to offset the gain **EXCEPT:**
    - (A) add closing costs from your original purchase.
    - (B) add capital improvements.
    - (C) deduct brokerage fees upon resale.
    - (D) deduct depreciation.

19. "Boot" is a factor arising in which of the following cases?
    - (A) When depreciating a property for tax purposes
    - (B) When there is a difference between the equity of two properties being exchanged
    - (C) When property is given a stepped-up basis at death
    - (D) When no loans are involved

❖ 20. A person aged 55 or older qualifies for up to a $125,000 tax exemption in which of these cases?
    - (A) When gain results from the sale of the taxpayer's principal residence only
    - (B) On any type of property just so long as the sales price is under $125,000
    - (C) Sale of property by married person
    - (D) When replacement of property found within 24 months

21. When applying for the "over 55 rule," if both spouses are over 55 years of age on the title transfer date, there is $125,000 profit tax exemption:
    - (A) per person.
    - (B) per marriage.
    - (C) per property.
    - (D) per year.

22. The amount that can qualify for the "over 55 rule" tax exemption is:
    - (A) the difference between the "adjusted sales price" and its "adjusted cost basis."
    - (B) the difference between the original purchase price and the total sales price.
    - (C) the difference between net sales price and total loans.
    - (D) the difference between original sales price and the listed price.

23. All are true about the $125,000 "over 55 rule" tax exemption **EXCEPT:**
    - (A) may be used only once in a lifetime.
    - (B) applies only to one marriage, not a subsequent remarriage.
    - (C) is limited to residential property.
    - (D) both spouses must be over 55.

❖ 24. Tax deductions on a personal residence include all of the following **EXCEPT:**
    - (A) loan points paid by purchaser.
    - (B) prepayment penalties.
    - (C) real property taxes.
    - (D) depreciation.

25. In qualifying for the "residence replacement rule" in which the taxpayer seeks tax deferral, the residence may be:
    - (A) vacant land where he or she lives in a tent.
    - (B) a mobile home or a houseboat.
    - (C) rental property.
    - (D) commercial property.

26. In determining the purchase price of a replacement principal residence for tax purposes, it is:
    (A) the initial purchase price only.
    (B) the initial purchase price plus some closing costs.
    (C) the depreciated value.
    (D) the market value.

27. For tax assessment purposes, which piece of information is the **LEAST** important?
    (A) Zoning
    (B) Location
    (C) Length of lease
    (D) Physical condition

28. In order to qualify for a tax deferral on capital gain, an owner must reinvest how much of the proceeds from the sale of his or her residence into the replacement residence?
    (A) 30 percent
    (B) 50 percent
    (C) 75 percent
    (D) No minimum

29. Items for which special assessments may be levied include all of the following **EXCEPT:**
    (A) sidewalks.
    (B) curbs.
    (C) street paving.
    (D) front yard beautification.

30. Real estate exchanges are advantageous because they are:
    (A) tax deferred.
    (B) tax-free forever.
    (C) tax exempt.
    (D) tax discounted.

31. If a broker exchanges a property listed by a co-broker with a property he or she has listed, under the usual cooperating situation:
    (A) the broker receives two sales commissions.
    (B) the broker receives the sales commission only on the property he or she listed.
    (C) the broker forfeits his or her commission.
    (D) the broker is paid a flat fee.

32. *J* brought a ten-year-old office building. The allowed method of depreciation with no recapture of depreciation would **MOST** likely be:
    (A) 100 percent.
    (B) straight line.
    (C) 150 percent.
    (D) 175 percent.

33. Straight-line depreciation provides for which of the following?
    (A) The same rate each year
    (B) The fastest amount of allowable depreciation in the first year
    (C) An adjustable rate
    (D) A steadily increasing rate

34. Tax-deferred exchange treatment is given on:
    (A) like property exchanged for like property.
    (B) a personal residence exchanged for a commercial property.
    (C) personal property traded for real property.
    (D) short-term leases.

❖ 35. Under which circumstance can one take depreciation on a single-family dwelling for federal tax purposes?
    (A) When one lives in it
    (B) When one sells it
    (C) When one exchanges it
    (D) When one rents it

36. *C* sold his three-year-old rental vacation home for a $30,000 gain. He immediately reinvested all the proceeds in a more expensive house in which to live. For income tax purposes *C* will:
    (A) have the gain deferred.
    (B) pay capital gains tax.
    (C) pay ordinary income tax.
    (D) pay no tax.

37. *W* purchased an investment condominium apartment three years ago and paid $82 per month as his pro rata share of real property taxes. In paying his federal income taxes for last year, *W* is able to deduct all those taxes paid from his taxable income. Assuming *W* was in a 32 percent tax bracket, how much less does he pay in taxes because of this real property tax deduction?
    (A) $246
    (B) $315
    (C) $669
    (D) $945

38. If a person purchases an apartment building as an investment and then sells it after nine months, profit on the sale is taxed as:
    (A) long-term capital gain.
    (B) ordinary income.
    (C) short-term capital gain.
    (D) tax-deferred income.

39. A broker is advising an investor about investing in real estate or in stocks. One big difference found in real estate is:
    (A) capital gain.
    (B) depreciation.
    (C) risk.
    (D) investment return.

40. The principal advantage of exchanging real estate, as opposed to selling, is:
    (A) depreciation.   (C) deferring tax.
    (B) less commission. (D) higher appraisal.

41. G sells the residence for $115,000 that he bought two years ago for $78,000. G added a bathroom for $2,500 and a basketball court for $6,000. G buys another house ten months later for $125,000. G's realized gain on the sale is:
    (A) $28,500.   (C) $38,500.
    (B) $34,500.   (D) $41,000.

42. Which of the following is true regarding a property having depreciation deductions that exceed the amount of income from the property?
    (A) The property will devaluate more rapidly.
    (B) It is always advantageous to show a loss on income property.
    (C) The loss must always be used to offset other income.
    (D) It can be carried over to reduce next years property income.

43. A couple buys a residence for $80,000. During the first year they have expenses of $4,100 in mortgage interest, $1,500 in real property taxes, depreciation of $3,300, and fire insurance of $520. They also added a guest room for $6,400. Deductions on their tax return for the year will be:
    (A) $1,500.   (C) $6,120.
    (B) $5,600.   (D) $12,520.

44. Which of the following expenses is deductible by the homeowner during the current tax year?
    (A) Painting
    (B) Family room addition
    (C) Property insurance
    (D) Mortgage interest

45. An investor receives 5 percent interest on a real estate loan. The IRS can claim a higher interest rate which is called:
    (A) implied interest.
    (B) imputed interest.
    (C) escalated interest.
    (D) inferred interest.

46. A couple owns their own principal residence plus a vacation cabin that they use three weeks a year and rent out the rest of the year. What can they deduct for the cabin?
    (A) Mortgage interest and property taxes only
    (B) Depreciation and repairs not to exceed income
    (C) Vacancy loss
    (D) No deductions allowed

ANSWERS

1. **B** Improvements such as sewers, street widening and curbs are all considered special assessments and are therefore taxed direct to the benefiting taxpayers and not the general public.

2. **A** "Boot" (anything received in an exchange of "unlike-kind" property) may be the only immediately taxable portion of a tax-deferred exchange.

3. **B** Vacant land does not qualify for depreciation; whereas, improvements are wasting assets and can be depreciated.

4. **D** Unpaid taxes on real property become a lien and could cause the involuntary sale of the property to pay the tax.

5. **C** Land does not qualify for depreciation, but improvements on investment property do.

6. **D** When specific properties are benefited by public improvements, the charge levied to pay for such an improvement is called an assessment or a special assessment (unlike a general tax).

7. **C** The profit tax deferral on a residence applies if the new residence is bought or is built within 24 months. "Within" means prior to or after the sale.

8. **D** Installment sale treatment is automatic, unless the taxpayer elects *not* to use it. As principal payments are received, only a portion is taxed as gain. The 30 percent maximum down payment rule has been eliminated by the IRS.

9. **C** Depreciation is a permissible deduction that allows the taxpayer to periodically deduct a portion of his or her investment from annual income before tax calculation. Thus, each dollar deducted from income is a dollar not taxed. For property put in service after 1980, the method used is called "cost recovery."

10. **D** A retired person generally is looking for net spendable income cash flow rather than other types that may offer tax shelter advantages to salaried persons or other persons with taxable incomes.

11. **C** Real property taxes are assessed according to improvement value and land value (an ad valorem valuation).

12. **A** *S* qualifies for a tax deferral because he purchased another principal residence within the 24-month period.

13. **A** An ad valorem tax is one that is levied in accordance with the value of the property.

14. **C** He or she would qualify for a tax deferral on the profit made from the sale of his or her principal residence. If he or she had purchased a less expensive house, then a portion of his or her profit would be taxable that year.

15. **B** Depreciation on land is not allowed; he could therefore depreciate only the improvements.

16. **C** Mortgage principal is not a deductible item on an owner's vacation home, a principal residence, or any other investment. However, the other choices are deductible on the residence as well as the vacation home.

17. **D** You get to deduct all the interest. Your net taxable income is taxed.

18. **D** Depreciation does not apply to one's personal residence. A, B and C are used to adjust the "basis" of the property.

19. **B** "Boot" arises during a tax-deferred exchange, and usually is the difference in the equities of the properties being exchanged.

20. **A** The exemption applies only to the taxpayer's principal residence. He or she or the co-owner spouse must be age 55 or older, and the seller must have owned and occupied the residence at least three of the five years before the sale.

21. **B** There is only one exemption per marriage. However, if two qualified owners not married to each other, such as two brothers or two partners, sell their jointly owned principal residence, then each co-owner can claim up to $125,000 of tax-free profits.

22. **A** "Adjusted sales price" is the gross selling price minus sales costs such as real estate sales commission, transfer tax and other selling expenses. "Adjusted cost basis" is the sum of the purchase price, closing costs not tax deductible at the time of purchase, and capital improvement costs added during ownership.

23. **D** The exemption can be taken once in a lifetime only; therefore, any unused portion will be wasted, since it cannot be saved for future use. Nor can a subsequent remarriage qualify either party to the exemption a second time. Only one spouse has to be 55.

24. **D** Loan points and prepayment penalties are fully tax deductible as interest in the year paid if the security for the loan is the borrower's personal residence. If the security is investment property, these charges are deductible over the term of the loan and not in the year paid.

25. **B** Although vacant land will not qualify for such a tax deferral, principal residences, such as single-family houses, condominiums, cooperative apartments, one unit in an apartment house owned by the taxpayer, mobile homes and even houseboats, will qualify.

26. **B** The purchase price includes initial purchase price plus closing costs that were not tax deductible at the time of the purchase, and capital improvements

made and paid for within a 24-month time period before or after the sale of the former principal residence.

27. **C** Taxes are based on the fee simple interest. There is not one tax for the leased fee and another tax for the leasehold estate.

28. **D** The law does not require any reinvestment of the sale proceeds into the replacement. Thus, a seller could get 100 percent financing on the replacement residence and pocket the tax-free cash from the sale of the previous principal residence.

29. **D** Items such as sewers, curbs, street paving and sidewalks are all included in special assessments. An owner's front yard is his or her own responsibility and does not fall into an assessment category by the taxing body.

30. **A** Although the taxpayer may defer the taxes on an exchange, taxes must be paid when he or she sells the newly acquired property.

31. **A** The broker will receive a sales commission on each of the properties because he or she has in effect sold two properties. He or she will also receive the listing commission on the property listed for sale. The broker should disclose to both parties this dual commission situation.

32. **B** Straight line is the only allowable method of depreciation. The accelerated depreciation rules were abolished by the 1986 Tax Reform Act. Now, all property must be depreciated on a straight-line basis over a specified number of years.

33. **A** Straight line is the only type of depreciation that provides the same amount each year.

34. **A** In order to qualify for a tax deferred exchange, there must be like properties that are held for productive use in business or for investment. Personal residences do not qualify, nor do leaseholds under 30 years.

35. **D** Depreciation is allowed on property held in a trade or business but not a personal residence.

36. **C** There is no deferral of gain unless the property is the principal residence of the taxpayer.

37. **B** Solution: $82 x 12 = $984. If taxed at a 32 percent bracket $984 would require approximately $315 in taxes that would have been due if the man didn't have this tax write-off.

38. **B** Long-term capital gain benefits were abolished under the 1986 Tax Reform Act. All gain is now treated as ordinary income.

39. **B** While investment real estate normally can be depreciated to the tax advantage of the owner, this is not true of stock.

40. **C** A properly structured IRC Section 1031 exchange will result in a deferral of capital gain tax on the sale.

41. **B** Realized gain is computed by subtracting original cost (plus improvements) from sale price. Whether the gain is recognized now or deferred until a later date is not material to this question.

42. **D** The extra deduction will help shelter other income from taxes, hence the term "tax shelter." Current tax limits offsets against other income (passive loss rules). Excess depreciation can be applied against that property's income in future years.

43. **B** On a residence (as opposed to an investment property) the deductible items are mortgage interest and real property taxes.

44. **D** A and C are not deductible and B is added to the *basis* to lessen the gain upon resale.

45. **B** The imputed interest rule allows the IRS to assert that 10 percent interest was actually earned.

46. **A** If they occupy more than 14 days or 10 percent of the total days rented, the cabin is no longer entitled to complete rental property deduction.

PART C   Financing of Real Estate

This part contains questions on the topics of

- Institutional sources of financing
- Government loan programs
- Seller carryback financing
- Functions of the secondary mortgage market
- Features of the mortgage document
- Foreclosure upon default of the mortgage

Expect about 20 percent of the general portion of the examination to contain questions on the topics covered in Part C.

Chapter 9   Sources of Financing: Institutional and FHA/DVA

The questions in this chapter will test your comprehension of the following topics:

- The operations of the secondary mortgage market
- The procedures for obtaining loans guaranteed by the Department of Veterans Affairs (DVA)
- The procedures for obtaining loans insured by the Federal Housing Administration (FHA)
- Installment land contracts from the seller
- Use of the sale and leaseback
- Graduated payment mortgages (FHA 245 program)

False Friends

The following words are often confused with one another. Note the difference in meaning of these false friends:

Novation/Substitution: Unlike a DVA loan assumption, the total release of liability of the seller is a novation, whereas a substitution involves the assumption by a veteran buyer who substitutes his or her DVA eligibility for that of the seller.

Debenture/Mortgage: Unlike a mortgage, a debenture involves a note without any collateral to secure it.

Installment Land Contract/Purchase Money Mortgage: Both involve seller carryback financing; the difference is that legal title remains with the seller in an installment land contract.

Second Mortgage/Secondary Mortgage Market: A second mortgage is a junior mortgage, whereas the secondary mortgage market refers to the selling of mortgages to investors.

A helpful way to compare the FHA and DVA loan programs is to review this chart:

COMPARISON OF FHA AND DVA LOAN PROGRAMS

Department of Veterans Affairs

1. financing available only to veterans and certain widows and widowers who haven't remarried
2. DVA financing limited to owner-occupied residential (1- to 4-family) dwellings—must sign occupancy certificate on two separate occasions
3. does not require down payment, though lender may request small down payment
4. methods of valuation differ—DVA issues a certificate of reasonable value
5. with regard to home loans, the law requires that the DVA loan may not exceed the reasonable value of the home
6. no prepayment penalty
7. guarantees the loan up to specified limits
8. secondary financing permitted (with limitations)
9. buyer prohibited from paying discount points (except in refinancing and certain defined circumstances); he or she can pay a 1 percent origination fee plus a DVA funding fee
10. DVA loan can be assumed by nonveteran with DVA approval

Federal Housing Administration

1. financing is available to veterans and nonveterans alike
2. financing programs for owner-occupied residential.
3. requires a larger down payment than DVA
4. different evaluation methods; like DVA there are prescribed valuation procedures for the approved appraisers to follow
5. FHA valuation sets the maximum loan FHA will insure but does not limit the sales price
6. no prepayment penalty
7. insures the loan by way of mutual mortgage insurance; premiums paid by buyer
8. no secondary financing in excess of maximum FHA loan permitted
9. buyer may pay a 1 percent origination fee; buyer or seller may pay loan points
10. FHA loan can be assumed with FHA approval

Courtesy of *Modern Real Estate Practice*, published by Real Estate Education Company, Chicago.

QUESTIONS

1. A mortgage banker generally can do all of the following **EXCEPT:**
   (A) service loans for its clients.
   (B) use its own money to make loans.
   (C) list for sale property financed by one of its clients.
   (D) quote terms and conditions of loans to prospective borrowers.

2. All the following agencies are a primary source of money for the secondary mortgage market **EXCEPT:**
   (A) Fannie Mae.
   (B) Department of Veterans Affairs.
   (C) Ginnie Mae.
   (D) Freddie Mac.

3. Under a DVA loan, a veteran can do which of the following?
   (A) Transfer the original DVA loan to another home
   (B) Sell the home and allow a nonveteran buyer to assume the loan with DVA approval
   (C) Use the DVA loan to acquire a commercial building
   (D) Use one loan to purchase two separate properties

4. A veteran seeking a DVA loan to purchase a three-family structure must:
   (A) agree to a loan amortization not to exceed 15 years.
   (B) sign a statement that there will be no negative cash flow.
   (C) agree to a 20 percent down payment.
   (D) agree to occupy part of the dwelling.

❖ 5. A case where the seller wanted to be relieved of all obligations under the DVA mortgage that another veteran buyer would assume and substitute eligibility would be **BEST** described as:
   (A) subordination.   (C) acceleration.
   (B) novation.   (D) subrogation.

6. The DVA is authorized to:
   (A) make direct loans to veterans.
   (B) regulate lending institutions that make DVA loans.
   (C) charge prepayment penalties.
   (D) guarantee repayment of loans up to a specified amount.

7. Which of the following statements regarding federally insured or guaranteed loans is true?
   (A) An FHA loan may be granted to a qualified buyer who indicates intent to rent the entire property for which the loan is obtained.
   (B) A DVA loan may be granted to an eligible veteran who indicates intent to rent the entire property.
   (C) FHA loans are freely assumable.
   (D) FHA loans insure the lender up to 100 percent of any loss suffered.

8. All of the following are transactions involving a collateralized debt **EXCEPT:**
   (A) chattel mortgage.   (C) mortgage.
   (B) debenture.   (D) deed of trust.

9. The DVA is authorized to make direct loans:
   (A) when the veteran agrees not to occupy the property.
   (B) in a rural area where the veteran cannot find a lender to lend at rates of interest competitive with those in other areas.
   (C) to anyone who can financially qualify.
   (D) provided there is no secondary financing on the dwelling.

10. A requirement of a borrower under an FHA-insured loan is that he or she:
   (A) have cash for a down payment and part of closing costs.
   (B) have the spouse sign as co-borrower.
   (C) certify that he or she will rent the premises.
   (D) have a minimum annual income of $25,000.

11. The FHA serves to do all of the following **EXCEPT:**
   (A) help stabilize the mortgage market.
   (B) improve housing standards.
   (C) make direct loans in the primary mortgage market.
   (D) stimulate housing activity.

❖ 12. The money used for Federal Housing Administration (FHA) loans is supplied by:
   (A) qualified lending institutions.
   (B) Fannie Mae.
   (C) the Federal Housing Administration.
   (D) the Federal Home Loan Bank.

❖ **13.** To qualify for a DVA loan on a dwelling all of the following are true **EXCEPT:**

(A) The applicant must sign a declaration that he or she intends to occupy the dwelling.

(B) There must be an appraisal from an appraiser approved by the DVA.

(C) The applicant must have a certificate of eligibility.

(D) The borrower must pay the discount points at closing.

14. When a loan is approved by FHA:

(A) the appraised value must not be less than the sale price.

(B) the government guarantees the value of the property.

(C) it must be for investment property only.

(D) there will be some required down payment.

15. The FHA will insure:

(A) first mortgages.

(B) second mortgages.

(C) wraparound mortgages.

(D) junior mortgages.

16. *A*, a veteran, who sells his house and permits the buyer to assume his DVA loan:

(A) has no further liability if he obtains a release from the buyer.

(B) has no further liability.

(C) has a primary liability until the loan is paid in full.

(D) has no further liability if he obtains a release from the lender and the DVA.

17. The discount charged by a lender on a federal DVA or FHA loan is a percentage of the:

(A) sales price.   (C) loan amount.

(B) appraised value.   (D) down payment.

18. An installment contract for the sale of real estate gives the buyer all of the following **EXCEPT:**

(A) the right to live on the property.

(B) the right to lease the property.

(C) the right of possession.

(D) legal title to the property.

19. The Department of Veterans Affairs:

(A) regularly makes direct loans up to certain amounts.

(B) does not apply to women.

(C) guarantees loans.

(D) insures conventional loans.

❖ **20.** When the amortized payment of a mortgage remains constant over the period of the loan, but leaves an outstanding balance to be paid at the end, this payment is called:

(A) an escalation payment.

(B) a balloon payment.

(C) a satisfaction payment.

(D) an acceleration payment.

21. The amount a lender will loan is generally based on:

(A) the listed price.

(B) the appraised value for loan purposes.

(C) the appraised value for loan purposes or the sale price, whichever is lower.

(D) the final sales price.

22. A borrower bought a $74,000 house with no down payment through a savings and loan association. The loan was probably a(n):

(A) conventional insured loan.

(B) DVA loan.

(C) FHA loan.

(D) conventional loan.

23. If title to real property remains in the seller's name after it has been sold on a monthly payment plan, the buyer would have purchased it under:

(A) FHA financing.

(B) a guaranteed loan.

(C) a land contract.

(D) an option.

❖ **24.** A promissory note providing for interest only to be paid during its term is **BEST** described as:

(A) an installment note.

(B) a straight note.

(C) an amortized note.

(D) a noninterest bearing note.

25. To compute the dollar value of a loan discount, each point is equal to:

(A) 1 percent of the amount to be loaned.

(B) 1 percent of the down payment.

(C) 1 percent of the appraised value.

(D) 1 percent of the sales price.

26. Most of the junior loans that are available today are secured through:
    (A) savings and loan associations.
    (B) private investors.
    (C) commercial banks.
    (D) mortgage bankers.

27. Usury means **MOST** nearly:
    (A) making loans without benefit of cosigners.
    (B) lending money at fluctuating interest rates.
    (C) being capable of multiple usage.
    (D) illegal interest.

28. If the seller agrees to provide financing on a non-recourse basis, which of the following is true after the buyer defaults?
    (A) The buyer is personally liable for the full amount of the note.
    (B) The seller can recover a deficiency judgment against the buyer.
    (C) The seller is limited to what the property brings at foreclosure.
    (D) The seller can recover punitive damages against the buyer.

29. When a seller takes back a purchase money second mortgage from the buyer, the seller is responsible for preparing and executing which of the following?
    (A) Deed
    (B) Second mortgage
    (C) Acknowledgment on the mortgage
    (D) Continuation of title

30. Which of the following is **LEAST** important to a loan company considering a loan application?
    (A) Length of employment
    (B) Irregular overtime pay
    (C) Other indebtedness
    (D) Base salary

31. Which one of the following is an agency of the Department of Housing and Urban Development?
    (A) Federal Deposit Insurance Corporation
    (B) Government National Mortgage Association
    (C) Department of Veterans Affairs
    (D) Mutual Mortgage Insurance Corporation

32. A prospective home purchaser can do which of the following?
    (A) Pay more than the Certificate of Value (CRV) but not more than the FHA appraisal
    (B) Not pay more than the CRV but pay more than an FHA appraisal.
    (C) Pay more than the FHA appraisal provided there is a second mortgage
    (D) Pay more than the appraisal provided it is in cash

33. A person would consider a purchase money mortgage under which of these circumstances?
    (A) When the buyer has only a small amount of cash for the purchase
    (B) When the owner wants to obtain a second mortgage to pay for home improvements
    (C) When an owner needs extra cash for adding a new bedroom wing
    (D) When the buyer will not take title until after paying all that is owed

❖ 34. The liquidation of a debt by periodic installment is **BEST** described as:
    (A) amortization.   (C) acceleration.
    (B) an annuity.   (D) assemblage.

35. Both DVA and FHA loans can be made by all of the following **EXCEPT:**
    (A) savings and loan associations.
    (B) commercial banks.
    (C) mortgage companies.
    (D) credit unions.

36. The amount of mutual mortgage insurance premium on a single family FHA loan is:
    (A) ½ of 1 percent of the average loan balance.
    (B) ½ of 1 percent of the annual loan balance.
    (C) ½ of 1 percent of the average annual loan balance.
    (D) an initial one-time payment to FHA.

37. A savings and loan association would be likely to make all of the following types of loans **EXCEPT:**
    (A) DVA.   (C) FHA.
    (B) Conventional.   (D) FNMA.

38. A borrower wishes to locate first-mortgage financing that will not charge a penalty if it is paid off before maturity. Which type of loan will **NOT** generally meet this need?
    (A) FHA
    (B) Conventional
    (C) Nonconventional
    (D) DVA

❖ 39. The term "refinancing" refers to:
    (A) obtaining a second mortgage on a property that already has a first mortgage.
    (B) the repayment of an existing mortgage loan from the proceeds of a new one.
    (C) changing one or more of the terms of an existing mortgage loan.
    (D) a secondary mortgage-market transaction.

40. The limit on the amount of a DVA loan is:
    (A) the listed price.
    (B) the amount of the Certificate of Reasonable Value.
    (C) there is no limit.
    (D) an amount three times the DVA entitlement.

41. Interest calculated on the total sum of unpaid principal and the simple interest accrued thereon is called:
    (A) simple interest.
    (B) compound interest.
    (C) penalty interest.
    (D) interest rate.

42. Of the following types of financing, which pairing is synonymous?
    (A) Take-out loan—Secondary financing
    (B) Construction loan—take-out loan
    (C) Interim loan—construction loan
    (D) Obligatory advances—installment loan

43. Which of the following is a source of primary mortgage funds for real estate developers?
    (A) Federal Deposit Insurance Corporation
    (B) Federal National Mortgage Association
    (C) Federal Home Loan Bank
    (D) Federal Savings and Loan

44. A debenture is:
    (A) a mortgage.
    (B) a collateralized note.
    (C) a trust deed.
    (D) an unsecured note.

45. *H* sold her residence and took back a purchase money first mortgage that she decided to sell. To do this, the seller would have to find a buyer in the:
    (A) primary mortgage market.
    (B) real property securities business with a permit.
    (C) secondary mortgage market.
    (D) business of arranging primary financing only.

46. A vendee is one who:
    (A) sells or offers to sell.
    (B) buys or offers to buy.
    (C) loans money.
    (D) borrows money.

47. All of the following elements are typical of junior financing **EXCEPT**:
    (A) balloon payment.
    (B) short term.
    (C) private lenders.
    (D) fully amortized.

48. An impound or reserve account **MOST** benefits the:
    (A) borrower.
    (B) lender.
    (C) trustee.
    (D) trustor.

49. The lender is not insured or guaranteed against a loss, by reason of the borrower's default in repayment, under which type of loan?
    (A) FHA loan
    (B) Conventional loan
    (C) DVA loan
    (D) GI loan

50. The lender under a conventional loan may compensate for the additional risks brought on by lack of government insurance by doing all of the following **EXCEPT**:
    (A) requiring higher down payments than would be required if the loan were insured.
    (B) charging higher interest rates.
    (C) requiring private insurance.
    (D) requiring title insurance.

51. A DVA loan may be granted for the purchase of a one-family to four-family dwelling if:
    (A) the veteran certifies the rent collected will equal the mortgage payments.
    (B) the loan will be amortized for not more than 20 years.
    (C) the down payment will be at least ten percent.
    (D) the veteran agrees to live there.

52. When a borrower defaults on an FHA-insured loan, any losses sustained by foreclosure are made up through:
    (A) the Federal Treasury.
    (B) the Mutual Mortgage Insurance Plan.
    (C) an attachment lien against the borrower.
    (D) an assessment against the lending institution.

❖ 53. A land contract (or contract for deed) and a seller-carryback purchase money mortgage are similar in that:
    (A) the seller assumes no financial risk.
    (B) the title is conveyed immediately to the buyer.
    (C) the seller is the lender.
    (D) a mortgage is required.

54. The Federal National Mortgage Association (FNMA) performs which of the following functions?
    (A) Regulates commercial banks
    (B) Makes DVA and FHA loans
    (C) Loans conventional mortgage funds
    (D) Operates in the secondary mortgage market

❖ 55. What element is peculiar to the sale and leaseback transaction?
    (A) The seller gets a return on the purchase in the form of rental.
    (B) The property is sold on condition that the new owner lease it back to the seller at the time title passes.
    (C) The buyer keeps capital in inventories, rather than in realty.
    (D) The rental that the seller pays is not income-tax deductible.

56. The seller under a land contract is called the:
    (A) grantor.   (C) vendor.
    (B) grantee.   (D) vendee.

57. Under a DVA loan, which of the following is true?
    (A) All closing costs must be paid in cash by the seller.
    (B) World War I veterans are eligible.
    (C) The buyer pays the discount points.
    (D) The loans do not contain prepayment penalties.

58. The Federal Housing Administration does all of the following **EXCEPT:**
    (A) insure loans to qualified buyers.
    (B) protect lenders in case of default.
    (C) require a down payment.
    (D) loan its own funds.

59. The payment of an old loan with a new loan is termed "refinancing." Which is the **LEAST** likely purpose for "refinancing" loans?
    (A) To acquire the property
    (B) To pay for rehabilitation or modernization
    (C) To get a more advantageous loan than was on the property
    (D) To raise money for purposes of satisfying a balloon payment

60. One function of FNMA (Fannie Mae) is selling seasoned mortgages and trust deeds to individual investors and financial institutions. A "seasoned mortgage" is a mortgage:
    (A) in existence for some time that has a good record of repayment by the mortgagor.
    (B) with a long record of assignments.
    (C) with a subordination clause.
    (D) on which a novation has been given.

61. Which of the following statements is true concerning the Federal Housing Administration?
    (A) It insures up to 80 percent of the loan amount.
    (B) It is a part of the Department of Housing and Urban Development (HUD).
    (C) It insures 60 percent or $46,000, whichever is less.
    (D) It makes loans only to veterans.

62. For which type of loan must the applicant be an owner-occupant?
    (A) DVA loan   (C) Conventional loan
    (B) Straight loan   (D) Amortized loan

63. The DVA can give direct loans:
    (A) when the borrower/veteran agrees to rent the property.
    (B) when the property is located in an area where conventional loans are not easily available.
    (C) if the borrower puts up additional down payment.
    (D) if the veteran agrees not to pay more than the CRV.

64. An FHA lender will allow all of the following **EXCEPT:**
    (A) the seller to pay all costs for the buyer.
    (B) the buyer to give the seller a second mortgage as part of the purchase price in which the total borrowed will exceed the maximum FHA loan.
    (C) the buyer to prepay the loan without prepayment penalty.
    (D) the buyer to refinance the loan when 80 percent of the loan can be paid off in 30 years.

❖ 65. Discount charges charged on a loan result in:
    (A) higher yield to the lender.
    (B) longer time period of loan repayment.
    (C) lower overall cost to borrower.
    (D) higher purchase price in the secondary mortgage market.

66. Which of the following is considered a conventional loan?
    (A) FHA insured
    (B) DVA guaranteed
    (C) Commercial Bank loan
    (D) FNMA mortgages

67. On a DVA loan, who pays the initial origination fee?
    (A) Veteran   (C) Mortgage broker
    (B) Lender   (D) Mortgage banker

68. When an applicant applies for DVA financing:
    (A) the DVA uses approved appraisers.
    (B) the DVA must accept an appraisal of an M.A.I.
    (C) an appraisal is not required.
    (D) an appraisal is required only if the applicant is applying for 100 percent financing.

❖ 69. Under an FHA graduated payment mortgage, which of the following fluctuates over the term of the loan?
    (A) Interest rate   (C) Finance charge
    (B) Monthly payments (D) Annual rate

70. A seller has owned the property for one year. The buyer is paying all cash. The seller is **MOST** likely to pay a prepayment penalty with which type of loan?
    (A) DVA   (C) Debenture
    (B) FHA   (D) Conventional

❖ 71. The maximum permissible "loan-to-value ratios" are:
    (A) based on sale price.
    (B) determined by federal statute in the case of FHA loans.
    (C) based on the banker's competitive market analysis.
    (D) fixed by law for conventional loans.

72. All of the following is true of conventional loans **EXCEPT:**
    (A) They are made to the buyer without governmental insurance or guarantee.
    (B) The policy requirements of their lenders are not uniform.
    (C) The requirements to qualify are uniformly fixed by state law.
    (D) They require a higher down payment than nonconventional loans.

❖ 73. All of the following transfers can result in the lender exercising its rights under the due-on-sale clause, based on the rules of Freddie Mac (FHLMC) **EXCEPT:**
    (A) recorded land contract.
    (B) lease with option to purchase.
    (C) unrecorded land contract.
    (D) second mortgage.

74. A buyer wants to take out an FHA loan. The broker should refer the buyer directly to:
    (A) any approved lending institution such as a bank or savings and loan association.
    (B) an FHA appraiser in the area.
    (C) the Federal Housing Administration Office.
    (D) the Federal National Mortgage Association.

75. The penalty for complete prepayment of an FHA-insured loan during the first ten years is:
    (A) 2 percent of the face value of the note at time of payment.
    (B) 90 days interest on the remaining balance.
    (C) one percent of the original amount of the loan.
    (D) nothing.

76. Who would most probably pay the initial one percent origination fee allowed by DVA on guaranteed loans?
    (A) Seller
    (B) Lending institution
    (C) Buyer
    (D) Escrow

77. The maximum amount that may be loaned to a qualified veteran on a DVA-guaranteed loan is limited to:
    (A) the assessed value of the property.
    (B) 60 percent of the appraisal.
    (C) $36,000.
    (D) the amount shown on the Certificate of Reasonable Value (CRV).

78. Which is true regarding the secondary mortgage market?
    (A) The Government National Mortgage Association (known as Ginnie Mae or GNMA) underwrites loan pools consisting of FHA and DVA loans.
    (B) The secondary mortgage market refers to lending institutions who loan money to homeowners, who then use their equity in the home as security in the form of a second mortgage.
    (C) The entire market is headed by a federal commissioner.
    (D) Loans are deemed securities and regulated by the Securities and Exchange Commission.

79. A conventional mortgage may be:
    (A) guaranteed by FHA.
    (B) a commercial loan.
    (C) approved by the DVA.
    (D) made at a rate of interest set by a government agency.

80. When you purchase property under an installment contract of sale (agreement of sale) you have all of the following **EXCEPT:**
    (A) an insurable interest.
    (B) an equitable interest.
    (C) legal title.
    (D) a transfer of possession.

81. As used in real estate financing, the term "impounds" **MOST** nearly means:
    (A) moratorium.   (C) attachments.
    (B) reserves.   (D) penalties.

82. A federal savings and loan institution must belong to which of the following?
    (A) Savings Association Insurance Fund
    (B) Federal Land Bank
    (C) Federal Reserve Board
    (D) Federal Depository Board

83. Which is to the seller's advantage in a sale and leaseback?
    (A) Lease payments are deductible.
    (B) Depreciation is deductible.
    (C) Interest is deductible.
    (D) Property tax is deductible.

❖ 84. Which of the following best describes the principal advantage of a sale and leaseback from the commercial buyer's point of view?
    (A) Capital is not tied up.
    (B) Rental payments are tax deductible.
    (C) Capital gain benefits result.
    (D) Allowable depreciation (cost recovery) can be claimed.

85. Which statement most accurately describes mortgage companies that act as mortgage loan correspondents?
    (A) They prefer negotiating loans that can be sold on the secondary market.
    (B) They are organized under federal laws and are subject to vigorous supervision.
    (C) They do not service the loans they originate.
    (D) They are not active in the field of government-insured loans.

86. When discount charges are charged on DVA loans, the purchaser may:
    (A) volunteer to pay them.
    (B) be charged a loan origination fee.
    (C) amortize them over the loan term.
    (D) make the seller pay the origination and DVA funding fee as well.

87. All of the following practices in a real estate transaction involving a federally related mortgage loan under the Real Estate Settlement Procedures Act (RESPA) are prohibited **EXCEPT:**
    (A) Lender requires specific title insurer.
    (B) Buyer pays referral fee to attorney.
    (C) Broker requests kickback.
    (D) Escrow requires fee for services.

88. When a property is sold under an agreement of sale (land contract):
    (A) legal title passes to the buyer.
    (B) buyer receives a deed at the close of initial escrow.
    (C) the vendor retains possession.
    (D) buyer has equitable title until satisfaction.

89. The definition of an institutional lender includes all of the following **EXCEPT**:
    (A) state charter of banks.
    (B) pension funds.
    (C) savings and loan associations.
    (D) commercial banks.

90. The secondary mortgage market is most affected by the policies of:
    (A) Fannie Mae.
    (B) unintentional investors.
    (C) government-owned agencies.
    (D) insurance companies.

❖ 91. A mortgage broker:
    (A) arranges loans between borrowers and lenders.
    (B) is a lender.
    (C) buys mortgages in the secondary mortgage market.
    (D) buys mortgages and resells them at a profit.

92. A federal savings and loan company must insure its deposits for at least:
    (A) $20,000.   (C) $50,000.
    (B) $40,000.   (D) $100,000.

93. A financing arrangement under which the buyer does not become the legal owner of record is:
    (A) a trust deed.
    (B) a land contract.
    (C) a purchase money mortgage.
    (D) a quitclaim deed.

94. Which of the following is a source of primary mortgage funds?
    (A) Federal Deposit Insurance Corporation
    (B) Federal National Mortgage Association
    (C) Federal Home Loan Bank
    (D) Federal Savings and Loan Association

95. The lender that specializes in real estate home loans, allows a high loan-to-value ratio, deals in nongovernment loans, services its own loans and makes many medium-term to long-term loans would be:
    (A) a savings and loan association.
    (B) a pension plan.
    (C) an insurance company.
    (D) a credit union.

96. In a sale-leaseback transaction, which benefits the seller-lessee?
    (A) The transaction makes working capital available.
    (B) The transaction always involves substantial capital gains tax savings.
    (C) Closing takes less time.
    (D) Conventional financing is easier to obtain.

97. Funds from all of the following institutions are a source of capital for real estate loans **EXCEPT**:
    (A) life insurance companies.
    (B) credit unions.
    (C) savings and loans.
    (D) mortgage brokers.

98. *C* wants to sell his industrial warehouse by way of a sale-leaseback. What would be the **LEAST** relevant factor for the buyer in such a transaction?
    (A) Amount of lease payments
    (B) Income tax deductions
    (C) *C*'s book value
    (D) Replacement cost

99. The Federal National Mortgage Association can do all of the following **EXCEPT**:
    (A) purchase conventional loans.
    (B) sell mortgages to institutions.
    (C) buy FHA-DVA loans.
    (D) originate federal loans.

100. When discount charges are charged on FHA loans:
    (A) the purchaser may not pay the discount points.
    (B) the purchaser is not allowed to pay them.
    (C) only the buyer may pay the charge.
    (D) the seller must pay all points.

101. Which of the following **BEST** describes the fee charged to make a loan?
    (A) Reversion fee   (C) Discount fee
    (B) Origination fee   (D) Transfer fee

102. *C* wants to buy five unoccupied rental units. He could obtain all the following loans **EXCEPT**:
    (A) DVA loan.   (C) conventional loan.
    (B) bank loan.   (D) credit union loan.

103. How long will an FHA conditional loan commitment be in effect?
    (A) One month
    (B) Three months
    (C) Six months
    (D) 12 months

❖ 104. L is purchasing a home by way of a DVA loan. The closing statement reveals a payment of $1,200 in discount points. How would this payment appear on the closing statement?
    (A) Reduction in the proceeds due seller
    (B) Addition to the principal due from buyer
    (C) Reduction in the buyer's down payment
    (D) Addition to the proceeds due seller

❖ 105. The seller has an existing first mortgage. In order to limit exposure to further liability on the mortgage note, the seller should find a buyer ready to:
    (A) take title subject to the mortgage.
    (B) subordinate his or her position to the mortgage.
    (C) assume the mortgage and note.
    (D) obtain his or her own financing.

106. When the lender under a deed of trust requires title insurance, who would be the **MOST** likely person to pay for it?
    (A) Mortgagee
    (B) Trustee
    (C) Trustor
    (D) Beneficiary

❖ 107. A purchases a fee simple property for $70,000 by way of assuming a first mortgage of $50,000, paying $10,000 in cash and having the seller take back a purchase money second mortgage for the balance. There is an existing $5,000 second mortgage on the property to be paid off. At the close of escrow, what is the correct order in which to record documents?
    (A) The assumption mortgage, the deed, the purchase money second mortgage
    (B) The deed, release of existing second mortgage, assumption agreement, purchase money mortgage
    (C) The purchase money second mortgage, the deed
    (D) The release of second mortgage, the deed, the purchase money second mortgage

108. C is purchasing a home for $78,000 and the lender is giving a 90 percent loan at ten percent interest, plus a two percent loan origination fee. How much is the loan origination fee?
    (A) $1,404
    (B) $1,560
    (C) $1,650
    (D) $7,020

109. When is legal title transferred to a vendee under an installment land contract (agreement of sale)?
    (A) Upon payment of the conveyance tax
    (B) Upon satisfaction of the purchase price
    (C) At the initial closing
    (D) Once the vendee can guarantee payment to the seller

110. What is the primary purpose of an FHA conditional loan commitment?
    (A) To insure a lender against default
    (B) To guarantee against a borrower's default
    (C) To qualify a buyer for an FHA loan
    (D) To establish the market value of a property

111. Which of the following statements about conventional mortgages is true?
    (A) They are insured by the federal government.
    (B) They may be neither prepaid nor assumed.
    (C) The buyer must be an owner/occupant.
    (D) They require a higher down payment than FHA or DVA.

112. Which is true regarding FHA loans?
    (A) The FHA will insure first and second mortgages.
    (B) To be insured, the loan must involve an FHA-approved mortgagee.
    (C) There is a small prepayment penalty.
    (D) They are funded by the federal government.

113. An owner is selling his or her house in a flood-prone area. Adequate flood insurance would be required in which case?
    (A) Sale by way of FHA-insured loan
    (B) Sale by way of purchase money mortgage to seller
    (C) Sale by agreement of sale (installment land contract)
    (D) Sale by all cash

❖ 114. A certificate of eligibility is a prerequisite for which type of loan?
(A) Conventional   (C) DVA
(B) FHA   (D) FNMA

115. The borrower obtains a government-insured loan that allows paying a lesser amount each month during a fixed period of time and a greater amount each month during the next period of time. Which type of loan is this?
(A) Conventional rate loan
(B) DVA direct loan
(C) FHA graduated payment loan
(D) FNMA convertible loan

❖ 116. In which one of the following ways does a mortgage broker differ from a mortgage banker?
(A) The broker services the loans he or she arranges.
(B) The broker arranges junior financing.
(C) The broker does not provide his or her own funds to originate the loan.
(D) The broker operates in the primary mortgage market.

❖ 117. Assume that a buyer is making fully amortized payments of $600 per month on a purchase money mortgage. Which of the following is true?
(A) The amount applying to principal decreases each month.
(B) The interest payment stays the same.
(C) Interest and principal payments are constant.
(D) The amount applying to interest decreases each month.

118. The borrower under a fixed rate Section 203b FHA loan is notified that the total monthly (PITT) payment will increase $15 per month. What is the **MOST** likely cause of such an increase?
(A) Inflation
(B) Interest rate escalation
(C) Prepayment
(D) Tax increase

119. Where would a private investor go to insure a conventional loan?
(A) Federal Housing Administration
(B) Federal Home Loan Bank
(C) Federal National Mortgage Association
(D) Private mortgage insurer

❖ 120. A veteran sells his or her property to another veteran who assumes the loan. Which of the following statements is true?
(A) The seller is automatically released from liability upon the assumption.
(B) The seller is immediately eligible for a maximum new DVA loan upon the assumption.
(C) There is a prepayment penalty.
(D) It may be assumed with DVA approval.

121. The ceiling on the amount of interest that can be charged by the seller in a real estate loan is most directly regulated by:
(A) Fannie Mae.
(B) Federal Home Loan Bank.
(C) Department of Veterans Affairs.
(D) state law.

122. All of the following statements are true about Freddie Mac **EXCEPT:**
(A) it is a federal agency called the Federal Home Loan Mortgage Corporation.
(B) it buys and sells mortgages in the secondary mortgage market from savings and loan associations.
(C) it requires the use of standard loan documents.
(D) it has a direct loan program up to $35,000.

123. Buyer signs a five-year interest-only installment land contract to purchase a farm for $100,000 with a $5,000 down payment. After diligently meeting his monthly payment obligations for three years, the buyer loses his job and defaults. A court would likely permit all of the following remedies **EXCEPT:**
(A) foreclosure and sale.
(B) buyer forfeits all payments.
(C) suit to hold buyer to the contract.
(D) suit for repossession and balance due under contract.

124. Which one of the following is a source for investor loans?
(A) FHA insured loans
(B) DVA guaranteed loans
(C) Ginnie Mae loans
(D) Conventional loans

125. Assume you have a couple who doesn't have enough combined income to qualify under acceptable "income-to-purchase price" ratios but whose prospects for rapid salary increases are great. For which type of financing program would it be most appropriate to apply?

   (A) FHA 206(b)   (C) FNMA loan
   (B) DVA loan   (D) FHA 245

126. Your client is purchasing a house under an installment contract called a contract for deed. At the initial closing, the seller signed the deed and placed it with an escrow agent who will hold it until the full amount is paid. Which of the following statements is true?

   (A) Upon default of the buyer, the seller can automatically get the property back, plus sue for the balance due.
   (B) Upon the seller's death, escrow should surrender the deed to the probate court.
   (C) If the seller dies during the contract period, the buyer will lose the house.
   (D) The death of the seller should have no effect on the buyer's interest.

127. If a buyer wants to pay more than the FHA loan amount, what can he or she do?

   (A) Increase the mutual mortgage insurance
   (B) Increase the down payment
   (C) Increase the points
   (D) FHA rules prohibit paying more than the loan amount

ANSWERS

1. **C**   Mortgage bankers often originate loans using their own money and then package them (warehousing) to larger investors and continue to regularly service these loans.

2. **B**   A guarantees loans. The Federal National Mortgage Association (called Fannie Mae) is now a private corporation that purchases DVA, FHA and conventional loans in the secondary mortgage market with money raised by selling debentures backed by the U.S. government.

3. **B**   DVA loans are assumable with prior approval of DVA based on DVA assumption guidelines. The DVA loans are not transferable and the veteran would need to have eligibility restored prior to getting a loan on another home. If the assuming buyer is also a veteran, the seller should see about getting the buyer to substitute his or her DVA eligibility. Otherwise, the seller couldn't get his or her own eligibility fully restored until the buyer paid off the loan.

4. **D**   Most DVA loans are amortized for longer than 15 years. Frequently, the expenses will exceed the income on the rented units, but there is no prohibition on negative cash flow, just a requirement that the veteran occupy one of the units.

5. **B**   Novation is the substitution of one obliged party for another. Note that the assuming buyer would have to substitute his or her own DVA eligibility.

6. **D**   DVA makes direct loans in rare cases, as in rural areas, where loans aren't readily available. While DVA does have certain lending standards, DVA does not regulate lending institutions, as do the Federal Reserve Board (banks) and the Federal Home Loan Bank Board (savings and loan associations).

7. **A**   FHA once had investor programs, but now requires the borrower to occupy the property. DVA limits its loans to veterans who will occupy a single-family residence or at least one unit in a property not to exceed four units. FHA and DVA loans now have certain restrictions and standards regulating loan assumption.

8. **B**   A debenture is an unsecured obligation. The FHA will sometimes offer to pay debentures to lenders who suffer a loss. A chattel mortgage uses personal property as the security.

9. **B**   The direct loan program is related to lack of comparable loans in certain areas and not to occupancy.

10. **A**   The borrower is restricted from obtaining second financing to pay for the down payment and closing costs.

11. **C**   FHA sets standards for the loans. It also sets minimum property requirements (MPRs) for the secured properties.

12. **A**   The private lender makes the loan, which is then insured by FHA.

13. **D**   DVA uses its approved appraisers and will lend only to owner-occupant veterans.

14. **D**   If the appraised value is less than the sale price, the purchaser must pay the difference in cash, not with a second loan. The government *insures* the lender against loss due to the borrower's default.

15. **A**   The FHA prohibits junior financing on properties it insures. After closing, the mortgagor can obtain further financing.

16. **D**   To get such a novation, the veteran could sell to a qualified buyer.

17. **C**   If it were a $100,000 loan on a $110,000 property with 4 points, the discount charge would be $4,000.

18. **D**   The seller (vendor) retains legal title as security for payment of the balance due; the buyer (vendee) receives equitable title and possession.

19. **C**   Direct loans are made in exceptional circumstances with the current limit around $35,000. DVA loans apply to male and female veterans and certain unremarried widows and widowers of veterans.

20. **B**   For example, a five-year loan could be amortized on a ten-year basis with a balloon payment due at the end of the fifth year.

21. **C**   Typically the appraised value is lower in a seller's market, since buyers are willing to pay higher prices to get the property.

22. **B**   There are no down payment requirements under DVA if the buyer and the property meet DVA requirements. Thus, 100 percent loans are possible.

23. **C**   A land contract is also referred to as an agreement of sale, an installment contract or a contract for deed.

24. **B**   An amortized note would include interest and principal payments.

25. **A**   The percentage is based on the amount loaned. The amount loaned would be based on the lesser amount of sales price or appraised value.

26. **B**   Choices (A), (C) and (D) tend to emphasize first loans, whereas noncommercial lenders, especially sellers, provide second financing.

27. **D**   Usury is a rate of interest that exceeds the legal maximum set by state law. Some courts will penalize the lender of a usurious loan by allowing recovery of principal only, no interest at all. Federal rules control over state law.

28. **C**   In non-recourse financing the seller's sole recourse upon default is to look at the property. The buyer is not personally liable if the foreclosure sale fails to bring enough money to pay the amounts due.

29. **A**   Because the buyer benefits from having a mortgage loan to purchase the property, the buyer would pay for the cost of preparing the mortgage. Also, the seller does not sign the mortgage. The seller is obligated by contract to convey title to the buyer, so the seller pays for the cost of the deed.

30. **B**   The lender is primarily concerned with steady income, not irregular overtime, which may greatly fluctuate.

31. **B**   Ginnie Mae functions in the secondary mortgage market, especially in government assisted projects.

32. **D**   The Certificate of Reasonable Value (CRV) is used in DVA loans. In either a DVA loan or an FHA loan, the buyer can pay more than the appraisal.

33. **A**   Purchase money financing often helps bridge the gap between the sales price and the amount of cash the buyer can produce through savings and other loans. While one could have a junior purchase money mortgage, choice (B) describes a mortgage loan not given as part of the acquisition of the property.

34. A A fully amortized debt is one in which there are equal periodic payments of principal and interest, resulting in a zero balance at the end of the stated period. While the amount is constant, the part of each payment intended for interest and that for principal varies, with the interest portion gradually decreasing and principal portion gradually increasing. An annuity is the periodic payment of money for the duration of a person's life or other designated period of time.

35. D Choices (A), (B) and (C) can make both conventional and nonconventional (DVA and FHA) loans.

36. D FHA insurance formerly was paid monthly, based on ½ of one percent of the average annual loan balance. The mortgage insurance premium (MIP) is now paid to FHA at the start of the loan. Along with a periodic servicing fee, the lender may allow the borrower to finance this premium with periodic payments to the lender. Monthly MIP payments to FHA are still permitted on condominium loans.

37. D All these loans are popular with savings and loan companies. FNMA does not originate loans.

38. B Many conventional loans restrict prepayment and/or have a substantial prepayment penalty. Certain nonconventional loans by law contain no prepayment penalties.

39. B An owner may pay off his or her five-year ten percent loan with the proceeds of a recently negotiated 25-year, nine percent loan (a primary market loan transaction). Naturally, the first lender would record a release of mortgage to clear the records of that encumbrance.

40. B The CRV sets the upper limit of a DVA loan.

41. B Many states prohibit the charging of interest upon the interest of a loan.

42. C The construction loan is generally short-term during the interim of completing the building, and this loan is paid-off or taken-out by the final permanent take-out loan.

43. D (A),(B) and (C) would not lend money directly to a borrower.

44. D A debenture is an unsecured note. Fannie Mae raises money by selling debentures.

45. C The selling of existing, primary loans involves the secondary mortgage market.

46. B The buyer under an agreement of sale (land contract) from a vendor is called a vendee, who has acquired equitable title in the property.

47. D Most junior loans are short-term, interest-only, or partially amortized with a balloon payment.

48. B An impound or reserve account is to hold monies in reserve to pay for future charges on the property, like taxes or insurance, thus assuring the lender that the security will not be exposed to liens for delinquent payments.

49. B Some lender may, however, require some private mortgage insurance like MGIC to protect against borrower's default.

50. D Lenders often require such extra compensation or else demand private mortgage insurance. Title insurance is required in most loans.

51. D The only requirement is that the veteran certify that he or she will occupy one of the units.

52. B The borrower formerly paid for the insurance monthly at the annual rate of ½ of one percent of the average annual loan balance. This fee is now paid at the start of the loan, or may be financed.

53. C Under a land contract, the seller retains legal title as security, whereas under the purchase money mortgage, the seller retains no title interest in the property, only the lien interest of a mortgagee.

54. **D** Fannie Mae buys and sells first mortgages in the secondary mortgage market. The Federal Reserve Board regulates commercial banks.

55. **B** The buyer is relatively confident the seller will be a triple-A tenant. Rent is tax deductible as a business expense.

56. **C** The vendor will become the grantor in the deed when the land contract is satisfied.

57. **D** The buyer can pay certain closing costs. DVA loans are available to certain veterans of World War II and afterwards.

58. **D** Through a mutual mortgage insurance plan paid for by the borrower, the FHA will give lenders financial protection in foreclosure situations. FHA requires owner-occupancy.

59. **A** When acquiring a property, the new buyer frequently obtains a loan to pay the seller the purchase price, the proceeds of which the seller uses to satisfy his mortgage.

60. **A** Note that FNMA also buys new mortgages from certain lenders that have a good track record in originating successful loans.

61. **B** FHA, a federal agency of HUD, insures up to 100 percent of the loan amount.

62. **A** A veteran can obtain a loan on a one-family to four-family dwelling, but he or she must occupy one of the dwellings. FHA loans are available to both owner-occupants and nonoccupants although the latter sometimes have to make a greater down payment (their loan-to-value ratio is lower).

63. **B** DVA does have a limit direct loan program, typically restricted to rural areas where financing is difficult to obtain.

64. **B** Secondary financing is prohibited under FHA regulations if it makes the total borrowed exceed the FHA amount for the property.

65. **A** For each point on a low interest loan, it is estimated the yield to the lender increases by ⅛ percent. Thus four points could increase a 9½ percent loan to a ten percent yield. Loans are sold at discounted or lower prices in the secondary market.

66. **C** FHA and DVA are considered nonconventional loans that involve the federal government as a party to the loan. In conventional loans the lender looks only to the borrower and the property in the event of default.

67. **A** The veteran cannot pay any of the loan discount points. These points are paid by the seller. The veteran may pay up to a one percent loan origination fee plus a one percent loan funding fee.

68. **A** DVA does not have to accept the appraisal of anyone except its own approved appraisers.

69. **B** Graduated payment mortgages appeal to younger people who expect their income to gradually increase so they will be able to handle higher payments in later years. Under an adjustable rate mortgage, the interest would fluctuate.

70. **D** Debentures are unsecured notes. FHA and DVA prohibit prepayment penalties. Private lenders often include prepayment penalties in their mortgages.

71. **B** Loan-to-value ratios are based on the lower of sales price or appraisal value.

72. **C** Each lender maintains its own unique practices and policies about originating conventional loans.

73. **D** As a result of the federal Garn-St. Germain law, federal lending institutions are permitted to call in or accelerate their loans in the event the borrower transfers title to the real property securing the loan. Any transfer of legal or equitable title (including options or long-term leases) will trigger the due-on-sale clause, with a few exceptions such as transfer between husband and wife. This law does not apply to junior mortgaging, since no transfer of legal or equitable title is involved.

74. **A** The FHA does not make the loan, the lending institution does.

75. **D** There is no prepayment penalty allowed on either DVA or FHA loans.

76. **C** Someone other than the veteran, usually the seller, must pay all discount points.

77. **D** The CRV sets the ceiling on the loan. Assessed value refers to tax value. DVA guarantees the loan up to 60 percent of the outstanding loan balance or $46,000, whichever is lower.

78. **A** The secondary mortgage market refers to the marketplace for buying and selling loans that originated in the primary market. Such a program results in an increase in the flow of money available for further origination of loans. GNMA is a government agency that is active in the secondary mortgage market of DVA and FHA loans.

79. **B** DVA and FHA agencies are not involved in the conventional mortgage marketplace.

80. **C** Because of the vendee's equitable title, insurance on the property can and should be obtained.

81. **B** An impound account is frequently required by mortgagees. The mortgagor would advance monies for future payments of certain carrying charges, such as taxes and insurance. This protects the lender against problems that could arise if the buyer defaults on those charges.

82. **A** Such membership is not required of state-chartered savings and loans, although many voluntarily carry deposit insurance with the S.A.I.F.

83. **A** Depreciation taxes and interest are deductible to the owner who is the buyer/lessor, but the seller/lessee can deduct the rent as a business expense.

84. **D** The buyer gets the tax advantages of ownership, plus the benefits of any later appreciation in value of the property.

85. **A** They favor loans made with the standardized FNMA and Freddie Mac application and document forms. Typically organized under state law, they often continue to service the loans they originate, which frequently are FHA and DVA loans.

86. **B** If the buyer were allowed to pay the discount, this would tend to defeat one of the purposes of nonconventional DVA loans—to keep the interest and down payment affordable. The buyer can pay if refinancing a loan.

87. **D** RESPA prohibits rebates, tie-ins, kickbacks and referral fees in connection with the closing of a real estate transaction.

88. **D** Legal title does not pass at the first closing; only equitable title passes when the vendee receives the agreement of sale. At the second closing, when the vendee satisfies the terms of the agreement of sale, the deed will pass the legal title.

89. **B** Institutional lenders are heavily regulated by federal and state agencies. Pension funds are private lenders.

90. **A** At first, Fannie Mae was a federal agency but later it became a private corporation.

91. **A** A mortgage *banker* could be a lender as well as an arranger.

92. **D** Each deposit is insured up to $100,000 by the Savings Association Insurance Fund (S.A.I.F.).

93. **B** Under a land contract, the buyer has equitable ownership, but the seller keeps record title.

94. **D** Choice (A) insures deposits, (B) operates in the secondary mortgage market and (C) regulates savings and loan associations.

95. **A** Savings and loan associations have been key participants in the residential real estate marketplace.

96. A   There are no capital gains tax advantages. The seller gets back his or her development capital to help operate his or her business.

97. D   Credit unions are rising fast in popularity as a source of residential financing. While life insurance companies seldom make individual residential loans, they do operate in the secondary market, thus providing mortgage funds. Mortgage brokers do not lend money.

98. C   How *C* carries the property on his books has little relevance to current value. Book value is the price paid, plus any improvements, less tax depreciation taken.

99. D   Fannie Mae operates only in the secondary mortgage market.

100. B   Anyone, including the borrower (not necessarily the seller) may pay the discount. The purchaser may pay an origination fee not to exceed one percent.

101. B   Many lenders immediately sell their loans in the secondary mortgage market, so they make their profit in the origination and service charges.

102. A   DVA would allow up to four units, provided the veteran occupied one of the units.

103. C   The FHA may give its approval to a project developer, subject to obtaining qualified buyers within the time limit. This is known as a conditional commitment.

104. A   The seller would be debited the amount of the discount points.

105. D   If the buyer obtains financing, the seller will get cashed out and can pay off the existing mortgage. The seller would not be primarily liable if the buyer assumed the note, although he or she would remain secondarily liable.

106. C   The trustor is the borrower (the mortgagor). The lender is the beneficiary.

107. D   The existing second will be paid off, so a release or satisfaction piece must be recorded. Nothing need be recorded concerning the assumption since the obligation to assume will be stated in the deed. This is recorded an instant before the purchase money second mortgage.

108. A   A 90 percent loan would be: $70,200 times two percent equals $1,404.

109. B   The conveyance tax (transfer tax) is paid when the agreement of sale is recorded. When the vendee pays in full and satisfies all the terms and conditions of the contract, then legal title will be transferred. Until then, the vendee has equitable title.

110. C   With an FHA conditional loan, the property is appraised and loan values are approved, subject to the qualification of buyers.

111. D   Conventional loans do not involve government insurance (FHA) or guarantee (DVA). Depending on the loan provisions, they may be prepaid and assumed, or sold subject to. Nonconventional loans would be DVA and FHA loans. Through use of an acceleration clause, a lender may decide to limit a borrower's ability to sell the property to a buyer who would assume the loan. (The lender could call the full amount of the loan.) DVA and FHA loans can be freely prepaid with no penalty.

112. B   FHA insures only first mortgages given by approved lenders.

113. A   Lending institutions subject to FDIC regulations require flood insurance in order to loan on property in a designated flood zone. Private lenders are not subject to such regulations.

114. C   The Department of Veterans Affairs requires the veteran certify eligibility for its guaranteed nonconventional loans. The eligibility remains with the property until the loan is paid off or another veteran assumes the loan and substitutes his or her eligibility.

115. **C**   A financing innovation is the FHA 245 loan program—monthly payments in the loan's early years are lower than the amortized payment, but such payments graduate or increase as the loan matures. These loans appeal to borrowers who anticipate an increase in their earning power, especially younger married couples.

116. **C**   Unlike the broker, the mortgage banker is capable of originating loans as well as servicing the loans arranged for others. The mortgage banker operates in the primary mortgage market (originating loans) as well as in the secondary mortgage market (selling loans, especially to FNMA).

117. **D**   As each monthly $600 is paid, a portion is applied to reduce the principal balance of the debt. This results in a lower interest payment for the next month because interest is now calculated on a lower balance.

118. **D**   FHA loan payments are typically all-inclusive payments, which include a payment after taxes and insurance (as in a budget mortgage). The FHA interest rates are fixed.

119. **D**   Private Mortgage Insurance (PMI) is frequently used to insure a portion of a conventional loan. FHA does insure certain nonconventional loans under its Mutual Mortgage Insurance Plan.

120. **D**   To assume a DVA loan committed after March 1, 1988, a purchaser must be able to qualify based on DVA guidelines.

121. **D**   Choices (A),(B) and (C) do regulate certain loan transactions on a national level, but the interest rate ceilings are typically controlled by the individual state usury statutes.

122. **D**   Freddie Mac is most active in the secondary mortgage market for savings and loan association financing. Its requirements have caused considerable standardization of loan documents throughout the country.

123. **D**   If the seller elects to sue the buyer for the full contract price and also give the seller the property back, it would be a windfall. The seller is attempting to cancel the contract on one hand and then enforce the contract on the other hand.

124. **D**   Note that FHA discontinued its investor loan program in 1989.

125. **D**   The FHA 245 is the graduated payment loan program in which monthly payments start low but then increase as the loan matures, while the borrower's income is expected to increase as well. The 203(b) program is the most popular level payment home loan insurance program.

126. **D**   Most contracts for deed contain a forfeiture clause permitting the seller to repossess the property, or the seller could elect to seek money damages. Usually the seller cannot get both the property and damages. The recent trend, however, in cases where the buyer has built up a large equity, is to force a foreclosure sale and return any excess monies to the buyer. Since the deed has been placed in escrow, the death of the seller would normally have no effect on the deed. The principal determination to be made by the probate court is who is entitled to the payments of the balance due.

127. **B**   The FHA gives the buyer a choice to back out if the appraisal value (CRV) exceeds the sales price.

Chapter 10 Mortgages and Foreclosures

The questions in this chapter test your comprehension of the following topics:

- Clauses commonly found in mortgages
- Different classifications of mortgages
- Consequences of a default under a note and mortgage
- Assumptions and sales subject to a mortgage

False Friends

The following words are often confused with one another. Note the difference in meaning of these false friends:

Mortgagor/Mortgagee: The mortgagor (borrower) gives the mortgage to the mortgagee (lender) to secure the payment of money (note).

Acceleration/Alienation: An alienation clause (due on sale or restraint on alienation) triggers the acceleration of the full debt upon a transfer of title; it is a specific type of acceleration clause.

Subordination/Subrogation: To subordinate means to give up priority to an anticipated future mortgage or lien, whereas subrogation means to substitute a creditor who succeeds to the rights of another.

Trustor/Beneficiary: Under a deed of trust, the trustor (borrower) transfers title to a trustee for the benefit of the beneficiary (lender).

Estoppel Certificate/Reduction Certificate: The estoppel certificate is issued by the mortgagor to establish the amount of the debt and whether any defenses exist, whereas the reduction certificate is issued by the lender to someone who is about to assume the loan.

Foreclosure/Forfeiture: A foreclosure action extinguishes any claim the mortgagor may have to the real property securing a defaulted loan, whereas a forfeiture refers generally to the loss of a right to something as a result of nonperformance of an obligation or condition.

Subject to/Assumption: Both involve the sale of a property without paying off the underlying mortgage; however, only with an assumption does the buyer agree to become personally liable for any deficiency judgment upon default.

QUESTIONS

1. Upon the closing of the sale of mortgaged property, the seller **MUST** in every case:
   - (A) pay off the mortgage.
   - (B) deliver the deed to the grantee.
   - (C) obtain the approval of the mortgagee.
   - (D) obtain a new mortgage.

2. A mortgage is usually released by a:
   - (A) reversion.
   - (B) reconveyance.
   - (C) quitclaim deed.
   - (D) satisfaction piece.

❖ 3. A clause in a mortgage or lease, stating that the rights of the holder shall be secondary to a subsequent lien, is called:
   - (A) a subordination clause.
   - (B) an habendum clause.
   - (C) an escalation clause.
   - (D) a recapture clause.

4. If the mortgagee has the property sold at a foreclosure sale and it brings an amount inadequate to pay off the loan, what can the mortgagee do?
   - (A) Sue the mortgagor for the deficiency
   - (B) Cancel the sale
   - (C) Appeal to the Supreme Court
   - (D) Attach all other properties owned by the debtor

5. What will happen upon the sale of a mortgaged property by foreclosure?
   - (A) Any existing listing of the property with the broker is terminated.
   - (B) Foreclosure requires the payment of a commission to the listing broker.
   - (C) Any tenant may remain in occupancy until his or her lease is ended.
   - (D) The owner is forbidden from bidding at the foreclosure sale.

❖ 6. Mortgage satisfaction is evidenced by which of the following?
   - (A) Estoppel certificate
   - (B) Release of lien
   - (C) Reduction certificate
   - (D) Certificate of no defense

7. An "acceleration clause" found in a promissory note or mortgage would mean that:
   - (A) upon the happening of a certain event, the entire amount of the unpaid balance becomes due.
   - (B) payments must be made more frequently at a future specified date.
   - (C) the interest rate can increase.
   - (D) payments may not be made more frequently than specified.

8. Which of the following occurs when the mortgagor is declared bankrupt?
   - (A) Mortgagor retains equitable title to the property but forfeits legal title.
   - (B) Mortgagor no longer owes any money under the mortgage note.
   - (C) The mortgagee will give the mortgagor one year to pay back the debt.
   - (D) Title will pass to the receiver in bankruptcy.

9. An individual, partnership or corporation to whom title to or an interest in a property is conditionally conveyed as security for a loan is known as:
   - (A) the mortgagor.
   - (B) the borrower.
   - (C) the mortgagee.
   - (D) the lessee.

❖ 10. Which of the following must sign the mortgage and the note?
   - (A) Mortgagor
   - (B) Mortgagee
   - (C) Trustee
   - (D) Beneficiary

11. Of the following, who is benefited by an acceleration clause in a mortgage or trust deed note?
   - (A) The borrower
   - (B) The lender
   - (C) A future purchaser upon resale of property
   - (D) The trustee

12. The mortgagor's right to reestablish ownership after default is known as:
   - (A) redemption.
   - (B) reestablishment.
   - (C) acceleration.
   - (D) subordination.

13. A trust deed must be signed by:
   - (A) the beneficiary.
   - (B) the trustor.
   - (C) the lender.
   - (D) the trustee.

❖ 14. The main advantage of a wraparound mortgage is that:
  (A) the borrower gains additional financing at a higher rate than the market interest rate.
  (B) the originator of a wraparound mortgage is the primary mortgage holder.
  (C) the wraparound mortgage specifically finances subdivisions.
  (D) the effective interest rate is typically lower than the prevailing rate on new mortgages.

15. Which of the following mortgage loans would LEAST likely be classified as a second mortgage?
  (A) Wraparound   (C) Seller-assisted
  (B) Construction   (D) Junior loan

❖ 16. All of the following are true of the "promissory note" used to finance real property EXCEPT:
  (A) It is the written promise of the borrower to repay the loan.
  (B) It is the fundamental loan document.
  (C) It is typically recorded.
  (D) It is signed by the mortgagor.

17. The certificate executed and acknowledged by the mortgagee, stating the amount due on the mortgage, is known as:
  (A) the estoppel certificate.
  (B) the reduction certificate.
  (C) the deed of trust.
  (D) the novation certificate.

18. Which of the following is true when the seller takes back a mortgage from the buyer as part payment for the sale?
  (A) The seller is entitled to possession of the property until the debt is paid.
  (B) The seller retains legal title.
  (C) No second mortgages may be placed on the property by the buyer.
  (D) The mortgage is a purchase money mortgage.

19. The use of an acceleration clause in a mortgage or a deed of trust is:
  (A) to require the mortgagor to make more payments per month.
  (B) to increase the amount of the monthly payments.
  (C) to require the entire balance be paid at once when exercised.
  (D) to pressure the mortgagor into making payments.

20. A written acknowledgment that a mortgage has been satisfied is BEST called:
  (A) a subordination.
  (B) a promissory note.
  (C) a release of lien.
  (D) an estoppel certificate.

❖ 21. In the event a first mortgagee fails to record his or her mortgage and a good faith second mortgagee records his or her mortgage first, all of the following would be true EXCEPT:
  (A) The second mortgagee has priority.
  (B) The borrower is personally liable to both lenders.
  (C) The first lender will still be able to collect the money owed.
  (D) An unrecorded mortgage cannot be enforced and collected upon.

❖ 22. What type of mortgage may permit a builder to obtain the release of lots, one at a time, as they are developed?
  (A) Blanket mortgage
  (B) Package mortgage
  (C) Open-end mortgage
  (D) Conventional mortgage

23. Which of the following events results in the release of a mortgage lien?
  (A) Foreclosure sale
  (B) Sale by mortgagor
  (C) Lease of property
  (D) Further encumbrance

24. A promissory note creates which of the following?
  (A) Secured mortgage
  (B) Personal obligation
  (C) Specific lien
  (D) General lien

25. A conditional conveyance of land designed as security for the payment of money or the performance of some act that will become void upon such payment or performance is:
  (A) a lien.
  (B) a deed of trust.
  (C) a general warranty deed.
  (D) an option.

26. If mortgaged property is sold, and the buyer assumes and agrees to pay the mortgage debt:
    (A) the lender can recover the balance from either the seller or the buyer or both.
    (B) the seller no longer has any liability for the debt.
    (C) only the buyer has any liability.
    (D) the property cannot be sold at foreclosure if the buyer defaults.

27. In researching records at the office of public records, you can usually distinguish between a first and second mortgage by:
    (A) the date of instrument.
    (B) the words "first" or "second" preceding the phrase "this indenture."
    (C) notations made by the recorder.
    (D) the date of recording.

28. Which of the following best describes a reduction certificate?
    (A) It shows the balance due on a mortgage.
    (B) It shows the sales price has been reduced on the listing.
    (C) It shows the property has gone down in value since it was last appraised.
    (D) It shows the interest rate has been reduced from the original loan rate.

29. By which means could a deed of trust be discharged?
    (A) By default
    (B) By reconveyance to the trustor
    (C) By refusal of the beneficiary to release control
    (D) When the seller can prove clear title to the property

30. A $150,000 interest-only loan at ten percent in which the entire principal is due at the end is **BEST** described as which type of loan?
    (A) Graduated   (C) Amortized
    (B) Term   (D) Declining balance

31. A clause that advances the time for payment of a debt is:
    (A) an acceleration clause.
    (B) a balloon payment clause.
    (C) a prepayment clause.
    (D) an escalation clause.

32. When you use real property as security for a loan, you do which one of the following?
    (A) Pledge it   (C) Assign it
    (B) Hypothecate it   (D) Devise it

33. A second mortgage is:
    (A) equal in standing and value with a first mortgage.
    (B) a junior lien on real estate that has a prior mortgage.
    (C) always made by the seller.
    (D) used in practically all real estate purchases.

34. A promissory note that provides for payment of interest only, during the term of the note, would be:
    (A) an installment note.
    (B) a straight note.
    (C) an amortized note.
    (D) a nonnegotiable note.

35. In real estate financing, the debt is evidenced by:
    (A) a mortgage.
    (B) a promissory note.
    (C) a chattel mortgage.
    (D) a financing statement.

❖ 36. The clause in a mortgage note that permits the loan to be paid off at any time without a penalty is called:
    (A) a subordination clause.
    (B) an acceleration clause.
    (C) an "or more" clause.
    (D) a nonresponsibility clause.

37. A partial release clause is used commonly in:
    (A) a lease.
    (B) a blanket encumbrance.
    (C) an attachment.
    (D) a judgment lien.

38. When the seller finances the buyer's purchase of a home, it is **MOST** precisely described as:
    (A) a conventional mortgage.
    (B) a chattel mortgage.
    (C) a purchase money mortgage.
    (D) home financing.

❖ 39. A "balloon payment" on a mortgage refers to the:
    (A) first payment.   (C) middle payment.
    (B) last payment.   (D) total payments.

40. In the absence of an agreement to the contrary, the mortgage that normally has priority is:
    (A) the mortgage for the largest amount.
    (B) the first mortgage executed and delivered.
    (C) the mortgage recorded first.
    (D) the construction loan mortgage.

41. Which would be an example of involuntary alienation?
    (A) Trust deed
    (B) Tax sale
    (C) The first mortgage
    (D) The construction mortgage

42. Which one of the following is true about a promissory note?
    (A) It may not be executed in connection with a loan on real property.
    (B) It is an agreement to do or not do a certain thing.
    (C) It is the primary evidence of a loan.
    (D) It is a note that is guaranteed or insured by a government agency.

43. The person to whom a mortgage is made is the lender, also called:
    (A) the mortgagor.   (C) the lessor.
    (B) the mortgagee.   (D) the trustee.

44. Buying real property "subject to the mortgage" is:
    (A) a type of conditional loan.
    (B) a mortgage bought by FNMA and sold to GNMA.
    (C) the taking of title to property by a grantee with no personal responsibility to the lender for paying the mortgage loan.
    (D) the right to foreclose without going to court.

45. The party who is similar to a mortgagor in a transaction involving a deed of trust is **BEST** called:
    (A) the borrower.   (C) the beneficiary.
    (B) the trustor.   (D) the trustee.

46. The seller has a 20-year amortized first mortgage, which the buyer is to assume. Which is true?
    (A) The loan must be a conventional loan to be assumable.
    (B) The buyer's loan will be an amortized loan.
    (C) Amortized loans are not assumable.
    (D) Upon assumption the terms of the loan are usually changed.

47. What accompanies the mortgage document in a real estate loan transaction?
    (A) Promissory note   (C) Abstract
    (B) Deed   (D) Appraisal

48. The difference between the value of the property and the amount of the outstanding mortgage balance is **BEST** described as which of the following?
    (A) Mortgagee's statutory equity
    (B) Mortgagor's equity
    (C) Value owing
    (D) Debt service

❖ 49. An escalation clause in a mortgage usually provides for:
    (A) an adjustment of the interest rate under specified conditions.
    (B) immediate payment of the full debt upon any default.
    (C) a method of speeding up the payment to pay off the loan sooner.
    (D) a locked-in interest rate in the event that interest rates increase.

50. Which statement can be made concerning a secured real estate loan?
    (A) Charging a rate of interest higher than the legal maximum is called "points."
    (B) Subordination clause is a clause by which a prior lien holder permits subsequent lien(s) to step ahead in priority.
    (C) Prepayment is the lender's charge for making a loan.
    (D) Each point is equivalent to two percent of the loan amount.

❖ **51.** A mortgage that covers several parcels of land and may contain a provision for sale of an individual parcel, thereby reducing mortgage payments, is:

(A) a direct reduction mortgage.

(B) an amortized mortgage.

(C) a blanket mortgage.

(D) a declining balance mortgage.

52. If a buyer of real property agrees in the contract of purchase to assume an existing loan:

(A) the seller is entirely relieved of all responsibility to pay the note in full.

(B) the seller remains solely responsible for repayment of the note.

(C) the buyer can only lose the property through foreclosure but cannot be sued for a deficiency judgment.

(D) the buyer could be held liable if loan payments are not made.

53. Where there is a default on a mortgage, which of the following can occur?

(A) The lender can foreclose without the need of going through judicial proceedings if there is a "power of sale" clause in the mortgage.

(B) After the foreclosure sale, the borrower has a ten-year statutory right to redeem the property by paying all cash.

(C) The mortgagor can pay up all of the back payments at any time and thus remain in good standing with the lender.

(D) Only if there is an escalation clause in the mortgage can the lender foreclose.

❖ **54.** An equitable period of redemption refers to a time within which:

(A) a lender can foreclose on a borrower who is in default.

(B) the debtor can reclaim the property by payment.

(C) a prospective purchaser can bid on the property.

(D) the court may take possession of the secured property.

55. When the foreclosure sale of mortgaged property does not yield enough to pay off the mortgage(s), the lender(s):

(A) must pay for the expenses of collection.

(B) may pursue other assets of the borrower for the deficiency.

(C) may cancel the sale and repossess the property.

(D) accepts debt that stays with the property and transfers to the new buyer.

56. In preparing the mortgage document, one should note that:

(A) the mortgagor is not named in the mortgage.

(B) the mortgagee is not named in the mortgage.

(C) the mortgagor does not sign the mortgage.

(D) the mortgagee does not sign the mortgage.

❖ **57.** If the foreclosure sale proceeds are less than the outstanding debt and foreclosure expenses, which of the following remedies is available?

(A) There is no remedy.

(B) The mortgagee must absorb the loss, since the mortgagor is liable only for foreclosure expenses.

(C) Owner has the statutory right of redemption.

(D) Mortgagee may obtain a deficiency judgment against the mortgagor.

58. The monthly payment on a loan remains the same, yet the amount applied to interest decreases and the amount applied to principal increases as the loan gets older. This is an illustration of which of the following?

(A) Amortization   (C) Subrogation

(B) Depreciation   (D) Inflation

59. In the mortgage, the lender can establish which of the following?

(A) The right of redemption

(B) The length of the redemption period

(C) Usurious rate of interest

(D) The terms of repayment

❖ 60. What advantage to the borrower does a 20-year amortization loan have over a 15-year amortization loan?
(A) A lower amount of interest
(B) Lower monthly payments
(C) Higher monthly payments
(D) Lower down payment

❖ 61. Which of the following is true?
(A) The acceleration clause is placed in a mortgage document for the benefit of the mortgagor.
(B) The escalation clause is placed in the mortgage contract to facilitate foreclosure.
(C) The defeasance clause tells when the payments are due and defines any late charges.
(D) Charging more than the legal rate of interest is called usury.

62. A deed that conveys title to a mortgagee from a mortgagor and prevents legal action to recover the lender's collateral is known as a deed:
(A) of surrender.
(B) in lieu of foreclosure.
(C) of release.
(D) of reconveyance.

63. Of the following all statements are true concerning a purchase money mortgage **EXCEPT:**
(A) It can be given by the purchaser to the seller to secure partial payment.
(B) It allows the buyer to obtain title to the property.
(C) Any mortgage that is part of the purchase price of the property is a purchase money mortgage.
(D) It is only used for second mortgages.

❖ 64. A mortgage that allows for advances to a mortgagor up to a certain maximum is:
(A) a package mortgage.
(B) an open-end mortgage.
(C) a purchase money mortgage.
(D) a wraparound mortgage.

65. Upon the satisfaction of a debt secured by a deed of trust, the title is reconveyed to the borrower by:
(A) the trustor.   (C) the lender.
(B) the beneficiary.   (D) the trustee.

66. An example of written evidence of a promise to repay borrowed money is:
(A) an abstract.
(B) an acknowledgment.
(C) a covenant.
(D) a promissory note.

67. A deed of trust is used to do which of the following?
(A) Convey land to a trustworthy friend
(B) Secure a loan of money by real property
(C) Convey land to a trustee for a minor
(D) Secure a loan of money by trade fixtures

68. A mortgagor's right, in some states, to reclaim the foreclosed property from the successful bidder after the foreclosure sale is:
(A) satisfaction of mortgage.
(B) equitable right of redemption.
(C) an action for judgment.
(D) statutory right of redemption.

69. A blanket mortgage does which of the following?
(A) Covers several parcels of land
(B) Finances the furniture and appliances in a dwelling
(C) Covers any property being financed, whether real or personal
(D) Covers the total payment of principal, interest, taxes, insurance and so on

❖ 70. A buyer purchased a furnished, fee simple home. He is going to assume the existing mortgage. The settlement company will arrange to have drawn up all the following with the exception of:
(A) bill of sale.
(B) note and mortgage.
(C) assumption agreement.
(D) warranty deed.

❖ 71. A statement from a borrower, setting forth the amount of the balance unpaid, the interest rate, and any claims he or she may have against the lender, is called a:
(A) lender's certificate.
(B) title certificate.
(C) estoppel certificate.
(D) financial certificate.

72. A clause in a mortgage that may permit the lender to call the entire balance due if the property is sold or otherwise conveyed by the mortgagor is called:
    - (A) defeasance clause.
    - (B) alienation clause.
    - (C) subordination clause.
    - (D) escalation clause.

73. A mortgage may be discharged by all of the following **EXCEPT**:
    - (A) satisfaction.
    - (B) power of sale.
    - (C) death.
    - (D) release.

74. The points of conventional loans are computed and based on:
    - (A) sales price.
    - (B) listing price.
    - (C) loan amount.
    - (D) closing costs.

75. A secured loan with a payback based on 25 years but which is to be paid in full in ten years is all of the following **EXCEPT**:
    - (A) a balloon mortgage.
    - (B) an installment contract.
    - (C) an amortized loan.
    - (D) a graduated payment mortgage.

76. A mortgage that permits the interest charge to range up and down according to the money market is called:
    - (A) an escalation mortgage.
    - (B) a net mortgage.
    - (C) an open mortgage.
    - (D) a variable rate mortgage.

77. Which is true concerning the typical purchase money mortgage?
    - (A) The seller takes back a mortgage as part of the purchase price.
    - (B) The seller is disposing of a mortgage loan.
    - (C) The buyer is denied the prepayment privilege.
    - (D) The seller is denied the prepayment penalty.

❖ 78. When a buyer "assumes and agrees to pay" an existing loan on the property, which of the following is true?
    - (A) The seller is relieved from liability.
    - (B) The buyer and the seller are liable on the loan.
    - (C) Only the seller is liable.
    - (D) Only the buyer is liable.

❖ 79. Which of the following terms **BEST** describes the right to pay off a mortgage debt after default?
    - (A) Foreclosure
    - (B) Prepayment
    - (C) Redemption
    - (D) Escalation

80. All of the following persons in a real estate purchase transaction using a purchase money trust deed signs the deed of trust **EXCEPT**:
    - (A) borrower.
    - (B) trustor.
    - (C) trustee.
    - (D) purchaser.

81. A mortgage contains a clause providing for the assignment of rents. Who benefits from this clause?
    - (A) Mortgagor
    - (B) Mortgagee
    - (C) Purchaser
    - (D) Trustee

82. Which of the following parties to a real estate sales transaction would have the **MOST** exposure to liability?
    - (A) Grantor of quitclaim deed
    - (B) Grantor in a loan assumption
    - (C) Grantee taking subject to the loan
    - (D) Grantor selling subject to the loan

83. *H* owns a house subject to a first mortgage. His property is said to be:
    - (A) restricted.
    - (B) subordinated.
    - (C) executed.
    - (D) encumbered.

❖ 84. Under an adjustable rate mortgage, which of the following may occur?
    - (A) The term of the loan may not be extended.
    - (B) The interest rate may decrease one percentage point.
    - (C) The number of lenders involved changes each year.
    - (D) No prepayment is allowed.

85. When is a mortgagor released from liability under a mortgage?
    - (A) Upon a sale subject to the mortgage
    - (B) Upon an assumption of the mortgage
    - (C) Upon a sale under a land contract
    - (D) Upon an assumption and novation

❖ 86. Which of the following statements regarding the interest on a long-term amortized mortgage loan is true?

(A) Unless otherwise provided, interest is usually charged in arrears, meaning at the end of each period for which interest is due.

(B) The interest portion of each payment remains the same throughout the entire term of the loan.

(C) The monthly payment will remain the same, and out of each monthly payment, the same amount will be applied to principal and toward interest.

(D) Amortized loans must have a floating interest rate.

87. A borrower obtains a home improvement loan secured by his or her house that is neither insured nor guaranteed by a government agency. This borrower has obtained which type of loan?

(A) Wraparound   (C) Subordinated
(B) Purchase money   (D) Conventional

88. The mortgage clause that permits the borrower to pay off the entire debt ahead of schedule without being charged a premium penalty is called:

(A) an acceleration clause.
(B) an escalation clause.
(C) a level off payment clause.
(D) a prepayment clause.

89. A borrower goes to a savings and loan to obtain a $39,000 second mortgage on his or her home. Which of the following statements is true?

(A) In order to create a valid mortgage loan, the borrower must sign two separate instruments, a mortgage and a note.

(B) A service charge of three points on this loan would be $300.

(C) This would be called a purchase money mortgage.

(D) There would be a subordination clause in the second mortgage.

90. Mortgaged real property is generally conveyed by:

(A) refinancing the loan.
(B) written approval of the mortgagee.
(C) delivery of a deed.
(D) satisfaction of the mortgage.

91. Which one of the following illustrates a voluntary transfer of legal title?

(A) Eminent domain   (C) Deed of trust
(B) Adverse possession   (D) Foreclosure

92. All of the following is true about a recorded mortgage instrument EXCEPT:

(A) It creates a specific lien.
(B) It is a security device for a promissory note.
(C) It secures the loan with the property.
(D) It is a debenture.

93. Which of the following statements is true concerning an amortized mortgage?

(A) There is a gradual decline in the monthly payments.

(B) The amount of the borrower's equity in the property is gradually reduced.

(C) It creates an unsecured loan.

(D) The last payment is equal to the third payment.

94. All of the following statements regarding a loan assumption are true EXCEPT:

(A) The grantee becomes liable for the original promissory note.

(B) Both grantee and grantor are liable for repayment of the loan.

(C) If the grantee defaults, the grantor is secondarily liable.

(D) The grantor is released from liability.

95. Which of the following BEST describes the upset price?

(A) The lowest price offered in a foreclosure sale

(B) The price below which the property will not be sold

(C) The price that is the final bidding price

(D) A concealed price that beats out all others

96. In a real estate purchase, the buyer assumes the mortgage. On the closing statement, such assumption would appear as:

(A) a debit to seller, credit to buyer.
(B) a credit to seller, debit to buyer.
(C) a credit to buyer and seller.
(D) a debit to buyer and seller.

97. *H* purchased a vacant lot under a 15-year mortgage. He intends to build a residence there in five years. From *H*'s point of view, the mortgage should contain which type of clause?

    (A) Subrogation   (C) Subordination

    (B) Release   (D) Escalation

98. Which of the following is directly involved in a nonjudicial foreclosure of real property?

    (A) The public advertising and sale of mortgaged property

    (B) The appointment of a commissioner

    (C) Summons and complaint

    (D) Court approval to sell

99. *A* buys an older home for renovation that she expects to begin when she moves into the house in several years. The **BEST** mortgage to obtain would be:

    (A) an open-end.   (C) a package.

    (B) a blanket.   (D) a piggyback.

❖ 100. A clause in a blanket mortgage that permits mortgagors to assign parcels of property covered by the mortgage upon payment of a specific amount is **BEST** termed:

    (A) a partial assignment.

    (B) a release.

    (C) a novation.

    (D) a due-on-sale.

❖ 101. All of the following are incorrect regarding similarities of a mortgage to a trust deed **EXCEPT**:

    (A) Both have the same number of parties.

    (B) Both have similar foreclosure processes.

    (C) Both transfer the same interest to the lender.

    (D) Both involve a promissory note.

102. Why would a seller most likely lend money to a buyer on a purchase money mortgage?

    (A) To obtain a secure investment

    (B) To provide long-term income

    (C) To facilitate the sale

    (D) To obtain a high rate of interest

103. In an assumption of mortgage transaction, the seller pays for all but which one of the following?

    (A) Deed

    (B) Title insurance

    (C) State conveyance tax

    (D) 1/2 escrow fee

104. A construction lender might require the lessor/owner to do what in order to lend the money?

    (A) Refinance

    (B) Subordinate the fee

    (C) Accelerate the loan

    (D) Depreciate the fee

105. There is a $50,000 mortgage at 14 percent for 15 years; monthly payments are $664.80. The loan principal is reduced by 3.7 percent during the fifth year. How much interest is paid during the 5th year?

    (A) $6,128   (C) $7,658

    (B) $7,000   (D) $7,977

106. A loan in which the mortgagor receives monthly payments for life with the balance of the mortgage to be paid at death is called:

    (A) index mortgage.

    (B) rollover mortgage.

    (C) wraparound mortgage.

    (D) reverse annuity mortgage.

107. Which of the following is least likely to contain a partial amortization clause?

    (A) Agreement of sale

    (B) Wraparound mortgage

    (C) Straight note

    (D) Balloon mortgage

108. Which type of mortgage financing is designed for elderly homeowners?

    (A) Growing equity

    (B) Reverse annuity

    (C) Interim

    (D) Graduated payment

109. Which of the following would most likely trigger a due-on-sale or alienation clause in a mortgage?

    (A) A one-year lease

    (B) A transfer into trust

    (C) A transfer to a spouse

    (D) A foreclosure sale

110. *I* has $120,000 equity in her duplex home. She buys a new home before her duplex sells. What type of loan would she likely obtain?

    (A) Package loan   (C) Swing loan

    (B) Blanket loan   (D) Take out loan

111. In comparing a Growing Equity Mortgage (GEM) to a 30-year amortized loan, all is true of the GEM loan **EXCEPT**:
    (A) GEM amortizes over shorter period.
    (B) GEM total interest paid is less.
    (C) GEM equity grows more slowly.
    (D) GEM payments increase over term of loan.

112. Upon a foreclosure, which is true?
    (A) Mortgagor gets balance of sale proceeds after all debts are paid.
    (B) Mortgagor's attorney will get paid out of sales proceeds.
    (C) Mortgagee will not recover attorney fees out of sales proceeds.
    (D) Mortgagor has a two-year right of redemption.

113. A loan in which the lender cannot obtain a deficiency judgment upon foreclosure is called:
    (A) non-recourse.   (C) balloon.
    (B) satisfaction.   (D) straight.

114. All of the following appear in a promissory note **EXCEPT**:
    (A) interest.
    (B) points.
    (C) term of lease.
    (D) purchase price of property.

❖ 115. Under what type of program can a financial institution underwrite an FHA loan?
    (A) Direct establishment
    (B) Direct endorsement
    (C) Direct capitalization
    (D) Direct programming

ANSWERS

1. **B** Without delivery of the deed, there would be no transfer. The existing mortgage could be paid off, assumed or taken subject to.

2. **D** This is also called a release. A reconveyance is used in a trust deed. Though a quitclaim deed would be possible, a satisfaction piece is more usual.

3. **A** This clause is frequently found in second mortgages that allow the mortgagor to refinance the first mortgage. A recapture clause is found in shopping center percentage leases, an habendum clause is likely in a deed, and an escalation clause covers increases or decreases in payments.

4. **A** Most states allow a deficiency judgment but some states (like California) have antideficiency laws that limit the recovery to the property itself.

5. **A** A foreclosure sale is an involuntary sale, thus the broker is not the procuring cause of the sale.

6. **B** Another name for a release is a satisfaction piece. The estoppel certificate (also called Certificate of No Defense) is used when assigning a mortgage. It confirms the terms of the mortgagor's debt to prevent later dispute over any of the terms.

7. **A** The note will accelerate upon default. It is called a due-on-sale or alienation clause if the note will accelerate upon a *transfer* of the property. This clause is also found in installment land contracts.

8. **D** The title passes to the receiver in bankruptcy. The mortgagor still owes the debt but lenders usually rely on the sale of the secured property to obtain reimbursement for the loan. As a secured creditor, the mortgagee would receive a preference in the bankruptcy distribution.

9. **C** This is especially true in a title-theory state. Upon full payment, the mortgagee will lose its conditional title in the secured property, as a result of the defeasance clause.

10. **A** The note evidences the debt and the mortgage transfers an interest in the secured property; thus the borrower, not the lender, will sign.

11. **B** The lender can declare the entire amount due upon default and then sue to foreclose.

12. **A**   After foreclosure, some states provide for a statutory right of redemption such as one year after the foreclosure sale; other states provide for an equitable right of redemption only up to the actual foreclosure sale.

13. **B**   The trustor is the borrower who must sign; the beneficiary is the lender, and the holder of naked title is the trustee.

14. **D**   A wraparound is a junior mortgage; but because the lender puts out only the cash difference between the existing mortgage and the total loan, the interest rate tends to be lower than the prevailing rate (but is usually higher than the existing mortgage's rate). The wraparound mortgage is actually a junior mortgage that overstates its principal by the amount of the surviving, underlying prior mortgages (i.e., the principal balance of the wrap loan includes the principal balances of all existing mortgages). For example, a buyer gets a mortgage for $140,000 at 9 percent, which wraps around the seller's existing mortgage of $100,000 at 7 percent, even though the current rate of interest is 11 percent. The wraparound lender puts up only $40,000 in cash and uses the buyer's monthly 9 percent payments to pay both the existing first mortgage ($100,000) and the wrap loan ($40,000). It is like a consolidation loan, with the wrap lender disbursing all the monthly payments.

15. **B**   The construction lender typically insists on being in first lien position. Choices (A) and (D) by definition are not first mortgages, and most seller loans are designed to help finance the difference between the buyer's first mortgage and the balance due on the purchase price.

16. **C**   The mortgage, not the note, is recorded because the note does not create an interest in real estate; also, lenders often do not want the terms of the loan made public.

17. **B**   The reduction certificate is used when a buyer assumes a mortgage or takes title subject to a mortgage. The estoppel certificate is executed by the mortgagor to assist the mortgagee in assigning the loan.

18. **D**   Possession and title pass to the buyer but the seller retains a security interest pending full payment of the debt. Sellers usually do not restrict the buyer's right to seek junior financing.

19. **C**   Such a clause does make the borrower think twice about defaulting. Without this clause, the lender would have to bring suit each month that a scheduled payment is missed.

20. **C**   Another name for this is satisfaction piece.

21. **D**   Recordation determines priority of mortgage liens (in the absence of a subordination clause). Even if a mortgage is not recorded, the mortgagor is obligated under the note, for the debt is still effective between the borrower and the lender. An unrecorded mortgage is still valid against the mortgagor; it is just *not* valid against the claim of a good faith second mortgagee who records first.

22. **A**   Blanket mortgages are often used in developing subdivisions. These mortgages should contain carefully worded partial release clauses to release individual lots from under the umbrella of the mortgage as they are sold.

23. **A**   The foreclosure sale would extinguish the security interest in the property but not necessarily the debt (there could be a deficiency judgment).

24. **B**   The mortgage creates the secured obligation; the note is evidence of the debt.

25. **B**   A deed of trust, like a mortgage, is a specific type of lien that involves a conditional conveyance of real property to a trustee to secure a debt.

26. **A**   Unless released, the seller (original mortgagor) is secondarily liable for payment of the debt; in a sense, the seller is a surety or guarantor. If the seller is released, this is called a novation.

27. **D**   Date of recordation determines priority. Here is an exception: If the earlier recorded mortgage contained a subordination clause, the latter mortgage would take priority.

28.   A   A reduction certificate is signed by the mortgagee to show the terms of the loan to a buyer who is assuming or taking title subject to the loan.

29.   B   Default would trigger the foreclosure process. When the debt is paid, the trustee conveys back to the borrower (trustor) by a reconveyance deed.

30.   B   A term or a straight note is an interest-only note with the full principal balance due in one lump sum at maturity. Under choices (A), (B) and (C) there are payments to principal during the loan.

31.   A   A balloon payment is the final payment in an amount that exceeds the regular monthly payment; it is not found in a fully amortized loan.

32.   B   To hypothecate is to put up as security *without* surrendering possession (in a pledge there is a surrender of possession). To devise is to transfer real property by will.

33.   B   It is subordinate to earlier mortgages and may be taken by the seller or any other lender.

34.   B   Amortized notes include payments of principal and interest; notes are typically negotiable and thus easily transferable.

35.   B   To secure the note, the lender obtains a mortgage. A financing statement is used in financing personal property under the Uniform Commercial Code.

36.   C   Also called the prepayment privilege clause, prepayment is allowed if, for example, the monthly payment is listed as "$600 or more."

37.   B   Release clauses enable the borrower to sell off subdivision parcels free and clear of the underlying blanket mortgage; these releases also are used in some condominium sales.

38.   C   Conventional mortgages are usually considered by lending institutions to be non-government assisted loans. Chattel mortgages involve a personal property loan transaction. There are many types of home financing alternatives.

39.   B   Balloon payments are popular in installment land contracts and nonamortized purchase money second financing.

40.   C   Recordation determines priority, lacking a subordination agreement.

41.   B   A tax sale is not voluntary; it results from failure to pay taxes. A deed of trust, like a mortgage, is a voluntary alienation (transfer) of real property to secure a loan.

42.   C   The note evidences the debt and the mortgage secures it. Choice (B) defines any contract.

43.   B   The lender is the mortgagee; the borrower is the mortgagor. Note the two e's in *lender* and the two o's in *borrower*.

44.   C   Upon default, the buyer would lose the property but would not be obligated for the seller's loan (as he would if he had "assumed" the loan).

45.   B   The best answer is the trustor, who is also the borrower.

46.   B   DVA or FHA loans are also assumable with approval. Unless the parties agree otherwise, the terms of the assumed loan remain the same. The word "recasting" refers to changing the terms.

47.   A   Without the note, the mortgage is not an effective lien. An appraisal report usually precedes the decision to make a loan. In the case of a home improvement loan, there would be no deed involved—choice (B).

48.   B   Any excess over the balance due the lender after a foreclosure sale belongs to the mortgagor, after other expenses have been paid.

49.   A   The modern version of the escalation clause is the variable rate mortgage. Choice (B) is the acceleration clause.

50.   B   An owner selling a vacant land to a developer might take back a purchase money mortgage and subordinate it to a construction loan, so the developer can complete the project, and thus begin to repay the owner. Choice (A) is usury.

51. C   Popular in subdivision developments, blanket mortgages must be carefully checked for definite and unambiguous partial release provisions.

52. D   Both buyer and seller are personally liable, unlike in a "subject to loan," choice (C). Seller is not relieved unless there is a novation, as there frequently is under "modern" assumptions.

53. A   Nonjudicial foreclosure is often permitted provided the mortgage contains a power of sale clause. Statutory redemption periods, if any, usually do not exceed one year. There is however, an equitable right of redemption up to the time of the foreclosure sale. Under choice (C), not all mortgages contain the right of "reinstatement."

54. B   In many states, to redeem the property, the borrower must pay back the entire debt, not just the overdue payments. The purpose of foreclosure is to cut off this right to redeem.

55. B   Unless it is a nonrecourse loan or there is antideficiency legislation, the mortgagee can seek a deficiency judgment, which could act as a general judgment lien when it is filed. The expenses are typically applied against the mortgagor's debt.

56. D   The mortgage transfers a security interest and thus the transferee need not sign (just as a grantee usually does not need to sign the deed).

57. D   The mortgagee will not be able to obtain a deficiency judgment, however, if there is state antideficiency legislation or if it is a nonrecourse loan.

58. A   Note that in the early years of the loan most of the monthly payment is applied to interest and very little to principal.

59. D   The right and period of redemption are controlled by state law and cannot be waived by contract.

60. B   Although the principal amount and the rate of interest are the same, the fact that the payments are spread over five more years results in lower monthly payments.

For example on a $100,000 loan at 12 percent, the monthly payment on a 15-year amortization is $1,200.22. The payment is $1,101.12 based on 20 years.

61. D   The acceleration clause benefits the lender; the escalation clause permits fluctuations in the interest rate to reflect changes in the money market.

62. B   The lender must check to see if there are any other liens on the property, since this type of deed will not cut off the rights of other lienholders as does a foreclosure action.

63. D   Compare this with seller-assisted financing by means of an installment sales contract in which the buyer gets equitable, not legal, title.

64. B   Such mortgages are not very popular today, especially due to the frequent transfer of mortgages in the secondary mortgage market. They usually can't exceed the original amount of the loan.

65. D   A deed of reconveyance goes back to the trustor from the trustee.

66. D   If secured by real property, a mortgage is also involved.

67. B   Choice (C) is a deed *in* trust.

68. D   The equity of redemption is that period up to the foreclosure sale. Many states also allow a redemption period after a tax sale.

69. A   Choice (B) is a package mortgage.

70. B   The deed usually contains an assumption clause obligating the grantee to take on the grantor's obligations under the existing note and mortgage. There would be a new note and mortgage if the seller is to be relieved of all liability (or novation).

71. C   It is important for purchasers of the mortgage in the secondary mortgage market to obtain this estoppel certificate. Most mortgages have provisions requiring the mortgagor to execute an estoppel certificate upon request of the mortgagee. The mortgagor states that he or

she has no claims, set-offs, or defenses to assert against the debt.

72.   B   Alienation clause is a specific type of acceleration clause (also called a due-on-sale clause). The defeasance clause terminates the lender's interest in the property upon full payment.

73.   C   The estate of the deceased mortgagor is responsible for existing contracts and debts. Some mortgagors obtain a term life insurance policy to cover this situation.

74.   C   If the lender charged three points on a $60,000 loan involved in the purchase of an $80,000 property with $2,000 in closing costs, the charge for the points would be $1,800.

75.   D   The loan is paid in installments, which are computed using a 25-year amortization with a balloon payment in ten years. A graduated payment is a loan for the full term.

76.   D   A similar effect can be obtained by an escalation clause in a mortgage.

77.   A   Technically, any loan to acquire the property is a purchase money mortgage, although the term is most commonly treated as a seller-assisted loan.

78.   B   The buyer is primarily liable, and the seller is secondarily liable. In a sale "subject to the mortgage," the buyer is not liable to the lender.

79.   C   The right to pay off a mortgage debt at any time up to the foreclosure sale is called the equity of redemption. Some states give an additional time after the foreclosure sale—this is called the *statutory* right of redemption.

80.   C   The trustee merely holds the legal title as security for payment of the debt by the trustor-purchaser-borrower.

81.   B   The lender is the mortgagee and would usually seek an assignment of rents as additional security when lending money secured by a rental property.

82.   D   The grantor selling subject to a loan would remain primarily liable for the debt and secondarily liable as a surety in a loan assumption. The grantor of a quitclaim deed would have the least exposure.

83.   D   The mortgage lien is an encumbrance on the title. The facts given do not indicate any public or private restrictions on the property.

84.   B   An adjustable rate mortgage may increase or decrease depending on the terms of the loan. If there is an increase, the monthly payments could stay the same but the term may be extended.

85.   D   With a novation, there is a substitution of the new buyer for the seller and the lender agrees to the release of liability of the seller.

86.   A   Interest is paid in arrears; therefore, the payment due September 1 covers interest for the August period. The amount of the monthly payment applied to interest gradually decreases as the principal on the loan is slowly paid off.

87.   D   The borrower has obtained a conventional home improvement loan. It is not a purchase money loan since the funds are not used to purchase or acquire the property.

88.   D   This is a prepayment privilege clause.

89.   A   The mortgage, not the note, would be recorded. The charge would be $1,170.

90.   C   Mortgaged property may be sold by assumption, subject to refinancing satisfaction, but in these cases, there must be transfer of legal title as shown by delivery of a deed.

91.   C   In a deed of trust, the borrower transfers legal title to a trustee as security for a loan from the beneficiary.

92.   D   The mortgage is a lien on the property and is security for payment of the note (this is evidence of the debt). Debentures are unsecured notes.

93. D   There are equal monthly payments but, as the loan matures, the amount applied to principal increases (thus increasing the buyer's equity), and the amount applied to interest decreases.

94. D   The grantee is primarily liable, with the grantor being secondarily liable for the debt. A novation results in a full release.

95. B   In some foreclosure actions, the court determines an upset price (a bottom price) below which offers to buy will not be considered.

96. A   The buyer's assumption represents money the seller will not receive at closing (thus a debit); it is how the buyer will pay a portion of the purchase price (thus a credit).

97. C   In order to obtain a construction loan, the lender usually will require the existing first mortgagee to subordinate his loan position (to be junior) to the construction lender.

98. A   Some states permit a form of foreclosure in which the mortgaged property is sold at a public auction after proper notice of sale has been given in newspaper ads if the mortgage contains a "power of sale" clause. By statute, states may permit a period of redemption after the foreclosure sale (statutory right of redemption) or up to the time of the sale (equitable right of redemption).

99. A   Under an open-end mortgage A can obtain additional monies for renovation later on without having to renegotiate a new mortgage—up to the amount of the original loan.

100. B   A release clause, or partial release clause, will remove a specific parcel from the lien of the blanket mortgage. Partial assignments typically involve the transfer of all of the lease term as it applies to a portion of the leased premises.

101. D   The trust deed and mortgage are devices used to secure the repayment of a debt. The trust deed uses a trustee to hold title and has a more expeditious foreclosure mechanism.

102. C   While (A), (B) and (D) may all be factors the seller considers, the most popular reason for carry-back financing is to facilitate the sale, since this opens up the market to more potential buyers.

103. B   Buyer pays for added cost of title insurance (above cost of certificate of title paid by seller); also, there is no need to prepare new mortgage and note.

104. B   The security is more valuable if the lender has an interest in the fee simple as well as the leasehold estate.

105. A $664.80 x 12 = $7,977.60

$50,000 x 3.7% = $1,850 principal reduction, less $7,977.60 = $6,128

106. D   These have not proven to be very popular.

107. C   A straight note is for interest only.

108. B   The lender pays the borrower a monthly annuity secured by the equity in the home. In a growing equity mortgage, the monthly amount gradually increases, which results in a faster pay down of the principal due.

109. B   Transfer into a trust is a *voluntary* movement of title.

110. C   A swing or bridge loan uses the equity in the unsold home as a part of the security for the new loan.

111. C   Monthly payments gradually increase with more going to reduce principal.

112. A   Any equity goes to borrower/mortgagor.

113. A   The lender must look to the property to satisfy any default on the loan.

114. D   The purchase price is found in the sales contract; the note states the amount of the loan.

115. B   In 1983 the FHA set up a direct endorsement program to enable certain recognized lenders to handle the evaluation and loan qualification process, thus helping to reduce the typical red tape found in the FHA loan process.

PART D Transfer of Property Ownership

This part contains questions on the topics of

- Different ways of transferring title to real property
- Types of deeds
- Elements of adverse possession
- The function of escrow to close a transaction
- Types of evidence of title
- Recordation of documents in the public records

Expect about 15 percent of the examination to contain questions on the topics covered in this Part D.

Chapter 11   Acquisition of Title: Deeds

Questions in this chapter will test your comprehension of the following topics:

- Warranty and quitclaim deeds
- The importance of delivery and recording of deeds
- The essential elements of a valid deed
- Covenants found in a warranty deed
- Use of adverse possession to transfer title

False Friends

The following words are often confused with one another. Note the difference in meaning of these false friends:

Grantor/Grantee: The grantor (seller) transfers legal title to the grantee (buyer) using a deed.

Covenant/Condition: A covenant is a promise to do something (as in a covenant of quiet enjoyment in a deed), whereas a condition is a contingency upon which a property right is gained or lost.

Deed/Bill of Sale: A deed transfers legal title to real property, whereas a bill of sale transfers legal title to personal property.

QUESTIONS

1. A quitclaim deed would always convey good legal title to real property in which of the following cases?
   - (A) The grantor was living on the property at the time of the conveyance.
   - (B) The grantor had good legal title to the real property.
   - (C) The grantee has received a certificate of title from a licensed title company.
   - (D) The grantor acquired title under a forged deed.

2. The grantor delivers a signed deed to his or her attorney, but the grantee's name is omitted. The grantor dies before any name is inserted. The deed is:
   - (A) invalid when made but valid when the grantee fills in his or her name.
   - (B) invalid when made but valid when recorded.
   - (C) valid if the deed is delivered to the grantee.
   - (D) invalid.

❖ 3. *H* executes a deed of his farm to *S*. *H* keeps the deed in his safe-deposit box. Upon his death, the box is opened and attached to the deed is a note to give the deed to *S*. Who has title to the farm?
   - (A) *S*
   - (B) *H*'s heirs
   - (C) The state
   - (D) *S*'s heirs

4. A quitclaim deed is frequently used to:
   - (A) remove a cloud on a title.
   - (B) remove an escrow.
   - (C) terminate a power of attorney.
   - (D) evict a tenant.

5. Following the execution of a sales contract, a deed is usually executed. To be valid, the deed must contain which of the following?
   - (A) Seller's name but no signature
   - (B) Buyer's name and signature
   - (C) Names of buyer and seller
   - (D) Date

❖ 6. When does legal title to real property pass from the seller to the buyer?
   - (A) On the date of recording of the deed
   - (B) When the closing statement has been signed
   - (C) When the deed is placed in escrow
   - (D) When the deed is delivered

7. A quitclaim deed transfers the interest of:
   - (A) the grantee.
   - (B) the mortgagor.
   - (C) the grantor.
   - (D) the lessee.

8. Which of the following is covered by the covenant against encumbrances in a general warranty deed?
   - (A) Undisclosed subsurface waterpipe easement
   - (B) Restrictive zoning ordinance
   - (C) Public restrictions
   - (D) Riparian rights of neighboring owners

9. For a deed to be valid, which of the following must be true?
   - (A) The grantee must execute the deed.
   - (B) It must be delivered during the lifetime of the grantor.
   - (C) The deed must be dated.
   - (D) The grantee must have legal capacity to contract.

10. Effective delivery of a deed depends upon:
   - (A) the knowledge of its existence by the grantee.
   - (B) mere physical transfer of the deed to grantee.
   - (C) the intention of the grantor.
   - (D) prior acknowledgement of the grantor's signature.

11. In order to be admissible to record in the appropriate public record office, a deed must be:
   - (A) signed by grantor and grantee.
   - (B) a printed form.
   - (C) signed by the grantee.
   - (D) signed by the grantor.

12. A quitclaim deed is **NEVER** used to accomplish which of the following?
   - (A) Transferring an interest to a co-tenant in common
   - (B) Removing a cloud from title, such as a possible dower interest
   - (C) Warranty title forever
   - (D) Correct record title

13. For a deed to be valid, which of the following must be set forth in the deed?
    (A) The exact consideration paid for the property
    (B) The amount of the loan
    (C) The grantor's age
    (D) The grantee's name

14. A person to whom real estate is conveyed, the buyer, is also called:
    (A) the assignee.   (C) the grantee.
    (B) the offeror.   (D) the optionee.

15. Which one of the following situations would make a deed void?
    (A) Grantor has signed under a power of attorney.
    (B) The deed is made to a fictitious grantee.
    (C) Grantee is not named but is sufficiently described in other terms.
    (D) Signature of grantor is spelled differently from the typed spelling on the deed.

❖ 16. For adverse possession, all of the following elements are required EXCEPT:
    (A) hostile.   (C) continuous.
    (B) notorious.   (D) tacking.

17. A deed prepared and signed but not delivered is:
    (A) invalid as between the parties, but valid as to subsequent recorded interests.
    (B) valid as between the parties.
    (C) valid as between the parties, but invalid as to subsequent recorded interests.
    (D) invalid as between the parties.

18. The word *hostile* as applied to adverse possession means:
    (A) the tenant hates the landlord.
    (B) the possessor claims ownership, rejecting other claims.
    (C) the possessor will defend land by force if necessary.
    (D) the possessor has fenced off the land.

❖ 19. The deed that limits the liability of the grantor to his or her own acts and all persons claiming by, through and under him or her is known as:
    (A) a special warranty deed.
    (B) a general warranty deed.
    (C) a quitclaim deed.
    (D) a trust deed.

20. In a valid deed, which of the following statements about the grantee is correct?
    (A) A deed may be used to convey title to a person with an assumed name.
    (B) The grantee in a deed may be a fictitious person.
    (C) The grantee must be of legal age.
    (D) The grantee's name may be omitted from the body of the deed, just as long as his or her signature is present.

21. A private individual would most likely acquire fee title by all of the following EXCEPT:
    (A) devise.
    (B) adverse possession.
    (C) demise.
    (D) voluntary conveyance.

22. The presence of a corporate seal on a deed:
    (A) means that consideration was paid.
    (B) implies that the proper or authorized person signed the deed.
    (C) would indicate that title is being conveyed to a corporation.
    (D) indicates there has been a valid delivery.

23. A quitclaim deed provides which of the following warranties?
    (A) Covenant of further assurance
    (B) Covenant of quiet enjoyment
    (C) Quiet title
    (D) No warranties

24. All of the following are necessary to the validity of a deed EXCEPT:
    (A) grantor execution.
    (B) delivery to grantee.
    (C) recording the deed.
    (D) designating the grantee.

❖ 25. The clause that defines or limits the quantity of the estate being conveyed is:
    (A) the partition clause.
    (B) the revocation clause.
    (C) the habendum clause.
    (D) the reversion clause.

❖ 26. In order for a deed to be valid, which of the following must occur?
    (A) There must be manual delivery of the deed.
    (B) The deed must be signed by the grantor and grantee and then recorded.
    (C) The deed must have a habendum clause.
    (D) The deed must be in writing.

27. In order to ascertain if title to private property could be acquired by adverse possession, one must check:
    (A) state law.
    (B) clouds on the title.
    (C) with a previous owner.
    (D) any previously recorded deeds.

28. *H* hands *C* a deed with the intent to pass title and asks *C* not to record the deed until *H* dies. When is the deed valid?
    (A) Upon *H*'s death
    (B) Immediately
    (C) It is void.
    (D) When *C* records the deed

❖ 29. Which of the following deeds offers the **LEAST** protection to the grantee?
    (A) Bargain and sale   (C) General warranty
    (B) Special warranty   (D) Quitclaim

30. All of the following are necessary to acquire title by adverse possession **EXCEPT**:
    (A) hostile use.
    (B) continuous use against the will of the owner for the statutory period.
    (C) payment of just compensation.
    (D) to have claim or color of title.

❖ 31. A declaration made by a person to an official stating that a deed has been freely and voluntarily executed is called:
    (A) an acknowledgment.
    (B) an authorization.
    (C) an authentication.
    (D) an execution.

❖ 32. Which of the following parties is in the weakest position against a claim of title by a stranger?
    (A) A nonoccupant holder of a warranty deed
    (B) A nonoccupant holder of an unrecorded quitclaim deed
    (C) One who holds an unrecorded deed
    (D) One who holds a recorded quitclaim deed to the property

33. If the grantor delivers a deed to the grantee in which the name of the grantee has been left out inadvertently, the deed is:
    (A) invalid.   (C) valid.
    (B) voidable.   (D) forged.

34. Deeds may be prepared by which of the following?
    (A) A licensed appraiser
    (B) An attorney or the owner of the property
    (C) A licensed salesperson
    (D) A principal broker only

35. When a buyer uses a quitclaim deed to extinguish his or her interest in a recorded agreement of sale, the quitclaim deed should be signed by:
    (A) the vendor.
    (B) the vendee.
    (C) the original notary.
    (D) the broker.

❖ 36. The recording of a warranty deed:
    (A) guarantees title.
    (B) insures ownership.
    (C) verifies title.
    (D) constitutes constructive notice of ownership.

37. *S* signs a deed of his property to *P* and delivers it to a neutral escrow company with irrevocable instructions to deliver it to *P* upon *S*'s death. Upon *S*'s death, what is the status of the property's title?
    (A) The property passes to *S*'s heirs.
    (B) The property passes to *P*.
    (C) It escheats to the state because there was no will.
    (D) *P* will receive only a life estate in the property.

38. In the transfer of real property by deed, ownership changes hands when the deed has been:
    (A) signed.   (C) recorded.
    (B) delivered.   (D) notarized.

39. In the event that a deed to a property was drawn to *A* and she died prior to the date of the deed's delivery, which of the following statements would be true?
    (A) The property would revert to government ownership by escheat.
    (B) The property would become part of *A*'s estate and be passed on to her heirs.
    (C) The deed would be considered invalid.
    (D) The deed would be considered valid.

40. Of the following, which statute or act creates the need for a deed to be in writing?
    (A) Statute of Descent
    (B) Recording Act
    (C) Statute of frauds
    (D) Statute of limitations

41. The covenant in a deed stating that the grantor has full possession of the premises in fee simple, or any other estate he or she purports to convey, is called the covenant of:
    (A) seizin.   (C) quiet enjoyment.
    (B) habendum.   (D) further assurance.

42. The covenant against encumbrances in a deed of conveyance warrants against the existence of all of the following undisclosed matters **EXCEPT:**
    (A) mortgages against the land.
    (B) judgment liens against the land.
    (C) easements that adversely affect the land.
    (D) zoning ordinances that limit the use of the land.

43. Which of the following is true relating to a conveyance of real property?
    (A) An illiterate grantor is incompetent.
    (A) A conveyance by an unmarried minor transfers absolute title.
    (C) A grantor cannot sign with an "X."
    (D) A grantee can be a minor.

44. In order to convey title to real property, a deed must contain which of the following?
    (A) Words of conveyance
    (B) An offer and acceptance
    (C) Grantor's marital status
    (D) Acknowledgments of grantor and grantee

45. Which of the following must sign a deed for it to be valid?
    (A) Seller or transferor
    (B) Grantee or transferee
    (C) Broker handling the transaction
    (D) Lender if there is financing involved

❖ 46. Which of the following statements regarding the recording of deeds is true?
    (A) An unrecorded deed is not enforceable between grantor and grantee.
    (B) A deed must be signed by the grantor in order to be recorded.
    (C) A deed with the grantee's name omitted is acceptable for recording.
    (D) An unacknowledged deed is void.

47. As far as its validity between grantor and grantee is concerned, a deed that is not dated, acknowledged or recorded is:
    (A) invalid because of these omissions.
    (B) void.
    (C) revocable by the grantor.
    (D) valid despite these omissions.

48. A claim for adverse possession is most nearly valid if:
    (A) the occupant makes improvements, fences the area, and cultivates the land.
    (B) the claim is under the mistake of right.
    (C) the person occupies the premises for the statutory period with or without the owner's consent.
    (D) the possession is hostile against the owner.

49. Which of the following is an essential element of a valid deed?
    (A) Legal description of the property
    (B) Grantee is of age and of sound mind
    (C) Recording
    (D) Acknowledgment

❖ 50. Marketable title to real property is **LEAST** likely to be conveyed:
    (A) to a minor.
    (B) by a quitclaim deed.
    (C) by a minor.
    (D) by a special warranty deed.

51. A valid deed in completion of a sales contract must be signed by which of the following?
    (A) Buyer
    (B) Seller
    (C) Buyer and seller
    (D) Seller and listing agent

52. A valid deed must contain which of the following groups of elements?
    (A) Competent grantor, valuable consideration, habendum clause
    (B) Property description, words of conveyance, covenants of title, execution
    (C) Habendum, grantor's signature, delivery and acceptance
    (D) Named grantee, competent grantor, delivery, grantor's signature

53. A deed signed by the grantor only is:
   (A) invalid until recorded.
   (B) valid and title will pass when the deed is delivered.
   (C) valid only when recorded.
   (D) invalid as far as subsequent purchasers are concerned.

54. A document in which legal title to real property is transferred from one person to another is:
   (A) a contract of sale.   (C) a deed.
   (B) a lease.   (D) a listing.

55. In a deed the grantee must:
   (A) be of sound mind and memory.
   (B) be of legal age.
   (C) be named.
   (D) sign the deed.

56. A deed whereby the grantor makes certain covenants and warrants to defend against certain claims that arose only during the period of ownership is:
   (A) a quitclaim deed.
   (B) a general warranty deed.
   (C) a nominal deed.
   (D) a special warranty deed.

❖ 57. Deeds that purport to convey an interest but make no warranty of good title are called:
   (A) bargain and sale deeds.
   (B) quitclaim deeds.
   (C) habendum deeds.
   (D) release deeds.

58. All of the following deeds are valid **EXCEPT**:
   (A) a deed to a partnership.
   (B) a deed to an actual person under an assumed name.
   (C) a deed to a fictitious human person.
   (D) a deed to a foreign corporation.

59. Which of the following statements is true concerning a general warranty deed?
   (A) It must be signed by the grantee if he or she is a trust beneficiary.
   (B) It insures title.
   (C) The grantor's warranty is limited to his or her own acts only during the time he or she was in possession of the title.
   (D) It is the most protective deed a grantee can receive.

❖ 60. Which of the following has **NO** effect on the validity of a deed?
   (A) Proper signature
   (B) Lack of money consideration
   (C) Delivery
   (D) Competent grantor

61. At which point in a real estate transaction does legal title to real property pass?
   (A) Execution of option
   (B) Exercise of option
   (C) Delivery of agreement of sale
   (D) Delivery of deed

62. Which of the following statements is true concerning recording a deed?
   (A) A forged deed is made valid by recording.
   (B) A delivered deed is not valid until it is recorded.
   (C) A deed must be signed by grantor and grantee in order to be recorded.
   (D) Recording is not needed to make a deed valid.

63. A warranty deed would be used to convey all the following **EXCEPT**:
   (A) fee simple estate.
   (B) life estate.
   (C) less than freehold estate.
   (D) fee conditional estate.

64. *C* delivers a valid deed to *B* who fails to record the deed. *B* then loses the deed and dies with *C* in an accident before it is found. Who owns the property?
   (A) *C*   (C) The government
   (B) *B*'s heirs   (D) *C*'s heirs

65. The buyer should keep the original recorded deed because:
   (A) it is the only evidence of title.
   (B) if lost, the buyer loses title.
   (C) it is needed to transfer title.
   (D) it is proof of title.

❖ 66. Which one of the following is **LEAST** likely to be signed by both parties?
   (A) Purchase contract
   (B) Listing
   (C) Lease
   (D) Warranty deed

67. Which of the following statements regarding a bargain and sale deed is true?
    (A) It transfers possession but not legal title.
    (B) It is used when the grantor is unsure whether or not he or she has good title.
    (C) It contains a covenant of seizin.
    (D) It has no covenants, but does have an implication that the grantor has good title.

❖ 68. For which of the following reasons would a grantor decide to use a special warranty deed rather than a general warranty deed?
    (A) The grantor is unsure whether there are any encumbrances on the title.
    (B) The grantor wants to limit liability to defects occurring during ownership.
    (C) The grantor wants to give as many warranties as possible.
    (D) The grantor is aware of recent defects in the title.

❖ 69. Which of these statements about deeds is true?
    (A) The special warranty deed contains the most covenants.
    (B) The quitclaim deed is no different than a bargain and sale deed.
    (C) The quitclaim deed gives the least protection to the grantee.
    (D) The general warranty deed offers the least liability to the grantor.

70. One tenant in common attempts to convey the entire fee simple interest in the property to a grantee using a general warranty deed. Which covenant in the deed would be violated?
    (A) Covenant of further assurance
    (B) Covenant of seizin
    (C) Covenant of quiet enjoyment
    (D) No covenants would be violated

71. Upon examination of the public records, the examiner discovers a deed with an assumption of mortgage. Which of the following would MOST likely not be found in the deed?
    (A) A granting clause
    (B) Grantor's signature
    (C) Grantor's age
    (D) Grantee's signature

72. Which of the following is false regarding a transfer of title by adverse possession?
    (A) The transfer of title is governed by state law.
    (B) The transfer is involuntary.
    (C) The transfer is voluntary.
    (D) A prescriptive period is involved.

73. Assume that a deed is signed by the grantor on Sunday and delivered to the grantee on Tuesday. Which of the following statements is true?
    (A) The deed is invalid.
    (B) The deed is not acceptable for recordation.
    (C) The deed is voidable.
    (D) The deed is effective to transfer title.

74. A grantor is willing to make the standard covenants of good title, but wants to limit his or her liability to claims arising during the ownership term. The grantor should execute which type of deed?
    (A) General warranty   (C) Quitclaim
    (B) Gift deed   (D) Special warranty

75. Which of the following is LEAST likely to contain a legal description of a parcel of real property?
    (A) Deed
    (B) Tax statement
    (C) Mortgage
    (D) Preliminary title report

76. Which of the following documents is MOST likely to be incorporated by reference in a warranty deed?
    (A) Power of attorney
    (B) Bill of sale
    (C) Declaration of restrictions
    (D) Assignment of lease

77. Of the following terms, which does NOT describe the type of occupancy needed for adverse possession?
    (A) Open and notorious
    (B) Continuous
    (C) Exclusive
    (D) Lawful

78. Which of the following statements best describes the covenant of quiet enjoyment in a general warranty deed?
    (A) Guarantee will not be disturbed by unnecessary noise.
    (B) Guarantor will not enter the property without prior notice.
    (C) Guarantor has the rights, title and ownership that he or she claims to have.
    (D) Guarantor will pay for any damages caused by improper drafting of the deed.

79. For adverse possession to be effective, all of the following must be present **EXCEPT**:
    (A) uninterrupted and continuous possession.
    (B) open and notorious possession.
    (C) occupied by original adverse possessor.
    (D) exclusive and hostile possession.

❖ 80. A deed has been properly escrowed with an attorney and closing is scheduled for 13 days later. If the seller dies before closing, when does legal title pass?
    (A) When the deed was placed into escrow
    (B) The estate must now provide another deed
    (C) The escrow dies with the seller so that no deed or legal title will pass at closing
    (D) Upon closing

ANSWERS

1. **B**   Quitclaim deeds transfer the interest of the grantor, *if any*. For example, a trespasser living on the property could not convey good title, but the real owner could. The title company could be mistaken.

2. **D**   A valid deed must contain the names of grantor and grantee; the grantee's name should be filled in by the grantor or his or her agent; recording does not make an invalid deed become valid. The attorney does not have authority to fill in the deed after the grantor's death. Delivery must occur during the life of the grantor.

3. **B**   There is no delivery; i.e., *H* did not give up *control* over the deed during his lifetime as he would have if he had handed it to *S* or put it into an escrow. To ac-

complish his purpose, *H* should have prepared a will. Unless revoked, a will would have the effect of transferring title upon *H*'s death.

4. **A**   A quitclaim deed might be used where there is doubt as to whether some distant heirs of a grantor have a valid claim. To clear the title, the heirs might be asked to execute quitclaim deeds. Other uses would be to remove possible dower claims or encroachment claims.

5. **C**   These are both essential elements to a valid deed; as are delivery and acceptance and legal description. Also, it must be in writing and signed by grantor.

6. **D**   Delivery is the key; recording is not necessary, though strongly recommended.

7. **C**   The title of the grantor is transferred to the grantee, regardless of the type of deed.

8. **A**   Because the easement was not disclosed, the grantee could recover for the loss in value caused by this easement (an encumbrance). Zoning laws, public restrictions and riparian rights are matters of public knowledge and therefore not covered under the covenant against encumbrances.

9. **B**   Only the grantor need sign unless the grantee assumes some obligation, as in a loan assumption. Only grantor need be competent.

10. **C**   The grantor can hand it to the grantee with instructions to have it reviewed by an attorney—thus, (B) is false. The grantee's acceptance is often presumed when grantee had no knowledge about the deed (before the grantor's death)—thus, (A) is false. Acknowledgment is generally necessary for recording but deeds do not have to be recorded to be valid, just delivered—thus, (D) is false. In all cases, the grantor must possess the mental intention to transfer legal title to the grantee for a valid delivery to have been accomplished.

11. **D** Only the grantor need sign a deed.

12. **C** A quitclaim deed contains no warranties. Often one co-tenant transfers his or her entire interest to another co-tenant by way of a quitclaim deed. A title report may reveal the lack of a wife's release of dower in some conveyance in the chain of title—a quitclaim deed signed by the wife can cure this title defect.

13. **D** Only sales contracts require the actual consideration, although fiduciary deeds do state the actual consideration. Often, deeds just state a nominal consideration. While marital status may be required by state law in order to record a valid deed, it is not needed in order to make the deed valid. A deed is not valid unless a grantee is named, although a deed to "someone's youngest sister" is adequate to identify the grantee.

14. **C** The buyer may be the offeror in a sales contract. As far as a conveyance is concerned, the buyer is the grantee. One who receives real property by gift (donee) or by devise (devisee) is also called the grantee.

15. **B** There must be a grantee in existence (e.g., a properly formed corporation). Grantors sometimes use assumed names for business purposes; such use may cause title searching problems, but delivery depends on the grantor's intention and not the name used. A deed to "John Smith and wife" would be adequate even though the wife's name hasn't been given.

16. **D** Tacking refers to meeting the continuous time element by linking together successive periods of possession of different occupants, such as a father's four years added to his succeeding son's ten years.

17. **D** Without delivery, there is no valid deed. The undelivered deed is invalid as between the parties and invalid as to any other interests in the property.

18. **B** A person who occupies the property with the consent of the landowner could not assert an adverse possession claim. This explains why tenants in common cannot usually claim adverse possession against each other unless there is a clear ouster by one tenant.

19. **A** Special warranty deeds are frequently used by fiduciaries such as guardians and trustees. In a general warranty deed, the warranties extend to defects arising even before the grantor acquired title—fiduciaries will not usually assume this risk.

20. **A** While the grantee can use a fictitious name, it must be a person in existence (i.e., you could not convey your property to Mickey Mouse or your pet poodle.) One could, however, transfer property to a trust with directions to the trustee to allow the poodle to live there in regal splendor.

21. **C** Demise is a conveyance for years, as in a lease. Devise is a gift of real property by a decedent's last will and testament. Adverse possession requirements vary according to state law but involve a hostile claim to land of another for a definite minimum period of time.

22. **B** A corporate grantor may use a seal, although a seal is usually no longer a legal requirement. In ancient times, deeds were sealed and not signed.

23. **D** There are no warranties in a quitclaim deed. These warranties are found in the general warranty deed.

24. **C** Although recording is not necessary for the validity of a deed, a prudent grantee, however, should record to give constructive notice to third parties and thus protect his or her interest.

25. **C** Also called the "to have and to hold" clause, the habendum clause is not an essential element for a valid deed but is customarily included. It would indicate that the grantor is conveying a fee simple or life estate, for example.

26. **D** Delivery in escrow could be sufficient; deeds need not be signed by the grantee, nor recorded, to be valid.

27. **A** Each state has different rules concerning adverse possession. For example, California requires five years whereas Hawaii

requires 20 years of continuous, hostile possession. Also, one may acquire title although there are clouds on the title.

28. **B**   Delivery is effected by the grantor's intention, and not by recording. Here, *C* received title, but simply did not record it. Recording is not necessary to validate a deed.

29. **D**   The correct choice (D) is followed in order of increasing protection by (A), then (B) and then (C). In a bargain and sale deed, there are no warranties, but the grantor does assert ownership of title.

30. **C**   Just compensation is involved in cases of eminent domain. "Color of title" would be where one is in possession under a defective deed, such as a forged deed or one improperly delivered.

31. **A**   Acknowledgments are usually taken by a notary public and are partially designed to eliminate forgery of documents. Therefore, notaries should require proper identification. Acknowledgments also are evidence that the document is authentic.

32. **B**   This grantee has given no constructive notice of the rights of recording or possession and has no warranties to assert against the grantor in the event the stranger proves to have a superior title.

33. **A**   Only the grantor or the grantor's authorized agent can fill in the essential element of the grantee's name. Until such time, the deed is void (not voidable), since it is missing an essential element.

34. **B**   Preparing a deed *for another* can be done only by a lawyer in most states. However, a few states do allow the use of standard forms for deeds that can be completed by title companies.

35. **B**   This quitclaim deed will release from record title any trace of the buyer's (vendee's) equitable title.

36. **D**   The whole world now is charged with notice of the grantee's rights and the contents of the deed. A title insurance policy is used to insure good title.

37. **B**   Most courts will relate delivery back to the date when the deed was first put into escrow, and they will hold that there was a valid delivery during *S*'s life. In effect, this legal fiction of the courts hold that *P* had title but *S* kept a life estate.

38. **B**   Execution is not enough, while recording and acknowledgment are not required, to make a deed effective. Delivery is the key. Delivery by a properly appointed escrow agent acting for the grantor is effective.

39. **C**   Delivery must take place within the grantee's lifetime; otherwise the deed is invalid. Proper delivery includes acceptance by the named grantee.

40. **C**   An old English statute (1677) adopted in differing forms in all jurisdictions requires that the transfer of any interest in real property be in writing and signed by the party to be charged, to be enforceable.

41. **A**   Thus, if grantor asserts ownership of a fee simple yet grantor only owns a life estate, there would be a breach of the covenant of seisin (also spelled seizin).

42. **D**   Zoning ordinances are matters of public knowledge and would not be covered by the covenant against encumbrances.

43. **D**   An illiterate cannot read or write but usually is quite aware of the nature of his or her actions. An illiterate grantor may sign by a "mark" that should be witnessed. Although some states treat a minor's deed as being voidable, most treat it as being void. A problem will arise when the minor later wants to convey the property; or guardianship proceedings will be required if the grantor is a minor. The grantee can be incompetent.

44. **A**   Sales contracts (not deeds) need to contain a meeting of the minds as evidenced by an offer and acceptance. (C) and (D) may be required to *record* a deed.

45. **A**   Only the grantor need sign, unless the grantee is assuming the mortgage.

46. **B**   The unrecorded deed is valid between the parties but may be unenforceable against a subsequent purchaser for value who records first. The signature of the grantor is a requirement for recordation.

47. **D**   The date is useful to prove when it was delivered but it is not required, nor is recording or acknowledgment.

48. **D**   Hostile claim is the key. The occupant under (A) could be a lessee and (C) is wrong because adverse possession cannot be with the owner's consent.

49. **A**   A street address is usually insufficient as a legal description and thus a metes and bounds description or a subdivision description should be used. The grantor must be of age and of sound mind. The grantee could be an insane minor when title is passed, but would need a guardian appointed to later transfer the interest.

50. **C**   Provided the grantor of the quitclaim deed had good title, that good title could be transferred, although a grantee would be wise to inquire why the grantor is not giving any warranties of title. If there is any doubt of a clear title, the obtaining of a title insurance policy is recommended. A deed by a minor is voidable. A guardian must be appointed and empowered by the court to convey.

51. **B**   Seller is the grantor; grantee (buyer) need not sign.

52. **D**   Deeds need not contain a valuable consideration (it could be good consideration, such as love and affection), a habendum clause, nor covenants of title (quitclaim).

53. **B**   Grantee need not sign but there must be delivery; recording is not necessary, but recommended.

54. **C**   Contract of sale transfers equitable interest; lease transfers possession; and a listing employs a broker to solicit prospective buyers for the seller's property.

55. **C**   It is the grantor that must be competent and sign. The grantee must merely be identified and in existence.

56. **D**   The quitclaim deed contains no specific covenants; the general warranty deed covers claims arising from defects existing even before the grantor acquired title.

57. **A**   A bargain and sale deed may be used by a grantor who has good title but does not want to make any warranties with respect to title. In this sense, it is slightly more beneficial to the grantee than a quitclaim deed (which is often used when the grantee is unsure whether he or she has any title to the property).

58. **C**   The grantee must exist at the time of delivery. Thus, a deed to S's grandchildren would not be valid if S is only ten years old at delivery.

59. **D**   Trust beneficiaries do not have the power to sign contracts or other documents involving the trust; only the trustee has the power. Trustees sign a special warranty deed, not a general warranty deed. Title insurance, not the deed, would insure the title.

60. **B**   It could be a gift deed involving only good consideration. Only contracts need valuable consideration; deeds are conveyances.

61. **D**   In (A), (B) and (C) the buyer may receive some equitable title, but receives legal title only when the deed is delivered.

62. **D**   While deeds should be recorded, recording is not legally required to make them valid. Note that recording will not validate an otherwise invalid deed.

63. **C**   The deed should state, however, in the granting clause or the habendum clause, which type of estate is being conveyed. This is important because a life estate terminates upon death. Choice (C) would be a lease.

64. **B**   After delivery, C no longer has an interest in B's property. In any dispute with C's heirs, B's heirs would have the burden of proving delivery was made.

65. **D**   The deed is one way to prove title. While recording is not usually mandatory, a recorded copy will aid the grantee in proving title if the original is lost or destroyed.

66. **D** A deed is a conveyance signed by the grantor. The listing is signed by both seller and broker.

67. **D** A bargain and sale deed transfers legal title. If the grantor is unsure of the title, a bargain and sale deed should not be used. The grantor should use a quit-claim deed, since there is an implication of good title when a bargain and sale deed is used.

68. **B** The special warranty deed restricts liability to defects occurring after the seller acquired title, whereas the general warranty deed is a warranty "forever" covering prior defects as well.

69. **C** As far as the grantor's liability is concerned, the general warranty deed gives the most exposure; then the special warranty deed (only covers the time the grantor owned the property), and then the quitclaim deed (with no liability).

70. **B** Because the grantor does not have the complete estate, the other tenants in common would have to join in the deed. Here the grantor would be liable under the covenant of seizin, since the grantor is not well seized of the *whole* estate.

71. **C** A granting clause would distinguish the deed from a mortgage. The grantee signs the deed, promising to pay the loan obligation.

72. **C** Each jurisdiction has its own particular time requirements but most agree on the essential elements of open, notorious, continuous (tacking is allowed) and, most important, hostile possession.

73. **D** Deeds signed on Sunday are just as valid as if signed on any other day of the week and will be accepted for recordation on any day the public record office is open for business.

74. **D** The general warranty covers claims arising prior to as well as during the grantor's ownership, whereas a special warranty deed only covers claims arising by, through, or under the actions of the grantor. The quitclaim deed makes no

covenants of title and the gift deed usually does not contain all the standard covenants of title.

75. **B** Deeds and mortgages are conveyances of real property; therefore, they must contain a legal description of the property. The title report must describe the particular property it covers. The tax statement generally lists just the address or tax identification number.

76. **C** It is common practice among subdividers to record a master declaration of restrictions on the permitted uses in the subdivision. They then refer to this declaration rather than retype all the restrictions on each deed.

77. **D** The occupancy is technically a trespass, and, if it is continuous for the statutory period, then title is acquired by way of adverse possession. If the occupant was on the property with the owner's permission, then the "hostile" element would be missing.

78. **C** If, for example, the guarantor (grantor) did not have good title because the prior deed was forged, then the grantee could sue the guarantor for breach of the covenant of quiet enjoyment. Choice (D) describes the covenant of further assurances.

79. **C** The Possession must be Open, Actual, Continuous and Hostile (POACH), as well as exclusive (or, Continuous, Actual, Notorious, Open and Exclusive—CANOE). A successor in interest to the original adverse possessor (for example, through a purchase agreement or will), can "tack on" his or her possession to the original period of possession to meet the statutory period.

80. **D** The rule is that a deed is valid only if the grantor is alive at the time of delivery. When death occurs during escrow, most courts will create the legal fiction that delivery occurred when the deed was first deposited in escrow and at that time the grantor was alive. Although delivery relates back, actual passing of legal title does not take place until closing.

Chapter 12   Settlement Procedures: Escrow, Evidence of Title and Recording

The questions in this chapter test your comprehension of the following topics:

• The purpose and effect of the state recording law
• The different types of evidence of title
• Key features of a title insurance policy
• The role of an escrow in real estate transactions
• The federal Real Estate Settlement Procedures Act

False Friends

The following words are often confused with one another. Note the difference in meaning of these false friends:

Chain of Title/Cloud on Title: The chain of title reveals the succession of owners in the history of a property, whereas a cloud on title is a defect or impairment in the title.

Quiet Enjoyment/Quiet Title: Quiet enjoyment is the right to uninterrupted use of the property, whereas quiet title is the name of a legal action to prove valid title to real property.

Acknowledgment/Affidavit: An acknowledgement is a formal declaration by the signer of a document, whereas an affidavit is a sworn statement that the facts contained in the affidavit are true and correct.

QUESTIONS

1. The chronological record of all conveyances and encumbrances affecting the record title to real property is known as:
   - (A) a title insurance policy.
   - (B) a chain of title.
   - (C) a cloud on title.
   - (D) a title report.

2. Which of the following statements regarding title insurance is true?
   - (A) When a lender requires an ALTA extended policy of title insurance to cover his or her interest, the policy is not assignable.
   - (B) When a buyer acquires title insurance to protect his or her equity, the policy may be passed on to the next buyer when the property is later sold.
   - (C) It protects the seller from negligence by the title or abstract company doing the search.
   - (D) It protects against losses suffered due to defects in the title.

❖ 3. The standard form title insurance policy insures against:
   - (A) governmental actions.
   - (B) forgery of a deed.
   - (C) rights of parties in possession.
   - (D) water and mineral rights.

4. When a title search reveals that there is a broken chain of title, this is **BEST** cured by:
   - (A) a quitclaim deed.
   - (B) a general warranty deed.
   - (C) partition.
   - (D) quiet title proceeding.

5. A system of land title registration in which the state guarantees title is:
   - (A) the Pennsylvania system.
   - (B) the Torrens title system.
   - (C) the Colorado system.
   - (D) the regular system.

6. The best way to discover a flaw in the recorded title to a piece of real property is by:
   - (A) calling the county surveyor.
   - (B) taking out property insurance.
   - (C) undertaking a search of title.
   - (D) hiring a lawyer.

7. In order for a prospective buyer of real estate to investigate the validity of the title, the buyer should request:
   - (A) a survey.
   - (B) a title search.
   - (C) an estoppel certificate.
   - (D) a warranty deed.

❖ 8. A broker finds a prospective buyer for a single-family dwelling, and the subject of title insurance has come up. The buyer wants the greatest owner protection available. Which of the following should the broker recommend?
   - (A) Certificate of title
   - (B) Standard coverage policy of title insurance
   - (C) Abstract of title
   - (D) Extended coverage policy of title insurance

❖ 9. When a title company issues an ALTA extended policy, such a policy usually extends beyond the risks normally insured under the standard policy to include all of the following **EXCEPT**:
   - (A) unrecorded mechanics' liens.
   - (B) unrecorded physical easements.
   - (C) the effect of zoning regulations.
   - (D) the rights of parties in possession.

10. Which of the following types of evidence of title gives the least protection to a buyer?
   - (A) Abstract of title
   - (B) Title search
   - (C) Certificate of title
   - (D) Policy of title insurance

❖ 11. Which of the following functions does an abstract of title perform?
   - (A) Guarantees a clear title
   - (B) Insures the title
   - (C) Gives the abstracter's opinion of the title
   - (D) Offers a condensed history of all recorded documents

❖ 12. Tracing the conveyances and encumbrances of real property is known as:
   - (A) chain of title.
   - (B) title search.
   - (C) cloud on title.
   - (D) recordation of title.

13. A property on which there will be a mortgage recorded is likely to have an on-site inspection under which of the following?
(A) An ALTA extended policy
(B) A standard coverage policy
(C) Only upon request by a mortgagor
(D) An inspection is necessary for any type of title insurance policy

❖ 14. A standard policy of title insurance insures against all of the following **EXCEPT:**
(A) matters of record.
(B) forgery.
(C) mining claims.
(D) contractual capacity.

❖ 15. When transactions involving the sale of real estate are placed in escrow, this means:
(A) a designated agent agreed to by the parties holds the necessary documents until the terms are met.
(B) they are completed in secrecy.
(C) the broker holds the papers until the registration of title is completed.
(D) the broker is no longer involved.

16. Which of the following would provide the **BEST** surety of good title?
(A) Certificate of title   (C) Quitclaim deed
(B) Title insurance   (D) Color of title

❖ 17. If escrow instructions differ from the deposit receipt or sales contract, and the escrow instructions have been signed by both the buyer and seller, which of the following is correct?
(A) A new deposit receipt must be written.
(B) Escrow instructions take precedence.
(C) Deposit receipt takes precedence.
(D) Everything is void; the parties must start over.

18. A proper escrow, once established, should be:
(A) managed by a licensed broker.
(B) void at the seller's option.
(C) voidable at option of either buyer or seller.
(D) not subject to the control of any one interested party.

19. A standard form policy of title insurance protects against loss resulting from all of the following **EXCEPT:**
(A) encroachments on the property.
(B) failure to deliver an earlier recorded deed.
(C) lack of capacity of the grantor.
(D) forgery in the chain of title.

20. In an escrow transaction, the escrow officer is:
(A) a representative of the title company, to assure title validity.
(B) an officer of the land court.
(C) an agent for the broker.
(D) an agent to the buyer and seller and holder of all pertinent papers.

21. To what does the term "chain of title" refer?
(A) Recording law
(B) Will beneficiaries
(C) Title companies
(D) Succession of property owners

22. When handling an escrow for both parties, the escrow holder is acting as:
(A) an agent of the seller.
(B) an employee of the buyer.
(C) an independent contractor.
(D) a beneficiary.

23. A valid escrow is **LEAST** likely created in connection with which one of the following?
(A) Sale of property
(B) Mortgage loans
(C) Bankruptcy
(D) Real property exchange

24. Earnest money deposits are **LEAST** likely held in escrow by which one of the following?
(A) Broker
(B) Licensed escrow company
(C) Attorney
(D) Salesperson

❖ 25. An abstract of title is **BEST** described as:
(A) a brief digest of the title to a particular property.
(B) a summary of each deed in a title search.
(C) an appraisal of the lands and the improvements.
(D) a summary of all the improvements and encroachments on the property.

26. Which of the following concerning escrow is true?
    (A) An escrow cannot be altered by either party except with the consent of both parties.
    (B) The escrow company is the agent of the grantor.
    (C) A salesperson may perform the escrow function.
    (D) An escrow may be canceled by a dissatisfied buyer.

27. An owner's title insurance policy protects the owner against:
    (A) loss of property due to mortgage foreclosure.
    (B) loss of title to a claimant with superior right of title.
    (C) losses due to fire damage.
    (D) monetary loss resulting from personal judgment liens against the owner.

28. Which of the following statements about evidence of title is true?
    (A) Title insurance insures the lender against loss in case of a default and foreclosure.
    (B) An abstract of title insures the buyer against loss due to any matters that could be disclosed in a title search and also those due to "off record" risks.
    (C) An abstract of title is the most secure evidence a buyer can receive.
    (D) An abstract of title offers no guarantee of title.

29. An examination of the records to assemble in chronological order the "chain of title" is called:
    (A) cloud on title.
    (B) affidavit of title.
    (C) title insurance policy.
    (D) abstract of title.

❖ 30. When money in a pending purchase of real property is held in escrow, the broker can obtain out of escrow an advance on earned commission:
    (A) if only the buyer gives written consent.
    (B) if only the seller gives written consent.
    (C) without the need for consent.
    (D) only when both buyer and seller give their written consent.

❖ 31. Which of the following statements about title insurance is correct?
    (A) Dollar coverage under a mortgagee's policy of title insurance remains constant.
    (B) Dollar coverage under an owner's policy of title insurance declines as the loan declines.
    (C) The buyer pays annually for coverage as long as the policy is in effect.
    (D) The insurance coverage on a mortgagee's policy is based on the declining balance of the loan.

32. Where is the **BEST** place to find a cloud on title?
    (A) Application for title insurance
    (B) Appraisal
    (C) Warranty deed
    (D) Title search

33. When a mortgagee requires a title insurance policy on the secured property:
    (A) the policy protects the interests of the lender and the owner.
    (B) the policy is assignable.
    (C) the policy is for the life of the mortgagor.
    (D) a mortgagee will require both an owner's and lender's policy.

34. After signing a contract for the sale of real estate, the deed is delivered to the buyer or held by a third person designated as:
    (A) the principal.   (C) the grantor.
    (B) the assignor.   (D) the escrow.

35. An abstract of title accomplishes which of the following?
    (A) Insures the title
    (B) Gives a history of the title, including the recorded encumbrances against the property
    (C) Guarantees validity of title
    (D) Protects the purchaser against any forgeries in the record

36. An owner's title insurance policy terminates all coverage of the owner:
    (A) whenever the owner becomes a grantor under a deed of conveyance.
    (B) when the mortgage is paid off.
    (C) when the grantor buys a new property.
    (D) upon written mutual cancellation.

37. *A*, the only daughter in a large family, inherits a condominium apartment from her father after a lengthy probate proceeding in which there were many conflicting claims to the apartment. Before selling the property *A* would be **BEST** advised to obtain:
    (A) a termite report.
    (B) a new mortgage.
    (C) a title opinion.
    (D) a survey.

38. The usual standard policy of title insurance insures against loss due to:
    (A) forgery in the chain of recorded title.
    (B) encumbrances not disclosed by official public records.
    (C) rights of parties in possession.
    (D) actions of governmental agencies.

39. Which type of evidence of title requires the least amount of search through the records?
    (A) Abstract of title
    (B) Torrens certificate
    (C) Title insurance
    (D) Regular certificate of title

40. If a title policy reveals the existence of numerous liens not disclosed in the sales contracts, the title is said to be all of the following **EXCEPT:**
    (A) clouded.
    (B) unmerchantable.
    (C) unenforceable.
    (D) unmarketable.

❖ 41. There are several requirements in a valid escrow concerning the sale of real property. One of them is:
    (A) a claim of marketable title.
    (B) the services of a real estate licensee.
    (C) a valid and enforceable written contract for the sale of the land.
    (D) that the escrow holder has an interest in the subject matter.

❖ 42. Escrow is often used for all of the following purposes **EXCEPT:**
    (A) to determine that outstanding and unpaid liens will be satisfied.
    (B) to see that the purchase price is paid and all checks have cleared the bank.
    (C) to offer properties for sale to prospective buyers.
    (D) to disburse funds from a sale to the appropriate people.

43. A written instrument of value is deposited with a disinterested third party who will deliver it upon the fulfillment of some condition. This **BEST** describes which of the following?
    (A) Bill of sale
    (B) Promissory note
    (C) Escrow
    (D) Hypothecation

44. Against which of the following risks does a standard owner's policy of title insurance normally afford protection?
    (A) Encroachments
    (B) Rights of parties in possession
    (C) Zoning ordinance
    (D) Minor's deed

45. Recording a deed is for the greatest benefit of:
    (A) the grantor.
    (B) the public trustee.
    (C) the attorney.
    (D) the grantee.

46. In real estate transactions, all of the following documents are usually recorded **EXCEPT:**
    (A) deed.
    (B) offer to purchase.
    (C) second mortgage.
    (D) purchase money mortgage.

❖ 47. It is common procedure to record all of the following instruments **EXCEPT:**
    (A) a land contract.
    (B) a quitclaim deed.
    (C) an assignment of a mortgage.
    (D) a promissory note secured by a mortgage.

48. For a deed to be validly recorded in most states, all of the following are true **EXCEPT:**
    (A) It must be acknowledged.
    (B) It must be recorded in the proper sequence of the chain of title.
    (C) It must be signed by the grantee.
    (D) It must be signed by the grantor.

❖ 49. An unrecorded deed is valid and binding:
    (A) between parties to the deed.
    (B) upon a later bona fide purchaser for value who first records the deed.
    (C) even if not delivered.
    (D) when signed by the grantee.

❖ 50. Constructive notice of a fact is established by:
    (A) entering it on public record.
    (B) acting openly in accordance with the fact.
    (C) direct communication of the fact to each interested party.
    (D) testifying to the existence of the fact under oath in open court.

51. Deeds are recorded to provide:
(A) actual notice.
(B) constructive notice.
(C) proof of validity.
(D) evidence against forgery.

52. A deed made and delivered, but not recorded, is:
(A) valid between the parties and valid as to the third parties with notice.
(B) valid between the parties and valid as to subsequent recorded interests.
(C) valid between the parties and invalid as to subsequent donees (recipient by gift) of the property.
(D) invalid between the parties.

53. A sells Blackacre Farm to B who does not record the deed. A then makes a gift of Blackacre to C by way of a deed, which C then records.
(A) Because C recorded his deed before B, C has better title to Blackacre than B.
(B) B has better title than C, since C is not a bona fide purchaser for value.
(C) B has superior title to C because the deed was given to B first.
(D) A recorded deed takes priority over all others, regardless of how the grantee acquires title.

54. Which of the following is protected by the recording laws?
(A) A person who acquires title by will
(B) A person who acquires title by gift
(C) A person who acquires title in good faith and for value
(D) A person who acquires property free of title defects

❖ **55.** A buyer is interested in buying property in another state without an inspection. You should advise the buyer to obtain:
(A) a quitclaim deed.
(B) an abstract of title.
(C) a bargain and sale deed.
(D) an extended coverage title insurance policy.

56. Someone who cannot act as a notary on a deed is:
(A) an attorney at law.
(B) a real estate broker.
(C) an interested person.
(D) an employee in the recording office.

57. Which of the following is true?
(A) Recording a deed guarantees its validity.
(B) The venue shows the place where property has been purchased.
(C) Recording protects against defects in the deed.
(D) Recording gives constructive notice.

58. All of the following are true **EXCEPT**:
(A) An acknowledgment is a formal declaration made before some public officer, usually a notary public, by a person who has signed a real estate document or other instrument stating that the signature is genuine and given freely.
(B) In order to give constructive notice to the public, a document affecting a piece of real estate should be recorded.
(C) Recording is the best security against an unmarketable title.
(D) The recording laws protect those who rely on what is contained in the public records.

59. H, bona fide purchaser for value who records his deed, would take precedence over a grantee with a prior unrecorded deed:
(A) if H has actual knowledge of the prior unrecorded deed.
(B) if the prior unrecorded deed's grantee had taken possession of the property and was living in a house on the property.
(C) because the prior deed came first in time.
(D) because H has a right to rely on what he finds in the records.

60. The recording system performs which of the following functions?
(A) Insures title against loss due to third-party claims
(B) Cures major defects in title
(C) Protects against fraud and forgeries
(D) Gives notice to all of the existence of documents

61. Deeds are recorded for which of the following purposes?
(A) To provide constructive notice of their existence
(B) Because the law requires it
(C) Because an unrecorded deed is not valid
(D) To make title marketable

62. An acknowledgment may be void if:
    (A) made before an officer who did not witness the signature.
    (B) made before an officer who has an interest, such as the lessor.
    (C) not made at the time the instrument was signed.
    (D) not made upon oath or affirmation.

63. A person must record an instrument within what period of time after it is signed and delivered?
    (A) 30 days   (C) One year
    (B) 90 days   (D) No time limit

64. All of the following is an insurance policy against losses suffered due to defects in the chain of title to a specific parcel of real estate **EXCEPT**:
    (A) mortgagee's policy.
    (B) insurer's policy.
    (C) owner's policy.
    (D) joint owner-lender policy.

❖ 65. How frequently are title insurance premiums paid?
    (A) Semiannually during ownership
    (B) Bimonthly during ownership
    (C) Only at the time of issuance
    (D) At the start and end of the policy term

66. A standard title insurance policy offers protection to an owner against which of the following?
    (A) Defects arising after the date of the policy
    (B) Encroachments
    (C) Costs of defending a lawsuit challenging the title
    (D) Unrecorded mechanics' liens

❖ 67. The Real Estate Settlement Procedures Act (RESPA) is designed to regulate which of the following?
    (A) Disclosures of closing information
    (B) Procedures for recording titles to real estate
    (C) Ceilings on interest rates charged
    (D) Those who are qualified to prepare a settlement statement

68. In closing a real estate transaction, various expenses and carrying charges are apportioned between the buyer and seller. These apportionments appear on the settlement statement as:
    (A) profits and losses.
    (B) debits and credits.
    (C) debits only.
    (D) those that always have an offsetting entry.

69. Which of the following statements about escrow officers is true?
    (A) They can disburse money and documents when all conditions of the escrow have been satisfactorily met.
    (B) They must be individually licensed by the real estate licensing agency.
    (C) Anyone can perform the escrow function.
    (D) They are used only when the property involves financing.

❖ 70. Under the rules and regulations of RESPA, which is true?
    (A) The buyer may not use his or her attorney at closing.
    (B) The lender can require the use of a designated closing agent.
    (C) The lender cannot charge points on the loan.
    (D) The borrower receives an explanation of settlement charges.

71. Which of the following documents serves as the **BEST** evidence of good title to a property?
    (A) Warranty deed   (C) Abstract
    (B) Bill of sale   (D) Mortgage

72. Which is true concerning a properly established escrow?
    (A) Voidable at the option of the seller
    (B) Voidable at the option of the buyer
    (C) Voidable at the option of buyer's or seller's broker
    (D) Voidable at the option of both buyer and seller acting together

❖ 73. When a property is sold subject to an existing lease that has nine months before it expires, all of the following statements regarding the settlement statement are true **EXCEPT**:
    (A) The security deposit is a credit to the buyer.
    (B) Prepaid rent is a credit to the buyer.
    (C) The security deposit is a debit to the seller.
    (D) Prepaid rent is a credit to the seller.

74. An escrow company does which of the following functions?
    (A) Collects all monies and pertinent documents for distribution
    (B) Determines that title is marketable
    (C) Represents either the buyer or the seller
    (D) Performs the title search

❖ 75. Which one of the following documents is **LEAST** likely to be recorded?
    (A) Quitclaim deed
    (B) Satisfaction of mortgage
    (C) Power of attorney
    (D) Offer and acceptance

❖ 76. When *C* deeds a property to *J*, who fails to record, and then *C* subsequently deeds the same property to *A*, which one of these statements is true?
    (A) *J* owns the property based on his having the first deed.
    (B) *A* is the owner if she first records without notice of *J*'s rights.
    (C) *A* and *J* are now tenants in common.
    (D) *C* remains the owner because both deeds are void.

77. All of the following can act as an escrow agent to close a transaction **EXCEPT**:
    (A) lender.
    (B) attorney.
    (C) real estate broker.
    (D) home inspection company.

78. Escrow will prepare all of the following **EXCEPT**:
    (A) deed.
    (B) escrow instructions.
    (C) closing statements.
    (D) conveyance tax certificate.

79. A seller sells a 5-unit rental building. How are the tenants' security deposits treated on the closing statement?
    (A) Credit seller
    (B) Debit buyer
    (C) Debit seller, credit buyer
    (D) Credit seller, debit buyer

80. On the closing statement, the earnest money deposit is:
    (A) a double entry.   (C) credited to buyer.
    (B) prorated.   (D) debit to seller.

81. A sales transaction closes on August 15th. Lease rent of $900 has been paid for the month. What is the proration?
    (A) Debit buyer $450
    (B) Credit seller $450
    (C) Debit buyer $480
    (D) Credit buyer $480

82. Which of the following events must happen upon the closing of a real estate purchase transaction?
    (A) The conveyance document must be recorded at the county recording office.
    (B) The buyer must be given occupancy of the property.
    (C) The buyer must pay the entire purchase price in cash at that time.
    (D) The deed must be delivered.

❖ 83. How would a purchase money second mortgage given by the purchaser to the seller appear on the settlement statement upon closing the real estate sale?
    (A) Credit to purchaser and debit to seller
    (B) Debit to purchaser and credit to seller
    (C) Only as a debit to the buyer
    (D) Only as a credit to the seller

84. For which of the following is the escrow agent responsible?
    (A) To make certain that all encumbrances on the title are removed prior to closing
    (B) To make certain that the buyer is in possession of the property prior to closing
    (C) To conduct a search of public records
    (D) To disburse all funds according to the agreement of the parties

85. All of the following would be covered in a standard title insurance policy **EXCEPT**:
    (A) special assessments.
    (B) prescriptive easements.
    (C) recorded mortgages.
    (D) competency of parties.

86. The settlement agent at closing is responsible for making payments for all of the following **EXCEPT**:
    (A) balance due on seller's mortgage.
    (B) title insurance premiums.
    (C) recording fee.
    (D) salesperson's commissions.

ANSWERS

1. **B**   Usually a title company or licensed abstracter conducts a title search of the chain of title in the public records to see what, if any, clouds on title there may be. A title insurance policy would then insure against losses suffered due to certain undisclosed title defects.

2. **D**   A lender's extended title insurance policy is assignable in order to facilitate the commercial transfer of mortgages in the secondary mortgage market. Because the owner's policy is not assignable, a new buyer would have to pay a one-time fee to cover any defects up to the time of purchasing a personal policy. (ALTA is the American Land Title Association.)

3. **B**   All title insurance policies cover hidden risks, such as forgery in the chain of title. An extended policy like an ALTA policy would cover against (C) and (D), but few policies would extend to (A).

4. **D**   A lawsuit to quiet the title would clearly establish the rights of parties after a gap in the title is found. In a few cases where the gap is obvious, a quitclaim deed from the interested party or heir could be helpful.

5. **B**   The Torrens system of title registration was designed from ship registration procedures in which title can be transferred or encumbered only by notation on the proper registration of title (certificate of title).

6. **C**   A title search would be needed to discover the flaw. Assuming a reputable title company gives its opinion, it is not usually necessary to hire an attorney.

7. **B**   The survey would reveal physical defects like encroachments. The warranty deed would only give a right to sue the grantor in the event there was a title defect.

8. **D**   An extended coverage title policy will insure against hidden risks and matters that an inspection of the property would reveal, such as mechanics' liens, undisclosed easements, or rights of parties in possession.

9. **C**   It would be an unusual endorsement even on an extended coverage policy that would cover matters of zoning and governmental regulation.

10. **B**   The title search is the actual process of running through the chain of title. At least with (A), (C) and (D), there would be some protection given to the buyer in the event of improper or negligent searching through the title.

11. **D**   An abstract is a document that summarizes (digests) the various recorded instruments found in the chain of title. It neither insures nor guarantees the title, although the abstracter would be liable for negligence in conducting the search if something such as a recorded second mortgage were overlooked.

12. **B**   In a title search, one runs through the chain of title to discover any clouds on title.

13. **A**   A standard policy generally confines itself to defects in the records, like forgery, whereas ALTA policies extend to physical defects (such as encroachments) because many lenders want this extra protection (which the borrower pays for anyway).

14. **C**   Mining and water claims are more likely to be excluded in the standard title insurance policy than any of the other choices.

15. **A**   Escrow acts as the stakeholder, a middleman between buyer and seller to make sure the parties perform their respective obligations before title and money pass.

16. **B**   In the event of loss due to a title defect, the title insurance carrier would most likely make good the insured's loss in the same way a surety company would. There are no warranties with a quitclaim deed. For there to be liability under a certificate of title, there needs to be some title company negligence.

17. **B**   Since the conflicting matter in the mutually agreed-upon subsequent escrow instruction is a modification of the original contract, the escrow agreement will usually take precedence. In a counteroffer, it is the offer that is modified.

18. **D**   Escrow does not take individual "change orders" from either party; both parties must consent to any change in the original contract or escrow instructions.

19. **A**   Encroachments would be physical matters not on the public records, such as overhanging trees, which could only be covered in an extended title insurance policy.

20. **D**   Escrow is a neutral party but is agent for seller as far as holding title and agent for buyer as far as holding money. It is a fiduciary.

21. **D**   Each *link* in the chain of title refers to a successive ownership to that particular property. There must be no gap in the chain of ownership.

22. **C**   Escrow is really a neutral third party hired by both buyer and seller to achieve a certain result.

23. **C**   Transfers of a bankrupt's property are usually handled through the federal court and subject to court approval.

24. **D**   A salesperson can only act as a subagent of the broker's principal.

25. **A**   An abstract of title not only summarizes deeds but also all recorded documents affecting the title, such as leases, options and mortgages.

26. **A**   The escrow company is the agent of both grantor and grantee. Once the transaction is in escrow, it is placed out of the unilateral control of either party.

27. **B**   Mortgage foreclosures would occur when the owner defaults on the mortgage. Title insurance is concerned with title losses.

28. **D**   Title insurance would protect the lender against a title defect or challenge to title to the secured property. An abstract neither guarantees not insures title. Off-record risks include forgery and incapacity.

29. **D**   The abstract tends to be a long document because it is the actual summary of documents found in the chain of title and not just the title companies' opinion of title.

30. **D**   Both parties must consent before the broker can draw from escrow against earned commission. Otherwise, there could be a problem in a case where the buyer is entitled to the return of his or her deposit.

31. **D**   Coverage is steady for an owner, but it declines for the lender as the loan decreases (like a term life insurance policy). There is a one-time payment.

32. **D**   The application for title insurance won't reveal anything.

33. **B**   The policy protects only the lender, but for a small premium the owner can and should get protection under a joint lender-owner policy, which is not assignable by the owner.

34. **D**   Escrow would hold the deed until both parties have fully performed their obligations under their existing contract of sale.

35. **B**   The abstract would reveal such recorded encumbrances as judgment liens, easements or mortgages.

36. **D**   The policy is not assignable to any buyer of the property. If, however, the grantee later sues the grantor for breach of warranty of title, the title company would defend the suit and protect the grantor based on their policy. Mutual cancellation would result from a settlement dispute.

37. **C**   Because the probate proceeding might not effectively settle all the claims of heirs to the property, *A* should be advised to obtain a title policy insuring her title. This would make her property more marketable.

38. **A**   The standard policy limits its coverage to matters of public record, including hidden risks such as forgery, nondelivery of a deed or incapacity.

39. **B** In a Torrens search there is only one major document to check—the certificate of title registration.

40. **C** A buyer might agree in the sales contract to take the property subject to all the disclosed liens. The key is disclosure.

41. **C** Escrow, which is a disinterested stakeholder, cannot carry out the terms of an unenforceable agreement.

42. **C** Escrow will often use the funds generated by the buyer to pay off unpaid taxes and mortgages so that buyer will get the free and clear title promised by the seller in the sales contract.

43. **C** Escrow might, for example, hold the buyer's funds pending delivery of the seller's deed. Hypothecation refers to mortgaging.

44. **D** The title policy usually protects against recorded conveyances that are ineffective due to incapacity.

45. **D** The grantee puts the world on notice of his or her rights in the property when the deed is recorded.

46. **B** Most sales contracts involve a short-lived transaction and are not recorded.

47. **D** A note does not involve an interest in real property. Also, most lenders do not want the details of the loan to be made public.

48. **C** Acknowledgment is usually required to lessen the risk of forgery. If, for example, the document is recorded before the transferor gets title, it will not be found in a regular chain of title search of the grantor-grantee index and, therefore, it is not constructive notice of the rights of the parties.

49. **A** The validity of the deed between the parties is not affected by failure to record. Most states rule that a good faith purchaser for value, without notice who first records, will have superior title to that of a prior grantee under an unrecorded deed.

50. **A** The law presumes people to have notice of matters published in the public records even though a person may not have actual notice.

51. **B** Anyone who deals with a property without first checking the public records does so at his or her own risk. Actual notice means direct knowledge of a fact.

52. **A** If the deed is not recorded, a subsequent purchaser for value (from the original grantor), without notice of the first unrecorded deed, could get superior title by recording the subsequent deed first. Donees are not protected under the recording law (nor are devisees).

53. **B** The recording laws do not protect a subsequent donee who gets property after an earlier unrecorded deed, even though the donee first records. In this case, the first in time, first in right rule would apply.

54. **C** Recording laws are designed to protect subsequent good faith purchasers for value who first record. (In certain "notice" jurisdictions, first recordation is not necessary.)

55. **D** In this situation the buyer should obtain an extended title insurance policy to cover against matters that would be revealed by an inspection, such as encroachments, adverse possession and mechanics' liens.

56. **C** An interested person, like a grantee, could not notarize the grantor's signature, even though properly licensed as a notary.

57. **D** Recording an invalid deed will not make it valid. The venue refers to the jurisdiction where the notary is authorized to take acknowledgments of signatures.

58. **C** To lessen the chances of forgery, most states require a document to be acknowledged by a notary public as a prerequisite for recording. Recording will not cure a defective title.

59. D Recording laws will only protect subsequent purchasers for value without actual or constructive notice. Possession can give constructive notice of the rights of the person in possession, thus illustrating the importance of a property inspection.

60. D The recording system neither insures nor corrects title defects; it merely gives constructive notice of the rights of people as to certain property.

61. A Recording laws are voluntary and not required. In Torrens system property, however, registration of title is required.

62. B The signature need not take place before the notary, but the disinterested notary must identify the person as the one who signed of his or her own free will. Choice (D) would be an affidavit.

63. D By not recording, however, the person risks losing the property.

64. B The insurance company is the insurer. The mortgagee has an insurable interest, as does the owner. The borrower is often required by the lender to obtain a mortgagee (lender) policy. Because this policy protects only the lender, the owner should, for a slight extra charge, obtain a combined policy that will protect both the borrower and the lender in the event of a loss.

65. C The premium is paid once at the beginning of the coverage and covers defects occurring up to the date of the policy.

66. C The title policy covers defects of record that occurred up to the date of the policy, including costs to defend even an unfounded lawsuit. Choices (B) and (D) are covered under an extended policy.

67. A RESPA is a federal law requiring certain disclosures of closing data, such as estimated closing costs, to consumers.

68. B Profits and losses appear on an income statement, whereas debits (or charges) and credits are accounting terms used in a closing statement.

69. A Most states require licensing of escrow companies but not individual escrow agents.

70. D The buyer is free to use an attorney and the lender can use any settlement agent, but RESPA prohibits the lender from dictating the use of one particular agent.

71. C As abstract of title is a summary of those documents found in the chain of title after a title search has been run. The warranty deed, like the bill of sale, does not prove the title; it merely promises that title is as represented and conveyed.

72. D A proper escrow is beyond the control or unilateral action of any one party, although both may agree to cancel or modify.

73. D Prepaid rent is a debit to the seller and a credit to the buyer, since the seller has already received this income for the unused period. The seller who has this money must return it to the buyer, who will eventually return it to the tenant, provided there are no damages at the time of lease termination. This is a broker level question.

74. A Escrow is a neutral stakeholder that holds the deed pending payment by buyer and clearing of any checks. A title company renders its opinion as to the marketability of title.

75. D Most contracts of sale are not recorded, because there is a relatively short time between signing and closing. If the attorney-in-fact is to sign a document that will be recorded, then the power of attorney must first be recorded (under the "equal dignities rule").

76. B The recording laws would protect A if she is a bona fide purchaser for value who first records.

77. D Also, a salesperson cannot act as escrow agent.

78. A Attorneys usually prepare the deed.

79.   C   Seller keeps the security deposit money, yet the buyer will have to return it to tenant at end of lease. Buyer should confirm amount with tenant.

80.   C   It is a single entry item.

81.   D   Seller has been paid rent for the last 16 days of the month. $900 ÷ 30 = $30 per day x 16 = $480. Note also that with expenses like taxes, that the seller pays up to the day of closing and that the buyer takes over on day of closing.

82.   D   While recording is recommended, it is not required. Delivery is a prerequisite to transfer of legal title at closing. The seller may be given a period of time after settlement in which to relocate—the buyer would then be wise to obtain a rental agreement.

83.   A   The loan is credited against the purchase price owed by the purchaser. It represents cash the seller will not receive at the time of settlement. This is a broker level question.

84.   D   Escrow is responsible for making certain that the parties have performed their respective contractual obligations prior to closing—the buyer may have agreed to take title subject to certain encumbrances or to delay taking possession.

85.   B   The standard title insurance policy covers matters of public record, questions of delivery, and competency. Only an extended policy would cover matters that an inspection would reveal, such as a prescriptive easement.

86.   D   The proper person to pay the salesperson is the broker.

Chapter 13   Real Estate Settlement Exercises

On the broker examination, there will be several questions requiring a general knowledge of how to prepare a settlement or closing statement, including the mathematics of prorations. Salesperson candidates should be able to complete the proration problems in this section. You will not have to complete a settlement statement on the exam. In all prorations, one should use a 360-day year and a 30-day month.

To assist the broker candidate in knowing how to prepare the settlement statements, a settlement statement guide has been prepared, showing most of the possible items that may be encountered in a problem, and whether these items are to be shown as a debit or credit to the buyer or seller. There is no definite order in which these entries appear on a settlement statement, although purchase price is typically first and the last entries are the balance due from buyer and net proceeds due to seller. Note that a few of these entries may differ from custom and practice in your area (especially items like title insurance). Also, few closing statements will contain all these entries but they are listed here for study purposes. A properly prepared sales agreement, however, will expressly state which party is to pay what expense. Using this guide and the Student Settlement Statement Worksheet, you should have no difficulty answering questions about the settlement statement. Special emphasis should be given to learning what items are typically debits and credits to the buyer and seller.

STUDENT SETTLEMENT STATEMENT WORKSHEET

SETTLEMENT DATE:	BUYER'S STATEMENT		SELLER'S STATEMENT	
CLOSING DATE	DEBIT	CREDIT	DEBIT	CREDIT
1. Consideration (purchase price)	X			X
2. Initial deposit		X		
3. New first or second mortgage (deed of trust)		X		
4. Existing mortgage payoff (deed of trust)			X	
5. First or second purchase-money mortgage (deed of trust) with seller		X	X	
6. Mortgage assumed (deed of trust)		X	X	
7. Land contract (agreement of sale)		X	X	
8. Interest arrears (assumption)		X	X	
9. Interest on new loan	X			
10. Interest on mortgage payoff			X	
11. Taxes in arrears		X	X	
12. Taxes in advance	X			X
13. Delinquent taxes			X	
14. Insurance assumed/advance	X			X
15. Rent collected in advance		X	X	
16. Rent owed	X			X
17. Preparation of deed			X	
18. Abstract or certificate of title			X	
19. Title search			X	
20. Title insurance	X			
21. Appraisal fee (requested by lender)	X			
22. New conventional mortgage (loan fee)	X			
23. Discount points (VA)			X	
24. Loan origination fee (VA)	X			
25. Prepayment penalty			X	
26. Mortgage assumption fee	X			
27. Conveyance tax			X	
28. Mortgage release			X	
29. Recording mortgage release			X	
30. Recording deed	X			
31. Recording mortgages	X			
32. Escrow fees	X		X	
33. Commission			X	
34. Survey		Negotiable		
35. Inventory (separate bill of sale)	X			X
SUB TOTALS	X	X	X	X
36. Balance due from buyer		X		
37. Net proceeds due to seller			X	

SETTLEMENT STATEMENT GUIDE

1. *Consideration (purchase price).* The full amount is credited to the seller and the full amount is debited to the buyer.
2. *Initial deposit.* The amount of the earnest money deposit is credited to the buyer.
3. *New first or second mortgage (deed of trust).* The full amount of the mortgage will be shown as a credit to the buyer, since it is the means by which the buyer will pay the purchase price.
4. *Existing mortgage payoff (deed of trust).* Will show as a debit to the seller.
5. *First or second purchase money mortgage (deed of trust) carried by seller.* Enter the full amount as a credit to the buyer and a debit to the seller (the mortgagee).
6. *Mortgage assumed (deed of trust).* The full amount will show as a credit to the buyer and a debit to the seller (because the seller will be receiving less cash at closing).
7. *Land contract (agreement of sale).* The full amount will show as a credit to the buyer and a debit to the seller (since the seller does not receive it in cash at the closing).
8. *Interest in arrears (when buyer is assuming existing mortgage).* Prorate the interest and enter this amount as a credit to buyer and debit to the seller.
9. *Interest on new loan.* This amount will be shown only as a debit to the buyer because he or she has to pay interest from the date of closing until the first loan payment date, which is usually the first day of the following month.
10. *Interest on mortgage payoff.* This amount will be shown only as a debit to the seller.
11. *Taxes in arrears.* Prorate the taxes and enter the amount as credit to the buyer and a debit to the seller.
12. *Taxes in advance.* Prorate the taxes and enter the amount as a debit to the buyer and a credit to the seller.
13. *Delinquent taxes.* If taxes are delinquent, enter this amount only as a debit to the seller.
14. *Insurance assumed (if paid in advance).* Prorate the insurance and enter it as a debit to the buyer and a credit to the seller.
15. *Rent collected in advance.* If the property being purchased is presently being rented, the rent collected in advance from the tenant will show as a credit to the buyer and a debit to the seller.
16. *Rent owed.* If the property being purchased is being rented and the rent has not yet been collected from the tenant, that amount will be shown as a debit to the buyer and a credit to the seller.
17. *Preparation of deed.* This will be a debit to the seller.
18. *Abstract or certificate of title.* Debit this amount to the seller.
19. *Title search.* Debit this amount to the seller.
20. *Title insurance.* Debit full amount to the buyer.
21. *Appraisal fee.* Charged to buyer if requested by lender.
22. *New conventional mortgage loan fee.* Debit to the buyer.
23. *Discount points (DVA).* Debit to the seller except in FHA negotiated interest rate loan programs.
24. *Loan origination fee (DVA).* Debit to the buyer.
25. *Prepayment penalty.* Debit this amount to the seller.
26. *Mortgage assumption fee.* If there is a charge for assuming the existing mortgage debit this amount to the buyer.
27. *Conveyance tax.* This will show as a debit to the seller.
28. *Mortgage release.* A mortgage release from the lender will be shown as a debit to the seller.
29. *Recording mortgage release.* Seller will want the lender's release recorded, therefore it will show as a debit to the seller.
30. *Recording deed.* This will be a debit to the buyer.
31. *Recording mortgages.* The recording of any mortgages will show as a debit to the buyer.
32. *Escrow fees.* Escrow fees are usually split in half, therefore they will show as a debit to both buyer and seller.
33. *Commission.* The commission, which is a percentage of the sales price, will show as a debit to the seller.
34. *Survey.* Who pays for surveying and staking varies from state to state, and is therefore negotiable and to be determined between the parties.
35. *Inventory.* If the buyer is to purchase inventory, which is on a separate bill of sale, this will show as a debit to the buyer and a credit to the seller.
36. *Balance due from buyer.* This is the amount shown after subtracting the buyer's credits from his or her debits. It will be entered as a credit if it is needed to balance a double entry system.

37. *Net proceeds due to seller.* This is the amount the seller will receive from the buyer and may be determined by subtracting the seller's debits from his or her credits. It will be entered in his or her debit column.

QUESTIONS

Closing Statement Preparation—Part 1

Indicate where the following entries would be entered on a closing statement as a debit or credit for buyer and seller:

1. Purchase price:

2. Earnest money deposit:

3. New first mortgage:

4. Second purchase money mortgage (with seller):

5. Taxes arrears:

6. Insurance assumed:

7. Preparation of deed:

8. Title insurance:

9. Recording deed:

10. Commission:

Settlement Statement Prorations—Part 2

❖ 1. The tax year is Jan.1 to Dec. 31. The first half of the tax year has been paid. Closing is Sept. 1, of the same year. Taxes are $432 per annum. What is the actual entry?

2. A fire insurance policy has an unused portion of 6 months, 10 days. The policy costs $151.20 for three years. What was the actual entry?

3. Annual taxes are $3,600 paid in advance on Jan. 1. Closing is Sept. 1. What is the tax proration?

❖ 4. Closing date is Dec. 15. Fire insurance is $720 for three years, paid in advance on Feb. 15 of the same year. What is the actual entry?

5. The balance of the mortgage assumed is $40,000 at 11 percent interest. Payments are due on the 10th of the month. Closing date is Mar. 1. What is the actual interest proration?

❖ 6. A property for sale has a rental cottage. Rent of $600 is payable in advance on the 10th of the month. Settlement date is July 20. What is the actual entry shown for the buyer and seller?

7. Taxes are $648 yearly. Closing is Dec. 15. The last half of the calendar year is unpaid. What is the actual entry?

8. There is an old mortgage of $50,000 at 8 percent being paid off. There will also be a new mortgage of $60,000 at 12 percent. The old mortgage is due on the 1st of the month, the new mortgage on the 15th. The settlement date is July 15. What is the actual entry if any for both mortgages and interest?

9. Closing date is Mar. 15. Taxes, $480 per year, are unpaid. What is the actual entry for the unpaid portion?

10. Closing date is Oct. 10. Mortgage assumed is $21,400 at 9 percent. Mortgage payments are paid on the 20th of each month. What is the actual entry?

11. One year insurance policy for $900 paid through December 31 of this year. Closing will be December 15 of the same year. What will be the amount of the proration?

ANSWERS

Closing Statement Preparation— Part 1

1. Purchase price: Debit buyer, credit seller

2. Earnest money deposit: Credit buyer

3. New first mortgage: Credit buyer

4. Second purchase money mortgage: Credit buyer, debit seller

5. Taxes arrears: Credit buyer, debit seller

6. Insurance assumed: Debit buyer, credit seller

7. Preparation of deed: Debit seller

8. Title insurance: Debit buyer

9. Recording deed: Debit buyer

10. Commission: Debit seller

Settlement Statement Prorations— Part 2

1. Credit buyer, debit seller $72 each. $36 per month × 2 months = $72

2. Debit buyer, credit seller $26.60 each. $4.20 per month × 6 ⅓ months

3. Debit buyer, credit seller $1,200 each. $300 per month × 4 months

4. Debit buyer, credit seller $520 each. $20 per month × 26 months

5. Credit buyer, debit seller $244.44 each. $4,400 per year of $366.66 per mo. × ⅔ months (Interest paid in arrears, due on 10th. Thus owed from Feb. 10 to Mar. 1)

6. Credit buyer, debit seller $400. Tenant paid entire amount in advance, thus seller must be charged ⅔ month, which is also credited to the buyer.

7. Credit buyer, debit seller $297 each. $54 per month × 5½ mos.

8. Debit seller $50,000 for mortgage payoff and $166.66 for interest in arrears. New mortgage will be shown as $60,000 credit to the buyer. There will be no interest proration on the new mortgage at this time. $333.33 per month × ½ month.

9. Credit buyer, debit seller $100. $40 per month × 2½ months

10. Credit buyer, debit seller $107. $1,926 annual interest. $160.50 per month × ⅔ month

11. Credit seller, debit buyer $40. $2.50 per day × 16 days.

PART E Real Estate Brokerage

This part contains questions on topics of

- Law of agency
- Fiduciary relationships
- Listing agreements
- Elements of a valid sales contract
- Provisions in a sales contract
- Option contracts
- Anti-discrimination under the Federal Fair Housing Act
- Truth-in-Lending disclosures
- Lease agreements
- Property management
- Securities

Expect about 35 percent of the examination to contain questions on the topics covered in this part E.

Chapter 14   Agency

Questions in this chapter will test your comprehension of the following topics:

- Fiduciary obligations of agent to principal
- Difference between listing agent, subagent and buyer's agent
- Real estate commissions
- Disclosure of material facts
- Use of power of attorney

False Friends

The following words are often confused with one another. Note the difference in meaning of these false friends:

Selling Agent/Seller's Agent: The selling agent works with a buyer making an offer, whereas the seller's agent is the listing agent.

Cooperating Agent/Subagent: The selling agent from another firm is called the cooperating agent, and may be either a buyer's agent or a subagent of the seller. If a subagent, then the cooperating agent owes fiduciary duties to the seller.

Principal/Principle: The client is the principal in an agency relationship; or, the debt in a loan. Sometimes principal is misspelled as *principle*.

QUESTIONS

1. The responsibilities of a real estate sales agent in a listing agency relationship include all of the following **EXCEPT**:
   - (A) exercise of due care.
   - (B) accountability.
   - (C) obedience.
   - (D) repair of defects.

❖ 2. After showing a property a number of times and not securing an acceptable offer, the broker decides to buy the property himself or herself. He or she must do which of the following?
   - (A) Wait until the listing expires and then make an offer to purchase
   - (B) Make his or her true position known to the seller
   - (C) Wait until he or she receives an offer and then offer a higher price
   - (D) Wait for at least 30 days and then offer full asking price

3. The listing broker owes a direct fiduciary responsibility to whom?
   - (A) The listing salesperson
   - (B) The buyer
   - (C) The buyer's broker
   - (D) The seller

❖ 4. A subagent of a seller would **BEST** be described as which of the following?
   - (A) Special agent
   - (B) General agent
   - (C) Buyer's broker
   - (D) Universal agent

5. The **BEST** description of a special agent would be a person who:
   - (A) is an attorney.
   - (B) is a broker.
   - (C) has limited authority.
   - (D) has contractual authority.

6. All of the following are fiduciaries **EXCEPT**:
   - (A) principal.
   - (B) trustee.
   - (C) guardian.
   - (D) receiver.

7. A salesperson employed by a real estate broker to show and sell property listed with the broker is **BEST** described as:
   - (A) an agent of the broker, who is an agent for the principal.
   - (B) an agent for the principal.
   - (C) a principal party to the transaction.
   - (D) an independent contractor not an agent.

8. An agency agreement to sell a specific piece of real property will be terminated by all of the following **EXCEPT**:
   - (A) death of the broker.
   - (B) bankruptcy of the seller.
   - (C) revocation of the listing salesperson's license.
   - (D) insanity of the broker.

9. When a salesperson makes a misrepresentation of a fact, the salesperson is liable only:
   - (A) when the statement was made with a malicious intent.
   - (B) if the salesperson is licensed.
   - (C) when the statement is a material fact.
   - (D) if the salesperson has a listing agreement.

10. An owner requests a broker to list a property for sale at $70,000. Upon inspection, the broker believes the property is worth $80,000. The broker should:
   - (A) get a listing for the property at $70,000.
   - (B) buy the property for $70,000.
   - (C) suggest that the owner list the property for $75,000, so there will be room for bargaining.
   - (D) inform the seller that the property is worth $80,000.

❖ 11. The broker's responsibilities in presenting to the seller a written offer to purchase include all of the following **EXCEPT**:
   - (A) making known to the seller all written offers before seller accepts an offer.
   - (B) making known the ramifications and practical effects of an offer.
   - (C) presenting only the offers that are within 10 percent of the asking price.
   - (D) presenting all offers as rapidly as they are received.

❖ 12. When a property is advertised "principals only," which of the following groups is **EXCLUDED**?
   - (A) Agents
   - (B) People who are willing and able
   - (C) Persons wanting to live on the property
   - (D) Financially capable brokers interested as buyers

❖ 13. The position of trust assumed by the broker as an agent for the principal is described **MOST** accurately as:
   - (A) trustee relationship.
   - (B) trustor relationship.
   - (C) confidential relationship.
   - (D) fiduciary relationship.

14. As agent of the seller, a real estate broker is usually authorized to do all of the following **EXCEPT**:
    (A) bind the principal under a sales contract.
    (B) advertise the listed property.
    (C) place a "for sale" sign on the listed property.
    (D) cooperate with other brokers to effect a sale.

❖ 15. A seller tells his or her broker that termites have destroyed the floor and that the swimming pool is in violation of the city setback requirements. Which of the following must the broker's salesperson disclose to a prospective buyer?
    (A) The condition of the floor only
    (B) The pool violation only
    (C) Both must be disclosed.
    (D) Neither must be disclosed if the seller asks that it be done that way.

16. In handling a real estate transaction, a broker should:
    (A) provide the client with a statement of the receipts and disbursements of client's money.
    (B) not reveal building code violations to the client.
    (C) reveal only those things that are part of the public record.
    (D) reveal only the items requested by the seller.

17. A fiduciary relationship usually exists between a principal and all of the following **EXCEPT**:
    (A) a trustee.   (C) an appraiser.
    (B) an administrator.   (D) a receiver.

❖ 18. Regarding financial agreements made by the client, the broker:
    (A) need not see that those agreements are put in writing.
    (B) is limited to setting the sales price and brokerage fee.
    (C) may delegate this responsibility to the sales manager.
    (D) is ethically bound to see that all contracts express specific written agreement of parties concerning the details of the transaction.

19. A broker usually pays a salesperson a share of the commission received by the broker from a sale when:
    (A) the salesperson submits sufficient earnest money deposit to the broker.
    (B) the sale is consummated and title is transferred to the purchaser.
    (C) there is a valid and binding offer and acceptance.
    (D) the contract and earnest money are placed in escrow.

20. Which is true about a fiduciary?
    (A) Is a disinterested third party
    (B) Looks after the principal's best interests
    (C) Must be an employee of the broker
    (D) Must be paid a fee

21. According to the laws of agency:
    (A) a broker must always charge a commission and put the amount on the listing form.
    (B) a broker may sue and collect a commission even though he or she had a forfeited license when the commission was earned.
    (C) the commission will be based on the listed price.
    (D) the principal and the client are the same person.

22. Most likely the real estate broker has an agency relationship with:
    (A) buyer.   (C) escrow.
    (B) seller.   (D) attorney.

23. The seller's broker negotiating a difficult sales contract between an experienced seller of real estate and a novice purchaser should do which of the following?
    (A) Not be concerned about the buyer's lack of experience
    (B) Refuse to continue negotiating with the purchaser
    (C) Insist that the purchaser employ an attorney
    (D) Suggest that the purchaser consider employing another broker or an attorney

24. An agent will usually be entitled to receive a commission if the agent:
    (A) presents a written offer to purchase during the term of a valid listing.
    (B) is the procuring cause of the sale.
    (C) has an open listing and the property is sold by another broker with an open listing.
    (D) holds an exclusive agency listing contract and the property is sold by the seller.

❖ 25. The commission rate for the sale of real estate is determined by:
    (A) silent agreement among brokers in a local area.
    (B) fixed schedules approved by the state licensing commission.
    (C) scarcity of real estate for sale.
    (D) negotiation between the broker and the seller.

26. The relationship between property owner and broker is that of:
    (A) seller and purchaser.
    (B) attorney and client.
    (C) principal and agent.
    (D) optionor and optionee.

27. A salesperson responds to an ad in the paper by a "For Sale by Owner." The owner gives the salesperson a key to inspect the property being sold. What type of agency is thereby created?
    (A) Fiduciary   (C) Contractual
    (B) Implied agency   (D) No agency

28. The cooperating broker in a real estate transaction may be any of the following EXCEPT:
    (A) listing broker.   (C) selling agent.
    (B) subagent.   (D) buyer's agent.

29. When a broker signs a contract to manage an owner's property, he or she becomes:
    (A) a lessor.   (C) a receiver.
    (B) a trustee.   (D) a fiduciary.

30. Salespeople may accept compensation of their predetermined share of the commission:
    (A) from the multiple-listing service.
    (B) from the owner of the property.
    (C) from their employing broker.
    (D) from a cooperating broker.

❖ 31. It is an unethical practice for a broker representing a seller to do which of the following?
    (A) Advise the seller of the highest price a prospective purchaser may be willing to pay
    (B) Advise a prospective purchaser of the lowest price the seller is willing to accept
    (C) Suggest to the buyer that the full asking price is an appropriate offer
    (D) Encourage broker from another company to try to sell the property

❖ 32. An attorney-in-fact, in executing the powers given to him or her under the provisions of a general power of attorney, usually has the right to do all of the following EXCEPT:
    (A) encumber the principal's property with attorney-in-fact as beneficiary.
    (B) sign the principal's name.
    (C) record the power of attorney in the county where the principal's property is located.
    (D) collect money for the principal.

33. A real estate broker may recover a commission in all of the following cases EXCEPT:
    (A) charging a 13 percent commission on raw land.
    (B) failing to give the owner a copy of the listing at the time it is signed.
    (C) charging more than six percent commission on residential land.
    (D) while holding an inactive license.

34. A broker who holds a bona fide option to buy a property is all of the following with respect to the property owner EXCEPT:
    (A) a principal.
    (B) an agent.
    (C) an optionee.
    (D) a prospective buyer.

❖ 35. An agent with a valid listing is generally considered to have earned a commission:
    (A) only if title is transferred.
    (B) when an offer has been secured from a prospective buyer.
    (C) when a ready, willing and able buyer who offers to buy on the principal's listing terms has been produced.
    (D) only when the principal signs a contract of sale.

36. Any person, partnership, association or corporation who authorizes or employs another, called the agent, to perform certain acts on his, her, or its behalf is **BEST** called:
    (A) the seller.   (C) the principal.
    (B) the broker.   (D) the assignor.

37. A real estate salesperson might lawfully accept an extra commission in a difficult sale from:
    (A) an appreciative seller.
    (B) a thankful buyer.
    (C) a broker-employer.
    (D) the mortgage lender.

38. A broker must open a separate account:
    (A) for each condominium project handled.
    (B) for each separate earnest money deposit handled.
    (C) into which he or she may place both client's money and his or her personal money.
    (D) that will be used to place all client's money and nothing more.

39. All of the following terminates an agency relationship **EXCEPT**:
    (A) the destruction of the subject matter.
    (B) making an offer.
    (C) death of the owner.
    (D) bankruptcy of the principal broker.

40. One who has the right to sign the name of the principal to a contract of sale is:
    (A) a real estate broker.
    (B) a special agent.
    (C) an attorney-in-fact.
    (D) an attorney at law.

41. When money is deposited in a client trust account, part of which will be used to pay the broker's commission:
    (A) the broker can withdraw the rightful share of the money before the real estate transaction is consummated or terminated.
    (B) accurate records must be kept on the account.
    (C) all interest belongs to the broker.
    (D) the broker can recover the advertising expenses of the sale out of this account before closing.

42. An agency has been breached. The court may declare the remedy to be any of the following **EXCEPT**:
    (A) rescission.
    (B) damages.
    (C) specific performance.
    (D) forfeiture.

❖ 43. The prime obligation of an agent to the principal is:
    (A) mutual trust.   (C) loyalty.
    (B) reverence.   (D) thrift.

44. All of the following have a fiduciary relationship **EXCEPT**:
    (A) lawyer to a client.
    (B) trustor to beneficiary.
    (C) listing broker to seller.
    (D) property manager to owner.

45. If a salesperson uses undue influence in a real estate transaction, all of the following would be true **EXCEPT**:
    (A) His or her license could be subject to suspension.
    (B) His or her license could be subject to revocation.
    (C) The broker of the salesperson would automatically lose his or her license.
    (D) The contract could be voidable.

46. All of the following have a fiduciary relationship **EXCEPT**:
    (A) agent to seller.
    (B) mortgagor to mortgagee.
    (C) attorney to client.
    (D) attorney-in-fact to principal.

47. Which of the following facts about a listed property can a broker conceal?
    (A) That the property is located within a 100-year flood plain zone
    (B) That the family den was built without a building permit
    (C) The type of neighbors that live in the surrounding area
    (D) The results of an engineer's report regarding the environmental hazards.

48. As a broker for a 30-unit condominium project, you discover that the exterior walls are 13½ inches from where they should be according to the building plans. You should do which of the following?
    (A) Disregard it as being insignificant
    (B) Seek an amendment to the plans
    (C) Retain an architect
    (D) Inform the client

❖ 49. A real estate broker who has entered into an agency contract with a seller may delegate responsibilities under the contract to one or more salespeople because:
    (A) all agency contracts are assignable.
    (B) the contract always contains this specific authority.
    (C) this is an implied authority arising out of custom.
    (D) the real estate licensing agency permits this.

❖ 50. A broker inspected the seller's house and discovered it was 600 square feet larger than the tax records had indicated. The extra area is an addition built without a building permit. The broker should tell the client all of the following EXCEPT:
    (A) The government could force the seller to remove the 600-square foot addition.
    (B) The seller should disclose this fact to any prospective buyer in order to avoid any claim of misrepresentation.
    (C) Because the addition has already been completed, it is no longer relevant to disclose this fact.
    (D) Inform the new buyers that they could be forced to tear down the illegal improvement.

51. The owner wants to sell property without the aid of a real estate broker. The owner may legally do all of the following EXCEPT:
    (A) evaluate the purchasing power of the buyer.
    (B) write up the sales contract between seller and buyer.
    (C) require that the buyer assume the present mortgage.
    (D) state preference for a buyer of the same religion.

52. When a buyer is about to buy a property, which of the following statements is true?
    (A) The listing broker can request the earnest money check be made payable to him or her.
    (B) The salesperson can request the check be made payable to him or her.
    (C) The salesperson should only accept cash for earnest money.
    (D) It is mandatory for the validity of a contract to take earnest money.

53. A power of attorney for a real estate sales contract is effective when:
    (A) it is not in writing.
    (B) either party dies.
    (C) it is signed by the principal.
    (D) it is signed only by the attorney-in-fact.

❖ 54. M Realty has a listing for $90,000. B makes an offer for $105,000. Without the knowledge of the seller, M Realty can do which of the following?
    (A) Offer to buy the property through a nominee for $90,000
    (B) Suggest that broker reduce the offer to $90,000
    (C) Buy directly from the seller for $95,000 and the next day resell to B for $105,000
    (D) Present the $105,000 offer to the seller

55. A power of attorney is still valid even if:
    (A) the principal dies.
    (B) the attorney-in-fact fails to use it for 90 days.
    (C) the principal records a declaration revoking it.
    (D) the attorney-in-fact dies.

❖ 56. The broker owes an obligation to do which of the following?
    (A) Divide the commission with another broker chosen or preferred by the buyer
    (B) Divulge to the buyer the lowest price at which the seller will sell
    (C) Present to the principal all written offers the broker receives including all of the terms and conditions of each offer signed by a prospective buyer
    (D) Keep the property in top condition

❖ **57.** As commission for negotiating the sale of a one million dollar hotel, a broker received title to a parcel of land valued at $30,000. The same day that the escrow on the hotel closed, the broker sold the land for $40,000. Which is true about the broker's actions in selling the land?

(A) Such action violates the licensing law because of the secret profit.

(B) Such action violates the licensing law if the broker does not give written notice to the hotel client of the sale.

(C) This would be illegal to receive land as a commission.

(D) This is proper behavior because the broker did not resell the land until after title to it was received.

58. The relationship between a real estate agent and principal is **MOST** similar to which of the following?

(A) Optionee and optionor

(B) Vendee and vendor

(C) Trustee and beneficiary

(D) Mortgagee and mortgagor

59. How does a person become an attorney-in-fact?

(A) By passing the law exam

(B) By operation of law

(C) By execution of a power of attorney

(D) By execution of a lease

60. What is the appropriate remedy for a broker against a seller who wrongfully refuses to pay an earned commission?

(A) File an attachment

(B) File a lawsuit

(C) File a lien against the property

(D) File a lis pendens

61. All but which one of the following are proper responsibilities of a real estate agent?

(A) Loyalty

(B) Skill

(C) Financing

(D) Accountability

❖ **62.** Under which of the following circumstances might a broker be liable for misrepresentation for negotiations with a prospective buyer?

(A) Broker states the land area is approximately one acre, when it is actually 44,000 square feet.

(B) Broker fails to mention that a structurally unsound grocery store is a nonconforming use.

(C) Broker passes on accurate information to the buyer that was given to him or her by the seller.

(D) Broker fails to disclose the height of the building.

63. Which of the following statements is true?

(A) A listing broker can tell a prospective buyer that the seller will accept less than the asking price if the seller will, in fact, accept the lower figure.

(B) A listing broker can refuse to transmit an offer to the seller if he or she thinks it is too low.

(C) The broker should present the first offer, then wait till that is accepted or rejected before presenting the next one.

(D) The broker must present all offers as soon as he or she receives them.

64. All of the following statements concerning the principal-agent disclosure are true **EXCEPT:**

(A) So long as a broker discloses that he or she is acting for a named principal, the broker usually is not liable if the principal defaults.

(B) A broker is personally liable for the principal's default of a contract that the broker negotiated without naming the principal.

(C) The broker may work for either the buyer or seller but not for both.

(D) The broker can act for both the buyer and seller in a transaction as long as his or her position is disclosed in writing to both parties.

65. To establish a firm legal contract between a broker and a seller, the prudent broker should:

(A) obtain an oral listing agreement from the seller.

(B) file a suit in a court of law.

(C) wait until a buyer is found and then seek to put the listing in written form.

(D) have his or her employment contract (the listing) in writing.

66. A real estate agent broker may lose the right to a commission in all cases, **EXCEPT** if he or she:
    (A) is guilty of a misstatement of known facts.
    (B) is not licensed when hired as an agent.
    (C) can show he or she had a written exclusive right to sell contract in force at the time of the sale.
    (D) quotes information to a buyer not authorized by a seller.

❖ 67. A listing broker receives an offer that fully matches the listing terms. Before presenting the offer, the broker receives two more offers, one for less than the listing price, but for cash and one for more than the listing price, but seller to take back a mortgage. What is the **BEST** approach for the listing broker?
    (A) Present the offer for the highest price
    (B) Present all offers at the same time
    (C) Present the cash offer first
    (D) Present the offers in the order received, one at a time

68. A real estate licensee should advise the use of legal counsel in which of the following cases?
    (A) In determining the value of a property before taking a listing
    (B) In comparing interest rates and discounts offered by several lenders
    (C) In determining which mortgage provisions are more advantageous to a borrower
    (D) In presenting an offer from a potential purchaser

❖ 69. Before obtaining a listing on a property that shares a driveway with the adjacent house, the owner insists that you (the broker) don't mention this fact to any prospective purchaser. Regarding this problem, you should:
    (A) inform a prospective buyer in spite of the seller's insistence.
    (B) not mention this fact unless a buyer asks.
    (C) refuse the listing if you can't persuade the owner to disclose.
    (D) do as the seller asks.

70. Broker S has a listing on a house that contains a provision that the house is to be sold in an "as is" condition. S learns of a major hidden defect in the property and, when showing a prospective purchaser, should:
    (A) advise the buyer of the defect.
    (B) only point out that the house will be sold in an "as is" condition.
    (C) mention the defect to the buyer only if asked.
    (D) inform the buyer that the seller has disclosed no defects.

❖ 71. Concerning a sale between a buyer and seller, the real estate licensee should:
    (A) advise them to have the title searched.
    (B) tell them the legal effect of the liens contained in the title commitment.
    (C) recommend the method of holding title.
    (D) advise the buyer against the use of a buyer's agent.

72. A broker can accept commissions from both buyer and seller under which one of the following conditions?
    (A) Only if there is a written listing from both
    (B) Under no circumstances
    (C) Only if both consent after full disclosure
    (D) Only if the total amount is under $10,000

73. Which one is most likely treated as an independent contractor?
    (A) Principal broker   (C) Broker in charge
    (B) Salesperson   (D) Secretary

74. The broker is in a hurry, so he or she persuades the seller to sign a blanket listing so that he or she can fill it out in a few days. This is a:
    (A) violation of the labor laws.
    (B) commonly accepted business practice.
    (C) bad business practice.
    (D) valid contract.

75. A listing broker offers subagency to outside brokers in the Multiple Listing Service. Broker B submits an offer on behalf of his buyer. B could be deemed any of the following **EXCEPT**:
    (A) buyer's broker only.
    (B) subagent of seller only.
    (C) dual agent.
    (D) finder only with no fiduciary duty to anyone.

76. A power of attorney that is effective even after the principal's subsequent disability or incapacity is called which one of the following?
    (A) Unilateral (C) Continuous
    (B) Durable (D) Fixed

77. All of the following are material facts that need to be disclosed by the real estate broker **EXCEPT**:
    (A) prior tenant has AIDS.
    (B) roof leaks.
    (C) drainage problem.
    (D) house not connected to sewer.

78. A buyer client asks the broker about the value of a particular property. The broker should:
    (A) provide an appraisal estimate of the property value based on comparable sales in the neighborhood.
    (B) indicate that the broker is not an appraiser but can provide information of prices that other properties have sold for recently.
    (C) provide an appraisal estimate based on a statistical analysis of MLS listing prices.
    (D) provide an appraisal estimate of the property value based on his or her best judgment.

ANSWERS

1. **D** The usual special agency involved between broker and seller normally does not include the repair of the listed property.

2. **B** It is not necessary that the listing first expire, but the agent must be extremely careful to disclose his or her interest in writing and avoid any possibility of self-dealing or secret profiting.

3. **D** The listing broker owes fiduciary duties to the seller, although he or she also has an ethical duty to treat fairly all parties to the transaction, including the buyer. The broker has a master-servant relationship with the salesperson (be it employee or independent contractor).

4. **A** The salespeople of the broker would be agents of the broker and subagents of the seller assigned to a special task and cloaked with limited authority—finding a ready, willing and able buyer to buy on the listing terms.

5. **C** An example is a real estate broker. A property manager, whose duties include many tasks, would most likely be a general agent. (A) and (B) are examples of a special agent.

6. **A** The principal is the one to whom the fiduciary duties are owed, as are the duties owed by a receiver to the bankrupt estate, the guardian to the ward's estate and the trustee to the beneficiary of the trust.

7. **A** The salesperson is a subagent of the seller who is authorized to carry out many of the duties of the broker. This is true regardless of whether the salesperson claims to be an employee or an independent contractor for tax purposes.

8. **C** An agency agreement is a personal service contract and will terminate upon death of either agent or principal. Bankruptcy results in the involuntary transfer of title to the receiver, so this will terminate the listing. Because the listing is a contract between the agent (broker) and the principal, what happens to the salesperson who obtained the listing will have no effect.

9. **C** For example, the fact the buyer is a veteran is usually not a material fact, except if the buyer is assuming a DVA loan. The salesperson is also liable for innocent misrepresentations (false statements made in ignorance or in good faith). Usually the salesperson is not a principal party to a transaction, such as buyer or seller.

10. **D** The broker has a fiduciary duty to protect the best interests of the client, which, in this case, would be to inform the owner of the true worth of the property and then discuss an appropriate listing price.

11. **C** Regardless of the order in which offers are received by the broker, the broker should present all written offers—even after an offer is accepted because it should be left up to the owner whether or not to accept a back-up contract. The broker plays a critical role in explaining the effect of an offer's contingencies, financing provisions, or time-is-of-the-essence clause.

12. **A**   The owner does not want to deal with intermediaries such as real estate agents.

13. **D**   The broker has the fiduciary duties of loyalty, care, obedience, skill, accountability and confidentiality.

14. **A**   Under the limited authority received in the standard listing contract, the broker cannot normally commit the principal to a sales contract (absent a power of attorney).

15. **C**   Failure to disclose material defects in property for sale could be grounds for misrepresentation by the agent (concealment of material fact) especially in view of the present consumer trend of the courts away from the former caveat emptor ("let the buyer beware") doctrine.

16. **A**   One of the fiduciary duties is to account for client monies. The agent can be liable for failure to reveal any pertinent fact about the property.

17. **C**   The appraiser is hired to render an independent evaluation of the property and is generally not entrusted with the client's properties nor authorized to act as an agent.

18. **D**   Practically speaking, in most states the parties rely on the broker, not an attorney, to protect them in their contract negotiations, especially regarding the financial commitments of the transaction (purchase contract terms such as price, financing, contingencies).

19. **B**   Although the broker and salesperson usually earn their commission when the contract is signed, payment of the commission is typically deferred until the sale is closed.

20. **B**   He or she is a very interested party who is held to a high standard of trust and confidence toward the principal's property.

21. **D**   The broker may waive any commission but cannot sue unless able to prove that he or she was licensed and employed by the owner (usually in writing).

22. **B**   As a general rule, the broker works on the seller's behalf to find ready, willing and able buyers. Under multiple-listing

service rules, a member broker may be presumed to be the subagent of the seller even though the seller has listed the property directly with another member broker.

23. **D**   You have a duty to treat all parties fairly, yet you owe your first and undivided loyalty to the seller. You should recommend that the buyer get assistance, so the buyer will be in an equal bargaining position. Otherwise, the buyer may try to cancel the contract later for alleged undue influence.

24. **B**   The written offer must be either on the listing terms or acceptable to the seller. Note, however, that it is less important for an agent to be the procuring cause in an exclusive-right-to-sell listing than in an open listing.

25. **D**   Any attempt to fix the rates by commission, local board, or groups of brokers would be in violation of state and federal antitrust laws.

26. **C**   It is a fiduciary relationship.

27. **D**   The salesperson has not been employed by the owner to sell the property. The owner has merely allowed the salesperson to arrange a convenient showing to a prospect.

28. **A**   The listing broker is the seller's agent. The licensed cooperating broker may represent either the seller as a subagent or the buyer as a buyer's agent; also called the selling agent.

29. **D**   The broker is placed in a special position of trust and confidence in this fiduciary management relationship.

30. **C**   The salesperson can receive money only from the broker; he or she can't take even a special bonus directly from the principal.

31. **B**   The broker would be breaching the duties of loyalty and confidentiality to reveal a price to a buyer other than that agreed upon by the owner in the listing or addendum. Rather than saying, "The property is listed at $100,000, but I know the owner will take $90,000," the broker should say, "The property is listed at

$100,000 and if you are going to submit an offer of less than that, I'll take the offer to the seller and see what he says."

32. **A** Such self-dealing action would violate fiduciary duty, since the agent-lender would have a conflict of interest.

33. **D** There is no limit on the amount of commission. Under most state license laws, the broker must give a copy of the listing at the time it is signed—failure to do so usually won't affect the right to a commission, but it might result in suspension or revocation of the license.

34. **B** Brokers can be principals for their own account. In such cases, they must disclose their license status.

35. **C** Even if the principal decided not to sign, the broker who was the procuring cause may have earned a commission if the offer matched the listing terms.

36. **C** Certain principal-agent relationships are fiduciary relationships. A seller is but one common example of a principal.

37. **C** A salesperson cannot receive compensation directly from anyone other than his or her broker.

38. **D** Many brokers use one client trust account, but have separate ledgers for each transaction.

39. **B** When the property is destroyed or when the purpose of the agency is accomplished, the listing terminates. This could be when a ready, willing and able buyer is produced with an offer at the listing terms or when the buyer's offer is accepted.

40. **C** An attorney-in-fact operates under a power of attorney. Under the equal dignities rule, this power should be in recordable form if the attorney is to sign the name of the principal to a recordable document such as a deed.

41. **B** The broker cannot withdraw money even though the commission has been earned.

42. **C** Courts will not force someone to perform a personal service agency contract; money damages will suffice to compensate for the breach.

43. **C** Undivided loyalty is the essence of the agency relationship.

44. **B** Trustor to beneficiary in a deed of trust is the relationship of debtor to creditor or borrower to lender.

45. **C** The contract may be voidable because of the actions of the principal's agents. For this reason it is important to select a competent and ethical agent. Need to prove broker failed to supervise (**NOT** automatic).

46. **B** This is a debtor-creditor relationship.

47. **C** The broker must disclose material facts to the buyer. Choice (A) is a material fact because the lender will require the buyer (borrower) to obtain federal flood insurance. Choice (B) is material because the concealment of a known building code violation amounts to fraud. Choice (C) however could involve a discrimination complaint based on steering.

48. **D** Because many legal questions are raised, this is an example of a situation in which the client or builder should be notified. The building discrepancy is a material fact that should not be disregarded.

49. **C** It is customary for a broker to delegate to the sales staff (as subagents of the principal) the performance of certain tasks, such as showing property or finding buyers.

50. **C** The seller should be told that the building department may have the power to force a removal of an illegal addition. Such a material fact must be disclosed to the buyer. If the seller orders the broker not to reveal this information, the broker may have to withdraw from the listing to avoid becoming a party to the concealment.

51. **D** An owner cannot violate federal and state anti-discrimination laws. Preparing one's own legal documents is permissible.

52. **A** The broker must then deposit the check into a client trust account or into escrow. Deposit checks cannot be made payable to the salesperson, who has no authority in this matter.

53. **C** Death terminates the agency power of attorney. Since the statute of frauds requires real estate sales contracts to be in writing, then, under the "equal dignities rule," the power of attorney must also be of the same dignity, that is, be in writing.

54. **D** If a broker decides to purchase property that is listed with the firm, it is essential to disclose in writing his or her true position. A straw man or intermediary cannot be used to buy for the broker in secret. The broker could lose his or her license for such self-dealing in obtaining secret profits.

55. **B** The power could be drafted for a period of longer than 90 days.

56. **C** The broker may not decide which offer would be the best to present to the seller.

57. **D** It is proper for the broker to accept land as commission, and there is no obligation to disclose to the client what becomes of the commission.

58. **C** The trustee in a deed of trust is a fiduciary who holds title to the secured property for the benefit of the beneficiary (lender). The trustor is the borrower.

59. **C** The power of attorney appoints the agent to perform those specified acts on behalf of the principal. In real property transactions, it is more appropriate to use a limited or special power of attorney rather than a general power of attorney.

60. **B** A broker can seek a money judgment against the seller but usually does not qualify as a laborer under the mechanic's lien law.

61. **C** Agents are not responsible for arranging financing, although they often use their skills to help their buyer-customer obtain needed financing on the best terms available.

62. **B** The use of the word *approximately* in citing land areas gives leeway for slight differences in square feet. The broker must disclose pertinent facts, such as the fact that because of zoning regulations the new buyer probably would not be able to make needed structural changes to the grocery store without risking loss of nonconforming use status. The building height is an obvious fact.

63. **D** A broker cannot quote a price less than the price authorized by the seller (usually the listing price) even though the broker knows the seller would accept. The broker has a duty of undivided loyalty and should encourage the buyer to make an offer, which the broker will transmit to the seller. The broker must transmit *all* written offers (not just the high ones) and let the seller make the final decision.

64. **C** The broker is not liable on the principal's contracts unless there are special facts involving misrepresentation. But if the broker fails to reveal his or her position as agent, then responsibility would fall to the broker for the contracts he or she signs. The broker may then seek damages against the undisclosed principal. Dual agency is permitted provided full disclosure is given and consent is obtained from the buyer and seller.

65. **D** Even in those states that permit oral listings, it is good practice to obtain such an employment agreement in writing to avoid disputes. A lawsuit is only necessary in those cases where a seller breaches the terms of an enforceable listing agreement.

66. **C** If a broker is guilty of misrepresentation, he or she may lose the right to a commission especially where the principal is an innocent party who suffers damage. To be entitled to a commission, the broker must be licensed at the time of the hiring and at the time of performance under the terms of the listing.

67. **B** The broker must try to immediately locate the seller to present offers as they are received. Since this is not always possible, the broker should keep the seller apprised of all offers received (or even ones that may be in the works). It would be improper practice to urge a seller to decide whether to accept or reject an offer before presenting other offers known to the broker.

68. **C** An attorney could best advise on the legal consequences of clauses such as prepayment, subordination or due on sale. (A) is an appraiser, (B) is a mortgage broker and (D) is a broker.

69. **C** A shared driveway could involve an encroachment or an easement and is the type of material fact that must be disclosed to the buyer, otherwise there could be a problem with unmarketable title or with misrepresentation. If a broker can't persuade the principal of the need to make this disclosure, the broker may have to refuse the listing so that he or she is not a party to a fraud. The broker must inform seller of all knowledge and offer recommendations. If the broker *already* has the listing, then choice (A) is a possibility.

70. **A** The use of the words "as is" does not protect the seller or broker from liability for misrepresentations due to concealment of material defects that can't be easily observed. In essence, this phrase informs the buyer that the seller intends to make no repairs to the obvious problems with the structure.

71. **A** It is sound advice to have the title searched to discover any defects. If the broker sees there are defects or if the client seeks information on the legal effect of various liens, the broker should refer the client to any attorney, since only an attorney is qualified to give legal advice. The listing broker should not discourage the buyer from seeking independent advice.

72. **C** Dual agency is permitted *provided* both buyer and seller give their informed consent in writing after full disclosure.

73. **B** The salesperson must not be compensated on a hourly basis. PB and BIC act in a supervisory capacity; also, secretary is an employee.

74. **C** The proper practice is to complete the essential portions of the agreement prior to the seller signing it.

75. **D** Most states do not recognize "middleman" status. In essence, *B* has to be someone's agent and he better disclose it early. A buyer's broker should reject the MLS offer of subagency; otherwise, a dual agency could arise.

76. **B** The written power of attorney must clearly show the intent to be *durable*.

77. **A** Licensing laws specifically exempts AIDS from material fact disclosure.

78. **B** The broker should not give professional advice unless the broker has the professional qualifications to do so and is willing to assume the risk.

Chapter 15   Listings

The questions in this chapter test your comprehension of the following topics:

- Types of listing contracts
- The multiple listing service
- Termination of listing agreements
- Responsibilities of the listing agent
- When a commission is earned

False Friends

The following words are often confused with one another. Note the difference in meaning of these false friends:

Exclusive Right to Sell/Exclusive Agency: The difference is that no commission is due under an exclusive agency if the seller finds the buyer.

QUESTIONS

1. In a multiple listing, a salesperson who negotiates a sale is directly responsible to:
   (A) the listing broker.
   (B) his or her employing broker.
   (C) the cooperating salesperson.
   (D) the seller.

❖ 2. A broker brought a buyer and seller together on a property deal and opened an escrow with a $500 deposit. Later the buyer and seller decided to rescind the contract and did so. How much commission would the broker earn?
   (A) $500   (C) Full commission
   (B) $1,250   (D) Nothing

❖ 3. A contract providing for the payment of a commission to the listing broker, no matter who sells the property, is called:
   (A) a net listing.
   (B) an open listing.
   (C) an exclusive-agency listing.
   (D) an exclusive-right-to-sell listing.

4. A listing contract will be terminated by all of the following EXCEPT:
   (A) destruction of the listed property.
   (B) death of the listing broker.
   (C) bankruptcy of the listing broker.
   (D) a sudden increase in market value.

5. When a broker gets a listing:
   (A) the listing should be prepared in writing.
   (B) any buyer must be furnished with a copy of the listing.
   (C) the seller may lawfully cancel it any time the seller decides the broker is not doing a good job.
   (D) there is no fiduciary relationship between a broker and the seller.

❖ 6. A property is listed with a broker at $65,000, although the broker is told that the owner will accept $62,000. A buyer prefers to sign an offer for $62,000, but indicates $65,000 could be offered. The broker should:
   (A) refuse to submit the $62,000 offer.
   (B) suggest a compromise of $63,500.
   (C) persuade the buyer to make a $65,000 offer.
   (D) persuade the buyer to go to another broker.

7. Except under specific conditions, an agent may serve only one principal at a time; however, a principal may contract to have more than one agent. Which of the following would BEST describe such a situation?
   (A) Multiple listing
   (B) Open listing
   (C) Exclusive agency
   (D) Exclusive right to sell

8. Under open listings, which of the following is true?
   (A) More than one broker may attempt to sell the listed property.
   (B) All brokers with open listings on the property will split the commission when the property is sold.
   (C) Each listing must be canceled in writing.
   (D) The listing must be submitted to the Multiple Listing Service.

9. A broker may provide for which of the following in an exclusive listing contract?
   (A) An automatic continuation of the term of the listing beyond the final termination date specified in the contract
   (B) Permission to post a sign on the property being listed
   (C) Permission for the salesperson to show the listing only to U.S. citizens
   (D) Permission to conceal presence of radon

❖ 10. Which of the following is true?
   (A) A broker must get the signatures of all owners on the listing form to be entitled to any commission.
   (B) A broker should not advertise without the written authorization of the owner.
   (C) A broker should place a sign on the property without written authority.
   (D) All other brokers showing the property must also have written authority to do so.

11. All of the following terminate an agency created by a listing EXCEPT:
   (A) insolvency of the listing broker.
   (B) fire destroying the listed property.
   (C) insanity of listing salesperson.
   (D) death of owner.

12. The listing contract creates:
    (A) a fiduciary agency relationship between broker and seller.
    (B) a special agency relationship between broker and salesperson.
    (C) an agency between the buyer and the seller.
    (D) an agency between the buyer and the broker showing the property.

❖ 13. Which of the following statements about listing brokers is true?
    (A) A listing broker can tell a prospective buyer that the seller will accept less than the asking price if the seller will, in fact, accept the lower figure.
    (B) A listing broker can refuse to transmit a "too-low" offer to the seller.
    (C) The broker only needs to present full price offers.
    (D) If the offer is not going to be full price, the broker should still encourage the buyer to make a written offer.

14. An agent for the seller is considered to have earned a commission:
    (A) only if a sale is completed and title is transferred.
    (B) if a purchaser is produced who is ready, willing and able to buy on terms acceptable to the purchaser.
    (C) when the agent presents a written offer if it is for full price, regardless of its terms.
    (D) if a binding contract to purchase is signed even if later the seller defaults, the broker is still entitled to a commission.

15. A salesperson holds two listings—an open listing on one property and an exclusive listing on another. Neither one contains a safety clause, and one week after both listings expire, the two owners get together and exchange properties without previously being shown the properties. The salesperson may:
    (A) sue for full commissions on both.
    (B) sue for commission on the open listing.
    (C) demand full commission on the exclusive listing.
    (D) receive no commission from either listing.

16. Which type of listing gives a broker the greatest protection?
    (A) Open listing
    (B) Net listing
    (C) Exclusive right to sell
    (D) Exclusive agency

17. When a broker has an exclusive-right-to-sell listing:
    (A) the seller may sell the property independently without the obligation to pay a commission.
    (B) the broker is entitled to a commission if a sale does not close due to the seller's fault.
    (C) only he or she is allowed to show or sell the property.
    (D) anything over the asking price is considered to be the broker's commission.

18. Under federal law, which of the following is prohibited?
    (A) Taking a net listing
    (B) Taking a listing in which the broker will receive all amounts of the purchase price in excess of an agreed amount
    (C) Signing a listing with more than one broker
    (D) Taking a listing that excludes sales to parents with children

19. After showing a listed property to a prospect, the broker with an exclusive-agency listing should:
    (A) make a record of it in the broker's files.
    (B) notify the seller of the prospect's identity.
    (C) send an office memo to the prospective buyer.
    (D) wait until the prospect makes a deal with seller.

20. To a real estate broker, the listing property owner is known as:
    (A) an agent.   (C) a prospect.
    (B) a fiduciary.   (D) a principal.

21. A copy of a listing agreement must:
    (A) be presented to the person signing the agreement.
    (B) include all the terms and conditions of the sale.
    (C) be given to the purchaser.
    (D) be given to the broker representing the purchaser.

22. An exclusive listing is terminated with no further liability by:
    (A) mutual agreement.
    (B) the principal's default.
    (C) the election of the seller.
    (D) the election of the broker.

23. In listing and marketing real property, it is important for the salesperson to do all of the following **EXCEPT** to:
    (A) check the survey stakes and boundaries.
    (B) determine who is in actual possession of the property.
    (C) select an escrow company to handle the closing.
    (D) obtain the signature of the seller(s).

24. To be enforceable, an open listing:
    (A) must have a specific termination date and be in writing.
    (B) must be signed by both buyer and seller.
    (C) must be canceled in writing by all listing brokers.
    (D) must state a specific asking price.

❖ 25. The owner of a property who signed a listing with a broker for 60 days was killed in an accident before the broker procured a buyer. This listing is:
    (A) binding upon owner's heirs to carry out the promises.
    (B) no good as an authorization, but binding if a buyer is secured later.
    (C) terminated immediately upon death.
    (D) still in effect as the owner's intent was clearly stated.

26. Death of either the principal or agent terminates:
    (A) the listing contract.
    (B) the contract for sale.
    (C) the deed.
    (D) the mortgage.

❖ 27. A broker can take part of the commission out of the client trust account prior to closing:
    (A) upon seller's permission.
    (B) provided there are enough funds left over to complete the closing.
    (C) anytime after the deposit is placed in escrow.
    (D) only upon written consent of the buyer and seller.

❖ 28. When a salesperson enters into a listing contract as agent of his or her broker, the salesperson must do all of the following **EXCEPT**:
    (A) execute the contract by signing the broker's name.
    (B) give a copy of the listing contract to the owner.
    (C) carefully explain all of the terms of the contract to the seller.
    (D) give a copy of the listing contract to the broker with whom the salesperson is associated.

❖ 29. A listing broker can do which of the following without written approval of the seller?
    (A) Buy the property directly from the seller/client and resell it immediately to a buyer for a higher price
    (B) Have a friend buy the property directly from the seller/client and resell it immediately to a buyer and split the profit with the friend
    (C) Quote a price considerably lower than that specified by the listing
    (D) Encourage a buyer to submit a written offer even if it doesn't match the asking price

30. In a typical real estate listing contract, the broker would be **BEST** described as:
    (A) a general agent.
    (B) a special agent.
    (C) the principal for the agent.
    (D) the principal for the subagent.

❖ 31. If the real property owner is a corporation, then the individual authorized to sign the listing agreement is:
    (A) the president.
    (B) the secretary.
    (C) the person named by corporate resolution.
    (D) the treasurer.

32. A listing held by a broker does not authorize acceptance of a deposit, but a purchaser is found who does give a deposit. The broker, solely for the purpose of holding the deposit, may retain it:
    (A) as the agent of the purchaser.
    (B) as the agent of the seller.
    (C) as the agent of the bank.
    (D) in the broker's personal bank account.

33. Which of the following statements about exclusive listings is true?
    (A) An exclusive-right-to-sell listing should be in writing.
    (B) An exclusive-agency contract can be terminated prior to the expiration date only by the sale of the property by the listing broker.
    (C) Death of the owner will not terminate it.
    (D) If the property is destroyed, the listing will still remain active.

34. When a broker has an exclusive-right-to-sell listing:
    (A) the seller may sell through his or her own efforts without obligation to pay a commission
    (B) the broker who procures a cash buyer on the listing terms is entitled to a commission regardless of whether the sale of the property is closed.
    (C) any price above the listed price goes to the broker.
    (D) the listing is given to more than one broker.

❖ 35. The type of listing in which the broker and seller are **LEAST** likely to know the amount of money that will be received as commission for the sale of the property is:
    (A) an open listing.
    (B) an exclusive authorization to sell.
    (C) a multiple listing.
    (D) a net listing.

36. A broker obtains an oral exclusive-right-to-sell listing for 13 months. The listing is usually:
    (A) valid.   (C) unenforceable.
    (B) binding.   (D) enforceable.

❖ 37. A broker has **MOST** likely earned a commission in which of the following cases?
    (A) Broker has communicated the acceptance of the seller to buyer.
    (B) Broker has obtained a substantial deposit with an offer.
    (C) Broker presents a written offer to the seller.
    (D) Broker finds a buyer who communicates an interest to pay the full asking price.

38. A seller has an exclusive-right-to-sell listing with one broker. Any offer from a prospective purchaser should be presented:
    (A) to the owner directly.
    (B) by the broker procuring the offer.
    (C) through the listing broker.
    (D) through a trustee.

39. The phrase "procuring cause" is **MOST** significant to a seller in relation to:
    (A) an exclusive agency.
    (B) an open listing.
    (C) an exclusive-right-to-sell listing.
    (D) a net listing.

❖ 40. Seller's broker was working with a buyer under an exclusive-authorization-to-sell listing and presented an offer at less than the listed price. At the same time, the owner was dealing with another buyer who offered more money for the property and all in cash. The owner sold to the buyer who paid all in cash at the higher price. The broker is entitled to:
    (A) a reasonable commission based upon the offer.
    (B) stop the sale of the property.
    (C) void the sale.
    (D) a commission based upon the higher selling price.

41. In the absence of a prior agreement as to when the broker's commission is earned, such commission is earned:
    (A) upon consummation of the deal.
    (B) upon a meeting of the minds of buyer and seller.
    (C) at the time the broker introduced buyer to seller.
    (D) when the deed is delivered.

42. An exclusive-right-to-sell listing contract does which of the following?
    (A) Provides that if the owner sells the property independently, the broker does not receive a commission
    (B) Terminates upon the death of the seller
    (C) Continues even if the owner or the broker goes through bankruptcy
    (D) Allows for verbal cancellation

❖ 43. After the sale, the listing broker refused to split the commission with the buyer's broker as agreed. Who is responsible to pay the buyer's broker?
(A) Listing salesperson
(B) Listing broker
(C) Seller
(D) Escrow service

44. The principal in the fiduciary relationship created by a listing agreement includes:
(A) the seller.
(B) the salesperson who got the listing.
(C) the broker.
(D) the buyer.

❖ 45. A broker secured a signed offer with a $5,000 deposit on the exact terms of a listing but the seller refused to accept it. Which of the following statements is true?
(A) The broker could maintain a suit for commission in court.
(B) The buyer could maintain a suit to force the seller to sell, since there was compliance with the listing.
(C) The broker should tell the seller that the seller must accept.
(D) The broker cannot collect a commission in excess of $5,000.

46. A broker can obtain a commission from both the buyer and seller in which case?
(A) With written permission of buyer and seller
(B) Under no circumstances
(C) When the broker holds the listing and then acts on behalf of the buyer in negotiating the purchase
(D) When the broker is working with a buyer who eventually buys a property listed in-house

47. A broker is holding an earnest money deposit, equal to the amount of the commission. The seller, at the closing, not only refuses to pay the broker a commission but also demands the broker pay him the entire deposit. The broker should:
(A) refuse to permit the closing of the deal.
(B) retain the earnest money as commission.
(C) file a complaint with the real estate licensing agency.
(D) pay the earnest money to the seller and then sue for commission.

48. The listing broker can usually show the buyer all of the following EXCEPT:
(A) subdivision map of the property.
(B) copy of the seller's recorded deed.
(C) listing contract.
(D) tax office data.

49. During the listing period under an exclusive-right-to-sell listing, the seller and buyer execute an option to purchase. If the option is not exercised until four months after the listing has expired, which is true?
(A) The broker has earned a commission based on the consideration paid for the option.
(B) The broker has earned a commission based on the purchase price.
(C) There is no commission earned for the option, only for the listing.
(D) The commission will be two full commissions earned for the listing and the sale on the option.

❖ 50. Which of the following statements about a listing is true?
(A) Having a listing in writing does not always give the broker the contractual right to take a deposit.
(B) The term "multiple listing" is the listing of the property with a number of different brokers.
(C) The broker earns a commission when the listing is signed.
(D) Once the seller signs the listing, the seller must pay the commission even if the seller doesn't like the terms of the offer.

51. Which is true concerning the printed words in a form listing contract?
(A) The parties may not cross out any of the printed words.
(B) Handwritten words take precedence over printed words if there is a conflict or inconsistency.
(C) Nothing may be added to the printed form except in those spaces that provide for such additions.
(D) If handwritten items are added, signatures must be acknowledged before a notary public.

52. The owner of a property gives broker an exclusive-right-to-sell listing. Broker produces a buyer who makes a full price cash offer without any contingencies. Which is true?
    (A) Broker has earned a commission even if the owner refuses to accept the offer.
    (B) Owner cannot refuse the offer.
    (C) The broker earns the commission only if the offer is accepted.
    (D) If the owner refuses the offer, the buy can sue for specific performance.

❖ 53. If a buyer presents a broker with an offer at the full listing price contingent upon financing:
    (A) the broker has earned commission.
    (B) the broker, provided so authorized in writing by the seller, could accept the offer and bind the principal.
    (C) the buyer is obligated to buy even if the contingency is not satisfied.
    (D) contingencies have no effect on the potential of the broker earning a commission.

54. Before visiting an owner of property in order to obtain a listing, a real estate licensee should do which of the following?
    (A) Perform a competitive market analysis
    (B) Order a formal appraisal from a bank
    (C) Have a completely signed contract
    (D) Obtain a title insurance policy

55. When a broker is preparing to take a listing on a residential house, he or she would find it helpful to do all of the following **EXCEPT**:
    (A) gather recent data on sales in the area.
    (B) consider the availability of mortgage funds.
    (C) obtain any relevant data from the available public records.
    (D) consider the seller's religious preference.

56. A listing broker inspects the property and discovers a shared driveway. The listing broker should reveal this fact on all of the following contracts **EXCEPT**:
    (A) the listing.
    (B) the offer to purchase.
    (C) the broker's agreement to split commission.
    (D) an option to buy the property.

❖ 57. In an exclusive listing with a 120-day expiration period, the owner sells the property to one of the broker's previous referrals on the 121st day. What commission is the broker entitled to receive?
    (A) None   (C) 75 percent
    (B) 50 percent   (D) Full

58. A person gives an option to sell while an exclusive right to sell is still in effect. The optionee exercises his or her option four months after the listing expires. Which one of the following regarding the broker's commission is correct?
    (A) The broker is not entitled to his or her commission since the sale takes place after the listing expires.
    (B) The broker is not entitled to his or her commission because he or she is given only an exclusive right to sell and not an option.
    (C) The broker is entitled to his or her commission because the option to sell was signed during the term of the listing.
    (D) The broker is entitled to his or her commission only if he or she had shown the property to the person who exercised the option.

ANSWERS

1. **B** Salespeople, as subagents, are always directly responsible to the broker who holds their licenses, whether their broker is the listing or the selling broker.

2. **C** Because the broker produced a ready, willing and able buyer, the commission established in the listing agreement has been earned.

3. **D** The commission is owed if the sale is produced "by me, by you or by anyone else." Under an exclusive agency listing, no commission is owed if the seller finds the buyer. Under an open listing, the broker must be the procuring cause.

4. **D** While the sudden increase wouldn't terminate the listing, a prudent broker would discuss with the owner the benefits of increasing the listing price and extending the term of the listing.

5. **A** It is good business practice to get the listing in writing even in those states where this is not required under either the statute of frauds or the licensing law. In choice (B), the listing is a private contract between broker and seller.

6. **C** The broker has a fiduciary duty to the principal (seller) to obtain the best possible price. Although the broker is ethically bound to treat all parties fairly, this does not mean the broker must make sure the buyer gets outside advice or representation.

7. **B** Only the agent under an open listing who is the "procuring cause" will be entitled to the commission. Under a multiple listing, there is only one listing contract and only one agent; the cooperating broker would be a subagent working with the listing broker.

8. **A** The agent with an open listing who proves to be the "procuring cause" of the sale will be entitled to the full commission; the others will get nothing. Disputes often arise as to who is the real procuring cause. The MLS generally does not take open listings.

9. **B** Courts disfavor automatic extension provisions in listings, especially since many unsophisticated sellers end up having to pay two commissions. For example, an owner thinks the 90-day listing has expired and so signs a new listing with Broker 2. When Broker 2 finds the buyer, Broker 1 also claims a commission under the earlier exclusive listing that ethnically had never been canceled in writing by the owner. Radon is a material fact the broker must disclose to the buyer.

10. **B** If one cotenant signed the listing, most courts will imply a promise by the signing tenant to obtain the authorization of the other cotenant. If later, when the broker produces a buyer, and the tenant can't get the authorization, then the broker can still get a commission from the signing cotenant. Prudent brokers, however, should take extra steps to protect themselves in these situations. Many states require written authorization for the broker to advertise, and it is good business practice to obtain this written permission in the listing.

11. **C** The agency agreement is between the owner and the broker, so the death or insanity of the salesperson would not affect the listing.

12. **A** The listing contract is between the seller and broker; the salesperson is a subagent under the broker and is authorized to perform certain tasks in accomplishing the purposes of the listing.

13. **D** Unless authorized by the seller, the broker may not quote a price other than that authorized in writing, even if the broker knows the seller would accept the lower price. The broker should encourage the buyer to submit an offer, which can then be discussed with the seller. The broker must submit all written offers for the seller's consideration.

14. **D** If the agent produced an acceptable buyer and later the buyer and seller decide to cancel the agreement, the broker has still earned commission. Choice (B) is false because the offer must match the listing or be on terms acceptable to the seller, not just to the purchaser.

15. **D** Because the listings had terminated and there is no mention of any safety clause (which would extend the term to cover any buyers registered with the owner), the salesperson is entitled to nothing.

16. **C** Under an exclusive-right-to-sell listing, the broker gets a commission regardless of who is the procuring cause, even if it is the seller who finds the buyer during the listing term.

17. **B** Only under an exclusive-agency listing (or open listing) would the seller not be obligated to pay a commission. If the seller is at fault (delivering an unmarketable title), then the broker has the right to sue. (Some brokers elect not to sue due to potential bad publicity.)

18. **D** Net listings are not prohibited by federal law, but they are illegal in some states. They are generally frowned upon (it would be easy to take advantage of unsophisticated sellers). Choice (D) violates Federal Fair Housing law.

19. **B** The broker will often send a registered or certified letter to the seller to prove the buyer was found by the broker. A memo in the broker's files does little good in establishing the fact that the seller knew this buyer had worked with the broker. This method helps prevent the seller from asserting that he or she found the buyer.

20. **D** The buyer is the prospect or customer and the broker is the agent or fiduciary.

21. **A** The broker must give a copy at the time the signature is obtained. While the general limits of the acceptable terms of sale may be outlined, it is usually the offer that details the actual terms and conditions of the sale.

22. **A** The parties to a contract usually may terminate it by mutual agreement, but default will trigger the remedy provisions of the contract.

23. **C** By locating the stakes, the salesperson might discover any obvious encroachment problems. It also should be ascertained if those parties in possession are just tenants or if they might be claiming some superior title to the premises. Selecting an escrow company or settlement agent should be left to the buyer and/or seller.

24. **D** The open listing is an employment agreement between broker and seller. Unlike exclusive listings, it does not need a specific termination date.

25. **C** Under general agency principles, death terminates an executory listing agreement.

26. **A** Death does not usually discharge contractual rights or obligations, except for personal service contracts, such as listings.

27. **D** The broker cannot touch the monies in the client trust account for a transaction unless both buyer and seller consent in writing to such a draw on the commission earned. This rule is designed to protect the parties in the event the deal is not consummated.

28. **A** The salesperson should not use the broker's name unless authorized in writing.

29. **D** These actions appear to violate the agent's duty to avoid secret profits in the real estate transactions of his principal. The fact the resale in choice (B) was immediate leaves little room for the broker to argue that the best interests of the principal were being served.

30. **B** The broker has limited authority specifically to find a ready, willing and able buyer on the listing terms. He or she does not have the authority to sign contracts binding the principal unless a power of attorney is held.

31. **C** The corporate resolution will reflect the fact that the board of directors has authorized the transaction and has designated the person(s) authorized to sign.

32. **A** A broker's authority is limited to finding a ready, willing and able buyer unless the owner expands that authority in the listing to include taking deposit money. Because this common-law rule appears quite unfair to the unknowing buyer, many listings include the authority to accept deposit money in their standard listing language. Without such authority, the listing agent is only a buyer's agent for the purpose of holding the deposit.

33. **A** Many states require exclusive-right-to-sell listings to be in writing to avoid disputes. The exclusive-agency contract could be terminated by mutual agreement, death or sale by the owner.

34. **B** The broker is entitled to a commission even if the seller is the procuring cause. Unless expressed or implied otherwise, earning the commission is not dependent on closing (especially if the seller is at fault in failing to close).

35. **D**   In a net listing, the broker will receive any amounts in excess of an agreed sales price; it could be nothing or it could be substantial.

36. **C**   If the state's statute of frauds requires the listing to be in writing, then an oral listing is unenforceable. Also, contracts that may not be performed within one year often must be in writing.

37. **A**   Under choice (A), there is now an accepted contract so it would not even matter if the sales price were less than the listing price, as it could be in choice (B).

38. **C**   The terms of the listing usually provide that all offers should be presented through the listing broker; the cooperating broker should avoid going directly to the owner.

39. **B**   The only broker entitled to the commission under an open listing is the one who is the procuring cause of the sale; this is not a requirement under exclusive listings, which might also be net listings.

40. **D**   Under the exclusive-authorization-to-sell listing, the broker earns commission based on the sales price regardless of who is the procuring cause of the sale.

41. **B**   The broker earns commission by procuring a buyer on the listing terms or on terms acceptable to the seller. In this case, the buyer and seller would have reached a mutually agreeable contract upon the meeting of the minds. Even if the deal were not consummated because of the seller, the broker has already earned the stated commission.

42. **B**   If it was an exclusive-agency listing, then the owner could sell and pay no commission. Death terminates personal service agency contracts such as listings.

43. **B**   The agreement to split any commission is between the listing broker and the buyer's broker. While the statute of frauds does not typically require this agreement to be in writing, the prudent broker will be sure it is done.

44. **A**   The principals to the listing agreement are the seller and the salesperson's broker, but the principal in the fiduciary relationship is the seller. The broker is the agent, and the salesperson is the subagent. The salesperson works for the broker.

45. **A**   The seller can be sued based on full performance by the listing broker, based on the agreed percentage of the listing price. The seller, however, is under no obligation to accept any offer, but is obligated to compensate a performing broker.

46. **A**   The broker must be careful to give both parties full written disclosure of a double compensation and obtain their approval. Such a practice is common in tax-deferred exchanges.

47. **D**   The broker has a fiduciary duty of obedience and a duty to account for all the client's monies. He or she cannot use client monies to set off or satisfy personal claims. A lawsuit may be the only answer.

48. **C**   The listing agreement is a confidential contract between the seller and the broker. Because it may contain some inaccurate information, the best procedure is to verify all material data and present them to the buyer in a separate fact sheet.

49. **B**   Most listings entitle a broker to a full commission on the exercise of an option that was entered into during the term of the listing. There will be one commission, which will be paid when the property is sold (to the buyer under the option). This will be split if there are two brokers, one representing the seller on the listing and another representing the buyer under the option. If there is only one broker acting for both parties, he or she will retain the entire commission, but will receive no more than that.

50. **A**   The right to take a deposit on the seller's behalf must be specified in the listing. This well illustrates the limited scope of authority of an agent under the standard listing. Also, the broker can't sign

contracts on behalf of the seller. There is just one exclusive listing in a multiple-listing situation and this listing is "pooled" among member brokers of the multiple-listing service. The commission is earned when the seller accepts a written offer at any price or refuses a full price offer that was for the terms and conditions specified in the listing.

51. **B**   The parties frequently cross out and initial inappropriate form language. Handwritten terms supersede printed words on the theory the parties have modified the form.

52. **A**   Broker has performed under the terms of the listing. Owner is under no obligation to the buyer to accept the offer, although still liable for the broker's commission. Owner may decide it would be better to reject the offer if the property has dramatically increased in value or if he or she is now unsure about selling. The buyer has no legal right to demand that the seller accept the offer. Only the broker can sue, and only for the amount of the commission.

53. **B**   On a contingent offer, the broker has not earned commission until the contingency is satisfied or waived. Although the usual listing gives the broker only limited authority, some sellers may add authority for their brokers to bind them to contracts (e.g., under a power of attorney).

54. **A**   Bank appraisals are not needed at the time of listing, especially where an experienced licensee can prepare an accurate comparable analysis using the market comparison approach.

55. **D**   Recent sales data will help in determining a comparable price for listing, and mortgage availability information is useful to foresee whether the seller might have to negotiate seller carryback financing with the buyer. Public information such as tax assessments, recorded zoning, setbacks and so on would be useful and may be needed by the buyer in making his or her decision to buy. A survey at that time would be premature and perhaps unnecessary.

56. **C**   The listing contract should detail all material facts concerning the property—the time of listing is the time to discover if there will be any encumbrances or defects. Naturally, this fact should be disclosed in writing to the buyer since the shared driveway could be an encroachment or involve an easement. Material facts should also be disclosed on the offer to purchase and the option to buy.

57. **A**   Unless the listing has a "safety clause," the broker gets nothing because the listing is terminated. Most safety or extender clauses allow a commission if the property is sold to a prior referral within a set period of time.

58. **C**   The buyer was found during the listing period. Note that there would be no full commission if the option was not exercised.

Chapter 16   Sales Contracts and Options

The questions in this chapter test your comprehension of the following topics:

- The essential elements of a valid contract
- The enforceability of contracts
- Default and remedies
- Use of options in real estate transactions
- Typical provisions in sales contracts
- Use of an earnest money deposit

False Friends

The following words are often confused with one another. Note the difference in meaning of these false friends:

Down Payment/Deposit: The down payment is the money required from the buyer to pay the purchase price in addition to the financing. It consists of the deposit money the buyer paid to demonstrate good intention to complete the purchase.

Executed/Executory: An executory contract is one that still needs to be performed, whereas an executed contract has been completed.

Option/Right of First Refusal: An option is a right to purchase property at a set price, whereas a right of first refusal is a right to purchase property only if it is offered for sale in the future.

Rescission/Restriction: Rescission is the remedy upon breach of contract in which the parties return to their respective positions before the contract (return to the status quo), whereas restriction is some limitation placed on the use of the property.

Unilateral/Bilateral: A unilateral contract involves one promise to perform (option contract), whereas a bilateral contract involves mutual promises to perform (as in a sales contract).

Void/Voidable: A void contract lacks the essential elements to be valid, whereas a voidable contract is valid except one of the parties has the ability to void it because of some wrongdoing.

Optionor/Optionee: The seller (optionor) gives the buyer (optionee) the right to purchase the property in return for the buyer paying option money.

Statute of Frauds/Statute of Limitations: The statute of frauds requires certain contracts to be in writing to be enforceable, whereas the statute of limitations sets time limits on the ability to file a lawsuit to enforce a right.

QUESTIONS

1. When withdrawing an offer to purchase before it is accepted by the seller, the offeror is first entitled to a refund of the deposit at which of the following times?
   (A) After the buyer obtains a court order
   (B) Immediately
   (C) After seller has had an opportunity to accept the agreement and declines
   (D) After the broker deducts earned commission

2. Certain elements must first be found in a real estate sales contract involving a single-family residence for it to be valid. Although the following elements are recommended, which one is NOT an absolute necessity?
   (A) Description of land
   (B) Type of deed
   (C) Names of the parties
   (D) Sales price

3. B agreed to build a house and sell it to H in 180 days. H agreed to pay the negotiated price within 45 days after completion. The contract, before completion of the house, may be referred to as:
   (A) an executory contract.
   (B) an implied contract.
   (C) a voidable contract.
   (D) an executed contract.

❖ 4. All of the following are an essential element of every real estate sales contract EXCEPT:
   (A) acknowledgment.
   (B) legality of object.
   (C) consideration.
   (D) reality of consent.

5. To be enforceable in court, a sales contract must have:
   (A) an earnest money deposit.
   (B) competent parties.
   (C) an acknowledgment.
   (D) a witness.

6. A contract in which H agrees to purchase C's real estate in 60 days is:
   (A) an option.   (C) a deed.
   (B) a lease.   (D) a contract of sale.

7. A sales agreement must contain which of the following?
   (A) Mortgage loan
   (B) Offer and an acceptance
   (C) Date of the offer
   (D) Legal description of the property

❖ 8. Which term BEST describes a court order to carry out the terms of a signed real estate sales contract?
   (A) Specific performance
   (B) Lis pendens
   (C) Attachment
   (D) Subpoena

9. A vendee is BEST described as one who:
   (A) sells or offers to sell.
   (B) buys or offers to buy.
   (C) loans money.
   (D) borrows money.

10. If it is to be a bilateral contract, the listing must be signed by:
   (A) buyer and seller.
   (B) seller and broker.
   (C) husband and wife.
   (D) buyer.

11. If you lost your home in a bankruptcy proceeding, you could recover your property by:
   (A) court action.
   (B) repurchase.
   (C) an automatic one-year right to repurchase.
   (D) the right to redemption.

12. A real estate contract signed by an unmarried minor is:
   (A) void.   (C) unenforceable.
   (B) voidable.   (D) indefeasible.

13. A novation is BEST defined as:
   (A) the substitution of one party for another in a contract wherein both the original parties remain liable.
   (B) the substitution of one party for another in a contract wherein the original contract is extinguished and the undertaking of the new party is a new obligation.
   (C) the same as an assignment.
   (D) a means of acquiring title by adverse possession.

14. Buyer and seller agree to the purchase of a house for $200,000 in which the buyer will make a $30,000 down payment and the seller will take back a ten-year purchase money mortgage for the balance. The sales contract usually will be valid even though the parties fail to provide for which of the following?
    - (A) Closing date
    - (B) Interest rate
    - (C) Sales price
    - (D) Signature of buyer and seller

15. Upon the seller's default, what should happen to the hand money or earnest money?
    - (A) It belongs to the broker.
    - (B) It should be returned to the buyer.
    - (C) It should be placed in an escrow fund.
    - (D) It should be retained by the seller.

16. Which of the following statements about certain provisions in a purchase agreement is true?
    - (A) "Time is of the essence" means there is a periodic tenancy.
    - (B) The agreement is voidable if the closing date is omitted.
    - (C) To accept the property "as is" means to accept obvious as well as hidden defects.
    - (D) If the sale is contingent upon the happening, or nonhappening, of some event, it must be stated in writing in the contract.

17. Which of the following constitutes a rejection of an offer?
    - (A) Mistake of law
    - (B) Lapse of time
    - (C) Counteroffer
    - (D) Mistake of fact

18. Which of the following phrases is out of place with the other phrases?
    - (A) Valuable consideration
    - (B) Offer and acceptance
    - (C) Words of conveyance
    - (D) Reality of consent

19. Buyer made an offer at less than the asking price. Seller then made a counteroffer. Buyer would not accept the counteroffer. If seller then agreed to accept the first offer, which of the following statements about the transaction is true?
    - (A) The buyer was legally bound to complete the deal.
    - (B) The broker had earned a commission.
    - (C) The buyer was released from the offer when the seller made a counteroffer.
    - (D) The broker is liable if the contract is unenforceable.

20. The law that bars legal claims after certain periods of time is known as:
    - (A) statute of frauds.
    - (B) statute of limitations.
    - (C) Administrative Procedures Act.
    - (D) real estate law.

21. An oral contract to lease real estate for a four-year period is:
    - (A) voidable.
    - (B) unilateral.
    - (C) void.
    - (D) unenforceable

22. A contract of sale cannot exist without an offer and which one of the following?
    - (A) An assignment
    - (B) A mortgage
    - (C) An assessment
    - (D) An acceptance

23. When a prospective buyer is in the locality and able to inspect the property, the prospect ordinarily has a right to rely on the broker's representations as to:
    - (A) future value of the property.
    - (B) nothing the broker says.
    - (C) everything the broker says.
    - (D) concealed details of construction of the building.

24. An indefeasible contract is one that:
    - (A) cannot be voided.
    - (B) is void.
    - (C) is voidable.
    - (D) is unenforceable.

25. A real estate sales contract will usually be terminated by:
    - (A) death of either party.
    - (B) delivery of the deed.
    - (C) assignment.
    - (D) either party changing his or her mind.

❖ 26. A written and signed real estate contract can be voided for which of the following reasons?
   (A) One of the parties failed to read the instrument before signing it.
   (B) One of the parties was an unmarried minor when the contract was signed.
   (C) One of the parties becomes sick.
   (D) The buyer fails to include a Social Security number.

27. The legal remedy **MOST** likely used by the seller upon abandonment and default by the buyer under a recorded contract of sale is:
   (A) trustee's sale.
   (B) lis pendens action.
   (C) partition action.
   (D) quiet title suit.

❖ 28. A buyer withdraws a written offer before the seller has signed. What is the broker's position in the transaction?
   (A) Broker splits earnest money with seller.
   (B) Broker charges commission later.
   (C) Broker gets nothing.
   (D) Broker is entitled to expenses.

29. An assignment of property rights in a real estate sales contract constitutes:
   (A) a lease.   (C) a lien.
   (B) an encumbrance.   (D) a conveyance.

30. A clause in a sales contract or a mortgage that requires punctual performance is described as:
   (A) specific performance.
   (B) time is of the essence.
   (C) escalation.
   (D) subrogation.

31. Which of the following is true concerning an assignable option?
   (A) It can be valid without a consideration.
   (B) It can be passed on to another.
   (C) It is binding only upon the assignor.
   (D) The assignment may be oral.

32. If the optionee dies prior to the exercise of the option, the option is:
   (A) terminated.   (C) valid.
   (B) voidable.   (D) unenforceable.

33. Which of the following terms is **LEAST** related to the other three?
   (A) Vendor   (C) Lender
   (B) Grantor   (D) Seller

34. Unless there are certain provisions to the contrary, the terms of the contract usually:
   (A) are not binding after closing because the terms of the contract are merged into the deed.
   (B) are enforceable after closing.
   (C) bind the lender as well as the buyer and seller.
   (D) are voidable at closing.

35. If fire destroys a home after the contract of sale is signed by both parties, but prior to closing, all of the following is true under the Uniform Vendors and Purchasers Risk Act **EXCEPT**:
   (A) The party in possession generally bears the risk of loss.
   (B) The seller bears the risk of loss if in possession and holding legal title at the time of the loss.
   (C) The buyer assumes responsibility upon signing the sales contract.
   (D) Responsibility generally passes to the buyer upon closing or occupancy whichever occurs first.

36. Which of the following is an essential element of any contract?
   (A) Written instrument
   (B) Words of conveyance
   (C) Consideration
   (D) Acknowledgment

❖ 37. The phrase "time is of the essence" means:
   (A) the buyer is in a hurry to take possession.
   (B) the closing must be held in a hurry.
   (C) things required to be accomplished by dates set forth in the agreement must be done on or before those dates.
   (D) time is unimportant.

38. If, after the signing of the contract for sale of land and before the closing, the seller dies, which of the following is true?
   (A) The contract is voidable at the option of the seller's representative.
   (B) The contract is voidable at the option of the buyer.
   (C) The deal is terminated by operation of law.
   (D) The death of the seller normally does not terminate the contract.

39. When a contract's terms have not been fully performed, it is known as:
   (A) an executed contract.
   (B) an executory contract.
   (C) a unilateral contract.
   (D) a bilateral contract.

❖ 40. The statute of frauds, as applied to real estate sales contracts, requires all of the following EXCEPT:
   (A) All contracts for the sale of real property, in order to be enforceable, must be in writing.
   (B) Such contracts must be signed by the party to be charged thereby.
   (C) Oral contracts are valid and enforceable.
   (D) Contracts for leases over three years must be in writing.

❖ 41. If an option contract is duly executed by seller and buyer, which of the following is true?
   (A) The owner may or may not sell.
   (B) The buyer must buy.
   (C) The owner must sell, but the buyer need not buy.
   (D) It is specifically enforceable by both parties.

42. The term "merchantable title" (or marketable title) means:
   (A) the title has no defects.
   (B) the seller can transfer interest by deed.
   (C) an abstract certified to date can be prepared.
   (D) the title appears to be reasonably free of unacceptable defects.

43. If the buyer withdraws an offer before it has been accepted, the deposit money goes:
   (A) one-half to broker and one-half to buyer.
   (B) all to the buyer.
   (C) all to the seller.
   (D) all to the broker.

44. A portion of a printed form contract is changed by typing in contrary provisions, which are then initialed by both parties. Which takes precedence?
   (A) Printing over typing
   (B) Neither—the contract is voidable because of the changes
   (C) Typing over printing
   (D) Neither—the parties may void the contract because of the change

45. All of the following are considered contracts EXCEPT:
   (A) mortgage.   (C) lis pendens.
   (B) net listing.   (D) escrow agreement.

❖ 46. Reality of consent in a contract means all of the following EXCEPT:
   (A) The terms of the contract must express the true intention of the parties.
   (B) The parties' consent to the contract must be genuinely given.
   (C) Both parties give their consent at closing.
   (D) Both parties are certain and clear about what is being offered and what is being accepted.

47. A contract for the sale of real estate is:
   (A) an executed agreement.
   (B) an expected agreement.
   (C) an executory agreement.
   (D) an anticipatory agreement.

48. In connection with a contract for the sale of real estate, a rider is:
   (A) an addendum.   (C) a lien.
   (B) a subrogation.   (D) a contract.

49. The phrase "time is of the essence" is most likely to be stated or implied in which of the following contracts?
   (A) Exclusive authorization and right to sell
   (B) Real estate receipt for deposit
   (C) Grant deed
   (D) Option

50. In the usual home purchase transaction, the offeror is MOST likely to be:
   (A) the vendee.   (C) the mortgagee.
   (B) the trustee.   (D) the lienee.

51. Where a contract of sale fails to mention the existence of a mortgage on the land, but there is such a mortgage, which of the following is true?
   (A) Seller can compel the buyer to complete the deal.
   (B) The signing of the contract of sale automatically makes the mortgage void.
   (C) The buyer has the right to demand a title free and clear of the mortgage.
   (D) The buyer must take title subject to the mortgage.

❖ 52. Which of the following statements concerning the assignment of sales contract is correct?
(A) The assignment of rights may be made only by the original seller.
(B) Sales contracts generally may be assigned.
(C) The contract becomes binding only upon the assignor.
(D) All contracts are assignable.

53. Prospective purchasers of property, as evidence of good faith, frequently make a deposit called:
(A) consideration.
(B) earnest money.
(C) collateral security.
(D) deferred purchase money trust.

54. The name of a contract that permits an investor to purchase property or not, for a stated sum within a limited period of time is known as:
(A) an assignment.
(B) an option.
(C) a deposit receipt.
(D) an agreement of sale.

❖ 55. In an option, the optionee is:
(A) the legal owner of record.
(B) the prospective purchaser.
(C) the assignor.
(D) the assignee.

56. When buyer and seller enter into a definite written purchase agreement with no special conditions except that no closing date is specified, the contract normally is:
(A) void for vagueness.
(B) voidable.
(C) enforceable.
(D) not acceptable by law.

57. Usually the right to declare a forfeiture of deposit money for breach of contract belongs to:
(A) the buyer.   (C) the lender.
(B) the seller.   (D) the broker.

58. The withdrawal of an offer before acceptance is called:
(A) reversion.   (C) rejection.
(B) rescission.   (D) revocation.

59. A licensed real estate broker who holds an option on a property must notify the prospective purchaser that he or she is:
(A) the optionee.   (C) the tenant.
(B) the optionor.   (D) the lessee.

❖ 60. Acceptance of a sales contract is accomplished when:
(A) the salesperson signs the sales contract.
(B) the offeree signs the sales contract.
(C) the offeror signs the sales contract.
(D) the broker signs the sales contract.

61. The granting of an option to purchase a farm requires all of the following **EXCEPT**:
(A) the holding of a real estate license.
(B) a valuable consideration to the optionor.
(C) that the contract be in writing to be enforceable.
(D) that the optionor sell if the option is exercised.

62. Under the statute of frauds, all contracts for the sale of real estate must be in writing. The principal reason for this statute is to:
(A) prevent the buyer from defrauding the seller.
(B) prevent perjury and fraudulent proof of a fictitious oral contract.
(C) protect the buyer from the broker.
(D) protect the general public from fraud due to unrecorded deeds.

❖ 63. A prospective purchaser has a legal right to demand which of the following?
(A) A copy of the broker's employment contract with the seller
(B) The return of the earnest money deposit prior to the seller's acceptance of the offer to purchase
(C) Copies of any offers from other interested buyers
(D) A copy of any appraisal that was previously done on the property

64. Assume that a contract to purchase for cash is signed by the unmarried seller and by *S* only as buyer. The tenancy is to be tenancy by the entirety. The contract is:
(A) enforceable.   (C) voidable.
(B) void.   (D) unenforceable.

65. Which of the following would be considered **MOST** like an offer to sell in a real estate transaction?
   - (A) Listing
   - (B) Advertisement
   - (C) Option
   - (D) Power of attorney

66. All of the following are a contract **EXCEPT:**
   - (A) closing statement.
   - (B) trust deed.
   - (C) listing.
   - (D) mortgage.

❖ 67. When a seller rejects an offer:
   - (A) such rejection should be noted on the offer by the seller or broker and a copy returned to the prospective buyer.
   - (B) it constitutes a counteroffer.
   - (C) the buyer will forfeit any deposit submitted with the offer.
   - (D) the broker is still entitled to a commission.

68. Undue influence on the part of a salesperson in obtaining a sales contract may result in all of the following **EXCEPT:**
   - (A) the contract being declared voidable by the injured party.
   - (B) revocation of the salesperson's license.
   - (C) automatic suspension of the broker's license.
   - (D) termination of employment of the salesperson with the broker.

69. All of the following statements are true regarding a buyer's deposit on an offer to purchase **EXCEPT:**
   - (A) The buyer can rightfully demand full repayment if he or she withdraws the offer prior to seller's acceptance.
   - (B) The deposit is subject to forfeiture to the seller in the event the buyer fails to consummate the accepted agreement.
   - (C) It must accompany an offer.
   - (D) It is recommended but not essential with a contract to purchase property.

70. In preparing an offer to purchase real estate, a broker should include provisions relating to all of the following **EXCEPT:**
   - (A) existing leases on the property.
   - (B) methods of financing the purchase.
   - (C) household items to include in the sale.
   - (D) terms and provisions of the seller's existing mortgage.

❖ 71. Which is true concerning an earnest money deposit?
   - (A) It serves as a source of payment of damages to the seller in case of a buyer's breach.
   - (B) It is essential to the contract for the sale of real property.
   - (C) It must equal ten percent of the purchase price.
   - (D) It may be kept by the broker as compensation if the offer is accepted.

72. Where money is actually paid as consideration for an option to purchase real property, the option:
   - (A) cannot be assigned by the optionee.
   - (B) must be in writing to be enforceable.
   - (C) is binding only on the optionee.
   - (D) may be withdrawn by the optionee.

73. In the typical real estate transaction, before a sales contract has been signed by the offeree, the earnest money belongs to:
   - (A) the broker.
   - (B) the offeree.
   - (C) the escrow.
   - (D) the offeror.

74. A nonnegotiable note used as an earnest money deposit with an offer to purchase is acceptable with the permission of whom?
   - (A) Broker
   - (B) Vendee
   - (C) Salesperson
   - (D) Vendor

75. If while an offer has been accepted and is in escrow prior to the closing date, the settlement officer discovers a cloud on the title and notifies the parties, the buyer can do all of the following **EXCEPT:**
   - (A) sue to quiet title.
   - (B) accept the title with the cloud.
   - (C) immediately refuse the deal and demand a refund of all monies.
   - (D) demand that the seller remove the cloud prior to closing.

76. When an offer is contingent on the buyer procuring a certain mortgage, the offer should state all of the following **EXCEPT:**
   - (A) the amount of the loan to be procured.
   - (B) the time period within which the buyer can procure the mortgage.
   - (C) the clauses to be included in the mortgage document.
   - (D) the maximum interest of the loan.

77. Riders in a real estate sales contract are valid in all the following cases **EXCEPT**:
    (A) only when incorporated with the original contract by reference.
    (B) only if signed or initialed by both parties.
    (C) even if obtained by fraud.
    (D) even if handwritten.

78. One of the principal purposes of the statute of frauds is to:
    (A) eliminate the perjury and fraud that may occur in trying to prove oral contracts.
    (B) set a time limit within which a lawsuit may be filed or barred.
    (C) regulate personal property transfers.
    (D) control the sale of business opportunities.

79. A present unconditional offer to perform is known as:
    (A) a tender.
    (B) a discharge.
    (C) a forfeiture.
    (D) a satisfaction.

❖ 80. A rescission of a contract is:
    (A) a ratification.
    (B) a return to the status quo.
    (C) an amendment to the terms of a contract.
    (D) an escrow arrangement.

81. An optionee in the usual real estate transaction has which of the following rights?
    (A) To collect rents during the option period
    (B) To legally enforce the exercise of the options even if the optionor no longer wishes
    (C) To occupy the property during the option period
    (D) To grant right-of-way easements across property

82. When there is a "meeting of the minds" which of the following has been accomplished?
    (A) Offer and acceptance
    (B) Satisfaction of the contract's major terms
    (C) Settlement has been held
    (D) Acknowledgment and delivery

83. Any of the following is normal method to discharge a contract **EXCEPT**:
    (A) divorce of either party.
    (B) operation of law.
    (C) agreement.
    (D) performance.

84. If an illiterate person signs a contract:
    (A) the contract is void.
    (B) the contract is presumed valid unless fraud can be proven.
    (C) the contract is voidable at the illiterate's option unless it was fully read aloud.
    (D) the contract is voidable at the illiterate's option if illiteracy can be established.

❖ 85. *H* gives *B* a check for $4,000 when *H* signs a contract to purchase *B*'s real property. The terms of the purchase are the $95,000 sales price paid as follows: $30,000 in cash from *H* and $65,000 by way of a first mortgage for 30 years at ten percent interest. Which of the following terms **BEST** describes the $30,000?
    (A) Down payment
    (B) Hand money
    (C) Earnest money deposit
    (D) Binder

86. All of the following statements concerning a sales contract are true **EXCEPT**:
    (A) It transfers legal title.
    (B) Both parties are legally bound by it.
    (C) It states the conditions under which the property is transferred.
    (D) It states the rights and duties of each party during the duration of the contract.

87. If an option is due to expire on July 15, and the owner of the property dies on July 5, the option is:
    (A) binding on the heirs.
    (B) valid, but must be exercised within the statutory period.
    (C) void.
    (D) voidable.

88. Who has the right to sign a binding sales contract?
    (A) An attorney-in-fact
    (B) A trust beneficiary selling trust property
    (C) The sales agent for the buyer
    (D) Any corporate officer of corporate-owned property

89. Any of the following terminates an offer to purchase real property **EXCEPT**:
    (A) marriage of buyer.
    (B) death of buyer.
    (C) destruction of property.
    (D) revocation of offer.

90. All of the following can be assigned **EXCEPT**:
    (A) a contract for deed.
    (B) an option.
    (C) trust deed.
    (D) warranty deed.

91. A broker promises to give a $20,000 bonus to the first salesperson who sells 20 houses. What type of contract is this?
    (A) Unilateral   (C) Bilateral
    (B) Executed   (D) Nominal

❖ 92. If no date of possession is mentioned in the sales contract, the buyer should receive possession:
    (A) upon the signing of the contract.
    (B) when the seller vacates the property.
    (C) upon signing the deed.
    (D) upon the transfer of title.

93. The usual offer to purchase would provide for all of the following conditions **EXCEPT**:
    (A) seller to pay cost of deed preparation.
    (B) conditions by which the buyers will purchase the property.
    (C) a requirement of early occupancy.
    (D) the closing date.

❖ 94. Which is true concerning real estate sales contracts?
    (A) A seller can be sued for "specific performance" if a contract is not performed.
    (B) A seller must sign an agreement to sell if the offer's terms are exactly in accordance with the listing agreement.
    (C) The sole remedy for default of the buyer is a suit for specific performance.
    (D) They must be on a printed form to make them binding.

95. If an option to purchase is exercised, which is true?
    (A) The option money is automatically applied to the purchase price.
    (B) The optionor can be forced to sell the property.
    (C) It is binding on the optionee.
    (D) The purchase price may be increased.

❖ 96. All of the following are true about liquidated damages **EXCEPT**:
    (A) enforced unless excessive in amount.
    (B) fixed and certain in amount.
    (C) limited to two percent of purchase price.
    (D) a discharge of the obligation.

97. S makes a written offer to purchase B's real property, stating it is good until Tuesday. Which is true?
    (A) B can create a contract by accepting the offer on Wednesday.
    (B) S can revoke her offer on Monday, even though B has not been given a chance to decide.
    (C) S cannot withdraw her offer until Tuesday.
    (D) If S wishes to withdraw the offer, the withdrawal must be in writing.

❖ 98. Buyer offered to buy property by assuming a $75,000 first mortgage. If, at closing, it turned out the loan balance was only $70,000:
    (A) buyer must pay the $5,000 in cash.
    (B) seller must accept a $5,000 note from buyer.
    (C) seller must give a second mortgage.
    (D) buyer can rescind the transaction.

99. All of the following are examples of real estate contracts **EXCEPT**:
    (A) an exclusive right to sell.
    (B) an agreement of sale.
    (C) a prospectus.
    (D) a lease.

100. A voidable contract is one that is:
    (A) legally insufficient and thus not recognized by law.
    (B) not binding upon either party.
    (C) signed on a holiday.
    (D) binding on one of the parties.

101. An executory contract is:
    (A) made by the executor of an estate for the sale of probate property.
    (B) yet to be performed.
    (C) performed completely.
    (D) not yet accepted by either party.

❖ 102. When a purchaser signs an offer allowing the seller three days in which to accept the offer:
    (A) the purchaser may not withdraw the offer before the expiration of the three days.
    (B) the purchaser may withdraw the offer only upon written notice prior to seller's acceptance.
    (C) the buyer puts up earnest money so that the seller may keep it if buyer withdraws his or her offer.
    (D) the buyer can revoke at any time prior to acceptance.

103. The transfer of rights under a contract without the release from obligation by the transferor is known as:
(A) assignment.
(B) novation.
(C) succession.
(D) supersedure.

104. If the sales contract does not specify otherwise, real estate sales contracts:
(A) are assignable.
(B) can only be assigned with the consent of the seller.
(C) may be oral.
(D) may be valid at the option of the buyer.

105. An illiterate person is considered:
(A) insane.
(B) incompetent to contract.
(C) one who can't speak.
(D) one who cannot read or write.

106. A binder given by a buyer in a real estate transaction:
(A) must be monetary.
(B) may be withdrawn by the buyer any time before the seller accepts and signs.
(C) must be in the form of a check.
(D) must be cash.

107. The printed matter in a sales contract will usually include some mention or reference to all of the following EXCEPT:
(A) evidence of title.
(B) assessment or liens.
(C) proration of taxes.
(D) amount of discount points.

108. Which is necessary for a valid contract for the sale of real estate?
(A) All of the essential terms and conditions of the sale
(B) The name of the broker representing the seller
(C) The tenancy of the buyer
(D) The name of the sales agent representing the purchaser

109. An offer that does not describe the method and terms of financing, but does state the price is:
(A) voidable.
(B) valid.
(C) one lacking a legal purpose.
(D) not binding.

110. Each of the following is an essential element for a real estate contract EXCEPT:
(A) legality of object.
(B) valuable consideration.
(C) words of conveyance.
(D) offer and acceptance.

❖ 111. In a contract of sale, the buyer:
(A) must make an earnest money deposit.
(B) will owe the broker a commission when the contract is accepted even if the sale is never consummated.
(C) will lose the earnest money if the buyer withdraws prior to acceptance.
(D) must give valuable consideration.

❖ 112. When a husband and wife desire to buy real property in both their names for cash and the husband is not available to sign the purchase contract, which of the following is true?
(A) The purchase contract is voidable if only the wife signs.
(B) The contract is void unless both husband and wife sign the contract.
(C) The husband must sign prior to closing.
(D) It is only when they desire to sell the property that both signatures are required.

113. An optionee can do which one of the following?
(A) Divert water from the property during the option period
(B) Collect rents during the option period
(C) Build a residence on the property during the option period
(D) Legally enforce the exercise of the option if the optionor decides against performing

❖ 114. All of the following are true under a contract of sale in which the date of occupancy is later than the settlement date EXCEPT:
(A) The buyer acquires legal title upon settlement.
(B) The contract should provide whether or not the seller is to pay any rent.
(C) The buyer has the risk of loss.
(D) The buyer will withhold the downpayment.

115. Which is true about valid contracts?

    (A) Money must be the consideration.
    (B) If the date is left off the contract, the contract is void.
    (C) Earnest money is essential consideration.
    (D) The consideration can be the mutual promises to perform.

116. All of the following are true of real estate options **EXCEPT**:

    (A) An option is a contract.
    (B) An option, to be enforceable, must be in writing.
    (C) Options are binding on the optionee.
    (D) The consideration put up by the optionee is the option money.

❖ 117. Which of the following **BEST** describes a clause in a sales contract providing for the buyer to obtain a new first mortgage, or the contract may be terminated if it cannot be obtained?

    (A) Defeasance clause
    (B) Subordination clause
    (C) Habendum clause
    (D) Contingency clause

118. The interest that a purchaser acquires when the offer to purchase has been accepted is:

    (A) a freehold estate.
    (B) an estate in fee simple.
    (C) equitable title.
    (D) legal title.

119. Reality of consent is lacking in a contract due to all of the following **EXCEPT**:

    (A) duress.
    (B) misrepresentation.
    (C) mistake.
    (D) illiteracy.

120. A person must be of the age of majority in order to do which of the following?

    (A) Hold title to real property
    (B) Pay federal income tax
    (C) Appoint an agent
    (D) Contract to buy necessities

121. *A* agreed to purchase *B*'s property and the written agreement was placed in escrow. *A* deposited the full purchase price but *B* refused to sign the deed. *B*'s action is an example of:

    (A) breach.   (C) rejection.
    (B) tender.   (D) rescission.

122. Which one is the **MOST** essential element for an enforceable real estate purchase contract?

    (A) Being in writing   (C) Date of contract
    (B) Witnessed   (D) Time of closing

123. *J*, 16 years old and unmarried, employs Rapid Broker under an exclusive authorization-to-sell listing to sell an apartment building *J* inherited from his father. Rapid finds Ready Buyer who executes a sales contract on the complete listing terms, which the seller accepts. Which of the following statements is true?

    (A) *J* can void the contract with Ready Buyer.
    (B) *J* is liable to Rapid Broker for the full commission.
    (C) The contract is voidable by the buyer.
    (D) The contract is binding on both parties.

❖ 124. At what stage in the typical real estate transaction is the sales contract signed by buyer and seller?

    (A) Prior to the issuance of the buyer's title insurance policy
    (B) Immediately after the lender commits to the loan
    (C) At the same time as recordation
    (D) Before the listing contract

125. All of the following would constitute a type of consideration required to enforce a real estate contract to purchase an $85,000 property **EXCEPT**:

    (A) an $85,000 cashier's check.
    (B) a written promise to pay $85,000 over five years at 11 percent interest.
    (C) an oral offer to purchase.
    (D) an earnest money deposit with a written offer.

❖ 126. Which is true of a right of first refusal given to a prospective buyer?

    (A) The seller must sell if the buyer decides to buy.
    (B) The seller must accept the buyer's offer.
    (C) The buyer must buy if the seller decides to sell.
    (D) The seller must offer the property to the prospective buyer if the seller decides to sell.

127. A broker reading that "time is of the essence" in the client's contract would know that it **MOST** nearly means:
    (A) the contract is a lease creating a tenancy for years.
    (B) the contract refers to that time period over which a property can be profitably used.
    (C) that the unity of "time" must be present.
    (D) that performance must be on the dates specified in the contract, with no extensions.

128. The failure to meet an obligation when due, as specified in a real estate contract, is best described as:
    (A) damages.   (C) default.
    (B) defect.   (D) distraint.

129. In a real estate sales contract, which party has the right, upon default, to declare the earnest money deposit forfeited?
    (A) Buyer   (C) Escrow
    (B) Attorney   (D) Seller

130. All of the following are essential elements of a real estate contract **EXCEPT**:
    (A) consideration.   (C) in writing.
    (B) performance.   (D) competent parties.

❖ 131. The provision in a real estate sales contract, providing for loss of the buyer's deposit money in the event of buyer default, is known as:
    (A) liquidated damages.
    (B) nominal damages.
    (C) punitive damages.
    (D) release damages.

132. *K* accepted an offer by *H* to purchase *K*'s house for $98,000 contingent on *H* obtaining conventional loan for $88,000 at 12 percent interest. *H* tried four lenders, but the best he could do was an $85,000 loan. Which of the following is true about this contract?
    (A) *H* will forfeit his earnest money if he does not purchase the house.
    (B) *H* is obligated to purchase if *K* offers to take back a second mortgage at 12 percent for $3,000.
    (C) He will have to continue to seek out another lender.
    (D) Because *H* cannot obtain the specified financing, the contingency will allow him the return of his earnest money with no further obligation.

133. On whom is a unilateral listing contract binding once the requested act has been performed?
    (A) Vendee   (C) Promisor
    (B) Broker   (D) Creditor

134. A buyer will only buy a particular property if the zoning can be changed. The buyer could put in an offer with a $5,000 earnest money deposit contingent on obtaining the zoning or he or she could negotiate a $3,000 option. Which is true if the zoning cannot be changed?
    (A) Under an option, the buyer is entitled to all the option money.
    (B) Under a contingency in a sales contract, the buyer forfeits all the earnest money deposit.
    (C) The money will be returned no matter which method is chosen by the buyer.
    (D) If the contingency in the offer is not met, buyer will obtain a refund.

135. A farm was listed by a seller. An interested buyer paid $5,000 for a 60-day option to purchase a farm for $85,000. After 45 days, the buyer submitted an offer to purchase the farm for $75,000. Which is true?
    (A) The option is terminated.
    (B) The seller must accept the subsequent offer.
    (C) A commission is owed when the seller gave a written option to the buyer.
    (D) Only if the seller accepts the offer will he or she owe a commission.

136. When an option states nothing to the contrary, which is ordinarily true regarding the optionee's rights?
    (A) Optionee can assign or sell the option.
    (B) Optionee can obtain a mortgage on the property.
    (C) The option gives the buyer legal title.
    (D) Title insurance is usually obtained before the option is exercised.

❖ 137. For a contract of sale to be valid, which is true?
    (A) It must be in writing and signed.
    (B) It must state an earnest money deposit.
    (C) It must have the signature of the agents for the buyer and seller.
    (D) It must have a purchase price.

138. All of the following are true concerning an option sale contract **EXCEPT**:
     (A) The optionee can enforce the sale.
     (B) The option money is usually forfeited if the purchase is not completed.
     (C) The optionee must sign the contract.
     (D) The optionor cannot require specific performance.

139. The closing date on a sales contract is March 1. On March 3, the seller declares a forfeiture of the earnest money deposit. What should be done with the deposit?
     (A) Return it to the buyer.
     (B) Give it to the seller.
     (C) Place the deposit in the listing broker's general account.
     (D) Obtain written instructions from buyer and seller.

ANSWERS

1. **B** The offeror can withdraw the offer anytime prior to the communication of acceptance. Since there is no contract, any earnest money deposit must be returned immediately.

2. **B** The sales contract that omits the type of deed is still enforceable although the seller might get away with just delivering a quitclaim deed. An adequate (not necessarily a legal) description, price, and names of both buyer and seller are essential.

3. **A** An executory contract is one that is yet to be performed.

4. **A** Acknowledgments are required only if the parties desire to record the sales contract. Reality of consent means that there was a voluntary meeting of the minds and no obstacles to consent, such as fraud, misrepresentation, duress, or undue influence, were present.

5. **B** If one of the parties were incompetent, the contract might be void or voidable depending on the type of incompetency. Earnest money is customary but not essential, since the mutual exchange of promises of performance by buyer and seller is the required valuable consideration.

6. **D** If it were an option, *H* would have the right but not the legal duty to purchase *C*'s real estate.

7. **B** An offer and acceptance is required to evidence a meeting of the minds. The sales contract could be for all cash (a "cash-out"). The date of the offer, while desirable, is not necessary. A general description of property will suffice.

8. **A** Upon the seller's default, a buyer could seek the equitable remedy of specific performance. A judgment for money damages may be insufficient to satisfy the buyer, since each piece of real property is unique and irreplaceable.

9. **B** The vendee is the buyer under an agreement of sale or land contract.

10. **B** Some listing contracts are unilateral contracts in which the broker is not obligated to perform. The modern trend is to interpret listing contracts as bilateral contracts so they are binding and enforceable the instant mutual promises of performance are exchanged.

11. **B** Once a bankruptcy receiver obtains title to real property, the bankrupt owner has no legal right to obtain a return of the property except by the eventual repurchase from the new owner.

12. **B** The minor is *able* to *void* the contract, but it is enforceable against the adult. An indefeasible contract cannot be voided.

13. **B** Choice (A) would be an example of a typical loan assumption agreement. However, if the lender elects to release the original borrower from liability, then there is a novation.

14. **A** Most courts will be able to supply a reasonable closing date based on local custom and practice. The interest rate is such an essential element of the financing that no court will be able to imply a reasonable interest rate—thus, the contract will fail for indefiniteness.

15. **B** The earnest money is to protect the seller against the buyer's default. If the seller defaults, the money must be

returned to the buyer. If the buyer elects to sue the seller for specific performance, the money will most likely be deposited into court.

16. **D** "Time is of the essence" means there must be punctual performance of the parties' legal obligations. If time is not made of the essence, most courts will imply a reasonable closing date for the contract to be valid. In those courts that won't imply a closing date, the contract would be void, not voidable. "As is" only covers obvious defects, not hidden defects known to the seller. Contingencies must be stated clearly.

17. **C** A counteroffer rejects the original offer, no matter how slight the change. Lapse of time would terminate an offer.

18. **C** Words of conveyance are essential for a valid deed. Reality of consent (mutual agreement), consideration, and offer and acceptance involve essential elements of a valid contract.

19. **C** If the seller makes any change to the offer, the buyer is free to reconsider or reject the property.

20. **B** Although the statute of limitations may be for six years, that period may be extended even further for various legal reasons—the defendant is a minor, parties are out of the state, and so on.

21. **D** Most statutes of frauds require long-term lease contracts be in writing to be enforceable.

22. **D** Offer and acceptance are the two elements needed to establish the required "meeting of the minds" to show mutual agreement.

23. **D** The broker would definitely be liable for misstatements of material facts, including concealment of material defects. However, matters of opinion or value usually are not considered to be material facts and thus some things the broker says, such as puffing, would not be held as misrepresentation.

24. **A** A defeasible contract would be a conditional contract such as: "I promise to sell you my house provided you don't marry

my daughter"; the marriage before closing would defeat the buyer's rights under the contract.

25. **B** Death does not usually terminate a real estate sales contract: such contract is binding upon the decedent's estate. Death would, however, terminate a personal services contract, such as an executory listing contract. Upon delivery of the deed, the contract is usually extinguished; only the deed survives as the controlling document.

26. **B** A person who signs a contract without reading it (or the fine print) does so at his or her risk. Most contracts of minors are voidable at the election of the minor. In some states, a minor who marries is treated as an adult. However, minors' contracts for necessaries, such as food or clothing, are not voidable.

27. **D** In order to clear the record of the recorded contract, court action may be necessary. An easier solution is to persuade the defaulting vendee to execute and record a quitclaim deed.

28. **C** Since there is no ready, willing and able buyer accepted by the seller, the broker gets nothing.

29. **D** Either the buyer or seller can usually convey rights to a sales contract, unless prohibited in the contract itself.

30. **B** For example, if it were important for the seller to close in a certain tax year, the seller would be advised to insert a "time is of the essence" clause so the buyer would not be able to delay even one day into the next tax year.

31. **B** An option must be supported by its own consideration. Whether or not it is assignable (transferred to an assignee) should be covered in the option agreement itself.

32. **C** The option is a valuable contract and the heirs of the optionee (purchaser) usually succeed to the option rights.

33. **C** The vendor, seller, and grantor all refer to the same person—the owner of real property who contracts to transfer title.

34. **A** Under the doctrine of merger, the contract does not survive the deed. Therefore, any important contract provisions that the parties want to remain should be inserted into the deed, or the contract itself should state that certain clauses "survive the closing" of the contract.

35. **C** Many states have adopted the rule that risk of loss does not pass to the buyer until either legal title or possession passes.

36. **C** Not all contracts need be in writing or acknowledged, but no contract is enforceable unless there is consideration to support the parties' obligations. Consideration may be the mutual exchange of promises or commitments to perform.

37. **C** Time is of the essence requires punctual performance—delays are not excusable.

38. **D** The contract is binding on the seller's estate and the buyer could bring an action against the estate for specific performance of the contract. The estate would receive the proceeds of sale, which would then be distributed to the heirs.

39. **B** Until the contract is fully performed (executed), it is said to be executory. In this sense, the word *executed* does not mean signed and delivered.

40. **C** An oral contract regarding real estate may be valid, but a court will not enforce it unless it satisfies the statute of fraud requirements. The parties to be charged are those who are to be held to the contract (the ones to be sued in the event of breach of contract).

41. **C** Since an option is a unilateral contract, the optionee is not obliged (nor can be ordered) to perform, but if he or she does elect to purchase, then the seller is bound to sell.

42. **D** If a title report or inspection reveals encumbrances *not disclosed* in the contract of sale, then the title is not as it was marketed by the seller. The buyer can therefore rescind or force the seller to clear those curable defects.

43. **B** Since there is no contract and thus no default, the earnest money binder belongs to the buyer.

44. **C** The typed-in changes are modifications to the contract and take priority since they were subsequently agreed to by both parties.

45. **C** A lis pendens is a formal notice that a lawsuit is pending concerning a particular property.

46. **C** If, for example, the buyer intended to buy Lot 1 and the seller intended to sell Lot 2, there would be no true meeting of the minds due to mutual mistake of fact. There must be no obstacle to genuine consent, such as fraud, duress, undue influence or misrepresentation (refers to consent at the time of the sales contract, not at closing).

47. **C** The contract of sale is yet to be performed in that buyer still has to produce the purchase price and seller must produce the deed.

48. **A** A rider is an addendum to a contract, such as the case when the parties agree to include the furniture in the sale after the contract is signed. An addendum or rider should reference the basic contract and be signed or initialed by all parties.

49. **D** If the optionee fails to exercise the option by the date specified, the option is terminated. If the purchase contract does not state "time is of the essence," most courts will allow a reasonable time to perform after the expiration of the stated closing date.

50. **A** Typically the buyer makes the offer after the seller has listed the property. The listing is not an offer to sell, just an employment agreement with a broker who is to solicit offers from prospective buyers (offerors). An example of a lienee would be one holding a mechanic's lien.

51. **C** The seller marketed a free and clear title and that is what he or she can be compelled to convey.

52. **B** Both sellers and buyers may assign their rights in a sales contract unless prohibited by the explicit terms of the agreement. Because of the rule that any sales contract may be assigned, some contracts have provisions stipulating that this particular sales contract cannot be assigned without consent. Listing contracts are not assignable.

53. **B** Earnest money is not essential to a valid sales contract, but it is prudent business practice to require it. It is not the consideration.

54. **B** Under an agreement of sale (D), the buyer would be obligated to purchase.

55. **B** "The optionee may wait and see!" Remember: the *or's* give and the *ee's* receive!

56. **C** Most courts will imply a reasonable closing date unless the facts indicate the parties intended that a specific closing date was essential to the contract. The best practice is always to include a realistic closing date.

57. **B** Sometimes the broker and the seller agree to a splitting of the deposit money as damages for the buyer's breach. The seller must elect which course to follow. For example, if he or she kept the deposit money, he or she could not sue for damages if the property were resold later at a loss.

58. **D** Rejection is the refusal to accept an offer; rescission is terminating an accepted offer (a contract), and reversion is the relating back to the original transferor (as in the reversion of title to the grantor upon the death of a life tenant).

59. **A** The broker-optionee must be careful that all parties know he or she has a license.

60. **B** When the seller signs the contract, this is typically the acceptance of the buyer's offer. Be sure that the seller or agent then notifies the buyer of the acceptance, to eliminate any chance the buyer may try to revoke his offer.

61. **A** Most optionors (sellers) would be non-licensees.

62. **B** Only certain important types of contracts need be in writing to be enforceable; they include real estate sales contracts.

63. **B** The listing is a confidential employment agreement between the seller and the broker. It should not be shown to the buyer; there could be inaccurate or unverified information on the listing. The buyer can revoke prior to acceptance.

64. **A** All cotenant buyers need not sign the contract of sale for it to be enforceable. It is good practice, however, to get all to sign. Note that the executory contract would not be enforceable against *S's* husband because he has not signed the contract.

65. **C** An option is actually an irrevocable continuing offer to sell supported by the optionee's payment (consideration) of option money.

66. **A** Closing statements are statistical summaries of the amounts paid, payable, received, and receivable in a real estate transaction. Choices (B) and (D) are used in loan transactions.

67. **A** The buyer should at least be advised that the offer was considered by the seller and then rejected. The rejection is only a counteroffer if so intended. Note that a counteroffer is also a rejection of the original offer.

68. **C** Undue influence on the part of the agent will make the contract voidable and is typically a ground for license revocation.

69. **C** The earnest money is really security for the buyer's performance—once there is a contract. It may be paid after acceptance.

70. **D** Since the buyer takes the property subject to existing leases, any leases should be noted. Financing methods should be clearly stated, as should any items not considered fixtures.

71. **A** Use of earnest money is both customary and prudent. It is not essential, as the buyer's promise to perform is sufficient consideration to support the seller's promise to sell.

72. **B** Options involve an interest in real property and thus, under the statute of frauds, must be in writing to be enforceable. Unless prohibited by its terms, most options would be assignable.

73. **D** Until acceptance, the deposit money belongs to the buyer (offeror). It is usually held in trust by broker or escrow.

74. **D** It is acceptable with the permission of the seller (vendor) because the seller will try to collect upon it in the event of buyers' default.

75. **C** Upon discovery of a title defect, the seller must be given a reasonable opportunity to correct the problem. The buyer has an equitable interest in the property and thus has grounds to sue.

76. **C** So that the contract does not fail for being indefinite, it is good practice to specify the limits of the loan, such as "a loan of not less than $100,000 for a term no less than 30 years at an interest rate not to exceed ten percent." It is a good idea to set a time limit for the buyer to meet the contingency so that the seller's property will not be tied up unduly. The contract usually does not contain all the clauses found in the mortgage.

77. **C** The riders must make reference to the basic contract or else the basic contract must make reference to the rider. All parties must sign or initial the rider. It is best to make reference in each document to the other document so that anyone looking at the contract alone will not think that is the total agreement. For example, "See Exhibit 'A' attached hereto and hereby incorporated by reference."

78. **A** Choice (B) refers to the statute of limitations.

79. **A** Before one party to a contract can claim the other party is in default, one must be ready to tender one's own performance.

80. **B** The concept of rescission is to return the parties to their relative positions that existed before they attempted to contract.

81. **B** The optionee has no rights to occupancy or rents until the option is exercised and the purchase is closed, provided it is not a lease option.

82. **A** There is said to be mutual agreement when there is reality of consent as evidenced by a valid offer, properly accepted.

83. **A** Despite divorce the contract is still enforceable against those parties who signed the contract.

84. **B** There are many illiterate people who are perfectly competent to understand their rights and obligations in a contract. They simply get someone to read it for them.

85. **A** The down payment includes the earnest money deposit (also called hand money or binder).

86. **A** The sales contract is an executory contract giving the buyer the right to acquire legal title upon satisfying the conditions of the contract.

87. **A** An option is a contract and death does not discharge contracts. The optionee could seek specific performance against the seller's estate. There is no statutory period for exercising an option, there is just a stated contract period.

88. **A** Only the trustee can effect a sale of the trust property. The beneficiary's interest is personalty. The corporate officer needs specific authorization to sign on behalf of the corporation.

89. **A** Choices (B), (C) and (D) would have a different effect *after* acceptance.

90. **D** Deeds cannot be assigned because they are not executory contracts, they are conveyances. There would have to be a new deed prepared to convey the legal title. A contract for deed is also known as a land contract, agreement of sale, or installment contract, as opposed to a sales contract.

91. **A** None of the salesmen are bound or obligated to sell 20 houses, but if they do perform this act, then the broker's promise to pay will become binding.

92. **D** Possession usually takes place upon delivery of deed, which often is several days after signatures are obtained on the deed, and a month or so after the sales contract is signed.

93. **C** The usual contract provides who will pay customary closing costs and contains the essential conditions of purchase.

94. **A** Specific performance is a powerful remedy given to the purchaser. Even if the buyer offers more than the listing price, the seller is under no obligation to accept, although the seller may be liable to the broker for breach of the listing contract to pay a commission. The seller can sue for money damages.

95. **B** Whether or not the option money is to be applied toward the purchase price is a question that should be addressed in the option itself; if it is not, then a court may have to decide what was the unexpressed intention of the parties. The optionor must sell if the optionee elects to buy.

96. **C** In fact, they often exceed two percent, although if too high (like 25 percent), then they will be treated as a penalty and hence unenforceable in many states.

97. **B** After the time of the offer lapses, the seller cannot create a contract by accepting. In effect, *B*'s late acceptance is a counteroffer and there is no contract unless it is accepted by *S*. An offeror can revoke the offer anytime prior to being notified of the acceptance.

98. **D** There has not been a meeting of the minds on the essential term of financing, and the buyer can rescind. The seller cannot force the buyer to pay the extra in cash or to take back a mortgage.

99. **C** A prospectus is an announcement or brochure describing a particular real estate offering, such as a new condominium project.

100. **D** A voidable contract is legally sufficient, but the law gives one of the parties the ability to void such contract where, for example, fraud, misrepresentation or a minor is involved.

101. **B** The contract of sale in which buyer and seller bind themselves to future performance is a classic example of an executory contract.

102. **D** Unless the seller pays consideration to make the buyer's offer irrevocable (this would then be an option to sell) the buyer can revoke at any time (even verbally) prior to being notified of the seller's acceptance.

103. **A** With an assignment, the assignor remains secondarily liable. A novation involves such a release of the transferor.

104. **A** They are generally assignable but some contracts specify that the buyer must first obtain the seller's consent.

105. **D** An illiterate is not incompetent to contract; he or she just cannot read or write.

106. **B** The binder or earnest money can be cash, a note, personalty or services rendered.

107. **D** If discount points are involved, they will probably be covered in the special conditions or financing sections.

108. **A** If the parties leave any essential term or condition for future agreement, the contract will be too indefinite to be enforceable. Tenancy usually can be provided later, if buyers are undecided.

109. **B** A cash sale would fit this question.

110. **C** A contract to build an illegal gambling casino would be void. "Good consideration" (love and affection) is not sufficient to support a contract, though it is permissible for a deed. Valuable consideration could be giving or promising something of value such as money or services in return for the performance of another or forbearance of a legal right (like waiving a debt).

111. **D** The consideration used to support most real estate contracts of sale is the mutual exchange of promises to perform by buyer and seller; therefore, earnest money is not legally required. Most buyers do not agree to pay the broker a commission upon default and so recovery from the buyer is quite difficult, if not impossible, unless the buyer had employed the broker.

112. **D** One buyer can sign the contract and request that title be conveyed to himself or herself and another. It is much more vital for all sellers to sign than it is for all buyers, although the best practice is to obtain the signatures of all parties. The broker should advise the seller as to why the husband is not signing.

113. **D** Even if the seller would suffer a hardship by having to sell, the optionee could obtain specific performance of the option contract.

114. **D** In a late occupancy, the seller gets to stay in possession after closing. Some provision should be made as to rent, and the rental agreement should be in writing.

115. **D** Services rendered, rather than money, could be the valuable consideration. Usually a date is not an essential term of a sales contract, though it is good practice to date the contract.

116. **C** An option is a unilateral contract. Since it involves an interest in real property, it must be in writing under the statute of frauds. The optionor is bound to perform.

117. **D** Clauses (A) and (B) are found in mortgages and leases and (C) in deeds.

118. **C** The vendee (purchaser) has the right to obtain legal title provided the condition is performed, mainly to pay the purchase price. This right is referred to as equitable title and involves the legal doctrine of equitable conversion.

119. **D** An illiterate person can still be competent to contract.

120. **C** A minor cannot appoint an agent (attorney-in-fact) to enter into contracts that the minor is not competent to execute. The minor would need a court-appointed guardian to act as an agent. Minors' contracts for necessaries (food, clothing) are valid.

121. **A** Violation of *B*'s obligation to convey title is a breach of contract and *A* would be free to seek the remedies of damages, rescission, or specific performance.

122. **A** The statute of frauds requires real estate purchase contracts to be in writing and signed by the party to be charged. Witnesses are not required in most states. While dates are helpful they are not essential. Most courts will be able to imply a reasonable time to close based on custom and practice in the community. In exceptional cases, however, the contract may specify that it is important for tax purposes that the contract close on time. In such a case, a court could find that the omission of a closing date was fatal.

123. **A** Contracts entered into with minors are usually voidable by the minor unless they are contracts for necessities of life such as food, clothing, or shelter. The minor is *able to void* the contract, not the adult.

124. **A** The real estate contract is typically entered into before the title report and prior to a loan. It is therefore important for the contract to contain language covering whether there are any major encumbrances on title and whether the offer is subject to loan approval (a contingency).

125. **C** A bargained-for promise to perform as well as money is sufficient to support a promise to sell.

126. **D** Regarding a right of first refusal, the seller cannot be forced to sell the property unless the decision has finally been made to sell and the price determined. An option price must be definite when the option is signed.

127. **D** The contract merely indicates that punctual performance is required, as in an option. Choice (B) refers to the appraisal concept of economic life.

128. **C** The most common default is failure to pay the amount due as in a purchase contract, promissory note, or lease. Distraint is a legal process brought by a lessor to seize a lessee's belongings for rents due.

129. **D** One of the seller's remedies upon buyer default is to retain the earnest money deposit as liquidated damages.

130. **B** Failure to perform a valid contract will, however, give rise to certain legal remedies, such as money damages or specific performance.

131. **A** A liquidated damage clause states, in essence, that because actual damages are difficult to estimate at the time of signing the contract, the parties agree upon an amount to liquidate or settle the contract in the event of buyer default. If the amount decided upon is excessive (say 20 percent of sales price), a court might not enforce such a penalty provision.

132. **D** Since the contingency was for H's benefit, he is not obligated to purchase unless the condition is met. The seller could not force him to accept an alternative method of financing.

133. **C** Once a broker finds a ready, willing and able buyer upon the terms of a unilateral listing agreement, the seller-promisor's promise to pay a commission becomes enforceable. Many listing contracts today are worded as bilateral contracts.

134. **D** Upon failure to exercise an option, the optionee usually forfeits all the option money. When the contingent event of zoning does not occur, the buyer is entitled to all his or her deposit money.

135. **D** An option is an enforceable contract and gives this buyer the *right* of election to purchase the farm for $85,000. The offer, only if accepted, would bind the seller to a separate contract; in which case the buyer would "lose" the $5,000 option money but would, under the accepted contract, be able to buy the farm for a lower price thus saving $5,000 on the deal.

136. **A** Like sales contracts, options are assignable unless prohibited by the terms of the option itself. The optionee does not have a mortgageable estate until the option is exercised. Until then, the optionee has a mere contract right and this is not the most attractive security to a lender.

137. **D** Technically, it need be signed only by the party to be charged (i.e., the party to be held to the contract), although it is best to get all to sign. For example, the seller could sign a letter confirming a prior oral agreement.

138. **C** The optionor must sign the option contract since he or she is the one who needs to be bound to his or her promise to perform; the optionee has given money as consideration, not a promise. The option is a unilateral contract in which one party promises to do something in return for the actual promise (to sell) of the other party. In practice, options are signed by both parties.

139. **D** Whoever holds the deposit money is reluctant to give the money to the seller unless the buyer consents. Perhaps the reason the buyer has not performed is because of an alleged misrepresentation or a claim that the seller's title is defective.

Chapter 17 Federal Fair Housing, Truth-in-Lending and Environmental Disclosures

The questions in this chapter will test your comprehension of the following topics:

- Grounds for discrimination
- Exemptions under the fair housing law
- Procedures for filing complaints
- Examples of discriminating practices
- Types of transactions covered or exempt under Truth-in-Lending
- Federal Environmental Disclosure

Because of the technical nature of the federal fair housing statute, parts of the law are reproduced here for your reference as you go through the questions:

CIVIL RIGHTS ACT, TITLE VIII—FAIR HOUSING

What Follows Are the Principal Parts of the 1968 Federal Fair Housing Act:

Policy

Sec. 801. It is the policy of the United States to provide, within constitutional limitations, for fair housing throughout the United States. Sec. 803. (b) Nothing in Section 804 (other than subsection [c]) shall apply to:

1. any single-family house sold or rented by an owner: Provided, that such private individual owner does not own more than three such single-family houses at any one time: Provided further, that in the case of the sale of any such single-family house by a private individual owner not residing in such house at the time of such sale or who was not the most recent resident of such house prior to such sale, the exemption granted by this subsection shall apply only with respect to one such sale within any 24-month period: Provided further, that such bona fide private individual owner does not own any interest in, nor is there owned or reserved on his behalf, under any express or voluntary agreement, title to or any right to all or a portion of the proceeds from the sale or rental of, more than three such single-family houses at any one time: Provided further, that after December 31, 1969, the sale or rental of any such single-family house shall be excepted from the application of this title only if such house is sold or rented (A) without the use in any manner of the sales or rental facilities or the sales or rental services of any real estate broker, agent, or salesperson, or of such facilities or services of any person in the business of selling or renting dwellings, or of any employee or agent of any such broker, agent, or salesperson and (B) without the publication, posting or mailing, after notice, of any advertisement or written notice in violation of section 804(c) of this title; but nothing in this proviso shall prohibit the use of attorneys, escrow agents, abstractors, title companies, and other such professional assistance as necessary to perfect or transfer the title, or,
2. rooms or units in dwellings containing living quarters occupied or intended to be occupied by no more than four families living independently of each other, if the owner actually maintains and occupies one of such living quarters as his residence.

(c) For the purposes of subsection (b), a person shall be deemed to be in the business of selling or renting dwellings if:

1. he or she has, within the preceding 12 months, participated as principal in three or more transactions involving the sale or rental of any dwelling or any interest therein, or,
2. he or she has, within the preceding 12 months, participated as agent, other than in the sale of his or her own personal residence in providing sales or rental facilities or sales or rental services in two or more transactions involving the sale or rental of any dwelling or any interest therein, or,
3. he or she is the owner of any dwelling designed or intended for occupancy by, or occupied by, five or more families.

Discrimination in the Sale or Rental of Housing

Sec. 804. As made applicable by Section 803 and except as exempted by Sections 803(b) and 807, it shall be unlawful:

1. to refuse to sell or rent after the making of a bona fide offer, or to refuse to negotiate for the sale or rental of, or otherwise make unavailable or deny, a dwelling to any person because of race, color, religion, sex, handicap, familial status or national origin.
2. to discriminate against any person in the terms, conditions, or privileges of sale or rental of a dwelling, or in the provision of services or facilities in connection therewith, because of race, color, religion, sex, handicap, familial status or national origin.
3. to make, print, or publish, or cause to be made, printed, or published any notice, statement or advertisement, with respect to the sale or rental of a dwelling that indicates any preference, limitation, or discrimination based on race, color, religion, sex, handicap, familial status or national origin, or an intention to make any such preference, limitation, or discrimination.

4. to represent to any person because of race, color, religion, sex, handicap, familial status or national origin that any dwelling is not available for inspection, sale, or rental when such dwelling is in fact so available.
5. to induce or attempt to induce for profit any person to sell or rent any dwelling by representations regarding the entry or prospective entry into the neighborhood of a person or persons of a particular race, color, religion, sex, handicap, familial status or national origin.

Discrimination in the Financing of Housing

Sec. 805. After December 31, 1968, it shall be unlawful for any bank, building and loan association, insurance company or other corporation, association, firm or enterprise whose business consists in whole or in part in the making of commercial real estate loans, to deny a loan or other financial assistance to a person applying therefor for the purpose of purchasing, constructing, improving, repairing or maintaining a dwelling, or to discriminate against him or her in the fixing of the amount, interest rate, duration, or other terms or conditions of such loan or other financial assistance, because of the race, color, religion, sex, handicap, familial status or national origin of such person or of any person associated with him in connection with such loan or other financial assistance or the purposes of such loan or other financial assistance, or of the present or prospective owners, lessees, tenants or occupants of the dwelling or dwellings in relation to which such loan or other financial assistance is to be made or given: Provided, that nothing contained in this section shall impair the scope or effectiveness of the exception contained in Section 803(b).

Discrimination in the Provision of Brokerage Services

Sec. 806. After December 31, 1968, it shall be unlawful to deny any person access to or membership or participation in any multiple listing service, real estate brokers' organization, or other service, organization, or facility relating to the business of selling or renting dwellings or to discriminate against a person in the terms or conditions of such access, membership or participation, on account of race, color, religion, sex, handicap, familial status or national origin.

Exemption

Sec. 807. Nothing in this title shall prohibit a religious organization, association, or society or any nonprofit institution or organization operated, supervised, or controlled by or in conjunction with a religious organization, association or society, from limiting the sale, rental or occupancy of dwellings that it owns or operates for other than a commercial purpose to persons of the same religion, or from giving preference to such persons, unless membership in such religion is restricted on account of race, color, sex, handicap, familial status or national origin. Nor shall anything in this title prohibit a private club not in fact open to the public, which as an incident to its primary purpose or purposes provides lodgings, which it owns or operates for other than a commercial purpose, from limiting the rental or occupancy of such lodgings to its members or from giving preference to its members.

Enforcement by Private Persons

Sec. 812. (a) The rights granted by Sections 803, 804, 805, and 806 may be enforced by civil actions in appropriate United States district courts without regard to the amount in controversy and in appropriate state or local courts of general jurisdiction. A civil action shall be commenced within one year after the alleged discriminatory housing practice occurred: Provided, however, that the court shall continue such civil case brought pursuant to this section or sections.
Sec. 812. (c) The court may grant as relief, as it deems appropriate, any permanent or temporary injunction, temporary restraining order or other order, and may award to the plaintiff actual damages and punitive damages, together with court costs and reasonable attorney's fees in the case of a prevailing plaintiff: Provided, that the said plaintiff in the opinion of the court is not financially able to assume said attorney's fees.

NOTE:
Conciliation. The Secretary of HUD shall attempt to obtain conciliation agreements with respect to the complaint.

Statute of limitations. An aggrieved person has one year after an alleged discriminatory housing practice to file a complaint.

Administrative Law Judge. Unless the parties elect to have the charge decided by a civil action brought by HUD in federal court, the charge is heard by a HUD administrative law judge who can award penalties of up to $50,000.

Interference, Coercion or Intimidation

Sec. 817. It shall be unlawful to coerce, intimidate, threaten or interfere with any person in the exercise or enjoyment of, or on the account of his having exercised or enjoyed, or on account of his having aided or encouraged any other person in the exercise or enjoyment of, any right granted or protected by Section 803, 804, 805, or 806. This section may be enforced by appropriate civil action.

The table below relates to the advertising rules under Truth-in-Lending.

QUESTIONS

1. The Federal Fair Housing Act exempts from its requirements which of the following?
   (A) Discriminating in the rental of rooms or units in a four-family dwelling where the owner actually resides in one of the units
   (B) Denying a person access to a multiple-listing service on account of race
   (C) Steering
   (D) Blockbusting

2. The Federal Fair Housing Act prohibits discrimination based on which of the following?
   (A) Race, national origin or color
   (B) Religion, sex or age
   (C) Religion, sex or military status
   (D) Race, sex or marital status

3. The Federal Fair Housing Act makes discrimination in housing illegal if based on all of the following **EXCEPT**:
   (A) marital status.   (C) physical handicap.
   (B) religion.   (D) sex.

4. Which of the following activities is a violation of the Federal Fair Housing Act?
   (A) A nonprofit church that denies access to its retirement home to a person because of race
   (B) A nonprofit private club that gives preference in renting units to its members at lower rates
   (C) A single-family homeowner selling his or her own home giving preference to a buyer based on sex
   (D) Discriminating in the sale of a warehouse based on sex

❖ 5. Which of the following is **NOT** covered under the Federal Fair Housing law because of the definition of "familial status"?
   (A) Condominiums that have a specific exemption defined under a "grandfathering" provision of state law
   (B) One or more individuals under the age of 18 living with a parent
   (C) Families where one or more members are pregnant ·
   (D) Housing projects intended for occupancy solely by individuals 62 years of age or older

Column A Trigger Terms	Column B Required Disclosures
Appearance of any of these items in Column A requires inclusion of everything in Column B	
• the amount or percentage of down payment • the amount of any installment • the finance charge in dollars or that there is no charge for credit • the number of installments • the period of repayment	• the amount or percentage of down payment • the terms of repayment • the annual percentage rate and if increase is possible

❖ 6. Under the Federal Fair Housing Act, which of the following is exempt?

(A) Private clubs operating a commercial boarding house

(B) Religious organizations giving preference to their members in renting church-owned housing

(C) Non-resident owner of a duplex renting one unit

(D) Real estate agent selling own home

7. Single-family housing privately owned by an individual owning less than three such houses may be sold or rented without being subject to the provisions of the Federal Fair Housing Act if:

(A) no more than two houses, in which the owner was not the most recent occupant, are sold in any two-year period.

(B) no more than one such house is sold in any two-year period.

(C) discriminatory advertising is used.

(D) the owner hires a real estate broker.

8. Which of the following is a protected person under the 1988 Fair Housing Law as amended?

(A) A person currently addicted to cocaine

(B) An alcoholic

(C) A person 50 years old seeking to lease a unit in a qualified retirement home

(D) A person with poor credit

9. Acme Savings & Loan would violate the Federal Fair Housing Act by denying a loan to Baker because of which of the following?

(A) Low earnings

(B) Too old

(C) Too many loans

(D) Minority background

10. White persons are protected by the Federal Fair Housing Act and have a right to bring suit in all of the following cases **EXCEPT**:

(A) They receive threatening phone calls for having sold their home to a minority family.

(B) Acts of discrimination deny them the opportunity to have neighbors who are members of minority groups.

(C) They are evicted by a landlord for having minority guests in their home.

(D) They are denied housing because they are Democrats.

11. *A*, a single parent with three children, applies to rent an apartment in a singles complex where her friend *B* lives. *A* is rejected because she has children. After *B* complains to the Secretary of HUD, *B* is evicted. Which is false?

(A) The rejection of *A* violates the Federal Fair Housing Act.

(B) Such reprisal action against *B* violates the act.

(C) The act applies to discrimination based on parental status.

(D) *B* can be held liable for filing a frivolous complaint.

❖ 12. Which of the following is probably a discriminatory practice under the 1988 Amendments to the Federal Fair Housing Law?

(A) Not allowing a family with children to keep a small dog

(B) Requiring a person with severe arthritis to carry a small dog while riding an elevator in a condominium project

(C) Requiring a partially deaf person to turn down the noise from a television set after midnight

(D) Requiring prospective tenants to fill out a credit report

13. A real estate broker enters a neighborhood bordering a blighted area and, in good faith, offers owners a reduced commission rate if they list with the firm and the property is sold within 180 days. There is no mention of the blighted area. Such practice is:

(A) blockbusting.   (C) redlining.

(B) steering.   (D) acceptable.

14. Under the Federal Fair Housing Act, which of the following practices is prohibited?

(A) A live-in owner's refusal to rent a unit in a two-family dwelling to any member of a certain religious group

(B) A broker's refusal to show a listed dwelling to a prospective purchaser because of the latter's ethnic background

(C) Refusal to rent because renter is in military

(D) Refusal to sell based on political preference

15. The authority under the Federal Fair Housing Act rests with:
    (A) the Secretary of the Interior.
    (B) the Attorney General.
    (C) the Federal Housing Authority.
    (D) the Secretary of Housing and Urban Development.

❖ 16. Any of the following acts is forbidden by the Federal Fair Housing Act EXCEPT:
    (A) racial discrimination in real estate board membership.
    (B) discrimination on the basis of national origin.
    (C) discrimination on the basis of age.
    (D) racial discrimination in home repair financing.

17. Which of the following is a legal reason for offering a shorter than normal mortgage term?
    (A) Physical frailty of borrower
    (B) Pregnancy of borrower
    (C) Short leasehold term
    (D) Mental handicap of borrower

18. Under the Federal Fair Housing Act:
    (A) an aggrieved person must file within 280 days of the alleged discriminatory practice.
    (B) the aggrieved person must first file his or her verified complaint with HUD before commencing any action in a U.S. District Court.
    (C) the aggrieved person has one year to file.
    (D) the aggrieved person must retain an attorney.

19. A complainant under the Federal Fair Housing Act must file his or her complaint:
    (A) directly with the governor's office.
    (B) within 45 days of the alleged discriminatory act.
    (C) within one year of the discriminatory act.
    (D) directly to the state attorney general.

20. Under the Federal Fair Housing Act, the burden to prove there was discrimination is on the:
    (A) court.   (C) respondent.
    (B) complainant.   (D) HUD secretary.

❖ 21. Under the Federal Fair Housing Act, it is permissible to:
    (A) approve a loan to a person who has stated the intention to rent the property only to members of a minority group.
    (B) refuse to grant loans on the basis of the financial condition of an applicant who is a member of a minority group.
    (C) refuse loans on properties because they are located in certain areas.
    (D) give preference in approving loans to members of a certain race.

22. The Federal Fair Housing Act does which of the following?
    (A) Makes it illegal for a lender to deny for any reason a loan to an applicant who is a member of a minority group
    (B) Exempts the owner of a private single-family residence if a real estate broker is not employed to sell the property and discriminatory ads are not used
    (C) Prohibits loans to minority college students
    (D) Exempts condominium owners from provisions of the act

23. Under the Federal Fair Housing Act, it is a discriminatory practice to deny a prospective buyer the services of all of the following if based on color EXCEPT:
    (A) title insurance company.
    (B) escrow company.
    (C) termite company.
    (D) moving company.

24. The Civil Rights Act of 1866 prohibits discrimination in housing on the basis of:
    (A) race.   (C) sex.
    (B) religion.   (D) marital status.

25. Which of the following is permitted under the Federal Fair Housing Act?
    (A) Charging a higher interest rate on a loan by a savings and loan association on the grounds the loan applicant intends to rent part of the subject property to members of a certain minority group
    (B) Advertising property for sale only in publications primarily aimed at a particular ethnic group and using models only of that same ethnic group
    (C) Giving preference to members of a certain sex in the selling of homes
    (D) Giving preference to members of the same political party.

❖ 26. The prohibitions of the 1968 Fair Housing Act apply to single-family housing in all of the following cases **EXCEPT**:
   (A) It is single-family housing owned by a corporation.
   (B) It is single-family housing privately owned by an individual who owns more than three such houses, or who sells, in any two-year period, more than one house in which he or she was not the most recent occupant.
   (C) A real estate broker uses discriminatory advertising to attract buyers.
   (D) The owner gives his or her home to his or her son.

27. In an effort to obtain more listings, a broker urges people in a certain neighborhood to sell because of the fact several minority types have recently moved in nearby and property values should decline. This is a violation of which law?
   (A) Federal Fair Housing Act on blockbusting
   (B) Federal Equal Credit Opportunity Act
   (C) Federal Truth-in-Lending
   (D) Federal Disclosure Act

28. The federal antidiscriminatory laws apply to:
   (A) sales by a broker of single-family homes.
   (B) private lodging for noncommercial purposes in a private club not open to the public.
   (C) sales of office buildings.
   (D) rentals of industrial property.

29. A renter complained to HUD about his or her landlord's discriminatory practices in the building. A week later the landlord gave the renter an eviction notice. Under which of the following situations would there be a violation of the Federal Fair Housing Act?
   (A) The renter is two months behind in his or her rent.
   (B) The landlord wants to get back at the "squealer."
   (C) The renter has damaged the premises.
   (D) The renter is conducting an illegal use on the premises.

❖ 30. A minority group is moving into an area immediately adjacent to an old subdivision. "X" Realty offers in good faith to list homes in the subdivision at a lower than usual rate if the owners list within 45 days. There is no mention of race. Which of the following is true?
   (A) The broker's license can be revoked.
   (B) This is blockbusting.
   (C) Such practice is not illegal.
   (D) Brokers cannot lower their standard rate of commission.

31. An apartment rents only to singles. Refusal to rent to which of the following would result in a violation of the Federal Fair Housing Act?
   (A) Families   (C) Military officers
   (B) Elderly persons   (D) Married couple

32. After HUD has filed a *charge* that a violation of the Fair Housing Law has taken place, the complainant may elect which of the following forums for the case to be heard?
   (A) Civil action in U.S. Bankruptcy Court
   (B) An Administrative Law Judge hearing
   (C) Board of REALTORS® arbitration
   (D) Binding mediation

33. A bank decides not to make real estate loans to the groups described below. Such refusal to which of the following groups would be a violation of the Federal Fair Housing Act?
   (A) Multiple groups seeking to live in one residence
   (B) Three "hard rock" musicians taking title as joint tenants
   (C) Four university professors
   (D) Three priests

❖ 34. A particular savings and loan association has blocked out certain regions of the community where it will not place loans because of the ghetto conditions. Such a practice is called:
   (A) redlining.   (C) warehousing.
   (B) steering.   (D) relocating.

35. The Federal Fair Housing Act provides that a *prima facie* (at first view) case against the broker for discrimination will be established in a complaint against the broker if he or she fails to do which of the following?
   (A) Display a HUD Equal Opportunity poster
   (B) Join an affirmative marketing program
   (C) Join the HUD antidiscriminatory task force
   (D) Attend mandatory classes on fair housing

36. A broker is discussing a new listing with a prospective minority buyer. The buyer wants to inspect the property immediately but the listing owner has instructed the broker not to show the house during the owner's three-week absence. The buyer insists on viewing the property. The broker should do which of the following?
    (A) Show the property to avoid a violation of the Federal Fair Housing Act
    (B) Request the Real Estate Commission arbitrate the problem
    (C) Inform the buyer of the seller's instructions
    (D) Notify the nearest HUD office

37. Several minority families recently moved into an all-white area. A broker advised his sales staff to try to obtain listings in this area but to avoid going to solicit these families because they were new purchasers and they probably would not be interested in selling as of yet. The broker's actions would violate which of the following laws?
    (A) Federal Fair Housing Act
    (B) Equal Credit Opportunity Act
    (C) Truth-in-Lending
    (D) Real Estate Settlement Procedures Act

❖ 38. All of the following acts on the part of a real estate broker would constitute steering and thus be prohibited under the FFH Act EXCEPT:
    (A) directing a prospective buyer of one minority group to work only with a salesperson of the same minority group and to look at areas dominated by that minority group.
    (B) directing a member of one minority group away from properties located in areas dominated by other races.
    (C) referring a member of one minority group to properties located only in areas dominated by members of the same group.
    (D) directing a minority buyer to an expensive subdivision.

39. S decides to use the services of OK Realty to locate a suitable home for his minority family. OK Realty assigns T, their only minority salesperson, who avoids showing S any properties outside of his minority neighborhoods despite the fact S had indicated an interest in houses in another district. OK Realty's discriminating action can BEST be described as:
    (A) redlining.
    (B) blockbusting.
    (C) steering.
    (D) conciliation.

40. A religious group bought a house in a subdivision and organized it into a commune. A broker, eager to make some quick profits, began to canvass this neighborhood, soliciting listings by inquiring whether the owners knew who had just moved into the area and leaving the firm's business card. Which term BEST describes the broker's marketing program?
    (A) Redlining
    (B) Lawful solicitation
    (C) Panic-peddling
    (D) Steering

41. Which of the following actions on the part of a federal credit union would violate the Federal Fair Housing Act?
    (A) Refusing to make loans on condominium conversion projects in a local neighborhood because of pending Congressional hearings
    (B) Refusing to make loans on apartment buildings in a local neighborhood because of a substantial increase in foreclosure over the past two years
    (C) Refusing to make loans to minority applicants whose credit is substantial
    (D) Refusing to make loans on commercial properties

42. All of the following are unlawful discrimination because of minority status and thus prohibited under the Federal Fair Housing Act EXCEPT:
    (A) using one set of credit standards for men and one for women.
    (B) canceling the leases of white residents who entertain minority guests.
    (C) referring minority prospects only to minority brokers or salespersons.
    (D) refusing to loan money to a minority applicant because of a poor credit rating.

43. Which of the following practices would be unlawful under the Federal Fair Housing Act?
    (A) Requiring all prospective residents to have recommendations from current residents, if most or all of the current residents are white Catholics
    (B) Selling lots only to builders approved by a realty company where no builder who is willing to sell to minority homeowners can get the necessary approval
    (C) Requiring an applicant to sign a form noting the applicant's religious preference
    (D) Requiring all applicants to submit a credit report

44. Which of the following practices is lawful under the Federal Fair Housing Act?
    (A) Requiring higher credit qualifications for minorities than whites
    (B) Requiring higher down payments from minorities than whites and prohibiting minorities from acquiring secondary financing
    (C) Requiring greater security deposits for military enlisted men than officers
    (D) When marketing housing in a minority neighborhood, putting "for sale" ads only in papers with a primarily minority readership in order to reduce the likelihood of integrating an area by selling to whites

45. Which of the following is considered discriminatory under the Federal Fair Housing Act?
    (A) Advertising in the "help wanted" section for a certain race
    (B) Rental of property to persons within certain income levels
    (C) Advertising in rental section for "military only"
    (D) Selling residential subdivision land only to Protestants

❖46. A owns a multi-family dwelling near a hospital in which she occupies one of the units. She rents out the other units and says she prefers to rent to foreign doctors. Which of the following statements is true under the Federal Fair Housing Act?
    (A) A is violating the act, assuming there are a total of three units in the dwelling.
    (B) A is not in violation of the act, assuming there are four units.
    (C) Indicating a preference for foreign doctors would not be a ground for discrimination under the act.
    (D) A is in violation of the act because she is intentionally acting to discriminate.

47. If a complainant files a discrimination lawsuit in a federal district court, all of the following remedies are available to the complainant **EXCEPT:**
    (A) permanent injunction.
    (B) actual money damages.
    (C) temporary restraining order.
    (D) triple damages.

48. A religious organization owns and operates a nonprofit condominium for its own members. It agrees to sell one of the units to a nonreligious group but to make an additional charge. Such action is:
    (A) lawful because the owners are a nonprofit religious organization.
    (B) lawful because condominiums are exempt from fair housing laws.
    (C) unlawful because HUD forbids surcharges of any kind.
    (D) unlawful because the owner's action was a violation of fair housing laws.

49. When you are taking a listing on an owner-occupied single-family residence, if the owner states that you are not to show the property to anyone of the Irish nationality, you should:
    (A) ignore the request and proceed with the listing.
    (B) comply with your principal's request.
    (C) make note of the fact in the listing and continue to list hoping that no Irish want to see the property.
    (D) refuse to take the listing.

50. A metropolitan transient home is owned and operated by a religious group as a nonprofit home for members of that group. S wants to rent and, because she is not a member of that religious group, she is required to pay a large surcharge. Which of the following is true?
    (A) This action is legal because it is a non-profit organization.
    (B) This action is legal because she is only renting and not purchasing.
    (C) This action is legal, if membership is not based on color, race, sex or national origin.
    (D) This action is not legal.

51. Under Truth-in-Lending, it is permissible to advertise which of the following statements alone?
    (A) $2,000 down
    (B) Ten percent interest
    (C) Reasonable monthly terms
    (D) $125 per month

52. The Federal Truth-in-Lending Act requires the lender to disclose which of the following when a purchase money mortgage is made?
    (A) Annual percentage rate
    (B) Right of rescission
    (C) Penalties for violating the act
    (D) Total closing costs

53. The annual percentage rate must be revealed to which of the following consumers?
    (A) Applicant for a residential first loan
    (B) Applicant for a commercial first loan
    (C) Applicant for an industrial first loan
    (D) Applicant for loan payable in three installments

❖ 54. Under Truth-in-Lending (TIL), a commercial bank lending on a first purchase money mortgage must do which of the following?
    (A) Disclose the total interest to be paid and the annual percentage rate
    (B) Require that both mortgagee and mortgagor sign the documents before Truth-in-Lending disclosure requirements become effective
    (C) Provide notice of a right of rescission
    (D) Disclose the annual percentage rate

❖ 55. The restrictions relating to advertisement of credit terms contained in the Truth-in-Lending law:
    (A) would permit the use of the phrase "no down payment" without further disclosure of financing terms.
    (B) apply to newspaper, TV, radio and magazine ads, but not to direct mail solicitation.
    (C) permit the advertisement of the interest rate without disclosure of the annual percentage rate.
    (D) require that an advertisement that specifies the monthly payment also state other key terms of the loan.

56. When computing an annual percentage rate for disclosure purposes under the Truth-in-Lending law, the creditor would include as finance charges all of the following loan expenses **EXCEPT:**
    (A) the service charge for making the loan.
    (B) loan finder fees.
    (C) credit check.
    (D) termite fee.

57. The Truth-in-Lending law is designed to do which of the following?
    (A) Limit the amount of interest charged the borrower
    (B) Limit the amount of closing costs
    (C) Disclose total closing costs
    (D) Disclose loan finance costs

❖ 58. The Truth-in-Lending law limits which of the following?
    (A) The number of discount points paid by the buyer
    (B) The number of discount points that can be paid by a seller
    (C) The amount of finance fees to be charged
    (D) The kind of advertising about points

59. Under the Truth-in-Lending law, the borrower (consumer), except in cases of a purchase money mortgage to acquire or construct a home, has a right of rescission upon notice for:
    (A) 24 hours.
    (B) three business days.
    (C) two calendar days.
    (D) 72 hours.

60. Truth-in-Lending laws apply to:
    (A) commercial loan transactions involving real property.
    (B) residential real estate mortgages.
    (C) all personal property transactions.
    (D) unconscionable contracts.

❖ 61. Regulation Z provides a right of rescission:
    (A) to first mortgages to finance the purchase of a residential condominium unit.
    (B) that expires three business days after the date of consummation of the transaction or the date on which the lender makes material disclosures, whichever is later.
    (C) to all residential loans on real estate.
    (D) that expires upon default of the loan.

62. All of the following are included in the "finance charge" under the Truth-in-Lending provisions **EXCEPT:**
    (A) points.   (C) attorney's fees.
    (B) loan finder fee. (D) service charges.

63. Regulation Z controls which of the following?
    (A) The amount of interest that can be charged in a credit transaction
    (B) What can be included in advertisements of certain credit transactions
    (C) The amount of points that can be charged
    (D) The length of the loan term

❖ 64. Under the advertising regulations of Regulation Z, all of the following are true **EXCEPT**:
    (A) Interest rates cannot be mentioned alone, but rather the "annual percentage rate" must be stated.
    (B) General terms such as "liberal terms available," "small down payments accepted" or "DVA or FHA financing available" may be used.
    (C) Violations are enforced by the Federal Trade Commission.
    (D) Real estate brokers are regulated as "arranger of credit."

65. The primary purpose of the Truth-in-Lending Act is to:
    (A) save the general public money in installment purchases.
    (B) establish a more uniform set of charges.
    (C) disclose to the consumer the cost and conditions of the installment purchase.
    (D) assist the federal government in controlling shady lending practices.

66. Exempt from the right of rescission under the Truth-in-Lending law is:
    (A) a conventional first purchase money mortgage on the borrower's principal dwelling.
    (B) a land contract to purchase raw land from a developer to build a dwelling.
    (C) a home improvement loan.
    (D) a home equity loan.

67. Which of the following is exempt from giving the rescission notice to a consumer purchasing a home according to the Truth-in-Lending Act?
    (A) Any second mortgagee
    (B) A seller carrying back a purchase money mortgage
    (C) A broker arranging credit for a fee
    (D) A home improvement lender taking a junior mortgage

❖ 68. Under Regulation Z, all of the following may be advertised alone **EXCEPT**:
    (A) five percent down payment.
    (B) 9½ percent annual percentage rate.
    (C) $73,600 cash price.
    (D) very low monthly payments.

69. The Truth-in-Lending law prohibits which of the following?
    (A) The advertising of credit terms
    (B) Advertising in general terms such as "quick financing available"
    (C) Advertising of interest rates
    (D) Advertising of only the percentage of down payment

70. Regulation Z requires lenders to:
    (A) properly inform buyers and sellers of commercial property of all settlement costs in a real estate transaction.
    (B) inform prospective home mortgage or trust deed borrowers of charges, fees, and interest involved in making a home mortgage or trust deed loan.
    (C) disclose the lender's margin of profit in each loan.
    (D) make loans to racial minority groups.

❖ 71. In accordance with the Federal Equal Credit Opportunity Act of 1974, a lender discussing a home loan with a young couple who both work may consider all of the following factors **EXCEPT**:
    (A) verification of bank and savings accounts.
    (B) age of either husband or wife.
    (C) credit references supplied by the couple.
    (D) verification of employment of husband and wife.

72. Under the Federal Equal Credit Opportunity Act, the property manager who requires a credit report on a prospective tenant can do which of the following?
    (A) Charge the tenant a fee for the cost of the report
    (B) Disapprove of the creditworthiness of the tenant based upon age
    (C) Disapprove creditworthiness based on the tenant's sex
    (D) Publish the report in the property manager association's monthly newsletter

73. Under the Consumer Protection Act, a homeowner sells his or her house to *A* and takes
back some financing. What does Regulation Z
require the homeowner to disclose to *A*?
    (A) Annual percentage rate
    (B) Financing charge
    (C) Three-day right of rescission
    (D) Nothing

74. Which is not required in the Truth-in-Lending
Disclosure statement?
    (A) Term of prepayment penalty
    (B) Finance charge
    (C) Annual percentage rate
    (D) Amount of interest per installment

75. Which federal law requires landowners to be
financially responsible for cleaning up hazard-
ous wastes that have been leached from toxic
wastes disposed of on a neighbor's property?
    (A) The Resource Conservation and Recovery
    Act of 1976
    (B) National Environmental Protection Act of
    1969
    (C) Superfund
    (D) The Toxic Substances Control Act

76. Which of the following environmental hazards
can be "friable"?
    (A) Asbestos
    (B) Formaldehyde
    (C) Radon
    (D) Polychlorinated Biphenyls (PCBs)

77. Which of the following environmental hazards
is indicated by leakage near electrical equipment such as transformers?
    (A) Asbestos
    (B) Formaldehyde
    (C) Radon
    (D) Polychlorinated Biphenyls (PCBs)

78. Which federal law requires landowners to be
financially responsible for cleaning up hazard-
ous wastes that have been dumped on their
property by prior owners or tenants?
    (A) Comprehensive Environmental Response,
    Compensation and Liability Act
    (B) National Environmental Protection Act
    (C) The Toxic Substances Control Act
    (D) The Clear Water Act

ANSWERS

1. **A** A limited exemption is afforded to an
occupant-lessor in a dwelling not to
exceed a fourplex, under Sec.
806(b)(2)—see text that follows. Choice
(B) is specifically prohibited under Sec.
806.

2. **A** Age is not yet a grounds for a discrimination violation under FFH. The present
grounds are race, color, sex, religion,
handicap, family or national origin.

3. **A** Marital status (the status of being single
or married) is not yet covered under
FFH.

4. **A** The church could be selective in denying
access on the basis of religion but not
race under Sec. 807. There is a specific
private club exemption under FFH.

5. **D** Housing projects for those 62 or over can
prohibit families. There is a limited
exemption for projects specially designed
for seniors 55 and over.

6. **B** Religious organizations and private clubs
can give preferences or restrict occupancy provided the establishment is not run
for a commercial purpose (it must be for
a nonprofit purpose) under Sec. 807.

7. **B** Frequent turnover of properties would
put the owner in the broker classification, thereby losing exempt status (see
Sec. 803(b)).

8. **B** Alcoholism is a disease and fits within the
physical and marital handicap provision.
A current drug user is not protected
although a reformed drug addict would
be protected.

9. **D** FFH prohibits lending practices based on
race, sex, religion or national origin,
under Sec. 805.

10. **D** (A), (B) and (C) are covered under the
FFH law, but political affiliation is not
covered.

11. **D** The FFH covers discrimination against
families. The FFH law does prohibit
intimidation and reprisal actions against
complainants (see Sec. 817).

12. B Is covered under the handicap provision requiring adjustment in the rules to accommodate the handicapped so long as this does not threaten the health and safety of others.

13. D Blockbusting or panic peddling is a broker's encouragement of owners to list before property values drop due to the arrival of certain minorities in the area. Steering is directing specific ethnic groups into or away from certain areas. Here, there is no connection between the reduced commission and any discriminatory ground.

14. B An owner is exempt provided he or she occupies one of the units in the dwelling, with no more than four units in the dwelling. It is no defense to the broker that he or she is obeying the owner's directions to discriminate. If this is true, then the broker should give up the listing.

15. D The complainant can go directly to HUD or to court. One advantage of going to the Secretary of HUD is that the activities of HUD in reviewing the case will help reduce the costs of the investigation.

16. C Age is not yet a ground for discrimination under FFH.

17. C Lenders cannot discriminate based on handicap or familial status, but they can deny loans based on sound economic reasons.

18. C The statute of limitations is one year, but the complainant has a choice of filing with HUD or in federal court. Both the complaint and the answer must be verified (made under oath).

19. C The Attorney General conducts litigation when the secretary of HUD acts as a party.

20. B In actual practice, however, the respondent often feels the obligation to prove there was no discrimination.

21. B Under choice (A) the borrower would be discriminating in the rental program and the lender can't be a party to the discrimination. A lender can refuse a loan for valid credit reasons, but not to discriminate against minority groups. Choice (C) is redlining.

22. B It is only illegal for a loan denial to be based on discriminatory reasons. Also, under choice (B) the owner cannot use discriminatory advertising.

23. D If based on color, it is an illegal act to discriminate against a person in the furnishing of facilities or services in connection with a real estate transaction (see Sec. 804(2)).

24. A A single-family owner who discriminates in the sale of his or her home based on race would not violate the FFH Act, but would violate the Civil Rights Act of 1866. The 1866 Act prohibits all racial discrimination, private as well as public, in the sale of real property.

25. D The loan decision cannot be based on ethnic reasons, only economic reasons. The FFH Act also prohibits discriminatory solicitation that would encompass this type of selected advertising due to its indirect effect on discrimination—it is selected on ethnic grounds.

26. D The exemption does not apply to commercial developers or to people deemed to be in the business of selling or renting dwellings (such as those who own more than three dwellings).

27. D Blockbusting is defined as "for profit, to induce or attempt to induce any person to sell or rent any dwelling by representations regarding the entry or prospective entry into the neighborhood of a person or persons of a particular race, color, religion, sex or national origin." A criminal does not fit into any of these categories.

28. A There is a limited exemption offered to single-family owners but not if they use the services of a broker (this is to avoid any tie-in between the government who licensed the broker and the discrimination).

29. B Retaliatory evictions are prohibited under FFH.

30. C For blockbusting to exist, there must be some actual or implied representation about the effect of the entry of minority groups into the area.

31. **A** FFH does not prohibit discrimination based on military, marital status or age, but does cover families.

32. **B** If both parties agree the case can be decided by an Administrative Law Judge rather than go to U.S. District Court. Unlike arbitration, mediation is not binding.

33. **D** Multiple groups might violate local zoning requirements but, like noisy people, they are not covered under the FFH.

34. **A** Redlining got its name from the alleged practice of outlining in red on a map those areas where loans would not be made by a lender. Because these areas are typically where minority groups are located, this practice has an indirect effect of discrimination.

35. **A** HUD does not strictly require that brokers display this small poster which states the broker does not discriminate in housing based on race, color, religion, handicap, familial status, national origin or sex. But failure to post it will result in a switch of the burden of proof from the complainant to the respondent in an FFH discrimination case. Affirmative marketing programs are entirely optional but are encouraged by REALTORS®.

36. **C** An agent must obey the instructions of the principal except where there is an illegal intent or act involved. Here, the owner is acting reasonably with no indication of any unlawful bias.

37. **A** Although the broker is probably acting in all good faith, the solicitation program is nevertheless based on skipping minority groups and soliciting only nonminority members of the neighborhood. Such action could create an indirect taint of discriminatory selection.

38. **D** Steering is discouraging the sale or rental of a dwelling because of the presence or absence of minority neighbors, whether actual, alleged or implied. Referring minority prospects to minority salespersons is treating people differently because of their minority status and such action is unlawful even though there may be a valid business purpose.

39. **C** Steering is the unlawful practice of discouraging the sale or rental of a dwelling because of the presence or absence of minority neighbors. Referring minority prospects to minority salespersons or directing people to, or away from, certain neighborhoods based on a discriminatory reason, is unlawful since it is treating people differently because of minority status even though there may be some valid business purpose.

40. **C** Panic-peddling is defined as soliciting of sales or rental listings, making written or oral statements creating fear or alarm, transmitting written or oral warnings or threats, soliciting prospective minority renters or buyers or acting in any other manner so as to induce or attempt to induce the sale or lease of residential property, either
    (a) through representations regarding the present or prospective entry of one or more minority residents into an area or
    (b) through representations that would convey to a reasonable person under the circumstances, whether or not overt reference to minority status is made, that one or more minority residents are or may be entering the area.

NOTE: The term *minority* means any group that can be distinguished because of race, sex, religion, color or national origin. Vigorous solicitation of sellers in a rapidly changing neighborhood is called panic-peddling.

41. **C** If refusal is based on sound economic reasons and not on any discriminatory basis, there is no violation. However, if the credit union decided not to make loans in certain ghetto areas based on racial problems that existed, then this would be the unlawful practice of redlining. The law applies to credit unions (also banks and savings and loans) and commercial loans on multi-family units.

42. **D** While discriminatory financial practices are unlawful, it is lawful to refuse to loan money if based solely on sound business practice. Assigning salespersons on the basis of minority status is to discriminate in the provision of services in connection with a real estate transaction.

43. **D**   The law prohibits not only direct discrimination but also practices that may be fair in form but discriminatory in operation. Even if the discrimination was unintentional and done through ignorance, the effect is discriminatory, and the result is a violation.

44. **C**   There may be sound economic reasons for distinguishing between officers and enlisted men; discriminating against the military, though not encouraged or endorsed, is usually not a violation of the Federal Fair Housing Act. Cases have held that a solicitation policy, as in (D), directed at blacks and excluding whites is a violation of the act.

45. **D**   Choice (A) does not cover a real estate transaction, and (B) is a typical factor to consider in renting.

46. **B**   Expressing a preference based on national origin is contrary to the provisions of the act. There is, however, an exemption to the owner-occupant of a dwelling occupied or intended to be occupied by no more than four families (a fourplex).

47. **D**   The complainant can persuade the court to issue orders preventing the respondent from continuing the illegal practices. Money damages are allowed for actual losses, but punitive damages are limited to $1,000. In cases involving willful intimidation, there is a fine or time in jail.

48. **A**   While making a surcharge is a discriminatory act (giving preference to a religious group), religious organizations are exempt if they are open to all to join and if they are run on a not-for-profit basis.

49. **D**   It is illegal under the Federal Fair Housing Act to accept a listing that involves a discriminatory act, such as denying access to people of a certain national origin.

50. **C**   To qualify for the religious exemption under the Federal Fair Housing Act, it is necessary that the home be operated for other than commercial purposes and that membership in the religion be open to all. Choice (A) is wrong because not all nonprofit organizations are exempt— only religious organizations and private clubs.

51. **C**   Advertising general credit terms is permissible but once the creditor starts to advertise specific terms, a full disclosure must be made of all credit terms.

52. **A**   While a purchase money lien is exempt from the need to disclose the finance charge and the total of payments, it still must disclose the annual percentage rate, which is the relationship of the total finance charge to the total amount to be financed.

53. **A**   Truth-in-Lending does not apply to commercial loans; it applies only to consumer (not corporate) loans of the household or family variety. A credit transaction involves payments in more than four installments.

54. **D**   Lenders need disclose only the annual percentage rate. A mortgagee does not sign the mortgage or the note.

55. **D**   The advertisement of "no down payment" would trigger the disclosure of all other credit terms because it means "100 percent financing." TIL also applies to direct mail solicitation.

56. **D**   All charges directly or indirectly related to making the loan are computed into the finance charge.

57. **D**   The law does not limit costs or charges, it merely requires their full disclosure. RESPA also regulates disclosure of closing costs.

58. **D**   The law requires disclosure of the points only, which, under DVA, must be paid by someone other than the borrower.

59. **B**   Note the difference between calendar and business days.

60. **B**   The law is designed to protect the ordinary consumer in credit transactions that affect household and family matters, not commercial investments. Personal property transactions over specified amounts (presently $25,000) are exempt.

61. **B**   First liens to acquire or construct a principal residence would be exempt. The right of rescission is designed to protect the homeowner from losing his or her home (this includes condominiums and mobile homes) because of a credit transaction that used his or her principal residence as security. Note that there is now a three-year statute of limitations if no disclosures are made.

62. **C**   Attorney's fees would be regularly incurred in closing the real estate transaction, regardless of whether or not credit was involved. Choices (A), (B) and (D) directly relate to the lending of money.

63. **B**   While state usury laws regulate the amount of interest, TIL controls the ads of those credit transactions that fit under Regulation Z.

64. **D**   The interest rate can be no more prominent in the ad than the annual percentage rate. Specific terms trigger the mention of all credit terms. The chart on page 194 indicates which specific terms would trigger certain required disclosures. Real estate brokers do not have to make the disclosures required of an "arranger of credit."

65. **C**   So that the consumer can best shop around for the most appropriate loan, the TIL law requires full disclosure of credit terms and use of a barometer of credit, i.e., the annual percentage rate.

66. **A**   Certain first liens are exempt (those to buy or build a home) if they are liens in connection with a "residential loan transaction" (i.e., a lien created in the consumer's principal dwelling to finance the acquisition or initial construction of that dwelling).

67. **B**   The lien to purchase is exempt.

68. **A**   Advertising that there is a five percent down payment requires disclosure of all the credit terms.

69. **D**   The advertising of credit terms is regulated, not prohibited.

70. **B**   Regulation Z (Truth-in-Lending) does not apply to commercial property transactions, just to residential transactions involving mortgages, trust deeds, or installment land contracts. Regulation Z does not pertain to discrimination.

71. **B**   Under ECOA, the lender cannot allow someone's old age to influence the loan decision. To do so would be illegal discrimination.

72. **A**   While a charge for the report is fair, it is illegal discrimination to deny services related to credit based upon being too old.

73. **D**   Since there are not facts indicating homeowner is a "creditor" (one who in the ordinary course of business extends credit), the Truth-in-Lending law does not apply.

74. **D**   The total amount of interest must be stated, not per installment.

75. **C**   Superfund imposes strict liability on landowners for clean-up expenses.

76. **A**   Asbestos can be "friable" or "non-friable." Friable means that it can quickly break up and be released as tiny fibers into the air that can be inhaled and cause lung damage.

77. **D**   PCBs can cause adverse reproduction effects in humans.

78. **A**   Congress has imposed clean-up responsibility through "Superfund" or as it is also known, Comprehensive Environmental Response, Compensation and Liability Act of 1980 (CERCLA).

Chapter 18   Property Management, Lease Agreements and Securities

The questions in this chapter test your comprehension of the following topics:

- The role and responsibilities of a property manager
- Property management agreements
- Rights and obligations of landlord and tenant
- Types of lease agreements
- Use of security deposits
- Common provisions found in lease agreements
- Types of transactions involving sale of securities

False Friends

The following words are often confused with one another. Note the difference in meaning of these false friends:

Security Deposit/Earnest Money Deposit: The security deposit is paid by the tenant up front to cover any default in the lease including damage, whereas the buyer puts up earnest money at the time of an offer to be forfeited in the event the buyer does not perform.

Tenancy at Will/Tenancy for Years: The tenancy for years lasts for a fixed period, whereas the tenancy at will may be canceled at any time by either landlord or tenant.

Eviction, Actual/Eviction, Constructive: In an actual eviction the landlord evicts the defaulting tenant; whereas in a constructive eviction, the landlord fails to provide the necessary services so the tenant is legally entitled to cancel the lease.

Leasehold/Leased Fee: The leasehold is the lessee's interest, whereas the leased fee is the landlord's interest represented by the value of the remaining rent plus the reversion.

Gross Lease/Net Lease: In a gross lease the tenant pays one amount and the landlord pays the expenses; whereas in a net lease, the tenant pays a net amount to the landlord and the tenant pays the expenses.

QUESTIONS

1. Among the major responsibilities of a property manager are all of the following **EXCEPT**:
   (A) obtain the highest possible return for the investor.
   (B) preserve the building.
   (C) maintain high occupancy.
   (D) obtain listing for resale.

❖ 2. A broker acting as a property manager of a building was instructed by the owner to paint the building for $1,000. Without the owner's knowledge and consent:
   (A) the broker could contract the job for $800 and keep the extra $200.
   (B) the broker could accept a rebate from the painter.
   (C) the broker could do the entire job and keep the $1,000.
   (D) the broker could do nothing that is not within the scope of the employment contract.

❖ 3. All of the following should be included as fixed operating expenses in the budget for property management **EXCEPT**:
   (A) property manager's fees.
   (B) ceiling replacement.
   (C) fuel costs.
   (D) maintenance.

4. A property manager's duties typically include all of the following **EXCEPT**:
   (A) collecting rents.
   (B) making minor repairs.
   (C) marketing space.
   (D) investing profits from clients' properties.

❖ 5. A properly drawn property management contract should contain all of the following **EXCEPT**:
   (A) a legal description of the property.
   (B) the terms and conditions of the employment.
   (C) outline of the expected duties.
   (D) the scope of the authority.

6. One of the most effective ways for a property manager to both provide income to the owner and advertise the manager's own abilities is through a well-run building that has:
   (A) as high or higher rents than other similar buildings.
   (B) satisfied tenants served by competent employees.
   (C) the most complete and up-to-date accounting reports.
   (D) the lowest paid employees.

7. All of the following should be a consideration in selecting a tenant **EXCEPT**:
   (A) size of the space versus the tenant's requirements.
   (B) tenant's ability to pay.
   (C) racial and ethnic backgrounds of the tenants.
   (D) compatibility of the business to other tenants.

8. Certified Property Manager (CPM) is a designation awarded to qualified applicants by:
   (A) local board of REALTORS®.
   (B) the National Association of Real Estate Boards.
   (C) state associations of real estate boards.
   (D) the Institute of Real Estate Management.

9. Included in the property management budget as fixed operating expenses are all of the following costs **EXCEPT**:
   (A) hazard insurance.
   (B) property management fee.
   (C) repair of damaged carpeting.
   (D) reserves for overhaul and maintenance of air-conditioning and heating equipment.

❖10. Property managers are responsible for all of the following **EXCEPT**:
   (A) protecting the condition of real estate.
   (B) maximizing income from real property.
   (C) handling rents.
   (D) drafting original legal documents for leasing of building.

11. A property manager, to secure the best return on the investment, would establish rental income by:
    (A) long-term rentals in the upper range of present rents.
    (B) long-term contracts at the mid-point of present day rentals.
    (C) long-term contracts with a built-in escalation clause.
    (D) month-to-month rental.

12. Which of the following is true?
    (A) The most common way of setting up a rent schedule for units of space in a building is to compare the space units with other similar units, in similar buildings, in similar neighborhoods and then to set competitive rents.
    (B) If the rent is not paid by the rental due date, the property manager should immediately evict the tenant.
    (C) The property manager should handle the listing and sale of the property.
    (D) The property manager should be well versed in all tax benefits of the property to the employer.

13. In negotiating a commercial lease for an absentee owner, a property manager may be permitted to do all of the following **EXCEPT**:
    (A) determine the limits of concessions, such as three months' free rent to be offered to prospective tenants.
    (B) initiate legal action against a tenant whose rent is in arrears many months.
    (C) require that the tenant list with the property manager other property for sale.
    (D) assist in determining the leasing prices.

14. All of the following are valid operating expenses for a building manager to put into the budget **EXCEPT**:
    (A) heating oil.   (C) debt service.
    (B) cleaning supplies.   (D) management fees.

15. Which is true regarding the role of a property manager?
    (A) The establishment of competitive rents is an important function of property management.
    (B) It is not the function of property management to investigate a prospective tenant's credit rating.
    (C) The quality of a tenant is of little concern to the property manager just so the tenant pays the rent on time.
    (D) The manager must evaluate the proper financing on the building.

16. When a broker signs a contract to manage an owner's property he or she becomes a:
    (A) lessor.   (C) receiver.
    (B) trustee.   (D) fiduciary.

17. A broker acting as a property manager should place which of the following into the general account?
    (A) Rents
    (B) Security deposits
    (C) Deposits for pets from tenants
    (D) Broker's earned commissions

18. In management of real estate, a broker may:
    (A) personally accept and keep rebates from suppliers.
    (B) commingle rents received with the broker's own funds.
    (C) invest security deposits in an interest-bearing account for the broker's own benefit.
    (D) not make a secret profit.

19. Assume that a property manager is a broker who is able to buy merchandise needed for the property through a relative at a lower price than from any other source. He or she should:
    (A) proceed with the purchases.
    (B) proceed with the purchases, charging the owner a portion of the costs saved for work done in securing a better price.
    (C) proceed with the purchases but inform the owner in writing that a relative owned the company from which purchases were made.
    (D) not purchase from a relative.

❖ 20. A properly drafted property management agreement should contain all of the following **EXCEPT**:

(A) names of owner and manager.

(B) requirement that the manager provide periodic reports to the owner.

(C) outlined duties of property manager.

(D) names of tenants in occupancy.

21. With reference to the function of a property manager, all of the following are the responsibility of a property manager **EXCEPT**:

(A) obtain the best possible return on the owner's investment.

(B) preserve the owner's investment.

(C) maintain the interior condition of rental units.

(D) interview prospective tenants.

22. Which is true regarding most properly drawn property management agreements?

(A) The manager obtains an exclusive listing to sell at any time.

(B) It defines the rights and obligations of owner and agent.

(C) The manager acts as the sales agent if the property is to be sold.

(D) The manager usually has an option on the property.

❖ 23. All of the following are true regarding property managers hired to keep the property fully occupied **EXCEPT**:

(A) Their management agreement must be in writing to be enforceable in court.

(B) One of the main functions is to protect their principal's investment.

(C) They have a fiduciary relationship with the owner.

(D) Their fees should be clearly outlined in the property management agreement.

24. All of the following should be covered in a properly drawn property management agreement **EXCEPT**:

(A) management fees.

(B) operating expenses.

(C) duration or term.

(D) manager's duties.

25. Which of the following would not be present in a typical property management agreement?

(A) Provision for monthly reports

(B) Long-term contract period

(C) Names of parties

(D) Amount of management fees

26. When describing the premises to be rented in a short-term office lease, the contract should include all of the following **EXCEPT**:

(A) legal description of the building.

(B) floor plan for the office.

(C) street address of the building.

(D) dimensions of the space.

❖ 27. A long-term lease is generally to the owner's advantage in all of the following cases **EXCEPT**:

(A) when negotiating a commercial lease with an escalation clause.

(B) when the owner has made significant alterations in the space to suit the tenant.

(C) when economic times cause excessively high demands for rental space.

(D) during predicted economic downturns and recessions.

28. Building rules and regulations generally do all of the following **EXCEPT**:

(A) protect the owner's investment.

(B) provide for the peaceful enjoyment of all tenants.

(C) keep rent increases to a minimum.

(D) serve the owner and offer benefits to the tenant.

29. A lease clause sometimes negotiated by a property manager that provides for increases of a predetermined amount of rent at specific times over the term of the lease is **BEST** described as:

(A) an index clause.

(B) a step-up clause.

(C) a percentage clause.

(D) an escalation clause.

30. A property manager **MOST** likely would conduct a market survey to determine:

(A) appropriate use of the building.

(B) appropriate rents to charge.

(C) required maintenance.

(D) availability of money.

31. A property manager should know that there will be an increased demand for apartment rental when there is an increase in:
(A) money supply.
(B) vacancy rates.
(C) mortgage rates.
(D) disintermediation.

32. A property manager of a commercial condominium project would normally perform all of the following functions **EXCEPT**:
(A) maintain the common elements.
(B) make repairs inside of units.
(C) maintain books and records.
(D) market space.

❖ 33. In inflationary times, a property manager would **NOT** want a long-term lease with rents based upon:
(A) graduated amounts.
(B) the consumer price index.
(C) the cost of living index.
(D) a fixed rate.

34. In negotiating a property management agreement with the owner of an apartment building, the property manager would **MOST** likely base the fee upon which one of the following?
(A) Percentage of gross collectible income
(B) Percentage of net income
(C) Flat rate
(D) Cost and expenses

35. In a lease, the right of first refusal most nearly means:
(A) tenant can cancel.
(B) tenant can extend.
(C) tenant can buy at foreclosure sale.
(D) tenant can match an offer to relet.

36. Which of the following events normally is a ground for terminating a lease?
(A) The death of either the landlord or tenant
(B) The sale of the property
(C) Abandonment by the tenant
(D) Foreclosure by a mortgagee with a prior recorded mortgage

37. A landlord and a tenant agree to terminate a lease. This is **MOST** specifically known as:
(A) release.
(B) rejection.
(C) abandonment.
(D) surrender.

38. What could happen when a commercial tenant who has been occupying a store on a ten-year lease refuses to vacate the premises at the end of the rental period?
(A) A tenant-at-sufferance condition exists.
(B) The landlord may hold the tenant liable for another ten-year period of rent payments.
(C) The tenant is entitled to one extension.
(D) The landlord can forcefully eject the tenant.

39. Which of the following statements is true concerning a sublease?
(A) The sublessee pays rent directly to the lessor.
(B) The sublessor is liable for any damages caused to the premises by the sublessee.
(C) Sublessor is no longer liable to lessor.
(D) A sublease transfers the entire remaining balance of the term.

❖ 40. The interest that a landlord has during a valid tenancy is known as:
(A) right to profits.
(B) reversionary interest.
(C) right of reentry.
(D) tenancy at sufferance.

41. In which case is the tenant relieved of the obligation to pay rent?
(A) Upon abandonment
(B) Upon constructive eviction
(C) Upon death of the landlord
(D) Because of external economic factors

42. The provisions of a lease may provide for all of the following **EXCEPT**:
(A) introduction of a non-conforming use.
(B) a 75 percent rent increase.
(C) rent increase based upon periodic appraisal.
(D) right of first refusal or option to renew.

43. All of the following are necessary parts of a lease **EXCEPT**:
(A) parties to the lease.
(B) term of the lease.
(C) option to purchase.
(D) terms of the rental payment.

44. Which of the following statements is true in respect to the assignment of a lease?
    (A) The original lessee is the sole party liable for the payment of the rent.
    (B) It is the same as a sublease.
    (C) The original lessee would still retain a right to use the property for a limited time.
    (D) The entire leasehold is transferred.

❖ 45. Under a net lease, the tenant usually pays for all of the following expenses **EXCEPT**:
    (A) utilities.   (C) taxes.
    (B) depreciation.   (D) insurance.

46. The term that **BEST** describes a tenant's interest in the property is:
    (A) a life estate.
    (B) a reversionary interest.
    (C) a remainder interest.
    (D) a leasehold estate.

47. Liability to a third person who sustains injuries on the leased premises normally belongs to:
    (A) the tenant.
    (B) the landlord.
    (C) mutual responsibility of landlord and tenant.
    (D) property manager.

48. A residential periodic lease will be terminated by:
    (A) mutual consent.
    (B) death of the landlord.
    (C) bankruptcy of the lessor.
    (D) outside claimants such as a trespasser.

49. A lease in which the rent will increase under certain circumstances is known as:
    (A) an upgrade lease.   (C) piggy-back lease.
    (B) a graduated lease. (D) sandwich lease.

50. Upon foreclosure against the landlord by the holder of a prior recorded mortgage, a subsequent tenant's lease:
    (A) remains unaffected.
    (B) may be terminated at the election of the mortgagee.
    (C) is affected even if the lease was signed before the mortgage.
    (D) is binding on the mortgagee.

51. A lease that requires the landlord to pay operating expenses of the property is called a:
    (A) net lease.   (C) graduated lease.
    (B) gross lease.   (D) percentage lease.

52. All but which one of the following provisions concerning the property should be included in a rental agreement for a residential condominium apartment?
    (A) Appraised value   (C) Amount of rent
    (B) Intended use   (D) Expiration date

53. Assume a mortgaged property is leased. Because of default in payment, the mortgagee forecloses on the mortgage. Which of the following statements is true regarding rights under the lease?
    (A) The lessee is automatically released from any further obligation on the lease.
    (B) The lease continues in effect despite the foreclosure.
    (C) The lease is void because the mortgagor has no right to give a lease on mortgaged property.
    (D) The lease may be terminated by the mortgagee but not by the lessee.

❖ 54. A lease of land only, on which the tenant agrees to construct a residence within a certain period of time, is **BEST** called a:
    (A) ground lease.   (C) net lease.
    (B) gross lease.   (D) percentage lease.

❖ 55. The sale of a property that is under a long-term lease has which of the following effects?
    (A) It terminates the lease upon 45 days' notice by the new owner.
    (B) It has no effect upon the term of the lease as far as the tenant is concerned.
    (C) It cannot be made unless the present tenant is notified of the intention to sell and given an opportunity to terminate the lease.
    (D) It terminates the lease and the tenant must negotiate a new lease with the new owner.

❖ 56. In a straight percentage lease, which of the following statements is true?
    (A) The owner usually has the right to examine the lessee's books.
    (B) There will be a minimum fixed rent in addition to percentage rent.
    (C) The tenant must pay expenses that occur on the property such as the taxes.
    (D) The tenant may choose any type of accounting system.

57. A recapture clause is frequently used in what type of lease?
    (A) Net lease
    (B) Gross lease
    (C) Percentage lease
    (D) Business lease

58. A lease that has a definite termination date is known as a:
    (A) tenancy for years.
    (B) periodic tenancy.
    (C) tenancy at will.
    (D) tenancy at sufferance.

59. *A* leases a warehouse to *B* who agrees to pay $1,000 per month to *A* in rent and pay the real property taxes, maintenance, insurance, and utilities. What is the type of lease most likely signed by *A* and *B*?
    (A) Net lease
    (B) Percentage lease
    (C) Gross lease
    (D) Sandwich lease

❖ 60. The right of first refusal gives the tenant which of the following?
    (A) The first choice to bid on the property upon foreclosure
    (B) The right to terminate the lease upon 30 days' notice
    (C) The right to re-rent (is binding on the lessor)
    (D) The right to get first choice to re-rent or buy if the owner decides to rent or sell

61. A graduated lease can be **BEST** defined as a lease:
    (A) that includes an option to purchase.
    (B) that provides for a possible increase in rent at a stated future time.
    (C) under which the landlord pays all ownership charges such as taxes.
    (D) that is passed intact from one owner to the next under terms of a contract.

❖ 62. A tenant rents a house at the beach from July 1 to August 31. This is known as:
    (A) a periodic tenancy.
    (B) an estate for years.
    (C) a tenancy at sufferance.
    (D) a tenancy at will.

63. The normal shopping center lease is which type?
    (A) Ground lease
    (B) Percentage lease
    (C) Gross lease
    (D) Sublease

64. A holdover tenancy is **MOST** likely created at the end of:
    (A) a tenancy in common.
    (B) a tenancy for years.
    (C) a tenancy at will.
    (D) a tenancy in severalty.

❖ 65. A tenancy at will is a tenancy of:
    (A) definite duration that either landlord or tenant can terminate at will.
    (B) indefinite duration that the landlord can terminate at will.
    (C) indefinite duration that either landlord or tenant can terminate at will.
    (D) definite duration that the tenant can terminate at will.

66. Which of the following statements concerning leases is true?
    (A) When a property with an existing lease is purchased, it is not necessary for the purchaser to honor the lease.
    (B) It is advisable for the lessee to obtain lease insurance against nonperformance of the lessor.
    (C) Lease rent includes principal and interest.
    (D) A lease may be terminated by surrender and acceptance.

❖ 67. By definition, an "estate for years:"
    (A) must last for a year or more.
    (B) must be for at least two years.
    (C) is for a fixed term, whether a week, a month or a decade.
    (D) requires a written lease.

68. If the lease does not cover the point:
    (A) the lessee is responsible for maintaining the interior of the premises and for waste.
    (B) the lessee is required to take out fire insurance on the leased premises.
    (C) the lease may not be assigned.
    (D) the lessor has the right to extend.

69. A tenant's rights under a lease:
    (A) are terminated when the property is sold.
    (B) are usually terminated when the lessor dies.
    (C) are superior to those of the lessor.
    (D) are usually binding even if the property is later mortgaged.

70. An instrument that transfers possession of real property, but does not transfer an ownership interest is a:
   - (A) deed.
   - (B) mortgage.
   - (C) land contract.
   - (D) lease.

❖ 71. Which of the following statements about leases is true?
   - (A) A gross lease is one where the rent is based on an agreed percentage of the gross income.
   - (B) A net lease is one where the rent is based on a fixed percentage of the net income.
   - (C) A percentage lease requires the tenant to pay a percentage of the property taxes on the property.
   - (D) A gross lease is one where the landlord pays the expenses normally incurred with property ownership.

72. An escalation clause in a lease provides for:
   - (A) adjustment of rental payments to cover contingencies.
   - (B) extension of the rental period.
   - (C) shortened rental term.
   - (D) more frequent payments on the rent.

73. Which of the following creates a lessor-lessee relationship?
   - (A) Life estate
   - (B) Agreement to lease
   - (C) Deed
   - (D) Lease

74. A reversionary interest in a leasehold situation:
   - (A) constitutes a breach of a lease.
   - (B) expires when a lease is executed.
   - (C) is a landlord's right to use of the property upon expiration of a lease.
   - (D) allows land to escheat at the termination of a lease.

❖ 75. H buys a small office building in which there are several existing two-year leases for commercial space. Which is true?
   - (A) The lessees can now be forced to pay higher rents to H.
   - (B) H takes title to the property subject to the terms of the lease.
   - (C) The leases are terminated upon the sale of the building.
   - (D) H may renegotiate the lease at his option within the first 60 days.

76. Which of the following types of leases typically does **NOT** require notice to quit?
   - (A) Month-to-month tenancy
   - (B) Tenancy at will
   - (C) Tenancy for years
   - (D) Tenancy for months

77. The term "lessor" is **MOST** likely to be used to describe:
   - (A) a tenant.
   - (B) an owner.
   - (C) a vendor.
   - (D) an optionor.

78. A leasehold interest lying between the primary lease and the sublease is known as:
   - (A) a percentage lease.
   - (B) a sandwich lease.
   - (C) an inactive lease.
   - (D) an undercapitalized lease.

79. A tenant who is constructively evicted by a landlord may consider the lease as being:
   - (A) renewed.
   - (B) terminated.
   - (C) assigned.
   - (D) sold.

80. Which of the following statements in reference to a lease is false?
   - (A) Rent is always payable in advance.
   - (B) Unless a contrary agreement is in effect, the lessee may sublet.
   - (C) A security deposit remains the property of the lessee until actual damages occur.
   - (D) A written lease can be altered by a witnessed, oral agreement.

❖ 81. Which of the following is true about the security deposit in most residential leasehold situations?
   - (A) It must consist of the first and last month's rent.
   - (B) It can only be applied to cover physical damage caused to the premises.
   - (C) It must be returned any time within one year.
   - (D) It may be put in an interest-bearing account.

82. In assigning a lease, the lessee of a lease that contains no provision covering assignment:
   - (A) remains liable for any unpaid rent.
   - (B) must obtain the written consent to such assignment.
   - (C) may not assign unless specifically stated so.
   - (D) only the assignee is liable for unpaid rent.

83. When the lessor in a net lease dies:
    (A) the lease terminates.
    (B) the lessee has the option to terminate the lease.
    (C) the lease is void.
    (D) the lease is not affected.

❖ 84. When leased premises reach a physical condition whereby the tenant is unable to occupy them for the purpose intended, the situation is legally recognized as:
    (A) a dispossess eviction.
    (B) an actual eviction.
    (C) a constructive eviction.
    (D) a passive eviction.

85. A leasehold estate at will is which of the following?
    (A) Tenancy for years
    (B) Tenancy at sufferance
    (C) Tenancy for an indefinite period
    (D) Life estate

86. The interest of a tenant who came rightly into possession by permission of the owner but continues to occupy the premises without permission is called:
    (A) a sandwich lease.
    (B) an estate at sufferance.
    (C) an estate at will.
    (D) an estate in remainder.

87. Which of the following best applies to a landlord-tenant relationship?
    (A) Tenancy in common
    (B) Tenancy at sufferance
    (C) Joint tenancy
    (D) Tenancy by the entirety

❖ 88. In the absence of specific agreement, rent on a commercial lease is due:
    (A) on the first day of the rental period.
    (B) on the last day of the month.
    (C) whenever the tenant wants.
    (D) at the end of the rental period.

89. Escalation clauses found in leases:
    (A) are reflective of changed market conditions.
    (B) are usually held by the courts to be unconstitutional.
    (C) demand the lease be terminated in the event of late payment.
    (D) allow the tenant to assign his lease.

❖ 90. A percentage lease is:
    (A) one that provides for the broker's percentage of commission.
    (B) one in which the usual rent is based upon the net profits of the tenant.
    (C) one that always allows the tenant to cancel the lease if his or her income falls below a desired amount.
    (D) one in which the tenant's usual rent is based upon gross receipts.

91. If it is not stipulated in the lease and the leased property is sold, the lease:
    (A) has to be renewed.
    (B) is binding on the new owner.
    (C) creates a tenancy from month to month.
    (D) is considered surrendered.

92. The lessor under a net lease pays the:
    (A) taxes.
    (B) special assessments.
    (C) maintenance.
    (D) mortgage principal payments.

93. The deposit that a lessee must pay:
    (A) is called an earnest money deposit.
    (B) is considered to be the property of the lessor during the term of the lease.
    (C) is called a binder.
    (D) is called a security deposit.

❖ 94. A lessee is responsible for all of the following on the leased premises **EXCEPT**:
    (A) waste by a third party.
    (B) injury to a third party.
    (C) hazardous holes or cracks in the sidewalk.
    (D) damage to the carpeting of the dwelling.

❖ 95. Upon which one of the following situations can the landlord take title to the tenant's bar stools, tables and chandeliers?
    (A) Commencement of the lease
    (B) Tenant's default for two months
    (C) Tenant's bankruptcy
    (D) Failure of the tenant to remove these items after the lease is terminated

96. All of the following are true under the Uniform Residential Landlord and Tenant Act **EXCEPT**:
    (A) A landlord cannot charge a security deposit equal to more than one month's rent.
    (B) The landlord must return the deposit within a specified number of days of the tenant vacating the premises, or specify reasons for withholding all or part of the deposit.
    (C) The landlord must make any requested repairs up to a maximum of $1,000.
    (D) The security deposit is the property of the lessee, but under the control of the lessor.

❖ 97. Where a lessee defaults on a lease and abandons the property in good condition, the lessee could be held liable for which of the following amounts?
    (A) The balance of the rent plus forfeiture of the security deposit
    (B) The balance of the rent plus the cost to find a new tenant
    (C) The balance of the rent
    (D) Overdue rent less legal fees

98. In a lease that contains an escalation clause, which of the following is true?
    (A) The rent could increase 100 percent.
    (B) The lessee has an option to renew for another term.
    (C) The lease payment remains fixed over the term.
    (D) The term of the lease may be extended indefinitely.

99. All of the following are features of a tenancy at will **EXCEPT**:
    (A) It terminates with proper notice by either party.
    (B) It has no definite duration.
    (C) Sale of the property will terminate it.
    (D) Death of the landlord will not affect it.

❖ 100. The conveyance of an estate by lease is **BEST** described as a:
    (A) devise.   (C) deed.
    (B) demise.   (D) decree.

101. If a landlord wants to regain possession of the leased premises, he or she gives notice to:
    (A) enjoin.   (C) quit.
    (B) attach.   (D) relinquish.

102. Which lease provides for certain adjustments in rent based upon specific time intervals?
    (A) Ground lease   (C) Graduated lease
    (B) Net lease   (D) Long-term lease

103. A lease for an apartment in a residential apartment project is usually which type of lease?
    (A) Ground lease   (C) Net lease
    (B) Gross lease   (D) Percentage lease

104. A lease based on gross revenues is a:
    (A) gross lease.   (C) percentage lease.
    (B) net lease.   (D) recapture lease.

105. *C* orally leases a store to *B* for one year. The lease is:
    (A) a valid tenancy for years.
    (B) unenforceable due to the statute of frauds.
    (C) a valid tenancy from year to year.
    (D) unenforceable due to the statute of limitations.

106. A lease is which of the following?
    (A) A contract
    (B) A conveyance
    (C) Neither a contract nor a conveyance but a separate document in itself
    (D) Both a contract and a conveyance

107. The basic title that the lessor holds during the term of a lease is **BEST** known as:
    (A) reversion.   (C) diversion.
    (B) remainder.   (D) revision.

108. Which of the following can assign a lease?
    (A) Tenant at sufferance
    (B) Tenant at will
    (C) Holdover tenant
    (D) Tenant for years

109. *A* leases a commercial warehouse to *B* for nine months. Which is true?
    (A) The lease must be in writing.
    (B) The rights and obligations of *A* and *B* are regulated by the Uniform Residential Landlord and Tenant Act.
    (C) *A* has the right to raise the rent after six months.
    (D) *B* has a less-than-freehold estate.

110. An escalation clause in a lease provides for:
    (A) increased rentals because of higher operating expenses.
    (B) term extensions.
    (C) renewal options.
    (D) distraint.

❖ 111. The tenant is usually responsible for all of the following under a net lease **EXCEPT**:
    (A) utilities.   (C) taxes.
    (B) insurance.   (D) depreciation.

112. Which of the following estates indicates a lessor-lessee relationship?
    (A) Life estate   (C) Fee estate
    (B) Estate for years   (D) Estate in common

113. C leases a farm to A for five years. When C dies two years later, it is discovered that he only had a life estate. What is the status of A's lease?
    (A) Valid lease
    (B) Tenancy at sufferance
    (C) Freehold estate
    (D) Tenancy for years

114. A three-year lease of a farm property from A to B is terminated by:
    (A) A selling the farm to C.
    (B) destruction of the farm by fire.
    (C) A selling the farm to B.
    (D) A mortgaging the farm.

❖ 115. Which of the following parties to a long-term ground lease is the holder of the leased fee?
    (A) Lessor   (C) Grantee
    (B) Lessee   (D) Grantor

116. When a developer obtains a ground lease and intends to obtain a construction loan to build a condominium project, what type of provision regarding financing should be included in the lease?
    (A) Acceleration clause
    (B) Escalation clause
    (C) Subordination clause
    (D) Subrogation clause

❖ 117. In the event the lessee, without good reason, abandons the leased premises, leaving it in good condition, to what degree is the lessee normally liable to the lessor?
    (A) For rent payable to the date lessee leaves the premises, plus security deposit
    (B) For rent payable to the date lessee leaves, plus security deposit, and a percentage of rent payable for balance of term
    (C) For rent due and payable for the remaining period of the lease
    (D) For rent due and payable for the remaining period of the lease, plus the expense in locating a new tenant

118. Under the provisions of the Uniform Residential Landlord and Tenant Act, which of the following is true?
    (A) The maximum amount of money the tenant can pay at the start of the lease is equal to three months' rent.
    (B) The lessor can put in the lease a requirement for lessor's consent prior to the lessee subletting the premises.
    (C) The lessee has a right of first refusal.
    (D) The lessor must place security deposits in an interest-bearing account for the lessor's account.

119. The clause in a lease giving the tenant the right to purchase the leased property at a specific price is a:
    (A) reversionary right.
    (B) holdover tenancy.
    (C) lease option.
    (D) right of first refusal.

120. During the term of the lease, whose property is the security deposit?
    (A) Lessor   (C) Lessee
    (B) Mortgagee   (D) Property manager

121. Which of the following must be contained in a commercial lease agreement for it to be valid?
    (A) Amount of taxes on the leased premises
    (B) Name of institution in which the security deposit is held
    (C) Assessed valuation of the property
    (D) Amount of rent to be paid and the method of payment (monthly, quarterly, and so on)

122. All of the following is true about selling interests in a **Real Estate Investment Trust (REIT), EXCEPT:**
    (A) The anti-fraud provisions of the Securities Act apply.
    (B) Salespeople need to be licensed under the securities law.
    (C) Violation of the law is a criminal offense.
    (D) Brokers need to be licensed under the real estate licensing law.

❖ 123. State laws that regulate real estate securities are called:
    (A) sunset laws.
    (B) blue-sky laws.
    (C) SEC laws.
    (D) RESPA laws.

124. A property manager asks a real estate broker to find partners for a venture that he or she will manage. The broker should do which of the following?
    (A) Contact the Attorney General
    (B) Check out the application of state and federal securities laws
    (C) Refuse to help
    (D) Charge a flat fee

125. All of the following are true concerning entities that are classified as Direct Participation Programs (DPP) **EXCEPT:**
    (A) Taxes are paid by the members of the entity.
    (B) People who sell these programs need a special securities license.
    (C) Examples of DPP entities include partnerships and S-corporations.
    (D) They are limited to 10 investors.

❖ 126. All of the following transactions involve the sale of a security **EXCEPT:**
    (A) an investment contract.
    (B) condominium apartment with mandatory rental pool.
    (C) shares in a limited partnership.
    (D) site of a commercial warehouse.

127. Selling a real property security without a securities license violates which one of the following laws?
    (A) 1933 Securities Exchange Act
    (B) 1934 Securities Exchange Act
    (C) 1935 Securities Act
    (D) 1936 Securities Investment Act

❖ 128. Which of the following security offerings are subject to the registration requirements of the 1933 Securities Act?
    (A) A private placement offering to less than ten investors
    (B) A security offering only to bona fide residents in one state
    (C) Shares in a residential real estate investment limited partnership
    (D) Interest in a profit-sharing retirement plan

129. The interstate sale of a subdivision could fall under the federal securities laws if the seller does which of the following?
    (A) Provides an inspection tour
    (B) Guarantees profits through a rental pool
    (C) Finances the sale
    (D) Covers the first year's property tax

130. Assume there is a 5-year lease at $5,000 per year. The lessor in year 3 usually cannot:
    (A) mortgage.
    (B) sell.
    (C) raise rent.
    (D) devise.

131. When buying an investment piece of real estate, the buyer should obtain which of the following?
    (A) Flood insurance
    (B) Estoppel letter from tenants
    (C) Reduction certificate
    (D) Tax withholding statement

132. On a triple net lease, the tenant usually pays for all of the following **EXCEPT:**
    (A) insurance.
    (B) utilities.
    (C) management fees.
    (D) mortgage payments.

133. When a group of investors and one or more sponsors acquire real estate, this is best called a:
    (A) rental pool.
    (B) time share.
    (C) syndication.
    (D) group investment.

134. If a person selling real property securities in the form of a REIT is guilty of fraud, all of the following could occur **EXCEPT:**
    (A) criminal penalty.
    (B) civil penalty.
    (C) rescission of contract.
    (D) actual damages multiplied by five.

135. Which of the following types of ownership is least likely to be subject to regulation by the securities law?
(A) Limited partnership
(B) Sub-chapter S corporation
(C) Syndication
(D) Joint tenancy

ANSWERS

1. **D** The property manager is a fiduciary but is not responsible for listing the property. This is an entirely different function from management.

2. **D** If the property manager is going to get a rebate, he or she must get the owner's permission, preferably in writing.

3. **B** Ceiling replacement would be a capital expenditure, the money for which would come from either reserve funds for replacement or a special assessment.

4. **D** Property managers handle rents, minor repairs and marketing of leases. They are not responsible for making investment decisions, such as handling real estate profits for their clients.

5. **A** While the property should be generally described, it need not be a legal description, such as a metes and bounds description.

6. **B** High rents (A) may not be the best barometer of an effective management program if there are excessive maintenance and other unnecessary costs.

7. **C** Such practice would violate the Federal Fair Housing Act and most state discrimination laws.

8. **D** IREM is an organization of the National Association of REALTORS®, which limits its membership to individuals (not firms) who meet minimum education and experience requirements in the area of property management.

9. **C** This is not a regularly occurring carrying charge.

10. **D** The property and its income are valuable assets of the owner, and the property manager is a fiduciary charged with the duty to protect and maintain them. Attorneys draft leases; property managers obtain signatures.

11. **C** Without an escalation clause, the landlord would suffer the effects of inflationary trends.

12. **A** Choice (B) is incorrect because the manager should first make contact with the tenant to find out the reasons behind the late payment, rather than immediately commencing legal eviction proceedings.

13. **C** Concessions are negotiable points in the lease, which are determined in the lessee's favor. If managers negotiate the lease, they should be sure that their authority extends to granting concessions. Most owners do not wish to be bothered with the hassles involved in eviction proceedings.

14. **C** Mortgage payments would not be a regularly occurring expenditure in an operating budget.

15. **A** The property manager plays a key role in establishing appropriate rents and screening prospective tenants.

16. **D** As a fiduciary, the property manager owes duties of loyalty, obedience, accountability, care and skill to the owner.

17. **D** The broker should establish a client trust fund account for rental management funds and keep these separate from the general fund and the residential sales client trust fund account. Broker fees can be kept in the general account once they are earned.

18. **D** The broker must fully disclose in writing any personal interest he or she may have in regard to the managed property.

19. **C** The point is to notify the owner of such a pertinent fact.

20. **D** The property management agreement is a contract, so the parties must be named. It is in the best interest of the owner to receive periodic reports. Although a list of tenants will be needed it does not have to be incorporated in the Property Management Agreement.

21. C   Protecting the investment in the property and maximizing the return are two major reasons why an owner hires a professional property manager. Interior work is usually the tenant's responsibility.

22. B   It is not the role of a property manager to handle the sale of the property; he or she markets the space in the building.

23. A   Although it is the best practice, the statute of frauds does not require property management agreements to be in writing to be enforceable. However, if the agent is authorized to lease real property for longer than the period called for in the statute of frauds, then such authority must be in writing to be enforceable.

24. B   These are contained in the budget.

25. B   Most owners would not want to get locked into a long-term property management agreement.

26. A   The lease will often contain an exhibit in which the space to be leased is outlined on a floor plan.

27. C   The escalation clause will aid in keeping the lease in line with inflationary trends and rising operating costs.

28. C   Properly prepared rules will help both owner and tenant.

29. B   Such a step-up clause is found in a graduated lease. An escalation clause allows for increases and decreases based on changes in a specified index, such as increased taxes or maintenance costs.

30. B   By comparison with similar buildings in the area, the manager will have better insight into the amount of rent to charge. Required maintenance is determined by inspection and observation; use or zoning and availability of money have little relevance.

31. C   As mortgage rates increase, fewer people can qualify to purchase a home and so must continue to rent. Disintermediation refers to savings account withdrawals.

32. B   The property manager works for the association of owners and would be unnecessarily exposing the association to liability for faulty work done within individual units.

33. D   Rental rates should allow for rising costs and expenses and should not be locked in for long periods of time.

34. A   Most property manager fees are based on a percentage of gross income (after deducting for vacancies and other rent loss) without taking into account operating expenses. Percentage fees are generally preferred to flat rates because they give the manager an incentive to increase the income from the property. The flat fee is often disadvantageous to the manager since it can be increased only by further negotiation with the owner.

35. D   If the lessor decides to lease the premises to a new tenant, the lessor must give a lessee with a right of first refusal the first chance to lease on the new terms. Sometimes a right of first refusal is worded so the lessee has the first chance to match an offer to purchase the property, if it is offered for sale.

36. D   A lease is a contract as well as a conveyance and neither death nor sale would affect the contract rights, i.e., the decedent's estate is bound by the terms of the lease and any purchaser takes the property subject to the lease. The tenant takes possession subject to the mortgage.

37. D   A surrender refers specifically to a lease terminated by mutual agreement—technically, a surrender and acceptance.

38. A   A tenant at sufferance is a tenant who remains on the property after lease expiration and before the landlord has consented to the continued occupancy. A landlord may elect to hold the tenant over to a new term but, because of the statute of frauds, most "holdover" tenancies are limited to one year (in some states, three-year oral leases are valid).

39. B   The sublessee pays the sublessor (original lessee) who is directly liable to the lessor for the rent and for full compliance with the provisions of the original lease. The sublessor does not avoid liability by transferring to the sublessee part of the interest.

40. **B**   The lessor has a reversion interest; he or she is entitled to recover the property, plus improvements, at the termination of the lease. The value of the leased fee is usually the rent (discounted to present worth), plus an estimated value attributed to this reversion interest. The grantor of a conditional fee estate has the right of reentry.

41. **B**   A tenant cannot avoid contractual obligations by abandoning the premises. But if the landlord substantially interferes with the tenant's right to peaceful habitability (for example, failing to provide plumbing or creating health hazards), then the tenant can leave the premises and be excused from paying rent.

42. **A**   By contract, the parties can agree to any rent increase, but they cannot agree to do something illegal, such as *commencing* a use that no longer conforms to the law.

43. **C**   A valid lease may or may not contain an option provision.

44. **D**   An assignment is a transfer of the entire leasehold, whereas a sublease transfers a portion by way of a separate agreement (such as the transfer of one-half of a ten-year lease).

45. **B**   The concept of a net lease has the tenant paying many of the carrying charges, such as utilities, insurance or taxes. Depreciation of the building is not a carrying charge and is handled by the landlord computing a recapture rate for the investment.

46. **D**   It might be noted, however, that a lessor has a reversionary interest in the leased fee (the lessor's interest).

47. **A**   Generally, the part with control over the leased property is liable for waste and injuries to third parties in those areas. The tenant typically has exclusive control over the leased premises, whereas the landlord would have control over areas such as hallways, stairwells and grounds.

48. **A**   By agreement, the lessee and lessor can reach a friendly surrender of their rights and obligations. Death usually does not terminate a contract, such as a lease (except an estate at will).

49. **B**   A graduated lease often is a long-term lease with increases (specified in a step-up clause) in the rent, structured to take place at established intervals at set amounts or at amounts to be reached by subsequent appraisal and arbitration.

50. **B**   A tenant takes a leasehold estate subject to the rights of prior recorded interests. The tenant would be advised, in these situations, to obtain a nondisturbance agreement from the mortgagee prior to executing the lease.

51. **B**   A triple net lease would have the tenant paying for all expenses whereas another net lease (called a modified net lease) might cover just taxes. Thus, it is important to review the exact requirements of each net lease.

52. **A**   Normally, the appraised value would have little bearing on the lessor-lessee relationship. The appraised value might become important in a long-term lease. If rent increases in later years, it will be negotiated based on value increases.

53. **D**   The mortgage has the choice of whether or not to terminate the lease, since the lessee acquired the leasehold estate subject to the existing mortgage.

54. **A**   These ground leases are often long-term, graduated net leases (55 or more years).

55. **B**   The purchaser takes the property subject to the rights of the lessee under the existing lease. This explains why it is important to inspect the property to discover the rights of parties in possession.

56. **A**   Inspection of books is typical, but a straight percentage does not provide for any minimum fixed rent.

57. **C**   The recapture clause would be found in a straight percentage lease. A landlord could recapture the premises and terminate the lease of a tenant not meeting specified income quotas.

58. **A**   The tenancy for years is the only type of lease that has a specific termination date. No notice to quit is needed to terminate the expired lease.

59. **A** The landlord nets a specific amount and the tenant must pay the carrying expenses.

60. **D** Depending on the wording, the right could be to match the first purchase offer or relet offer.

61. **B** Such a lease contains a step-up clause that details how and when the increases will occur (it could also have a step-down clause for decreases).

62. **B** The specific termination date is the key to a "tenancy or estate for years," a sometimes misleading classification because the term can be for less than a year.

63. **B** It could be a straight percentage lease, or one with a fixed minimum rent plus a percentage, or one of many other varieties.

64. **B** If a tenant under a lease for a set term stays on after the term, the landlord can elect to hold the tenant to another term (usually not more than a year).

65. **C** Either party can elect to terminate the tenancy, although most states now require a minimum amount of prior notice.

66. **D** Purchasers buy subject to the rights of existing lessees. Usually, commercial lessors can obtain insurance to protect against *lessee* defaults in failing to pay rent or damaging premises.

67. **C** If the estate for years period is less than one year, it may not have to be in writing to be enforceable under most statutes of frauds.

68. **A** The person in control usually has the responsibility for waste and injury. Unless required by the terms of the lease, the lessee need not take out insurance, although it is wise to be covered.

69. **D** Neither death nor sale of the property will terminate the lease. The mortgagee takes subject to existing leases.

70. **D** The lessee acquires exclusive possession, but not legal nor equitable ownership. A land contract transfers possession and equitable title.

71. **D** A percentage lease is based on a percentage of gross income.

72. **A** Such contingencies might include increases in energy costs or the cost of living index beyond specified levels; if so, rent would increase correspondingly.

73. **D** An agreement to lease does not transfer exclusive possession of the premises nor establish the parties as landlord or tenant.

74. **C** The landlord is entitled to obtain the possession of the fee plus any improvements on the property that the tenant either did not remove willingly or was not permitted to remove (by contract, the parties can deal otherwise with the improvements).

75. **B** The purchaser takes the property subject to the terms of existing leases and will have to wait until the two-year leases expire before being able to raise the rent.

76. **C** Even a tenancy at will would require some notice by either party that the tenancy is over.

77. **B** An optionor is usually the seller (vendor). Note that in a lease-option the owner would be a lessor and an optionor.

78. **B** The sandwich lessor is the lessee under the master lease, in the case where a ground lease is made between the owner and a developer, who then leases to the occupant. The developer is sandwiched in between the fee owner on one side and the fee user on the other side.

79. **B** Constructive eviction might be the case if the landlord allows the premises to become uninhabitable.

80. **A** Unless otherwise specified in the lease or state law, rent is payable in arrears, when the tenancy is at an end. Because of this ancient rule, most leases and most residential landlord-tenant codes provide for rent payments to be made in advance. Provided there are witnesses to prove the oral modification, most written leases can be orally modified, although the best business practice is to obtain such modification in writing to lessen the chance of dispute.

81. **D** The security deposit should not be earmarked as the last month's rent for then it would be taxable as prepaid rent. It belongs to the lessee and is held in trust as security against physical damage, failure to pay rent, failure to return any items on the premises (like keys), or failure to meet any other lease conditions.

82. **A** Written consent is required only if covered in the lease. The lessee (assignor) remains secondarily liable in the event the assignee defaults.

83. **D** Death does not alter the lease contract. The lessor's estate receives the rent and the property titleholder must uphold the lease.

84. **C** The tenant is thereafter relieved of rent payments once premises are vacated.

85. **C** The tenancy at will exists until either party terminates it, dies, or the property is sold. In a tenancy at sufferance, there is no lessor approval of the lessor-lessee relationship.

86. **B** An estate at sufferance is different than a trespass, and thus the tenant, who has the lowest estate in real property, cannot acquire title to the premises by way of adverse possession.

87. **B** Answers (A), (C) and (D) are methods of owning real property. A tenancy at sufferance indicates there once was a valid landlord-tenant lease relationship, which has now expired.

88. **D** Unless the lease provides otherwise (and most leases do), rent is not due until the end of the lease term.

89. **A** Escalation clauses are partially designed to keep rents in line with inflationary trends. It is a permissible constitutional exercise of one's freedom to contract for legitimate purposes.

90. **D** Naturally, the definition of "gross receipts" is quite an important part of the percentage lease (does it include returned merchandise, credit sales, mail orders, etc.?). "Profits" is a more difficult term to define precisely.

91. **B** The new owner takes the property subject to the lease unless the lease contains a cancellation clause, which provides that upon a sale of the property the owner may cancel the lease.

92. **D** The lessee pays the carrying charges but the lessor pays for the debt reduction.

93. **D** It is called a security deposit and is held in trust by the lessor, but it is the money of the lessee and can be used only to cover losses due to breach of the lease.

94. **C** Having exclusive control of the leased premises, the lessee is liable for damage caused by third parties (guests) and physical injury to third persons. Waste could be removal of topsoil, for example.

95. **D** These items are considered "trade fixtures" and remain the property of the tenant unless the tenant fails to remove them at the termination of the lease.

96. **C** The security deposit is limited and must be returned within a certain number of days; otherwise, the landlord may lose the right to withhold it. There is no requirement to make *any* requested repairs.

97. **C** The lessee is not responsible for more rent than required if the lease had not been breached and lessee had remained the full term. The key word here is *plus*. Costs are allowed only if the new tenant is found prior to the end of the full term.

98. **A** An escalation clause deals with rent increases, not a renewal option.

99. **D** In addition, the tenancy at will can be terminated by death of either party or sale of the property.

100. **B** A devise (A) is a conveyance of real property by will.

101. **C** To terminate a periodic tenancy the landlord would give a notice to quit. Also, prior to bringing an eviction action against a defaulting tenant, the landlord must usually give a notice to quit.

102. **C**   The graduated lease contains step-up clauses that frequently adjust the rent upwards.

103. **B**   The landlord (owner) gets a lump-sum payment each month, enough to pay carrying charges, such as taxes, maintenance or insurance. This is true even though the tenant usually pays for utilities.

104. **C**   Shopping center leases are typically percentage leases based on the tenant's gross revenues.

105. **A**   Most statutes of frauds permit oral leases for one year or less, although it is good practice to commit all leases to writing so as to lessen disputes between the parties.

106. **D**   A lease is a demise or conveyance of exclusive possession to the premises, and it is also a contract stating the rights and obligations of lessor and lessee.

107. **A**   A right of reversion can be transferred or assigned.

108. **D**   Neither (A), (B) nor (C) has an interest capable of transfer.

109. **D**   Most landlord-tenant codes cover residential leases only, not commercial leases.

110. **A**   Also included would be coverage for increased taxes. Distraint is the legal right of the landlord, under a court order, to seize a tenant's belongings for overdue rent.

111. **D**   The landlord is responsible for any losses caused by depreciation to the building, such as normal wear and tear deteriorations.

112. **B**   This nonfreehold estate specifies a definite duration.

113. **B**   *A* leased the property subject to the reversion interest of *C*'s grantor. Upon the end of the life estate, *A*'s interest in the property ceases and he is, at most, a tenant at sufferance until the owner determines whether or not to allow the tenancy to continue.

114. **C**   The lease is terminated because of the merger of the leasehold estate and the leased fee into *B*'s sole ownership. While the destruction of a residential apartment would terminate a lease, the destruction of a farm on leased property may not terminate the lease since many of the farming activities may continue. (This rule has a historical basis in our once agrarian society.)

115. **A**   The lessor holds the leased fee, which is valued as the discounted value of the rent plus the value of the reversionary interest. The lessee holds the leasehold estate.

116. **C**   Commercial interim lenders usually insist on being in a first position and thus would want the ground lessor to subordinate or make junior his or her leased fee position.

117. **C**   The lessor is entitled to the rent for the remaining term except when a replacement tenant is found, in which case the lessor is entitled to rent for the unoccupied period up to the new lease, plus the cost of finding that new tenant.

118. **B**   In the usual lease situation, the tenant pays the first month's rent in advance plus a security deposit (one month's rent). If the lessor does not put in a requirement for consent, then the lessee could assign or sublet without first obtaining the lessor's approval. State law determines if interest-bearing accounts are required.

119. **C**   In a lease option the price is fixed, whereas in a right of first refusal the tenant is given the right to purchase the property at whatever price is set by the seller and only if the seller decides to sell. The lessor's reversionary right refers to the fact that the land and improvements revert to the lessor at the end of the lease term.

120. **C**   The lessor (or lessor's agent) holds the security deposit for the lessee pending full performance of the lessee's obligation under the lease.

121. **D** Except in special commercial net leases, taxes aren't usually a relevant part of lease agreements. Though the lessee's property, the security deposit can be held by anyone and, in fact, is often spent by the lessor. Some states now require that security deposits in residential transactions be placed in interest-bearing trust accounts.

122. **D** REITs are securities and not real property; thus, real estate licenses are not required.

123. **B** Designed to prevent fraud such as "promoting the sky," federal securities laws are regulated by the Securities Exchange Commission (SEC).

124. **B** Selling interests in a partnership may be deemed to be selling a security and thus requires a special license.

125. **D** There is no limit. A "Direct Participation Program" is any entity in which the investors participate directly in the tax benefits (e.g., a partnership or S-corporation in which the taxes and deductions are passed through to the investors and not paid or taken by the entity.) The National Association of Securities Dealers (NASD), a self-regulatory organization that licenses securities dealers, has a new limited license for people who sell real estate securities or interests in DPPs (Series 22 license).

126. **D** A security involves any investment contract in which there is investment in a common enterprise for a profit motive, the profit to be obtained through the efforts of a third party (the sponsor). Resort condominiums with rental pool management often fit the definition of an investment contract.

127. **B** The 1934 Securities Exchange Act regulates people who sell securities, including real property securities and investment contracts. The 1933 Securities Act regulates the securities themselves and requires registration and disclosure. Note that states have their own securities laws, often called blue-sky laws, that often require the offering be fair, just and equitable.

128. **C** The 1933 Securities Act requires registration of securities unless exempt. One exemption is an offering to a limited number of investors; another exemption is the intrastate offering involving only one state. Note that even when a security is exempt from registration, the disclosure and antifraud provisions of the 1933 Securities Act still apply.

129. **B** The sale of an "investment contract" in which profits are guaranteed through the efforts of persons other than the investor constitutes a security.

130. **C** The rent is fixed for five years. Remember that with a five-year lease that the lessor should have paid a conveyance tax. If the lessor mortgages, sells or wills the property, it will be taken subject to the lease.

131. **B** The letter will *estop* the tenant from later denying the amount of rent owed, security deposit and length of lease term.

132. **D** The tenant pays for the carrying costs in addition to the basic lease rent. The lessor still makes the mortgage payments.

133. **C** The syndication frequently is structured as a limited partnership and may be subject to registration under state and federal law as a security.

134. **D** The anti-fraud provisions of the *federal* securities laws provide for stiff penalties, but not multiplied by five. The law applies to the seller and the broker.

135. **D** A security often involves stock or an investment contract, as when one invests in a venture with the expectation of making profits through the efforts of the promoter. The sale of an investment condo with a mandatory rental pool arrangement involves the sale of a security and thus requires registration with federal and state securities agencies.

Appendix I: Licensing Laws

The state test section of both the broker and the salesperson examinations contains questions concerning the state licensing law, including the rules and regulations. The questions on the real estate licensing law in this section cover a broad range of real estate license law in most states. Because of the many subtle differences among the laws of various states, there is a chance some of the following questions and/or answers may not be appropriate to your state. Therefore, the prudent student will obtain a current copy of his or her state's licensing laws.

QUESTIONS

1. A licensed broker can establish a main office in which of the following places?
   (A) In the bedroom of his or her residential-zone home
   (B) In the residence of one of his or her salespeople
   (C) In a commercially zoned office building
   (D) A post office

2. A principal broker may authorize a salesperson in the office to do which of the following?
   (A) Deposit client's money in the firm's trust fund
   (B) Withdraw client's money from the firm's trust fund
   (C) Divert client's money into the broker's account
   (D) Commingle personal funds with client's money

3. If you are a licensee selling your own real property, you must inform all of the following **EXCEPT:**
   (A) your principal broker of the proposed sale of the property.
   (B) the prospective buyers in writing of your interest in the property prior to the sale.
   (C) cooperating brokers of your interest.
   (D) buyer's loan officer.

4. The licensing laws usually require which of the following to be in writing?
   (A) The listing agreement for the sale of real property
   (B) The contract between two brokers cooperating on a real estate transaction
   (C) An appraisal
   (D) Attorney instructions

❖ 5. Monies may be paid out of the Recovery Fund in the event that:
   (A) a defrauded seller suffers a monetary loss in selling to a bankrupt broker who conceals that he or she is a licensed broker.
   (B) a salesperson does not get paid by his or her broker in accordance with the written agreement.
   (C) closing costs exceed the broker's estimate.
   (D) the broker withdraws from the transaction.

6. A licensed real estate salesperson may do which of the following?
   (A) Employ other real estate salespeople
   (B) Hang the license in his or her own home, zoning permitting
   (C) Buy property for his or her own account
   (D) Open a client trust account separate from the employing broker

7. Which of the following is true concerning a broker's conduct?
   - (A) A broker must get the signatures of all owners on the listing form in order to earn a commission.
   - (B) A broker can't advertise without the written authorization of the owner.
   - (C) A broker must hold open house.
   - (D) A broker cannot be a dual agent.

8. When a principal broker's license has been suspended or revoked, the salespeople:
   - (A) must return their wall certificate and ID cards to the licensing agency until they relocate.
   - (B) may continue to actively sell real estate throughout the remainder of that calendar year.
   - (C) must take the broker's examination.
   - (D) may be authorized to withdraw funds from the client's trust account.

❖ 9. Which one of the following is subject to licensing laws?
   - (A) Court-appointed guardian
   - (B) One buying property under a power of attorney
   - (C) Commissioner at foreclosure sale
   - (D) Buyer's broker

10. A person is NOT required to be licensed to:
   - (A) rent a friend's house for a fee.
   - (B) sell his or her own property.
   - (C) handle an exchange of two properties.
   - (D) sell an easement for another.

11. All advertisements relating to property for sale by a broker must:
   - (A) contain the selling price of the property.
   - (B) indicate the location of the property.
   - (C) name the listing broker.
   - (D) name the cooperating broker.

❖ 12. One of the responsibilities of the real estate licensing agency is:
   - (A) to arbitrate commission disputes between brokerage firms.
   - (B) to arbitrate between an employer-broker and his or her salespeople.
   - (C) to conduct real estate classes.
   - (D) to grant licenses.

13. A broker-salesperson employed by a corporation, as a salesperson, may do which of the following?
   - (A) Also operate as an independent agent
   - (B) Open a trust account for a client
   - (C) Show a buyer properties not listed by the corporation
   - (D) Sign contracts on behalf of corporate clients

14. A license is required for any person who sells or leases or attempts to sell or lease for others and for compensation all of these EXCEPT:
   - (A) freehold interests.
   - (B) leasehold interests.
   - (C) easement interests.
   - (D) personalty interests.

❖ 15. By statutory definition, which of the following activities, if done for compensation, constitutes real estate brokerage?
   - (A) Soliciting for prospective buyers
   - (B) Making a real estate feasibility study
   - (C) Negotiating a loan
   - (D) Conducting a survey

16. A real estate salesperson is unable to collect earned commission from his or her broker. What action can be taken?
   - (A) File a claim against the Real Estate Recovery Fund
   - (B) File a lawsuit
   - (C) Sue the Board of REALTORS®
   - (D) Place a lien on the client's trust account

17. In the event that a salesperson fails to pay for the renewal fee when due, whose license will be forfeited automatically?
   - (A) Salesperson's
   - (B) Salesperson's broker
   - (C) Principal broker's
   - (D) All salespeople in firm

18. A broker-salesperson employed by a brokerage company may accept compensation direct from the owner for which of the following services?
   - (A) Building a swimming pool
   - (B) Procuring a qualified buyer
   - (C) Negotiating the sale
   - (D) Helping to fill out the sales contract

19. Which of the following people need to be licensed?
    (A) Full-time surveyors
    (B) Condominium managers in charge of renting units
    (D) Loan officers
    (D) House painters

20. Commissions for the sale of real estate are all of the following **EXCEPT**:
    (A) are determined by agreement between the parties.
    (B) could be earned by the broker even though the one who signed the listing did not own the property.
    (C) are negotiable.
    (D) fixed by law.

❖ 21. Which is true concerning a broker's client trust account?
    (A) A broker can deposit a commission check received from a satisfied seller.
    (B) The real estate licensing agency can inspect the broker's records concerning these accounts.
    (C) The broker need not place rental deposits in the account.
    (D) Interest on the account belongs to the salesperson.

22. The buyer is entitled to receive from the broker:
    (A) a copy of the listing.
    (B) a copy of the accepted offer.
    (C) a copy of all appraisals.
    (D) a copy of the seller's tax returns.

23. All of the following funds should be placed in the real estate trust account **EXCEPT**:
    (A) installment land contract collection.
    (B) earnest monies.
    (C) rental collections.
    (D) petty cash.

24. When a licensee personally buys property that he or she has listed:
    (A) the licensee must disclose true position to the owner.
    (B) the licensee is under no obligation to advise the vendor of his or her status.
    (C) the licensee forfeits the commission.
    (D) the licensee is prohibited from buying listed property.

25. A broker-salesperson working for another broker is authorized to:
    (A) open a client trust account for one of the clients.
    (B) collect commission out of such account prior to losing.
    (C) sign contracts on behalf of the broker.
    (D) show buyers properties listed with the firm.

26. The real estate licensing agency requires at the time of renewal a current financial statement from which of the following real estate brokerage firms?
    (A) Corporation   (C) Joint venture
    (B) Partnership   (D) None required

27. The provisions requiring a person to be licensed as a real estate broker or salesperson shall apply to all of the following **EXCEPT**:
    (A) any person who leases, offers to lease, rents or offers to rent, any real estate or the improvements thereon.
    (B) any person who solicits for prospective purchasers.
    (C) any person who lists property for sale.
    (D) any person who sells his or her own house.

28. A broker's records of his client's account should contain all of the following **EXCEPT**:
    (A) the date and from whom the money was received.
    (B) the date and where deposited by the broker.
    (C) the amount of the money collected.
    (D) the amount of commission due.

❖ 29. An unlicensed secretary in a broker's office may:
    (A) give information to a caller about listings available.
    (B) take a listing by phone.
    (C) solicit for listings.
    (D) arrange for a salesperson to handle the sale.

❖ 30. Which of the following statements is true?
    (A) So long as the broker retains a written copy of the listing or other agreement, it is not necessary to deliver a copy of the agreement to the principal.
    (B) No broker shall be issued a license unless he or she maintains a definite place of business in an appropriately zoned area.
    (C) A salesperson who is an independent contractor can maintain an office independent from the broker.
    (D) A broker must withhold taxes from an independent contractor.

31. Which of the following people is required to have a real estate license as a salesperson or broker?
    (A) Tax consultant
    (B) Negotiator of real estate mortgage loans
    (C) Title officer
    (D) Cooperating broker

❖ 32. A salesperson can accept compensation directly from the:
    (A) buyer.
    (B) seller.
    (C) escrow officer.
    (D) employing broker.

33. A licensee may have his or her license revoked for:
    (A) representing more than one party in a transaction without the knowledge and written consent of both parties.
    (B) accepting a fee for an appraisal.
    (C) conducting an open house.
    (D) recommending an interior decorator.

34. Under the licensing laws, which of the following statements is **FALSE**?
    (A) A broker can hire two separate salespeople to work on the same property.
    (B) If the broker's license is suspended, the salespeople's licenses are subject to automatic forfeiture.
    (C) The broker owns the listing.
    (D) An inactive licensee can take a listing.

35. If a salesperson fails to obtain an earnest money deposit:
    (A) legal action could be taken against salesperson's broker.
    (B) this would be a violation of the license law.
    (C) the contract is voidable.
    (D) the contract is still binding.

❖ 36. A licensee can lose his or her license for which of the following?
    (A) Using monies received as commissions to pay office rent
    (B) Paying a commission to an unlicensed person
    (C) Splitting fees with a cooperating broker
    (D) Negotiating an exchange

37. To make a claim against the Real Estate Recovery Fund, one must do all of the following **EXCEPT**:
    (A) submit proof that the licensee cannot pay the entire judgment.
    (B) obtain a court judgment against a licensee.
    (C) notify the real estate commission.
    (D) post a surety bond.

38. A broker handles the rentals of several condominium apartments for an investor-client. The broker is permitted to place these rental monies into a:
    (A) general business account.
    (B) client trust fund account.
    (C) personal savings account.
    (D) mutual fund account.

39. A broker may have his or her license revoked for doing which of the following?
    (A) Refusing to split a commission with a cooperating broker
    (B) Quoting a price other than that agreed upon by the owner
    (C) Advertising property for sale
    (D) Refusing to list a property

40. One of the main purposes of the licensing laws is to:
    (A) protect the licensee from the effects of untrustworthy licensees.
    (B) protect the general public.
    (C) limit the number of licensees.
    (D) resolve disputes between licensees.

41. Assume that M & M Realty, Inc., is issued a broker's license. Which one of the following is the broker for the corporation?
    (A) Chairman of the board of directors
    (B) President of the corporation
    (C) Secretary-treasurer of the corporation
    (D) The person named in the license

42. Which of the following is exempt from obtaining a real estate license to sell real estate?
    (A) Salesperson from another state
    (B) Guardian
    (C) Part-time agent
    (D) Telephone solicitor of new listings

43. Which of the following actions by a licensed salesperson constitutes a violation of **MOST** states' licensing laws?
    (A) Splitting fees with unlicensed persons
    (B) Working more hours per week selling used cars than selling real estate
    (C) Refusing to take university real estate courses
    (D) Buying property listed with the firm

44. The state licensing agency can institute disciplinary action against a broker for which of the following types of conduct?
    (A) Being a party to a deed that recites a consideration of $10 while the actual price paid for the property was $100,000
    (B) Charging a commission in excess of the rates approved by the licensing agency
    (C) Commingling client's monies
    (D) Acting as an attorney-in-fact for a client

45. A nonlicensed secretary in a real estate office can perform which of the following functions?
    (A) Transmitting information from an MLS listing to a phone prospect if no one else is in the office
    (B) Verifying the accuracy of listing information supplied by a salesperson by checking the records at the state tax office
    (C) Filling out a sales contract with a client
    (D) Conducting an open house showing of a listed property

46. Which of the following must be licensed as a real estate broker?
    (A) Real estate escrow officer
    (B) Real estate mortgage loan officer
    (C) Real estate title officer
    (D) Listing agent

47. Assume a broker is going to rebate a portion of the commission in a real estate transaction. A direct rebate to which of the following is **LEAST** likely to be a cause for revocation of license under the real estate licensing law?
    (A) The salesperson for another broker
    (B) The personnel officer of the buyer's company for the referral
    (C) The mortgage loan officer
    (D) A principal in the transaction

48. A licensed broker may employ which of the following?
    (A) Another broker to act as a salesperson
    (B) An unlicensed person to solicit new listings
    (C) A salesperson to manage a branch office
    (D) A licensed salesperson from another state to show listings

ANSWERS

1. **C** The broker must have a definite place of business, owned or leased, and it should be zoned commercial.

2. **A** While salespeople usually are authorized to deposit their client's money into trust funds, the broker usually is the only one authorized to withdraw the money. In some states, salespeople can't handle money at all.

3. **D** The principal broker is responsible for the actions of the sales staff and should be kept apprised of all sales. Buyers should be made aware of the extra skills possessed by the seller-licensee. Cooperating brokers should be told of your interest and whether you are offering them subagency.

4. **A** While most states require listings to be in writing, the cooperating broker split is not covered under the statute of frauds, although good business practice would have it in writing.

5. **A** The Recovery Fund (the popular name given to state self-insurance programs required for all licensees) does not protect licensees, but it would cover the seller in choice (A) because of the misrepresentation.

6. **C** A salesperson cannot operate as a broker.

7. **B** A broker should get all signatures but he or she can hold liable only those who do sign. Most states' laws require written authorization to advertise.

8. **A** Since salespeople are employed by or associated with a broker, they can't exist independent of such broker.

9. **D** Choices (A), (B) and (C) are typical exclusions under the licensing requirements.

10. **B** Owners are exempt, not those who perform rental or sales activities for compensation.

11. **C** The ad must contain the name of the broker. This is to discourage brokers from using blind ads or bait advertising.

12. **D** The state licensing agency handles disputes between the consumer and licensees, but not disputes between licensees.

13. **C** Even a broker-salesperson (one with a broker's license who is working under another broker) cannot act independently as a broker.

14. **D** Freehold interests would include life estates and fee simple estates, whereas leasehold estates would include ground leases, net leases and periodic tenancies. Personalty refers to personal property.

15. **A** There are many services in connection with real estate that do not require licensing.

16. **B** Licensees normally cannot take advantage of the Recovery Fund provisions—these are reserved for consumers. However, the unpaid salesperson can seek recovery in a court of law.

17. **A** While a broker should make sure the sales staff is properly licensed, it would be too much of a penalty to forfeit the broker's license automatically.

18. **A** Construction is not one of those functions that requires a real estate license.

19. **B** Condominium rental managers involved in the leasing of units usually need a real estate license.

20. **D** Commissions are neither fixed by law nor by brokerage practice—they are determined by negotiations between broker and owner. If the broker finds a ready, willing and able buyer, then the person signing the listing is liable even though the signer does not own the property (an optionee, for example).

21. **B** A broker must not mingle his or her assets with clients' monies. The records are subject to spot checks to prevent commingling.

22. **B** Most license laws provide that the broker should give a copy of the contract of sale to all parties signing it at the time the signatures are obtained. The broker should not give a copy of the listing to the buyer.

23. **D** This would result in commingling, which could have the adverse effect of freezing clients' monies upon the death or bankruptcy of the broker.

24. **A** The owner relies on the judgment of the broker and should therefore be informed of whatever interest the broker may have as a buyer (i.e., assume the broker has an ownership interest in the buyer-corporation).

25. **D** A broker-salesperson is little more than an ordinary salesperson and thus cannot act as an independent broker.

26. **D** A financial statement or credit report may be required at the original issuance of the brokerage license.

27. **D** Choices (A), (B) and (C) must obtain a real estate license before they can conduct these stated activities.

28. **D** The broker's records should contain all the detailed information, plus be available for inspection by the real estate licensing agency. Commission monies do not belong in the clients' account.

29. **D** The unlicensed secretary cannot carry out functions like these that require a license.

30. **B** Copies of the listing should be given to those who sign at the time the signatures are obtained. A broker must have a definite place of business in an area zoned commercial.

31. **D** Some states require loan brokers to be licensed, but not as real estate licensees.

32. **D** A salesperson can accept compensation only from his or her broker.

33. **A** Dual agency is not permitted without written approval of both principals.

34. **D** New salespeople are frequently teamed up with other salespeople to sell a particular property. A salesperson must work under a properly licensed broker.

35. **D** There is no legal requirement to obtain an earnest money deposit, although good business practice dictates that there should be some monetary indication of the buyer's good faith desire to complete the transaction.

36. **B** It is illegal for a broker to pay a commission to an unlicensed person.

37. **D** The monies from the Recovery Fund are available up to stated limits in cases of judgments against licensees for misrepresentations or fraud when it turns out the licensee is judgment-proof and has no collectible assets.

38. **B** Placing these client monies into the broker's business account would be commingling.

39. **B** Refusing to split commissions as previously agreed could result in a lawsuit; the state licensing agency does not typically get involved in disputes between licensees. The broker must get the owner's permission to quote a price other than the listing price.

40. **B** The licensing law is designed to protect the general public in its real estate transactions by requiring competent and trustworthy licensees.

41. **D** A corporate broker must have an individual as its principal broker who may be a director, officer or even, in some states, an employee.

42. **B** Those who act in a legal capacity, such as a guardian or executor, are typically excluded since a court usually reviews their transactions to protect the public.

43. **A** Most states prohibit giving finder or referral fees to unlicensed persons. Both salespeople and brokers can be involved in real estate as a partial vocation.

44. **C** The broker cannot be a party to the naming of a false consideration. This is only a nominal consideration. Commission rates are negotiable and are not fixed by law.

45. **B** Giving information to a prospect would be considered solicitation and would thus require a license. Checking the accuracy of statements and facts does not require a license.

46. **D** None of these officers performs the functions of listing, selling or renting, which require real estate licenses.

47. **D** Splitting fees with unlicensed people is typically prohibited. However, splitting fees or giving rebates to buyer or seller is usually not regulated by licensing laws provided full disclosure is given to all principals.

48. **A** A salesperson is employed by the broker—this may include persons who have a sales or a broker's license. Branch offices must be managed by a broker.

Appendix II: Real Estate Mathematics

Almost one-fourth of the uniform section of the examination covers questions requiring basic arithmetic calculations. Most states now permit the use of a pocket calculator on the examination. The principal areas covered by the arithmetic problems are:

1. commission
2. interest
3. investment or income
4. profit and loss
5. depreciation and appreciation
6. taxes and insurance
7. prorations
8. ratio, proportion and scale
9. area

QUESTIONS

Commission

1. A three-bedroom house sells for $124,000 and the broker's total commission is 6 percent of the selling price. The commission is:
   (A) $744.
   (B) $6,000.
   (C) $7,440.
   (D) $20,667.

2. On a $78,000 sale of a house, the rate of commission is 6 percent: The salesperson gets 40 percent of the commission and the broker gets the remainder. How much does the broker get?
   (A) $1,872
   (B) $2,808
   (C) $4,680
   (D) $40,000

3. The commission on a house that sells for $96,000 is $4,800. What was the rate of commission?
   (A) 2 percent
   (B) 5 percent
   (C) 20 percent
   (D) 50 percent

4. A salesperson received $2,880 for selling a house. This was 40 percent of the total commission on the sale of a $120,000 house. What was the commission rate on the sale?
   (A) 3 percent
   (B) 4 percent
   (C) 6 percent
   (D) 12 percent

5. A house sold for $110,000 and the rate of commission was 6 percent. If the salesperson got $1,980, what percentage of the commission did the salesperson get?
   (A) 3 percent
   (B) 30 percent
   (C) 66 percent
   (D) 70 percent

6. A broker charges a rental management fee of one-third of the first month's rent, and 2 percent of each month's rent thereafter. He or she must pay a $100 "finder's fee" to an agent. If the house rents for $600 per month, how much does that licensed broker make in one year?
   (A) $100
   (B) $232
   (C) $332
   (D) $432

❖ 7. A broker gets 6 percent of the first $100,000 and 3 percent of any amount over $100,000. What would be the loss to the broker if a house listed for $180,000 has to be reduced by 20 percent?
   (A) $1,080
   (B) $7,320
   (C) $8,400
   (D) $15,720

Interest

8. Find the interest on $32,000 at 12¼ percent per annum (year) for 6 months.
   (A) $326
   (B) $1,320
   (C) $1,960
   (D) $2,640

9. If the interest on a loan at 13 percent per annum for 8 months was $5,400, what was the amount of the loan?

(A) $62,300   (C) $72,900

(B) $67,500   (D) $81,000

10. If the interest for 9 months on a loan of $80,000 was $7,200, what was the rate of interest per annum?

(A) 9.6 percent   (C) 12 percent

(B) 10.5 percent   (D) 13.5 percent

❖ 11. A purchase money mortgage carried back by seller for $60,000 at 10¾ percent was made February 1 and paid November 1. What was the total outstanding amount due at the time of payment?

(A) $48,375.00   (C) $64,837.50

(B) $55,162.50   (D) $66,450.00

12. A loan is made for 90 percent of the $96,000 appraised value of a house. The annual rate of interest is 12 percent. What is the bimonthly (every 2 months) interest payment?

(A) $684   (C) $1,728

(B) $864   (D) $8,208

13. On a simple interest loan of $15,000 that has an interest rate of 13 percent per annum, what is the total interest payment for 2 years, 6 months and 10 days?

(A) $2,403.30   (C) $3,033.33

(B) $2,433.30   (D) $4,929.20

❖ 14. A person receives a purchase money $30,000 loan from the seller at a reduced rate of 9 percent. Assuming the loan interest is calculated on a declining balance, if his or her payment is $250 per month, including interest, what is his or her balance after 3 payments?

(A) $29,898,86   (C) $29,949.81

(B) $29,924.43   (D) $29,975

Investment or Income

15. A property valued at $120,000 is earning an 8 percent return. What is the monthly return?

(A) $80   (C) $4,800

(B) $800   (D) $9,600

16. A property valued at $150,000 earns $750 per month. What is the annual percentage return?

(A) 6 percent   (C) 9 percent

(B) 7.5 percent   (D) 12 percent

❖ 17. A business shows a monthly profit of $1,050. If this is a 9 percent return, what is the value of the property?

(A) $9,450   (C) $94,500

(B) $14,000   (D) $140,000

❖ 18. A person owns a building with six apartments. Three of the apartments net him or her $200 each per month and the other three net him or her $150 each per month. For what amount should he or she sell the building to net the same profit if he or she invests the money at 9 percent?

(A) $12,600   (C) $126,000

(B) $105,000   (D) $140,000

19. A person rents each of his or her five apartments for $600 per month and has a total amount of expenses of $1,000 per month. He or she has an investment of $50,000 at 8 percent a year in the bank. He or she decides to use the bank interest to pay for better and more frequent property maintenance. What percent increase in rent per apartment must he or she obtain to offset this additional expense?

(A) 11.11 percent   (C) 33.33 percent

(B) 20 percent   (D) 66.67 percent

20. A store in a shopping center under a percentage lease pays a monthly rent of $600 plus 4 percent of the annual gross over $150,000. The gross yearly income was $250,000. If the lessor's interest in the store is valued at $150,000 what is the percentage return to the lessor?

(A) 7.5 percent   (C) 14 percent

(B) 11.2 percent   (D) 15 percent

21. A property is valued at $180,000 and is making an 8 percent annual net return on the investment. By what percentage must the monthly profit be increased to make a 10 percent annual return?

(A) 15 percent   (C) 25 percent

(B) 20 percent   (D) 30 percent

Profit and Loss

22. What percentage profit is made on a sale, if the selling price is $90,000 and the purchase price is $75,000?

(A) 12 percent   (C) 20 percent

(B) 15 percent   (D) 120 percent

23. If the purchase price of a property was $50,000, what should the selling price be to realize a 5 percent profit?

(A) $47,500   (C) $52,500

(B) $51,500   (D) $53,750

❖ **24.** A person buys a house for $50,000. He or she sells it for $60,000 with a 6 percent broker's fee and closing costs of $400. What was his or her percentage profit?

(A) 1.12 percent   (C) 11.2 percent

(B) 5.6 percent   (D) 12 percent

25. A house sells for $92,000, a 15 percent increase over the purchase price paid one year before. The seller paid the 9 percent interest on a 90 percent loan, taxes of $350, insurance of $150, and a 6 percent commission on the sale. What was the seller's return?

(A) Gain of $500   (C) Gain of $250

(B) Loss of $500   (D) Loss of $250

26. A house sells for $80,000. The seller pays 3 discount points to the lender on a 90 percent FHA loan and a 6 percent commission. If he or she bought the house for $50,000 five years ago, what was the annual rate of his or her profit?

(A) 6 percent   (C) 12 percent

(B) 9 percent   (D) 18 percent

❖ **27.** A person buys a house for $50,000 and wants to realize an 8 percent profit after paying a 6 percent real estate commission. What should the selling price be?

(A) $50,760   (C) $57,446

(B) $53,191   (D) $90,000

28. A house originally cost $30,000 to build. Over the next three years, costs went up 10 percent the first year, 20 percent the second year and went down 3 percent the next year. What would the construction cost of the same house be if building had been postponed three years?

(A) $25,608   (C) $38,412

(B) $33,000   (D) $39,600

Depreciation and Appreciation

29. A $90,000 house depreciates an average 3 percent each year. What is the house's value after seven years?

(A) $60,000   (C) $71,100

(B) $61,100   (D) $81,100

❖ **30.** A house depreciates 2½ percent per year for four years. If the house is now worth $108,000, what was it worth four years ago?

(A) $106,930.69   (C) $118,800

(B) $108,900   (D) $120,000

31. A house currently worth $153,000 was worth $180,000 five years ago. What was the depreciation per year?

(A) 2 percent   (C) 5 percent

(B) 3 percent   (D) 15 percent

32. A person has a $9,000 cottage that he or she depreciates using straight-line depreciation for 10 years. What is the dollar amount of depreciation each year?

(A) $900   (C) $1,100

(B) $1,000   (D) $1,800

❖ **33.** It cost $40,000 to build a house on a $20,000 lot six years ago. If the house depreciates at 3 percent per year and the lot appreciates at 5 percent per year, what is the total value now?

(A) $6,800   (C) $32,800

(B) $26,000   (D) $58,800

34. If a $30,000 house depreciates at 3 percent per year for five years under straight-line depreciation, what is it worth now?

(A) $2,550   (C) $15,000

(B) $4,500   (D) $25,500

35. If 3 percent depreciation on a $30,000 house were computed each year on remaining value, what would it be worth after five years?

(A) $25,762   (C) $27,380

(B) $26,558   (D) $28,227

Taxes and Insurance

❖ **36.** The tax assessment ratio for a house valued at $90,000 is 40 percent. If the tax rate is $3.50 per $1,000, what is the quarterly tax?

(A) $31.50   (C) $63.00

(B) $42.00   (D) $126.00

❖ **37.** If a person's semiannual tax on a $120,000 home is $243 and the tax rate is $6.75 per $1,000 of assessed value, what is the tax assessment ratio?

(A) 4 percent

(B) 6 percent

(C) 40 percent

(D) 60 percent

38. A person's semiannual tax on his or her $90,000 home is $78.75 and is based on a tax assessment ratio of 50 percent. What is the tax rate per $1,000 for his or her home?

(A) $1.57

(B) $3.14

(C) $3.50

(D) $35

39. A $120,000 home carries fire insurance on 80 percent of its value. If the rate is $3.50 per $1,000 of insured value for a three-year policy, what is the annual premium?

(A) $112

(B) $168

(C) $224

(D) $336

40. A person pays $168.75 each year for fire and home insurance. The rate is $3 per $1,000 of insured value for a two-year period. If his or her house is worth $150,000, what percent of that value is covered by insurance?

(A) 7.5 percent

(B) 25 percent

(C) 75 percent

(D) 85 percent

41. A property was conveyed for $60,000. If the conveyance tax rate was $0.07 per $100 value, what was the conveyance tax paid by the seller?

(A) $4.20

(B) $42

(C) $420

(D) $4,200

42. A property conveyed for $110,000 was charged a conveyance tax of $38.50. What is the tax rate per $100?

(A) $.035

(B) $.0385

(C) $.385

(D) $3.50

Prorations

43. The taxes of $390 have been paid for the entire calendar year. The seller sells on October 1. What is the amount of the remaining prepaid portion?

(A) $32.50

(B) $97.50

(C) $292.50

(D) $325

❖ **44.** A house is sold on May 1. On January 1 of that year the three-year insurance was paid in an amount of $441 and the semiannual tax of $180 was paid. How much should be debited to buyer and credited to seller?

(A) $332

(B) $392

(C) $422

(D) $452

45. The taxes on a house for the fiscal year July 1 to June 30 are $900, to be paid in advance. If the house is sold February 15, what is the amount of the prepaid portion owed back to the seller?

(A) $56.25

(B) $100

(C) $337.50

(D) $562.50

46. A house sold March 15. The taxes for the first six months of the year are $195 and have not been paid. How much of this does the buyer pay?

(A) $32.50

(B) $81.25

(C) $113.75

(D) $195

❖ **47.** The seller has made the October 1 payment on his or her mortgage at 8¾ percent, leaving a balance of $32,400. What is the amount of accrued interest as of the closing on October 20?

(A) $83.40

(B) $86.62

(C) $157.50

(D) $236.25

48. A property was sold April 15 and the three-year insurance premium of $426 was paid January 1 of the preceding year. How much does the buyer owe the seller?

(A) $11.83

(B) $24.26

(C) $118.30

(D) $242.52

49. On January 1, taxes of $600 are paid for the year and $120 is paid on the semiannual ground lease rent, both in advance. The house is sold April 10. How much is due the seller?

(A) $54.40

(B) $380.10

(C) $433.50

(D) $486.90

Ratio, Proportion and Scale

50. If 200 ft. of fence costs $900, what would 350 ft. of fence cost?

(A) $900

(B) $1,575

(C) $1,800

(D) $3,150

❖ 51. If a 9 x 12 ft. rug costs $1,500, what would a 14 x 16 ft. rug cost?
(A) $1,080 (C) $2,962.12
(B) $2,240 (D) $3,111.11

52. Lots A and B (see drawing below) have the same depth. Lot A is ¼ acre. How many acres are in Lot B?
(A) .031 (C) 3.1
(B) .31 (D) 31

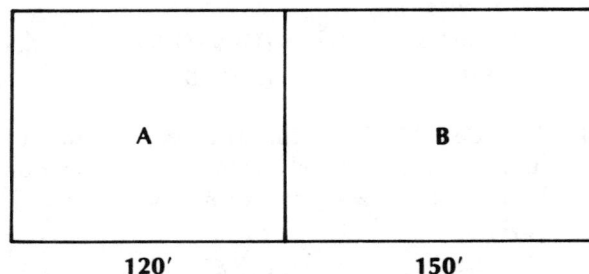

120'   150'

53. If 10 people take 8 hours to complete a job, how many hours would it take 15 people?
(A) 5.33 (C) 15
(B) 6.5 (D) 80

54. If a salesperson claims to sell three out of every five prospects, how many sales would result from 120 prospects?
(A) 18 (C) 72
(B) 36 (D) 120

55. In scale, if 2 in. represents a length of 6 ft., what would represent a length of 20 ft.?
(A) 2⅔ in. (C) 6 in.
(B) 3⅓ in. (D) 6⅔ in.

56. A back yard is drawn on a plan 6½ by 3 in. If the scale is ½ in. = 5 ft. and sod costs $15 per square yard, how much would it cost to sod this lawn?
(A) $1,625 (C) $3,250
(B) $2,160 (D) $6,500

Area

57. A lot is 70 x 120 ft. What fraction of an acre is this?
(A) ⅕ (C) ⅓
(B) ¼ (D) ½

58. What is the cost of the lot in the following illustration if the cost is $2.50 per sq. ft.?
(A) $562,500 (C) $2,500,000
(B) $1,125,000 (D) $4,500,000

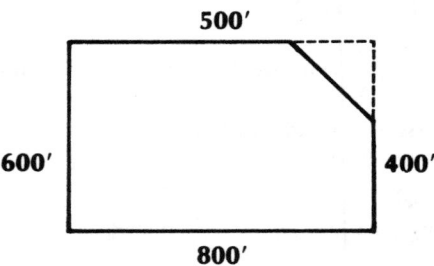

500'

600'   400'

800'

❖ 59. The house with the floor area shown below sells for $150,000. What is the cost per sq. ft.?
(A) $30 (C) $120
(B) $60 (D) $250

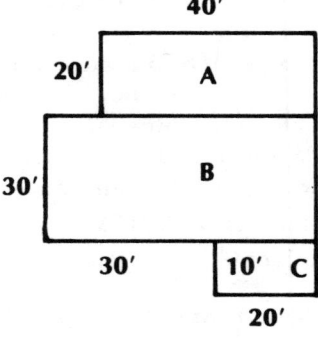

40'
20'   A
30'   B
30'   10' C
20'

60. Compute the cost of ready-mixed concrete for a driveway of 70 ft. long, 10 ft. wide, 3 inches deep at a cost of $30 per cubic yard.
(A) $44.80 (C) $82.20
(B) $54.80 (D) $194.40

❖ 61. A person buys the lot shown below for $12,000. To make way for the freeway, the state condemns the shaded area. What would be the market value of the shaded portion, assuming a 10 percent increase in value?
(A) $3,150 (C) $3,762
(B) $3,300 (D) $3,800

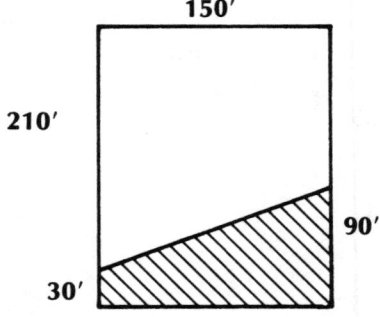

150'
210'
30'   90'

62. A property is for sale at $120,000. If the cost of the land is $15,000 per acre and the lot is rectangular with a 500 ft. frontage, what is the depth?

   (A) 696.9 ft.   (C) 966.8 ft.
   (B) 869.6 ft.   (D) 986.6 ft.

Miscellaneous

63. The owner of an apartment house with 8 apartments spends $1,000 on improvements. How much should he or she increase each rent to recoup this expense in 6 months?

   (A) $12.50   (C) $38.20
   (B) $20.83   (D) $125

64. A person buys a parcel of land for $1 million. He or she then subdivides it into eight lots to sell for $150,000 each. What percentage of return on the money is this?

   (A) 2 percent   (C) 20 percent
   (B) 4 percent   (D) 40 percent

65. A person has 6 apartments that he or she rents for $500 per month including utilities. If the utilities average $450 total per month, what would be the rent without the utilities?

   (A) $75   (C) $415
   (B) $85   (D) $425

66. A building with a net income of $10,000 was appraised at $100,000. What would be the value if the capitalization rate has decreased by one percentage point?

   (A) $90,909   (C) $105,263
   (B) $100,000   (D) $111,111

67. A salesperson is offered a straight salary of $2,000 per month or 40 percent of a 6 percent total commission. How much in monthly sales would make the two offers equal?

   (A) $50,000   (C) $124,600
   (B) $83,333   (D) $166,666

68. A salesperson gets $500 per month plus 40 percent of the 6 percent commission on sales. If he or she wants to earn $1,200 this month, how much must his or her sales be?

   (A) $20,833   (C) $50,000
   (B) $29,167   (D) $100,000

69. A house appreciates each year by 10 percent. This is equivalent to what percent for five years?

   (A) 50 percent   (C) 71 percent
   (B) 61 percent   (D) 81 percent

❖70. Acme Savings and Loan Association suggests the buyer can buy a home valued at 3½ times his or her yearly income. What should his or her minimum weekly salary be to buy a home worth $120,000?

   (A) $596.34   (C) $659.34
   (B) $634.59   (D) $695.34

71. On a ¼-acre of land, approximately what percentage is occupied by a 2,500 sq. ft. house?

   (A) 23 percent   (C) 34 percent
   (B) 32 percent   (D) 43 percent

❖72. A ¼-acre plot costs $5 per square foot. A house that is 60 x 40 ft. will cost $30 per square foot. What is the total cost?

   (A) $87,120   (C) $130,680
   (B) $126,450   (D) $174,240

73. The gross income on a property is $7,920. If this is a 6 percent return on cost, what is the cost?

   (A) $47,520   (C) $83,952
   (B) $74,448   (D) $132,000

74. On a 30-year mortgage in the sum of $110,000 at 11 percent, the monthly payment is $1,047.56. On the first payment, how much is applied to reduce the principal?

   (A) $3.92   (C) $1,008.33
   (B) $39.23   (D) $1,100

75. If the price of a house rises 10 percent the first year and 12 percent the second year, what is the percentage rise over the two years?

   (A) 13.2 percent   (C) 23.2 percent
   (B) 22 percent   (D) 120 percent

76. Find the cost of the lot below at $100 per square yard.
    (A) $28,800
    (C) $35,556
    (B) $32,000
    (D) $106,667

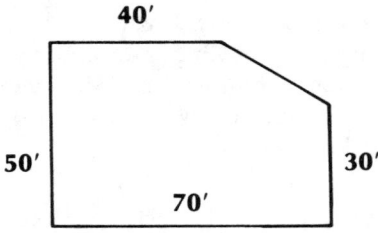

77. A 35 x 40 ft. house is on a ⅛-acre of land. What percentage is NOT taken up by the house?
    (A) 10 percent
    (C) 86 percent
    (B) 14 percent
    (D) 90 percent

78. A house originally cost $35,000 to build and the lot was $20,000. Lot prices have increased by 300 percent and building costs have doubled. What percentage did the entire property appreciate?
    (A) 36 percent
    (C) 136 percent
    (B) 73 percent
    (D) 500 percent

79. A person owns a house with a $32,000 mortgage and his or her payment is $260 per month. He or she rents the house for $600 per month, paying 10 percent to a broker and saving $75 per month for repairs. The annual profit he or she makes is what percent of his or her equity if the house would net $68,000 if he or she were to sell?
    (A) 1.3 percent
    (C) 13 percent
    (B) 3.6 percent
    (D) 36 percent

80. A house worth $90,000 is rented for a net profit of $400 per month. How much money invested at 12 percent would give the same net profit?
    (A) $40,000
    (C) $80,000
    (B) $45,000
    (D) $90,000

81. The mortgage payment on a house is $336 per month. How much money would have to be invested at 12.5 percent per annum to pay the monthly mortgage payment?
    (A) $25,326
    (C) $33,562
    (B) $32,256
    (D) $33,600

82. The buildings on a 150 x 220 ft. lot cover 30 percent of the lot. How many square feet are not covered by buildings?
    (A) 7,000
    (C) 23,100
    (B) 10,900
    (D) 33,000

83. A buyer applies at a bank for a loan to purchase a $60,000 home. The bank requires an 18 percent down payment on the first $30,000 and a 14 percent down payment on the remaining $30,000. What will be the bank's loan fee if they charge four points on the balance?
    (A) $2,016
    (C) $2,400
    (B) $2,184
    (D) $3,018

84. G earns $22,500 per year as a carpenter, and his spouse, S, is a secretary earning $15,000. They are selling their present home for $70,000 and will receive their equity of $35,000 at closing. They contact a lender who uses a 2.5-times rule of thumb. The most expensive home they would be capable of purchasing would be:
    (A) $75,000.
    (C) $93,750.
    (B) $89,750.
    (D) $128,750.

85. A buyer contracts to purchase a $75,000 home and puts up a good faith deposit of $1,500. The commission is 6.5 percent paid by the seller. The buyer gets a $260 credit for real property taxes paid in arrears. If buyer obtains an 80 percent conventional loan at 12 percent interest with three points, how much should he or she bring to the closing?
    (A) $15,040
    (C) $16,540
    (B) $15,300
    (D) $19,915

REAL ESTATE MATHEMATICS ANSWERS

Commission

1. C   Solution:

V $124,000   V = value
R   × .06   R = rate
I $7,440.00   I = income

---

2. B   Solution:

V $78,000   The commission is $4,680
R   × .06   Since the salesperson gets 40%,
I $4,680.00   the broker gets 60%

$4,680.00   ×   .60   = $2,808.00

---

3. B   Solution:

V $96,000   .05 = 5%
R   × ?   96,000) 4,800.00
I $4,800

---

4. C   Solution:

First determine the total commission: $2,880 is 40% of what?

          ?   7,200   The total commission was $7,200
        × .40   .40) 2,880
       $2,880

V $120,000
R   × ?   .06 = 6%
I $ 7,200   120,000) 7,200.00

---

5. B   Solution:

First determine the total commission:

V $110,000 $6,600 is total commission
R   × .06
I $6,600.00

Then the salesperson's commission was what percent of $6,600?

$6,600   .30 = 30%
  × ?   6,600) 1,980.00
$1,980

---

6. B   Solution:

1st month   200 $200 for the first month
                3) 600

each month $600
after   × .02   for 11 months $12 × 11 = $132.00
                 $12.00

The total commission is: $332.00
Less $100 "finder's fee":   – 100.00
                                $232.00

---

7. A Solution: NOTE: These types of multiple-step problems are more prevalent in the broker's exam than in the salesperson's exam.

Old commission $100,000 $80,000
                      × .06   plus   × .03
                    $6,000.00 $2,400.00

Total $6,000.00 + $2,400.00 = $8,400.00

New sales price   Old price $180,000   New price $180,000
                             × .20   – 36,000
                         $36,000.00 $144,000

New commission $100,000 $44,000
                     × .06   +   × .03
                   $6,000.00 $1,320.00

Total $6,000.00 + $1,320.00 = $7,320.00

Difference $8,400.00
               – 7,320.00
               $1,080.00

Interest

8. C Solution: V   32,000 $326.67   per month   326.67
                     R   × .1225   12) 3,920   × 6   months
                     I   3,920   1,960.02

---

9. A Solution: $5,400 for 8 months is $675 per month

                    $675   and is $8,100 for the year $675
                8) 5,400   × 12
                                                    $8,100

Then:
V   ?
R   × .13 $62,307.69
I $8,100   .13)   8,100

---

10. C Solution: The interest per month is $800

$$9 \overline{)\smash{7,200}} \quad \begin{array}{r} 800 \end{array}$$

The interest per year is $9,600

$$\begin{array}{r} 800 \\ \times\ 12 \\ \hline 9,600 \end{array}$$

Then:

V $80,000
R   × ?
I $9,600

$$80,000 \overline{)\smash{9,600}} \quad \begin{array}{r} .12 \end{array} = 12\%$$

---

11. C   Solution:

V $60,000
R   × .1075
I $6,450.00   total interest for the year

$$12 \overline{)\smash{6,450.00}} \quad \begin{array}{r} 537.50 \end{array} \quad \text{interest per month}$$

$537.50
×   9   months
$4,837.50   total interest for 9 months

Balance:

$60,000.00
+ 4,837.50
$64,837.50

---

12. C   Solution:

$96,000
× .90
$86,400.00 = amount of loan

$86,400
× .12
$10,368 = interest for the year

$$12 \overline{)\smash{10,368}} \quad \begin{array}{r} 864.00 \end{array} = \text{interest per month}$$

$864.00
×   2   months
$1,728.00

---

13. D   Solution:

V $15,000
R   × .13
I $1,950   interest per year

$$12 \overline{)\smash{1,950.00}} \quad \begin{array}{r} \$162.50 \end{array} \quad \text{interest per month}$$

$$30 \overline{)\smash{162.50}} \quad \begin{array}{r} \$5.42 \end{array} \quad \text{interest per day}$$

2 years:	2 × $1,950 =	$3,900.00
6 months:	6 × $162.50 =	975.00
10 days:	10 × $5.42 =	+ 54.20
		$4,929.20

---

14. B Solution:

1st payment:

V $30,000.00
R × .09
I $2,700.00

```
        $225.00
12 ) 2,700.00
```

$250.00 payment
− 225.00 interest
$25.00 to balance

$30,000 old balance
− 25 to balance
$29,975 new balance

2nd payment:

V $29,975.00
R × .09
I $2,697.75

```
        $224.81
12 ) 2,697.75
```

250.00 payment
−224.81 interest
$25.19 to balance

$29,975.00 old balance
− 25.19 to balance
$29,949.81 new balance

3rd payment:

V $29,949.81
R × .09
I $2,695.48

```
        $224.62
12 ) 2,695.48
```

$250.00 payment
−224.62 interest
$25.38 to balance

$29,949.81 old balance
− 25.38 to balance
$29,924.43 new balance

Investment or Income

15. B Solution:

V $120,000
R × .08
I $9,600.00 profit per annum

```
        $800      per month
12 ) 9,600.00
```

---

16. A Solution:

$750 monthly earnings
× 12
$9,000 yearly earnings

V $150,000
R × ?
I $9,000

```
              .06 = 6%
150,000 ) 9,000
```

---

17. D Solution:

$1,050.00 profit per month
× 12

$12,600.00 profit per year

V   ?
R   × .09

I $12,600.00

$$.09\overline{)12,600.00}^{\,\$140,000}$$

---

18. D Solution:

$200 $150 $600 $1,050
× 3   × 3   + 450   × 12
-----   -----   -----------------   ------------------
$600 $450 $1,050 per month $12,600 per year

V   ?
R   × .09

I $12,600.00

$$.09\overline{)12,600.00}^{\,\$140,000.00}$$

---

19. A Solution:

$50,000 $333.33 $66.67
× .08   12)‾4,000   5)‾333.33

$4,000.00 yearly

Raise each rent $66.67

V $600
R   × ?
I $66.67

$$600\overline{)66.67}^{\,.11}\; = 11\% \text{ increase}$$

---

20. A Solution:

$600 $250,000 $100,000
× 12   −150,000   × .04
-----------   ----------   ----------
$7,200 Fixed rent $100,000 $4,000

$7,200 + $4,000 = $11,200 yearly rent

V $150,000
R   × ?
I $11,200

$$150,000\overline{)11,200.00}^{\,.074}\; = 7.5\%$$

---

21. C Solution:

V $180,000
R   × .08 old rate
I $14,400.00 yearly

$$12\overline{)14,400}^{\,\$1,200} \text{ monthly profit (old)}$$

$180,000
× .10 new rate

$18,000.00 yearly

$$12\overline{)18,000}^{\,\$1,500} \text{ monthly profit (new)}$$

$1,500 new monthly profit
−1,200 old monthly profit
$300 gain

V	$1,200
R	× ?
I	300

$$1,200 \overline{)\,300} \quad \frac{.25}{} = 25\% \text{ increase}$$

Profit and Loss

22. C Solution:

$90,000
−75,000
$15,000 profit

$$75,000 \overline{)\,15,000} \quad \frac{.20}{} = 20\% \text{ profit and loss}$$

V	$75,000
R	× ?
I	$15,000

or

$75,000
× ?
$90,000

$$75,000 \overline{)\,90,000} \quad \frac{1.20}{} = 120\% \text{ return}$$

---

23. C Solution:

$50,000
× 1.05
$52,500

---

24. D Solution:

$60,000
× .94
$56,400.00
− 400.00
$56,000.00

$50,000
× ?
$56,000

$$50,000 \overline{)\,56,000} \quad \frac{1.12}{} = 12\% \text{ profit (112\% return)}$$

---

25. B Solution:

?
× 1.15
$92,000

$$1.15 \overline{)\,92,000} \quad \frac{\$80,000}{} \text{ purchase price}$$

$92,000
−80,000
$12,000 gross profit

Loan:

$$\begin{array}{r} \$80,000 \\ \times\ .90 \\ \hline \$72,000.00 \end{array} \text{ interest on loan}$$

$$\begin{array}{r} \$72,000 \\ \times\ .09 \\ \hline \$6,480.00 \end{array}$$

Commission:

$$\begin{array}{r} \$92,000 \\ \times\ .06 \\ \hline \$5,520.00 \end{array}$$

Total Expenses:

Interest	$6,480.00
Commission	5,520.00
Tax	350.00
Insurance	150.00
	$12,500.00

$$\begin{array}{r} \$12,000 \\ -12,500 \\ \hline -\ \ \$500 \end{array} \begin{array}{l} \text{Gross profit} \\ \text{Expenses} \\ \text{Loss} \end{array}$$

---

26. B Solution:

$$\begin{array}{r} \$80,000 \\ \times\ .90 \\ \hline \$72,000 \end{array} \text{ Amount of loan}$$

$$\begin{array}{r} \$72,000 \\ \times\ .03 \\ \hline \$2,160.00 \end{array} \text{ points (3\%)}$$

Commission:

$$\begin{array}{r} \$80,000 \\ \times\ .06 \\ \hline \$4,800.00 \end{array} \text{ Commission}$$

$$\text{Expenses} \quad \begin{array}{r} \$2,160.00 \\ 4,800.00 \\ \hline \$6,960.00 \end{array}$$

Profit:

$$\begin{array}{r} \$30,000 \\ -\ 6,960 \\ \hline \$23,040 \end{array}$$

$$5\,\overline{)\,23,040\,}^{\ \$4,608} \text{ profit per year}$$

B $50,000
% × ?
A $4,608

$$50,000\,\overline{)\,4,608\,}^{\ .09} = 9\%$$

---

27. C Solution:

$$\begin{array}{r} \$50,000 \\ \times\ .08 \\ \hline \$4,000.00 \end{array} \text{ profit}$$

$50,000 + $4,000 + .06SP = SP
or $54,000 = .94 × SP

$$.94\,\overline{)\,54,000.00\,}^{\ \$57,446.81} = \text{ selling price}$$

28. C Solution:

$30,000
× 1.10
$33,000 after 1 year
× 1.20
$39,600 after 2 years
× .97
$38,412 after 3 years

Depreciation and Appreciation

29. C Solution:

3% × 7 years = 21%

100% − 21% = 79%

$90,000
× .79
$71,100

---

30. D Solution:

2½% × 4 years = 10%   100% − 10% = 90%

?
× .90
$108,000

$$.90 \overline{) \begin{array}{c} \$120,000 \\ 108,000 \end{array}}$$

---

31. B Solution:

$180,000
× ?
$153,000

$$180,000 \overline{) \begin{array}{c} .85 = 85\% \\ 153,000 \end{array}}$$

100% − 85% = 15% for the 5 years

$$5 \overline{) \begin{array}{c} 3 \\ 15 \end{array}} = 3\% \text{ depreciation per year}$$

---

32. A Solution:

100% in 10 years = 10% each year
.10 × $9,000 = $900 per year

---

33. D Solution:

House: $40,000   3% × 6 = 18%
× .82   100% − 18% = 82%
$32,800.00

Lot: $20,000   5% × 6 = 30%
× 1.30   100% + 30% = 130%
$26,000

Total: $32,800
+ 26,000
$58,800

34. D Solution: 3% × 5 = 15% $30,000
                    100% − 15% = 85%   × .85
                                      $25,500

35. A Solution: $30,000
                     × .97
                    29,100.00   after 1 year
                     × .97
                    28,227.00   after 2 years
                     × .97
                    27,380.19   after 3 years
                     × .97
                    26,558.78   after 4 years
                     × .97
                    $25,762.02   after 5 years

Taxes and Insurance

36. A Solution: market value $90,000
                     × %   × .40
                    assessed value $36,000.00

                    assessed value (in thousands)   36
                     × rate   × 3.50
                    tax bill $126.00   annual tax

                                         $31.50
                    quarterly tax   4) 126.00

37. D Solution: $243 × 2 = $486 per year of tax

                    assessed value   ? $72
                     × rate   × 6.75   6.75) 486.00
                    tax $486.00

                    assessed value is $72 × $1,000 = $72,000

                    market value $120,000   .60 = 60%
                     × rate   × ?   120,000) 72,000
                    assessed value $72,000

38. C Solution: $78.75 × 2 = $157.50 tax per year

market value	$90,000	
× %	× .50	
assessed value	$45,000	

assessed value	$45	(in thousand)
× rate	× ?	
tax bill	$157.50	

$$45\overline{)157.50}\quad \$3.50$$

---

39. A Solution:

value	$120,000
× %	× .80
insured value	$96,000

insured value	$96	(in thousands)
× rate	× 3.50	
premium	$336.00	(for 3 years)

yearly = $112

$$3\overline{)336.00}\quad 112$$

---

40. C Solution: $168.75 × 2 = $337.50 for the 2 years

insured value	?	
× rate	× 3.00	
premium	$337.50	

$$3.00\overline{)337.50}\quad \$112.50 \text{ insured value (in thousands)}$$

market value	$150,000
× %	× ?
insured value	$112,500

$$150,000\overline{)112,500}\quad .75 = 75\%$$

---

41. B Solution:

value	$600	(in hundreds)
× rate	× .07	
tax	$42.00	

---

42. A Solution:

value	$1,100	(in hundreds)
× rate	× ?	
tax	$38.50	

$$1,100\overline{)38.50}\quad .035 = 3.5¢$$

Prorations

43. B Solution:
(a) time period: 3 months (Oct., Nov., Dec.)
(b) $390 per year ÷ 12 = $32.50 per month
(c) $32.50 × 3 = $97.50

44. D Solution: Insurance: $441.00 + 36 months = $12.25 per mo.
$12.25 × 32 mos. remaining = $392.00

Taxes: $180 + 6 = $30 per month taxes
$30 × 2 months remaining = $60

Total: $392.00 + 60.00 = $452.00

---

45. C Solution: $900 + 12 mos. = $75 per month
$75 × 4.5 mos. = $337.50

---

46. C Solution: $195 + 6 = $32.50 per month
Buyer pays for 3½ months $32.50 × 3.5 = $113.75

---

47. C Solution: V $32,400 $236.25 for the month
R × .0875   12) 2,835
I $2,835.00 $7.88 per day
30) 236.25

The seller owes for 20 days $7.88 × 20 = $157.50

---

48. D Solution: $426 + 36 months = $11.83 per month
$11.83 × 20½ months remaining = $242.52 due the seller

---

49. D Solution: Taxes: $600 + 12 = $50 per month
8⅔ months remain $50 × 8.67 = $433.50
Lease rent: $120 + 6 = $20 per month
2⅔ months remain $20 × 2.67 = $53.40
Total: $433.50 + $53.40 = $486.90

Ratio, Proportion and Scale

50. B Solution: $\frac{200}{900} = \frac{350}{?}$ 900 × 350 = 200 × ?

900 × 350 = 315,000   315,000 + 200 = $1,575

51. D Solution: $9 \times 12 = 108$ sq. ft. $\qquad$ $14 \times 16 = 224$ sq. ft.

Proportion: $\dfrac{108}{\$1,500} = \dfrac{224}{?}$ $\quad \dfrac{\text{area}}{\text{cost}}$ $\qquad$ $\$1,500 \times 224 = 108 = ?$

$\$1,500 \times 224 = \$336,000$ $\qquad$ $\$336,000 + 108 = \$3,111.11$

---

52. B Solution: $\dfrac{120}{.25} = \dfrac{150}{?}$

$150 \times .25 = 37.50$ $\qquad$ $37.50 + 120 = .31$ acre

---

53. A Solution: NOTE: This is an inverse proportion (as number of people goes up, hours go down)

$\dfrac{10}{?} = \dfrac{15}{8}$ $\qquad$ $8 \times 10 = 80$ (This is number of "man–hours")
$\qquad\qquad\qquad 80 + 15 = 5.33$ hours

---

54. C Solution: $\dfrac{3}{5} = \dfrac{?}{120}$ $\quad 3 \times 120 = 360$ $\quad 360 + 5 = 72$

---

55. D Solution: $\dfrac{2}{6} = \dfrac{?}{20}$ $\quad 2 \times 20 = 40$ $\quad 40 + 6 = 6\frac{2}{3}''$

---

56. C Solution: Scale ½ in. = 5 ft. would be 1 in. = 10 ft.

so $\quad \dfrac{1}{10} = \dfrac{6\frac{1}{2}}{?}$ $\qquad 10 \times 6\frac{1}{2} = 65$ ft.

$\dfrac{1}{10} = \dfrac{3}{?}$ $\qquad 3 \times 10 = 30$ ft.

So the yard is 65 ft. by 30 ft. = 1,950 square feet

Changing to square yards: There are 9 square feet to a square yard

$\dfrac{9}{1} = \dfrac{1,950}{?}$ $\qquad 9 \overline{)\ 1,950}^{\ 216\frac{2}{3} \text{ square yards}}$

Each square yard costs $15 so 216⅔ square yards cost 216⅔ × 15 = $3,250

Area

57. A   Solution: 70 ft. × 120 ft. = 8,400 square feet

$$\frac{1 \text{ acre}}{43,560 \text{ sq. ft.}} \times 8,400 \text{ sq. ft.} = ? \text{ acres} \qquad \frac{8,400}{43,560} = .193 \text{ (almost } \tfrac{1}{5} \text{ acre)}$$

---

58. B   Solution:

area = rectangle − triangle
= 600 × 800 − ½ (300 × 200)
= 480,000 − 30,000
= 450,000
cost = no. of sq. ft. × cost per sq. ft.
= 450,000 × $2.50
= $1,125,000

---

59. B   Solution:

area A = 40 × 20 =   800
B = 50 × 30 = 1,500
C = 10 × 20 =   200

total area = 2,500/sq. ft.

Cost per sq. ft. = 150,000 + 2,500 = $60

---

60. D   Solution:

(a) Finding volume in cubic feet

$$V = 70' \times 10' \times .25' \qquad (3 \text{ in.} = \frac{3}{12} = .25 \text{ ft.})$$

V = 175 cu. ft.

(b) Converting to cubic yards, 1 cu. yd. = 3′ × 3′ × 3′ = 27 cu. ft.

$$\frac{?}{175} = \frac{1}{27}$$

? = 175 ÷ 27 = 6.48 cu. yd.

(c) at $30 per cu. yd. the cost will be:
6.48 × $30 = $194.40

---

61. B   Solution:

(a) area of rectangle = 240 × 150 = 36,000 sq. ft.
(b) value of rectangle per sq. ft. $12,000 ÷ 31,500 = $0.33
(c) divided shaded area into 2 triangles
A = ½ (90 × 150) = 6,750
B = ½ (30 × 150) = 2,250
6,750 + 2,250 = 9,000 sq. ft.
(d) value = 9,000 × $.33 = $3,000
(e) with added 10% = $3,000 × 1.1 = $3,300

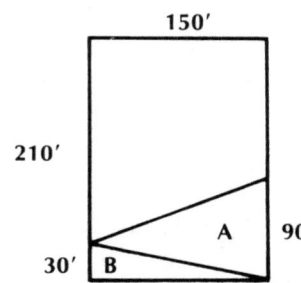

62. A Solution: (a) no. of acres = total cost ÷ cost per acre
                                                = \$120,000 ÷ \$15,000/acre
                                                = 8 acres

(b)   1 acre = 43,560 sq. ft.
        8 acres = 348,480 sq. ft.

(c)   Area = base × height
    348,480 = 500 × h
                h = 696.96 ft.

Miscellaneous

63. B Solution: \$1,000 shared by 8 apartments = \$1,000 ÷ 8 = \$125 each
                                in 6 equal payments = \$125 ÷ 6 = \$20.83

---

64. C Solution: 8 × 150,000 =   \$1,200,000
                                                    −1,000,000
                                                    \$200,000 increase

$$\frac{200,000}{1,000,000} = .20 = 20\%$$

---

65. D Solution: \$450 shared among 6 apartments = \$75 per apartment
                                Without utilities the rent would be \$500 − \$75 = \$425

---

66. D Solution: \$10,000 ÷ \$100,000 equals the capitalization rate of 10%
                                \$10,000 ÷ 9% is \$111,111

---

67. B Solution: 40% of 6% = .40 × .06 = .0240
Sales   ?   \$83,333.33
R   × .025   .024) ‾‾‾‾700‾‾
I   \$2,000

---

68. B Solution: \$700 commission; 40% × 6% = .024

Sales   ?   \$29,166.67
R   × .024   .024) ‾‾‾‾700‾‾
              \$700

---

69. B Solution: P(1.1) × (1.1) × (1.1) × (1.1) × (1.1) = P(1.61) = 61%

---

70. C Solution: $\dfrac{\$120,000}{3\frac{1}{2}}$ = \$34,285.71/year

$34,285.71 + 52 = \$659.34 per week

---

71. A Solution: 1 acre = 43,560 sq. ft.
¼ acre = 10,890 sq. ft.
2,500 + 10,890 = .229 = 23%

---

72. B Solution: ¼ acre = ¼ × 43,560 sq. ft. = 10,890 sq. ft.
10,890 × \$5 = \$54.450

60′ × 40′ = 2,400   2,400 × \$30 = $\underline{72,000}$
$\$126,450$

---

73. D Solution:

$$\begin{array}{r} ? \\ \times\ .06 \\ \hline \$7,920 \end{array} \qquad .06\,\overline{)\ \begin{array}{l}\$132,000\\ 7,920\end{array}}$$

---

74. B Solution:

$$\begin{array}{r} \$110,000 \\ \times\ .11 \\ \hline \$12,100\ +12 = \$1,008.33 \end{array} \qquad \begin{array}{r} \$1,047.56 \\ -1,008.33 \\ \hline \$39.23 \end{array}$$

---

75. C Solution: first year: 100 + (.10 × 100) = 110
second year: 110 + (.12 × 110) = 123.2
123.2 = 100 + (.232 × 100)

---

76. C Solution: Area = 70 × 50 − ½ (20 × 30)

= 3,500 − 300 = 3,200 sq. ft.
3,200 sq. ft. + 9 sq. ft./sq. yd. = 355.56 sq. yd.
355.56 × 100 = \$35,556

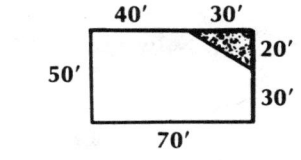

---

77. D Solution: ⅓ acre = 14,520 sq. ft.   35 ft. × 40 ft. = 1,400 sq. ft.

1,400 + 14,520 = .096 = 10% house
Therefore: 90% not house

78. C   Solution:

House	$35,000	× 2	=	$70,000
Lot	+20,000	× 300%	=	+60,000
	$55,000			$130,000
				−55,000
				$75,000 Appreciation

$$\frac{\$75,000}{\$55,000} = 1.36 = 136\%$$

---

79. B   Solution:

$600
−260 mortgage
340
− 60 to broker
280
−75 repair
$205

$205 ÷ $68,000 = .0030147
× 12
.03617 or 3.6%

---

80. A   Solution: $400 × 12 = $4,800/yr.

$$\frac{4,800}{.12} = \$40,000$$

---

81. B   Solution: $336 × 12 = $4,032/yr.

$$\frac{4,032}{.125} = \$32,256$$

---

82. C   Solution: 150 ft. × 220 ft. = 33,000   70% of 33,000 = 23,100 sq. ft.

---

83. A   Solution:

30,000 × 18% = 5,400   5,400 + 4,200 = 9,600
30,000 × 14% = 4,200   60,000 − 9,600 = 50,400 × .04 = $2,016

---

84. D   Solution: $37,500 × 2.5 = $93,750 is the amount of loan they would qualify for
Adding this to their $35,000 equity would mean they could purchase a
$128,750 home

---

85. A   Solution:

$1,500 deposit	$75,000	$75,000
+ 260 credit	× 80%	× 20%
$1,760	60,000	15,000 down payment
	× 3%	− 1,760
	$1,800 points	13,240
		+ 1,800
		$15,040

Appendix III: Salesperson's Practice Final Examination

This section contains a practice final examination for the salesperson candidate. It is similar in content and format to the test administered by Assessment Systems, Inc. (ASI).

The best way to prepare for the state exam is to work with exam material similar to that which will appear on the actual test. The actual test and this practice test have the same number of questions, type of questions, time limit and level of difficulty.

This following test is not, however, a copy of the actual test. It is copyrighted and may not be duplicated. The primary purpose of taking this practice test is to help you realize your weak areas so you can concentrate your studies on those areas.

General Information

1. The details about your state test may be found by contacting your state licensing agency. In addition, each testing agency prepares a special bulletin of information concerning the exam.
2. There is no scrap paper for math, so the test book must be used.
3. Battery-operated, hand-held, non-programable silent calculators may be used, although the math questions are designed to be answered without the need for one. However, you will find that the use of a calculator will cut down the amount of time spent on the math questions.
4. The test books are usually structured so that any page containing questions requiring arithmetic calculations contains 50 percent blank space or has a completely blank page fronting it for scratch work.

Specific Information

The ASI salesperson examination is divided into two separate tests, the General Test and the State Test.

The Salesperson General Test (80 questions) contains questions in the subject areas described below. The percentage distribution of each subject area is also shown. Approximately 20 percent of the test consists of questions dealing with arithmetic functions. These questions are distributed throughout the test.

Exam Content Outline and Allocated Percentage

Real Property and Laws Relating to Ownership (20)

Valuation of Real Estate (14)

Financing of Real Estate (20)

Transfer of Property Ownership (15)

Real Estate Brokerage (25)

Specialty Areas (6)

State Test

The State Test contains questions dealing with the real estate licensing laws, including the rules and regulations, as well as other aspects of real estate practices appropriate to the jurisdiction in which the test is being given. Examples of these other aspects include state statutes dealing with condominiums, subdivisions, fair housing, and administrative hearing procedures. Other aspects of real estate practice, which are not uniform, may also be included. Be sure to check with your state licensing agency for more details regarding this section.

SAMPLE SALESPERSON REAL ESTATE LICENSING EXAMINATION

1. Buyer and seller agree to the purchase of a house for $200,000 in which the buyer will make a $30,000 down payment and the seller will take back a ten-year purchase money mortgage for the balance. There is nothing in the contract to indicate that time is of the essence. The sales contract will be valid even though the parties fail to provide for which of the following?
   (A) Closing date
   (B) Interest rate
   (C) Signatures on the contract
   (D) Term of loan

2. If an option to purchase is exercised, which of the following is true?
   (A) The option money is automatically applied to the purchase price.
   (B) The optionor can be forced to sell the property.
   (C) The notice to exercise must be in writing.
   (D) Closing takes place the day the option is exercised.

3. A binder given by a buyer in a real estate transaction:
   (A) must be monetary.
   (B) may be withdrawn by the buyer any time before the seller signs his or her acceptance.
   (C) draws interest in favor of the broker.
   (D) must exceed 5 percent of sales price.

4. Which of the following is true under a contract of sale in which the date of occupancy is later than the settlement date?
   (A) The buyer does not acquire legal title upon settlement.
   (B) The contract should provide whether the seller is to pay any rent.
   (C) The buyer cannot obtain hazard insurance.
   (D) The seller is the legal owner until occupancy is ended.

5. If a lessee defaults on a lease and abandons the property in good condition, for which of the following could the lessee be held liable?
   (A) Balance of the rent plus forfeiture of the security deposit
   (B) Balance of the rent plus the cost to find a new tenant
   (C) Decrease in the market value of the property
   (D) Balance of the rent

6. Which of the following parties to a long-term ground lease is the holder of the leased fee?
   (A) Lessor   (C) Grantee
   (B) Lessee   (D) Grantor

7. Seller's broker was working with a buyer on an exclusive-authorization-to-sell listing, and presented an offer at less than the listed price. At the same time, the owner was dealing with another buyer who offered more money for the property and all in cash. The owner sold to the buyer at the higher price for all cash. The broker is entitled to:
   (A) a reasonable commission based upon the lower offer.
   (B) stop the sale of the property.
   (C) void the sale.
   (D) a commission based upon the higher selling price.

8. Which one of the following is true when the seller takes back a mortgage from the buyer as part payment for the sale?
   (A) The seller is entitled to possession of the property until the debt is paid.
   (B) The seller retains legal title.
   (C) No second mortgage may be placed on the property by the buyer.
   (D) This is a purchase money mortgage.

9. Buying real property "subject to the mortgage" is:
   (A) a type of conditional loan.
   (B) a mortgage bought by FNMA and sold to GNMA.
   (C) the taking of title to property by a grantee with no personal responsibility for paying the mortgage loan.
   (D) the right to foreclose without going to court.

10. A mortgage that covers several parcels of land and contains a provision for partial release upon the sale of an individual parcel is:
    (A) a direct reduction mortgage.
    (B) an amortized mortgage.
    (C) a blanket mortgage.
    (D) a declining balance mortgage.

11. In preparing the mortgage document, it should be noted that:
    (A) the seller assumes no financial risk.
    (B) the title is conveyed immediately to the buyer.
    (C) the seller is the lender.
    (D) a mortgage is required.

12. A buyer purchased a furnished fee simple home. He or she is assuming the existing mortgage. The settlement company will have drawn up all the following with the exception of:
    (A) bill of sale.
    (B) note and mortgage.
    (C) assumption agreement.
    (D) warranty deed.

13. Which of the following parties to a real estate sales transaction would have the **MOST** exposure to liability?
    (A) Grantor of quitclaim deed
    (B) Grantor in a loan assumption
    (C) Grantee taking subject to the loan
    (D) Grantor selling subject to the loan

14. If the foreclosure sale proceeds are less than the outstanding debt and foreclosure expenses, which of the following remedies is available?
    (A) There is no remedy.
    (B) The mortgagee must absorb the loss, as the mortgagor is liable only for foreclosure expenses.
    (C) Owner has the statutory right of redemption.
    (D) Mortgagee may obtain a deficiency judgment against the mortgagor.

15. *C* is purchasing a home by way of a DVA loan. The closing statement reveals a payment of $1,200 in discount points. How would this payment appear on the closing statement?
    (A) A reduction in the proceeds due seller
    (B) An addition of the principal due from buyer
    (C) A reduction in the buyer's down payment
    (D) An addition to the proceeds due seller

16. The Federal National Mortgage Association can do all of the following **EXCEPT**:
    (A) purchase conventional loans.
    (B) sell mortgages to institutions.
    (C) buy FHA-DVA loans.
    (D) originate federal loans.

17. A land contract (installment contract or agreement of sale) and a purchase money mortgage are similar in that:
    (A) the seller assumes no financial risk.
    (B) the title is conveyed immediately to the buyer.
    (C) the seller is the lender.
    (D) a mortgage is required.

18. A DVA loan may be granted for the purchase of a one-family to four-family dwelling if:
    (A) the veteran certifies the rent collected will equal the mortgage payments.
    (B) the loan will be amortized for not more than 20 years.
    (C) the veteran pays the points.
    (D) the veteran occupies one of the units.

19. The amount a lender will loan is generally based on:
    (A) the listed price.
    (B) the appraised value for loan purposes.
    (C) the appraised value for loan purposes or the sales price, whichever is lower.
    (D) the final sales price.

20. Under a Department of Veterans Affairs loan, a veteran can do which of the following?
    (A) Transfer his or her DVA loan to another home
    (B) Sell his or her home and allow a nonveteran buyer to assume the loan without DVA approval
    (C) Require a veteran buyer to agree in the sale contract to assume the loan and substitute his or her DVA eligibility
    (D) Obtain the DVA loan for a rental property

21. Regulation Z provides a right of rescission:
    (A) to first mortgages to finance the purchase of a residential condominium unit.
    (B) that expires three business days after the date of consummation of the transaction, or the date on which the lender makes material disclosures, whichever is later.
    (C) in all credit transactions.
    (D) that does not apply to loans made by commercial banks.

22. A person borrowed $85,000 and agreed to repay in monthly installments of $823.76 at 11½ percent annual interest. Of his or her first month's payment, how much was applied to reduction of principal?
    (A) $8.15
    (B) $9.18
    (C) $91.80
    (D) $814.58

23. *S* and *I* borrowed $85,000 at 11½ percent annual interest. Monthly payments on the loan are $823.76. In addition, they agreed to pay, into the "customer trust fund," the prorated monthly share of the annual taxes of $625.32, the semi-annual lease rent of $720, and a three-year homeowners insurance policy totalling $586.22. Their monthly payment would be:
    (A) $1,012.15.
    (B) $1,132.15.
    (C) $1,164.71.
    (D) $1,211.16.

24. On a long-term loan, the amount of semi-annual interest is $5,400 at an annual interest rate of 12 percent. How much money is invested?
    (A) $648
    (B) $45,000
    (C) $90,000
    (D) $180,000

25. What would be the FHA-insurable loan on a dwelling if the FHA valuation is $106,300 and the FHA insures 97 percent of the first $25,000, 90 percent of the next $10,000 and 80 percent of the remainder?
    (A) $9,029
    (B) $90,290
    (C) $92,900
    (D) $102,100

26. *E* and *D* agreed to buy an apartment on the following terms: first mortgage loan on a 90 percent loan-to-value ratio; seller to accept a second mortgage for one-half the remaining balance, the remainder to be paid in cash as down payment. If the down payment was $15,000, what was the amount of the first mortgage loan?
    (A) $27,000
    (B) $30,000
    (C) $270,000
    (D) $300,000

27. Which of the following statements regarding deeds is true?
    (A) The general warranty deed gives the least liability to the grantor.
    (B) The quitclaim deed gives the least protection to the grantee.
    (C) The special warranty deed gives the greatest protection to the grantor.
    (D) The bargain and sale deed is unlawful.

28. *H* executes a deed of his farm to *S*. *H* keeps the deed in his safe deposit box. Upon his death, the box is opened, and attached to the deed is a note to give the deed to *S*. Who has title to the farm?
    (A) *S*
    (B) *H*'s heirs
    (C) The state
    (D) *S*'s heirs

29. Which of the following is covered by the covenant against encumbrances in a general warranty deed?
    (A) Undisclosed subsurface waterpipe easement
    (B) Restrictive zoning ordinance
    (C) Rights of adverse possessor
    (D) Mining and water claims

30. The clause that defines or limits the quantity of the estate being conveyed is the:
    (A) partition clause.
    (B) revocation clause.
    (C) habendum clause.
    (D) reversion clause.

31. Which of the following parties is in the weakest position against a claim of title by a stranger?
    (A) A nonoccupant holder of a warranty deed
    (B) A nonoccupant holder of an unrecorded quitclaim deed
    (C) One who holds an unrecorded deed
    (D) One who holds a recorded quitclaim deed to the property

32. As far as its validity between grantor and grantee is concerned, a deed that is not dated, acknowledged or recorded is:
    (A) invalid because of these omissions.
    (B) void.
    (C) revocable by the grantor.
    (D) valid despite these omissions.

33. One who owns a life estate cannot:
    (A) sell one's interest.
    (B) mortgage one's interest.
    (C) devise one's interest.
    (D) lease one's interest.

34. Restrictions in a deed that benefit only the grantor:
    (A) can be removed by the grantor issuing a quitclaim deed.
    (B) must be more lenient than the current zoning use.
    (C) must be more strict than the current zoning use.
    (D) are irrevocable.

35. To the holder of the dominant tenement, an easement is:
    - (A) an encumbrance.
    - (B) an appurtenance.
    - (C) a license.
    - (D) an encroachment.

36. After *C* purchases a property, he has a survey made and finds that his neighbor, through error, has recently built an ornamental fence two feet over on *C's* land. This would be a basic example of:
    - (A) a party wall.
    - (B) an encroachment.
    - (C) an appurtenance.
    - (D) adverse possession.

37. Riparian rights are those rights possessed by:
    - (A) an owner living in a townhouse subdivision.
    - (B) an owner living on a waterway.
    - (C) a corporation.
    - (D) a business trust.

38. The word "fee" used in connection with real property means:
    - (A) the money charged by a broker for services.
    - (B) an estate of inheritance.
    - (C) the charge made for searching title.
    - (D) the leased land.

39. When a person dies intestate and no heirs can be found for intestate succession, real property will revert to the government through a process known as:
    - (A) reconveyance.
    - (B) reversion.
    - (C) escheat.
    - (D) succession.

40. What document is prepared to evidence that personal property is pledged to secure a loan?
    - (A) Bill of sale
    - (B) Chattel mortgage
    - (C) Bargain and sale deed
    - (D) Partial release

41. Which is true about apartment ownership?
    - (A) In a condominium, each owner is responsible for his or her own mortgage payments, as well as those of fellow apartment owners.
    - (B) In a typical cooperative association, if one or more members fail to pay their share of the mortgage, the other owners must make payments for the defaulting members, or risk foreclosure on the entire property.
    - (C) In a condominium, usually there is a blanket mortgage on the common area.
    - (D) Each owner receives an apartment deed.

42. What can the taxing agency do when a condominium apartment owner defaults in paying state real property taxes?
    - (A) Seek to foreclose against the apartment
    - (B) Seek to recover from the condominium association
    - (C) Force the owner to forfeit a bond
    - (D) Place a lien on the common elements

43. Under the Federal Fair Housing Act it is permissible to:
    - (A) approve a loan to a person who has stated the intention to rent the property only to members of a minority group.
    - (B) refuse to grant loans on the basis of the financial condition of an applicant who is a member of a minority group.
    - (C) require the applicant to sign a form that lists religion, sex and marital status.
    - (D) deny housing to a pregnant woman.

44. Which of the following is permissable under the Federal Fair Housing Act?
    - (A) Charging a higher interest rate on a loan by a savings and loan association on the grounds the loan applicant intends to rent part of the subject property to members of a certain minority group
    - (B) Advertising property for sale only in publications primarily aimed at a particular ethnic group and using models of only that same ethnic group
    - (C) Refusing a loan on a house based on the religion of the applicant
    - (D) Denying housing based on a prior criminal violence

45. *S* decides to use the services of OK Realty to locate a suitable home for his minority family. OK Realty assigns *T*, their only minority salesperson, who avoids showing *S* any properties outside of minority-speaking neighborhoods despite the fact *S* had indicated interest in houses in an all-white district. OK Realty's discriminating actions can be **BEST** described as:
    - (A) redlining.
    - (B) blockbusting.
    - (C) steering.
    - (D) conciliation.

46. A salesperson gets 60 percent of the commission on property he or she lists and sells for the firm. Which of the following transactions will earn the most money for the salesperson?
    (A) $60,500 at 7 percent
    (B) $63,500 at 6.5 percent
    (C) $63,750 at 6.5 percent
    (D) $64,000 at 6 percent

47. Working for the A-1 Real Estate Agency, the listing salesperson gets 20 percent of the total commission on a sale. The selling salesperson gets 45 percent of the remainder. How much would S receive if he were both the listing and selling salesperson on a $115,500 sale at six percent commission?
    (A) $2,494.80   (C) $4,504.50
    (B) $3,880.80   (D) $6,930

48. An owner requests a broker to list a property for sale at $70,000. Upon inspection, the broker believes the property is worth $80,000. The broker should:
    (A) get a net listing for the property at $70,000.
    (B) buy the property himself or herself for $70,000.
    (C) suggest that the owner list the property for $75,000 to have room for bargaining.
    (D) inform the seller that the property is worth $80,000.

49. A fiduciary relationship could exist between a principal and all of the following EXCEPT:
    (A) a trustee.   (C) an appraiser.
    (B) an administrator.   (D) a receiver.

50. A real estate salesperson might lawfully accept an extra commission in a difficult sale from:
    (A) an appreciative seller.
    (B) a thankful buyer.
    (C) a broker-employer.
    (D) the mortgage lender.

51. When money is deposited in a client trust account, part of which will be used to pay the broker's commission:
    (A) the broker can withdraw his or her share of the money before the real estate transaction is consummated or terminated.
    (B) accurate records must be kept on the account.
    (C) interest on the account is by law the property of the broker.
    (D) the salespeople can withdraw money prior to closing.

52. One who has the right to sign the name of a principal to a contract of sale is:
    (A) an attorney-in-fact.
    (B) a broker with a listing.
    (C) a special agent.
    (D) an attorney at law.

53. The relationship between a real estate agent and a principal is MOST similar to which of the following?
    (A) Optionee and optionor
    (B) Vendee and vendor
    (C) Trustee and beneficiary
    (D) Mortgagee and mortgagor

54. A property manager's duties typically include all of the following EXCEPT:
    (A) collecting rents.
    (B) making minor repairs.
    (C) marketing space.
    (D) investing profits from client's properties.

55. All of the following are a valid operating expense for a building manager to put into a budget EXCEPT:
    (A) heating oil.   (C) foundation repairs.
    (B) cleaning supplies.   (D) management fees.

56. A standard form policy of title insurance does NOT protect against loss resulting from:
    (A) encroachment on the property.
    (B) liens and encumbrances of record.
    (C) lack of capacity of the grantor.
    (D) forgery in the chain of title.

57. Escrow or a settlement agent is often used for all of the following purposes EXCEPT:
    (A) to determine that outstanding and unpaid liens will be satisfied.
    (B) to see that the purchase price is paid and all checks have cleared the bank.
    (C) to handle the signing of documents and the closing.
    (D) to prepare the legal and tax documents.

58. A deed made and delivered but NOT recorded is:
    (A) valid between the parties and valid as to third parties with notice.
    (B) valid between the parties and valid as to subsequent recorded interests.
    (C) valid between the parties and invalid as to subsequent donees of the property.
    (D) invalid as between the parties.

59. The recording system performs which of the following functions?
    (A) Insures title against loss due to third-party claims
    (B) Cures major defects in title
    (C) Gives constructive notice of documents
    (D) Handles the closing of real estate transactions

60. An insurance policy purchased January 10, 1989, was assumed by the purchaser effective October 30, 1990. Cost of the policy was $356.80 for a three-year period. The policy would be prorated as follows:
    (A) $142.05 credit to purchaser, debit to seller.
    (B) $142.05 credit to seller, debit to purchaser.
    (C) $214.75 credit to purchaser, debit to seller.
    (D) $214.75 credit to seller, debit to purchaser.

61. Prorate the prepaid taxes as of settlement date (June 15) if a property is valued at $120,000 and assessed at 55 percent value with a tax rate of $3.20 per $100 of valuation on a calendar year basis.
    (A) Debit both $968
    (B) Credit both $968
    (C) Credit buyer $1,144, debit seller $968
    (D) Debit buyer $1,144, credit seller $1,144

62. N sold her house August 31 for $112,000. Her mortgage balance is $63,200 and she has paid the taxes of $684 through December 31. She pays six percent commission to the agent. What is the amount due to the seller before other closing costs?
    (A) $42,308   (C) $105,280
    (B) $63,428   (D) $105,508

63. B, as manager of the Lua Overlook Apartments, collects $450 per month on each of six apartments. He makes monthly disbursements of $180 for utilities and $85 for insurance. If his management fee is ten percent of gross rent per month, how much does he send the owner each month?
    (A) $2,065   (C) $2,265
    (B) $2,165   (D) $2,365

64. A house sold for $115,500, with the purchaser assuming a mortgage loan of $83,526.23. Tax rates were as follows: state recording tax, $0.15 per $100 or part thereof; local recording tax, $.0.05 per $100 or part thereof; state transfer tax, $0.50 per $500 or part thereof, less assumed mortgage indebtedness. What were the total taxes applicable to this sale?
    (A) $32   (C) $231
    (B) $89.75   (D) $263

65. A 10-year-old, well-maintained house that is 36 ft. x 42 ft. is on a lot currently valued at $15,600. The current reproduction cost is $52 per sq. ft., excluding depreciation. The total depreciation for this structure is charged at $0.75 per sq. ft. What is the current value of the property to the nearest thousand?
    (A) $79,000   (C) $94,000
    (B) $93,000   (D) $95,000

66. Two years ago a property was assessed at $63,000. The tax rate was 90 mills. When the community was reappraised last year, the assessment was up ten percent, but the tax rate was down ten percent. The taxes paid were:
    (A) down by $56.70.   (C) up by $47.80.
    (B) the same.   (D) up by $56.70.

67. F is interested in an income property from which he would realize $1,500 per month net. If investment capital is attracted to a 15 percent return, what is the maximum he should pay for the property?
    (A) $22,500   (C) $120,000
    (B) $100,000   (D) $225,000

68. J is developing a subdivision with lots from ¼ to ¾ acre. There are four floor plans available in the house—1,000 sq. ft., 1,450 sq. ft., 1,600 sq. ft. and 1,850 sq. ft. The lots sell for $65,000 an acre and the houses $63.50 a square foot. What is the difference between the least and most expensive home?
    (A) $79,750   (C) $93,432
    (B) $86,475   (D) $166,225

69. Physical deterioration most closely means:
    (A) obsolescence.   (C) reversion.
    (B) wear and tear.   (D) recapture.

70. If the reproduction cost shows a higher dollar amount than the appraised value, which of the following **MOST** probably has occurred?
    (A) Accrued depreciation
    (B) Excessive appraisal
    (C) Economic obsolescence
    (D) Capitalization

71. Which of the following is true of real estate appraisers?
    (A) They may not advertise.
    (B) They usually base their fees on a percentage of appraised value.
    (C) They must have a professional designation such as MAI, SREA.
    (D) None of the above.

72. All of the following are examples of external obsolescence **EXCEPT**:
    (A) population density.
    (B) direct effect of the elements.
    (C) zoning.
    (D) special assessments.

73. In using the market comparison approach to appraisal, the appraiser considers:
    (A) the sales price of comparable properties.
    (B) the acquisition cost to the present owner.
    (C) the property tax rates.
    (D) the tax benefits.

74. A variance could be which of the following?
    (A) A large, new supermarket located in an area zoned for small retail shops
    (B) An old grocery store located in an area recently rezoned residential
    (C) A single-family home in a residential zone
    (D) A home more expensive than adjacent homes

75. The difference between police power and eminent domain can be **BEST** determined by:
    (A) whether or not the action was by sovereign power or by statute.
    (B) whether or not any compensation was paid to the owner.
    (C) whether or not the owner's use was affected.
    (D) whether or not the improvements are to be razed.

76. Which of the following statements is true?
    (A) All liens are encumbrances.
    (B) All encumbrances are liens.
    (C) Specific liens affect all property of the debtor located in the state.
    (D) Judgments are specific liens.

77. Which of the following liens would have top priority in the event of foreclosure of the subject property?
    (A) State income tax lien recorded first
    (B) Federal estate tax lien recorded second
    (C) Mechanic's lien for work commenced before any other lien was recorded
    (D) State property tax lien recorded last

78. The lender wants to insure the first priority of his lien. The lender should do all of the following **EXCEPT**:
    (A) make sure that all other liens are removed or subordinated from the property being used as collateral.
    (B) make sure the borrower has an absolute estate with no liens.
    (C) obtain an ALTA title insurance policy.
    (D) verify the health of the borrower.

79. The gross income multiplier is calculated by dividing the sales price by the:
    (A) monthly net income.
    (B) monthly gross income.
    (C) annual net income.
    (D) annual gross income.

80. All of the following appear in a promissory note **EXCEPT**:
    (A) interest.
    (B) commencement date.
    (C) term of loan.
    (D) purchase price of property.

ANSWERS

1. **A** Courts normally will imply a reasonable closing date, but not such as essential term as the interest rate.

2. **B** Whether or not the option money is applied to the purchase price is a negotiable point. The optionee can obtain specific performance against the optionor.

3. **B** A binder is like a deposit receipt. Although it usually is money, it could be some other form of valuable consideration (a boat or even a promise to do something).

4. **B** In a late occupancy, the seller gets to stay in possession after closing. Some provision should be made as to rent, and the rental agreement should be in writing.

5. **D** In no event could he be responsible for more rent than if he had not breached the lease and had remained for the full term. They key word here is *plus*.

6. **A** The lessor holds the leased fee, which is valued as the discounted value of the rent plus the value of the reversionary interest. The lessee holds the leasehold estate.

7. **D** Under the exclusive-authorization-to-sell listing, the broker earns commission based on the sales price, regardless of who is the procuring cause of the sale.

8. **D** Possession and title pass to the buyer, but the seller retains a security interest pending full payment of the debt. Sellers usually do not restrict junior financing.

9. **C** Upon default, the buyer would lose the property, but would not be obligated for the seller's loan (as buyer would if "assuming" the loan).

10. **C** Blanket mortgages are popular in subdivision developments. It is important to check if there are unambiguous partial release provisions.

11. **D** The mortgage transfers a security interest and thus the transferee need not sign (just as a grantee usually need not sign the deed).

12. **B** The deed usually contains an assumption clause obligating the grantee to take on the grantor's obligations under the existing note and mortgage. There would be a new note and mortgage if the seller is to be relieved from all liability (i.e., a novation).

13. **D** The grantor selling subject to a loan would remain primarily liable for the debt, whereas he or she would be secondarily liable as a surety in a loan assumption. The grantor of a quitclaim deed would have the least exposure.

14. **D** In a few states, however, such as California, there can be no deficiency judgments on purchase money mortgages. In effect, they are treated as nonrecourse loans.

15. **A** The seller would be debited the amount of the discount points since the buyer is prohibited by law from paying discount points on DVA loans.

16. **D** Fannie Mae only operates in the secondary mortgage market.

17. **C** Under a land contract, the seller retains legal title as security, whereas under the purchase money mortgage, the seller retains no title interest in the property, only the lien interest of a mortgagee.

18. **D** The only requirement is that the veteran certify he will occupy one of the units.

19. **C** Typically, the appraised value is lower in a seller's market.

20. **C** The DVA loans are not transferable by the veteran to his or her new home. The veteran would need to have eligibility restored prior to getting a loan on another home. DVA loans are assumable with prior approval.

21. **B** First liens to acquire or construct a principal residence (including condominiums) would be exempt. The right of rescission is designed to protect the existing homeowner from losing his or her home (including condominiums and mobile homes) due to a credit transaction that uses a principal residence as security. Not that there is now a three-year statute of limitations if no disclosures are made.

22. B

$$85,000$$
$$\times\ .115$$
$$\overline{9,775}\ /yr.$$

$$\frac{9775}{21} = \$814.58$$

$$\begin{array}{r} \$823.76 \\ -814.58 \\ \hline \$\ 9.18 \end{array}$$

23. A

Tax	$= \dfrac{625.32}{12} =$	\$52.11/month
Lease	$= \dfrac{720}{6} =$	\$120/month
Insurance	$= \dfrac{586.22}{36} =$	\$16.28/month
Loan	$=$	\$823.76/month
Payment		\$1012.15 Total

24. C

$$\begin{array}{c} ? \\ \times\ .12 \\ \hline 10,800 \end{array} \qquad \frac{10,800}{.12} = \$90,000$$

25. B

25,000	10,000	71,300	24,250
× .97	× .90	× .80	9,000
24,250	9,000	57,040	+57,040
			$90,290

26. C

15,000 down		?	$\dfrac{30,000}{.10} = 300,000$
15,000 2nd	× .10		× .90
30,000	30,000		$270,000

27. B As far as the grantor's liability is concerned, the general warranty gives the most exposure, then comes the special warranty deed (only covers the time the grantor owned the property), and then the quitclaim deed (no liability).

28. B There is no delivery because *H* did not give up control over the deed as he would have if he had handed it to *S* or put it in an escrow. To accomplish his purpose, *H* should have prepared a will.

29. A Since the easement was not disclosed, the grantee could recover for the loss in value caused by this easement, which is an encumbrance. Zoning laws are public restrictions and matters of public knowledge and thus not covered under this covenant.

30. C Also called the "to have and to hold" clause, it is not an essential element for a valid deed but is customarily included. It would indicate if the grantor is conveying a fee simple or life estate, for example.

31. B This grantee has given no constructive notice of his rights (recording or possession) and has no warranties to assert against the grantor in the event the stranger proves to have a superior title. Possession gives constructive notice (actual notice if a person is aware of the possession).

32. D The date is useful to prove when it was delivered but it is not required, nor is recording or acknowledgment.

33. C A *devise* is a transfer by will (do not confuse with *demise*, which is a transfer by lease). There is no estate left after the owner of the life estate (life tenant) dies. The buyer, lender or lessee take their interest subject to the life estate so their interests cease when the life estate ceases. Lenders rarely lend on a life estate; and, if so, they may require a term life insurance policy as further security. Incidentally, the buyer would own a "life estate pur autre vie."

34. A For example, assume a grantor of Lot 1 reserved an easement to benefit neighboring Lot 2. At any time, he could release the reservation interest in Lot 1 by way of a quitclaim deed. A more lenient deed restriction limiting a building to three stories would not control over a zoning law that permits only two stories, and vice versa.

35. B To the servient tenement, the easement is an encumbrance. To the dominant tenement, it is something that attaches to the land and benefits it.

36. B *C* could bring a lawsuit to seek removal of the fence. Failure to do so for a long enough time might result in the neighbor obtaining title to the disputed land by adverse possession. This would be an encumbrance on *C*'s land, not an appurtenance. A party wall is located on the property line.

37. B Such riparian owner would be the beneficiary of any increased land due to accretion.

38. B Fee refers to a fee simple, which is a freehold estate of inheritance. The broker typically earns a commission.

39. C Most state laws allow a long period between death and title passing to the government so that next of kin can file claims.

40. B In those states that have adopted the Uniform Commercial Code, the chattel mortgage is called a security agreement and it is a financing statement that is recorded.

41. B In a condo, the owners are not responsible for the mortgage payments of other owners. But in a co-op, there is usually one blanket mortgage, so all owners must make up the defaults of others to avoid foreclosure of the one mortgage. Of course, they would have a lien on the defaulting owner's interest to the extent of their cash advances. Co-op owners receive a proprietary lease, not an apartment deed.

42. A Most state laws require that state real property taxes be assessed against individual units and not the property as a whole.

43. B In choice (A), the borrower would be practicing discrimination in his or her rental program, so the lender cannot be a party to this. A lender can refuse a loan for valid credit reasons, but not to discriminate against minority groups.

44. D The loan decision cannot be based on ethnic reasons, only economic reasons. The FFH Act also prohibits discriminatory solicitation, which encompasses this type of selective advertising as indirect discrimination—it is selected on ethnic grounds. A proposed tenant who poses a threat to others can be denied housing.

45. C Steering is the unlawful practice of discouraging the sale or rental of a dwelling because of the presence or absence of minority neighbors. Referring minority prospects to minority salespersons may be unlawful, since it treats people differently because of minority status, even though there may be some valid business purpose.

46. A
$$A = \$4,144 \times .60 = \$2,486$$
$$B = \$3,840 \times .60 = \$2,304$$
$$C = \$4,128 \times .60 = \$2,477$$
$$D = \$4,235 \times .60 = \$2,541$$

47. B

115,500	6,930	6,930
× .06	× .20	− 1,386
6,930	1,386	5,544
		× .45
		2,494.80

2,494.80
+1,386.00
$3,880.80

48. D The broker has a fiduciary duty to protect the best interests of the client, which, in this case, would be to inform the owner of the true worth of the property and then discuss an appropriate listing price.

49. C The appraiser is hired to render an independent evaluation of the property and is generally not an agent entrusted with the client's properties.

50. C A salesperson cannot receive compensation directly from anyone other than the broker.

51. B The broker cannot withdraw money even though commission has been earned, unless the broker has the written consent of both seller and buyer.

52. A Brokers have too limited an authority under most listings. They could sign if they were attorney-in-fact under a power of attorney.

53. C The trustee in a deed of trust holds title to the secured property for the benefit of the beneficiary (lender).

54. D Property managers handle rents, minor repairs, and marketing of leases. They are not responsible for making investment decisions, such as handling real estate profits for their clients.

55. **C** Foundation work would not be a regularly occurring expenditure.

56. **A** Encroachments would be physical matters off the public records (such as overhanging eaves), which could only be covered in an extended title insurance policy.

57. **D** Escrow will often use the buyer's money to pay off unpaid taxes and mortgages so the buyer will get the free and clear title promised by seller. Escrow does not act as the attorney or accountant.

58. **A** If the deed is not recorded, a subsequent purchaser for value (from the original grantor) without notice of the first unrecorded deed could get superior title by recording this subsequent deed first. Donees are not protected under the recording law (nor are devisees).

59. **C** The recording system neither insures nor corrects title defects; it merely gives constructive notice of the rights of people in certain property.

60. **B** 21⅔ months elapsed since January 10, 1989.

$$\frac{356.80}{36} = \$9.91 \text{ month} \qquad \begin{array}{r} 21\frac{2}{3} \\ \times\ 9.91 \\ \hline \$214.75 \end{array}$$

$$\begin{array}{r} 356.80 \\ -\ 214.75 \\ \hline \$\ 142.05 \end{array} \text{ seller has already paid for the unused period}$$

61. **D**
$$\begin{array}{r} 120,000 \\ .55 \\ \hline 66,000 \end{array} \qquad 660 \times (320/100) = 2,112/\text{yr}$$

$$\frac{2,122}{12} = \$176/\text{month} \qquad \begin{array}{r} \$176 \\ \times\ 6.5 \\ \hline \$1,144 \end{array} \text{ months}$$

Seller has prepaid for the whole year and there is a 6.5-month unused portion that the buyer will benefit from unless some adjustment (proration) is made. In tax prorations, the debit and credit amounts are equal.

62. **A**
$$\begin{array}{r} 112,000 \\ \times\ .94 \\ \hline 105,280 \end{array}$$

$$\begin{array}{r} -63,200 \\ \hline 42,080 \end{array}$$

⅓ year: $\dfrac{\$684}{3} = \begin{array}{r} 228 \\ 42,080 \\ \hline \$42,308 \end{array}$

63. **B**
$$\begin{array}{r} 450 \\ \times\ 6 \\ \hline 2,700 \\ -\ 535 \\ \hline 2,165 \end{array} \qquad \begin{array}{r} 2,700 \\ \times\ .10 \\ \hline 270 \end{array} \qquad \begin{array}{r} 270 \\ 180 \\ +\ 85 \\ \hline 535 \end{array}$$

64. **D**
$$\begin{array}{r} 1,155 \\ \times\ .05 \\ \hline 57.75 \end{array} \qquad \begin{array}{r} 1,155 \\ \times\ .15 \\ \hline 173.25 \end{array} \qquad \begin{array}{r} 115,500.00 \\ -\ 83,526.23 \\ \hline 31,973.77 \end{array}$$

31,973.77 ÷ 500 = 63.9 (approximately 64)

$$\begin{array}{r} 64 \\ \times\ .50 \\ \hline 32 \end{array} \qquad \begin{array}{r} 57.75 \\ 173.25 \\ +\ 32.00 \\ \hline 263.00 \end{array}$$

65. **B**
$$\begin{array}{r} 36 \\ \times\ 42 \\ \hline 1,512 \end{array} \quad \begin{array}{r} 1,512 \\ \times\ 52 \\ \hline \$78,624 \end{array} \quad \begin{array}{r} 78,624 \\ +\ 15,600 \\ \hline 94,224 \\ -\ 1,134 \\ \hline \$93,090 \end{array} \quad \begin{array}{r} 1,512 \\ \times\ .75 \\ \hline 1,134 \end{array}$$

66. **C**
$$\begin{array}{c} 63,000\ +\ 6,300\ =\ 69,300 \\ \times\ .090\ -\ .009\ =\ \times\ .081 \\ \hline 5,670 \qquad\qquad 5,613.30 \end{array} \qquad \begin{array}{r} 5,670.00 \\ -\ 5,613.30 \\ \hline \$56.70 \end{array}$$

67. **C**
$$\begin{array}{r} 1,500\ /\text{month} \\ \times\ 12\ \text{months} \\ \hline 18,000 \end{array} \quad \begin{array}{r} ? \\ \times\ .15 \\ \hline 18,000 \end{array} \quad \frac{18,000}{.15} = \$120,000$$

68. **B** **Least**
$$\begin{array}{lll} \frac{1}{4} \times 65,000 & = & 16,250 \\ +\ 1,000 \times 63.50 & = & +\ 63,500 \\ & & \hline \\ & & 79,750 \end{array}$$

Most
$$\begin{array}{lll} .75 \times 65,000 & = & 48,750 \\ +\ 1,850 \times 63.50 & = & 117,475 \\ & & \hline \\ & & 166,225 \\ & & -\ 79,750 \end{array}$$

Difference   86,475

69. **B** Loss in value due to wear and tear is physical deterioration.

70. **A** If it costs $100,000 to reproduce a five-year-old building valued at $92,000, there has been an adjustment made for $8,000 of depreciation over the five years.

71. **D** Appraisers' fees are based upon the time and expenses; it would be unethical to have a contingent appraisal fee.

72. **B** Population changes, changes in zoning or an unusually high assessment might cause external obsolescence of the property. Direct effect of the elements (such as wind, snow) could result in physical deterioration.

73. **A** Since the market comparison approach uses prices of recently sold comparables, the acquisition cost of the property is irrelevant.

74. **A** Choice (B) is an example of a nonconforming use.

75. **B** If the value of property is lessened by government regulation under the police power as opposed to taking under eminent domain, there is no just compensation paid.

76. **A** Judgments are general liens. Easements are encumbrances but not liens.

77. **D** Priority typically depends on date of recordation except in cases of state real property tax liens and special assessments.

78. **D** Prior liens should be removed or placed junior through subordination. The lender usually would not want to lend on a conditional fee simple estate.

79. **D** The gross income multiplier, used to compare investment property in the market comparison appraisal method, is the ratio between the gross income and the sales price.

80. **D** The purchase price is found in the sales contract; the note states the amount of the loan.

Appendix IV: Broker's Practice Final Examination

This section contains a practice final examination for the broker candidate. Like the practice salesperson exam, this test is similar in content and format to the broker exam administered by ASI.

The best way to prepare for the state exam is to work with test material similar to that which will appear on the actual test. The actual test and this practice test have the same number of questions, type of questions, time limit and level of difficulty.

This following test is not, however, a copy of the actual test. It is copyrighted and may not be duplicated. The primary purpose of taking this practice test is to help you realize your weak areas so you can concentrate your studies on those areas.

Broker candidates should consider taking the salesperson's practice final examination as well for an additional exercise in test-taking.

General Information

1. The details about your state test may be found by contacting your licensing agency, and obtaining a special bulletin of information concerning the exam.
2. There is no scrap paper for math, so the test book must be used.
3. Battery-operated, hand-held, non-programmable silent calculators may be used, although the math questions are designed to be answered without the need for one. However, you will find the use of a calculator will cut down the amount of time spent on the math questions.
4. The test books are usually structured so that any page containing questions requiring arithmetic calculations contain 50 percent blank space or has a completely blank page fronting it for scratch work.

Specific Information

The ASI broker examination is divided into two separate tests, the General Test and the State Test.

The Broker General Test (80 questions) contains questions in the subject areas below. The percentage distribution of each subject area is also given. Approximately 20 percent of the test consists of questions requiring arithmetic calculations. These questions are distributed throughout the test.

Exam Content Outline

1. Real Property and Laws Relating to Ownership (23 percent)

   Questions in this area cover the following topics:

   Ownership of Property: components of real property (land, mineral rights, etc.), how personal property differs from real property, methods of land description, interests in real estate, forms of ownership.

   Transfer of Title: deeds, wills, governmental or judicial actions, power of attorney.

   Encumbrances: easements, encroachments, liens, priority among liens, covenants, conditions and restrictions.

   Public Power Over Property: eminent domain, escheat, property taxation, building codes, planning and zoning; hazard areas.

2. Valuation of Real Property (13 percent)

   Questions in this area cover appraisal, competitive market analysis and influences affecting value.

3. Federal Income Tax Laws Affecting Real Estate (7 percent)

Questions in this area cover the impact of federal tax laws on owner-occupied residences, real estate investments and other tax considerations.

4. Financing of Real Estate (20 percent)

Questions in this area cover the following topics:

Sources of Financing: institutional; seller financing; existing financing; secondary mortgage market.

Characteristics of Loans: amortization; interest rates; FHA, DVA, FmHA, conventional and private loans; nonrecourse financing.

Special Forms of Financing: wraparound, blanket, package, growing equity, bridge (swing), construction, home equity, sale-leaseback, other.

Financing Instruments: mortgages; notes; trust deeds; contracts for deed (land contracts).

Foreclosure and Redemption

Terms and Conditions: lender requirements, loan origination costs.

5. Settlement (12 percent)

Questions in this area cover evidence of title, reports and settlement procedures.

6. Real Estate Practice (25 percent)

Questions in this area cover the following topics:

Agency Relationships and Responsibilities: relationship of broker to principal and to the public; relationship of salespersons to broker, broker's principal and the public; salesperson as independent contractor or employee; broker or salesperson as principal; ethical responsibilities of brokers and salespersons; disclosure of agency relationship.

Listing of Real Property: characteristics of types of listing agreements; disclosure of material facts and discussion of defects; brokerage fee; physical data and other data; building codes; zoning and use permits; compliance with fair housing laws; ownership of record; homeowner's association bylaws and fees; right of first refusal; termination of listings.

Real Estate Sales Contracts: elements of real estate sales contracts; notice of acceptance, rejection, revocation or rescission; transmittal of offers and counteroffers; contract contingencies, options; earnest money deposits; personal property included; financing considerations; assignment; contract enforcement.

Other Federal Laws: fair housing laws; Truth-in-Lending Act (Regulation Z); Bulk Sales Act; Tax Reform Act (1986)

Specialty Areas: property management; common interest properties; securities laws affecting real estate investments.

State Test

The State Test contains questions dealing with the real estate licensing laws, including the rules and regulations, as well as other aspects of real estate practice appropriate to the jurisdiction in which the test is being given. Examples of these other aspects include state statutes dealing with condominiums, subdivisions, fair housing and administrative hearing procedures. Other aspects of real estate practice, which are not uniform, may also be included. Be sure to check with your state licensing agency for more details regarding this section.

SAMPLE BROKER REAL ESTATE LICENSING EXAMINATION— GENERAL SECTION

1. After showing a property a number of times and not securing an acceptable offer, the broker decides to buy the property himself or herself. He or she must do which of the following?
   (A) Wait until the listing expires and then make an offer to purchase
   (B) Make his or her true position known to the seller
   (C) Place his or her license on inactive status
   (D) Use a strawman

2. A seller tells his or her broker that termites have destroyed the floor and the swimming pool is in violation of the city setback requirements. The broker's salesperson must disclose to a prospective buyer all of the following **EXCEPT:**
   - (A) condition of the floor.
   - (B) pool violation.
   - (C) termite problem.
   - (D) the seller's lowest price.

3. It is an unethical practice for a broker representing a seller to do which of the following?
   - (A) Advise the seller of the highest price a prospective purchaser is willing to pay
   - (B) Advise a prospective purchaser of the lowest price the seller is willing to accept
   - (C) Advise a prospective purchaser of a cracked foundation
   - (D) Present written offers that are less than the listing price

4. When money is deposited in a client trust account, part of which will be used to pay the broker's commission:
   - (A) the broker can withdraw his or her share of the money before the real estate transaction is consummated or terminated.
   - (B) accurate records must be kept on the account.
   - (C) the broker usually keeps interest earned on the account.
   - (D) the broker can keep earned commissions in the account.

5. In real estate transactions all of the following documents are usually recorded **EXCEPT:**
   - (A) deed.
   - (B) offer to purchase.
   - (C) second mortgage.
   - (D) purchase money mortgage.

6. The recording system performs which of the following functions?
   - (A) Insures title against loss due to third-party claims
   - (B) Cures all defects in title
   - (C) Gives notice of documents
   - (D) Guarantees good title

7. The Real Estate Settlement Procedures Act (RESPA) is designed to regulate which of the following?
   - (A) Disclosures of closing information
   - (B) Procedures for recording titles to real estate
   - (C) Disclosure of agency
   - (D) Proration of expenses

8. Except under specific conditions, an agent may serve only one principal at a time; however, a principal may have more than one agent. Which of the following would **BEST** describe such a situation?
   - (A) Multiple listing
   - (B) Open listing
   - (C) Exclusive agency
   - (D) Exclusive right to sell

9. A property owner who signed a listing with a broker for 60 days was killed in an accident before the broker procured a buyer. The listing is:
   - (A) binding upon owner's heirs to carry out his or her promises.
   - (B) no good as an authorization, but binding if a buyer is secured later.
   - (C) terminated immediately upon death.
   - (D) still in effect, as the owner's intent was clear.

10. The phrase "procuring cause" is **MOST** significant to a seller in relation to:
    - (A) an exclusive agency.
    - (B) an open listing.
    - (C) an exclusive-right-to-sell listing.
    - (D) a net listing.

11. A broker is holding an earnest money deposit, equal to the amount of his or her commission. The seller, at the closing, not only refuses to pay the broker a commission but demands that the broker should pay him or her the entire deposit. The broker should:
    - (A) refuse to permit the closing of the deal.
    - (B) retain the earnest money as commission.
    - (C) file a complaint with the real estate licensing agency.
    - (D) pay the earnest money to the seller and then sue for commission.

12. Which of the following would be a debit to the buyer on the settlement statement?
    (A) Purchase price
    (B) Earnest money deposit given by the buyer
    (C) Assumed mortgage
    (D) New mortgage

13. An owner's title insurance policy protects the owner against:
    (A) loss of property due to mortgage foreclosure.
    (B) loss of title to a claimant with superior right of title.
    (C) lawsuits based on property condition.
    (D) loss due to a new tax law.

14. An abstract of title does which of the following?
    (A) Insures the title
    (B) Gives a history of the title, including the recorded encumbrances against the property
    (C) Guarantees the title
    (D) Covers encroachments

15. A property manager's duties typically include all of the following **EXCEPT**:
    (A) collecting rents.
    (B) making minor repairs.
    (C) marketing space.
    (D) investing profits from clients' properties.

16. *A* purchases a fee simple property for $70,000 by way of assuming a first mortgage of $50,000, paying $10,000 in cash and having the seller take back a purchase money second mortgage for the balance. There is an existing $5,000 second mortgage on the property. At the close of escrow what is the correct order in which to record the documents?
    (A) The assumption mortgage, the deed, the purchase money second mortgage
    (B) The deed, release of existing second mortgage, assumption agreement, purchase money mortgage
    (C) The purchase money second mortgage, the deed
    (D) The release of existing second mortgage, the deed, the purchase money second mortgage

17. Which of the following activities is a violation of the Federal Fair Housing Act?
    (A) A nonprofit church that denies access to its retirement home to a person because of race
    (B) A private club that gives preference in renting units to its members at lower rates
    (C) An owner-occupant of a duplex who refuses to rent to a woman
    (D) Refusing to rent to a teacher

18. A religious group bought a house in a subdivision and organized it into a commune. A broker, eager to make some quick profits, began to canvass this neighborhood, soliciting listings, inquiring whether they knew who had just moved into the area and leaving his or her business card. Which term **BEST** describes the broker's marketing program?
    (A) Redlining
    (B) Lawful solicitation
    (C) Panic-peddling
    (D) Steering

19. A broker is discussing a new listing with a prospective minority buyer. The buyer wants to inspect the property immediately but the listing owner has instructed the broker not to show the house during the owner's three-week absence. The buyer insists on viewing the property. The broker should do which of the following?
    (A) Show the property to avoid a violation of the Federal Fair Housing Act
    (B) Request the Real Estate Commission arbitrate the problem
    (C) Explain to the buyer why the property cannot be shown
    (D) Cancel the listing

20. A minority group is moving into an area immediately adjacent to an old subdivision. "X" Realty offers to list homes in the subdivision at a lower than usual rate if the owners list within 45 days. There is no mention of race and the broker acts in good faith. Which of the following is true?
    (A) The broker's license can be revoked.
    (B) This is blockbusting.
    (C) Such practice is not illegal.
    (D) Brokers cannot lower their standard rate of commission.

21. A properly drafted property management agreement should contain all of the following **EXCEPT**:

(A) names of owner and manager.

(B) requirement that the manager provide periodic reports to the owner.

(C) fee payment schedule.

(D) list of approved appraisers.

22. How would a purchase money second mortgage given by the purchaser to the seller appear on the settlement statement upon closing the real estate sale?

(A) Credit to purchaser and debit to seller

(B) Debit to purchaser and credit to seller

(C) Only a debit to seller

(D) Only a credit to buyer

23. Prorate the prepaid taxes as of settlement date (June 15) of a property valued at $120,000 and assessed at 55 percent value with a tax rate of $3.20 per $100 of valuation on a calendar year basis.

(A) Credit both $968

(B) Debit both $968

(C) Debit buyer $1,144, credit seller $968

(D) Credit buyer $1,144, debit seller $1,144

24. In order to close a $73,000 purchase of a home, the buyers paid a $5,000 earnest money deposit and secured a 75 percent conventional loan. The buyers' expenses included a five point loan discount charge, $425 survey, and they received a $275 credit on the tax proration. How much cash should the buyer bring to final settlement?

(A) $16,138   (C) $21,138

(B) $17,192   (D) $23,412

25. L sold his house August 31 for $112,000. His mortgage balance is $63,200 and he has paid the taxes of $684 through the end of the calendar year. He pays 6 percent commission to the agent. What is the amount due L before other closing costs?

(A) $42,308   (C) $105,280

(B) $63,428   (D) $105,508

26. A lot sold for $1,200 an acre. What would be the minimum selling price for three acres after one year if expenses are $500 per acre and the subdivider wants to make a ten percent profit?

(A) $4,510   (C) $5,100

(B) $4,960   (D) $5,610

27. Two lots with equal depth have front footages of 200 ft. and 350 ft. If the first lot has 20 acres, how many acres are in the second?

(A) 30   (C) 53

(B) 35   (D) 114

28. Which of the following transactions will net the seller the most money, assuming a broker's fee of seven percent?

(A) $50,900 sales price and $15 in miscellaneous expenses

(B) $51,200 sales price and $110 in miscellaneous expenses

(C) $52,000 sales price and $294 in miscellaneous expenses

(D) $52,500 sales price and $492 in miscellaneous expenses

29. In which of the following tenancies could a husband or wife seek partition if they cannot agree as to the sale of the property?

(A) Tenancy by entirety

(B) Joint tenancy

(C) Tenancy in severalty

(D) Tenancy for years

30. T and S take title to a farm as joint tenants. Assuming S dies, which of the following is true?

(A) T holds title with S's heirs.

(B) T holds title to the whole farm subject to the material interest of S's surviving wife.

(C) T holds title as a tenant in severalty.

(D) S's share passes according to his will.

31. A proper escrow, once established, should be:

(A) managed by a licensed broker.

(B) void at the seller's option.

(C) voidable at option of either buyer or seller.

(D) not subject to the control of any one interested party.

32. A deed made and delivered, but not recorded, is:

(A) valid between the parties and valid as to third parties with notice.

(B) valid between the parties and valid as to subsequent recorded interests.

(C) valid between the parties and invalid as to subsequent donees of the property.

(D) invalid as between the parties.

33. A written and signed real estate contract can be voided for which of the following reasons?
    (A) One of the parties failed to read the instrument before signing it.
    (B) One of the parties was an unmarried minor at the time the contract was signed.
    (C) The market value was less than the sales price.
    (D) The market value declines.

34. If an option contract is duly executed by seller and buyer, which of the following is true?
    (A) The seller may sell or not at his or her option.
    (B) The buyer must buy.
    (C) The seller must sell, but the buyer need not buy.
    (D) It is specifically enforceable by both parties.

35. A prospective purchaser has a legal right to demand which of the following?
    (A) A copy of the broker's employment contract with the seller
    (B) The return of the earnest money deposit prior to seller's acceptance of the offer to purchase
    (C) A copy of the plans and specifications of the home
    (D) A copy of the seller's financing statement

36. Which of the following is true regarding the assignment of sales contract?
    (A) An assignment of the sales contract by the buyer generally is valid.
    (B) Only the original seller can assign rights.
    (C) Assignments are illegal.
    (D) Assignment requires the consent of the seller.

37. *H* executes a deed of his farm to *S.* *H* keeps the deed in his safe deposit box. Upon his death, the box is opened, and attached to the deed is a note to give the deed to *S.* Who has title to the farm?
    (A) *S*   (C) The state
    (B) *H's* heirs   (D) *S's* heirs

38. The covenant against encumbrances in a deed of conveyance warrants against the existence of all of the following undisclosed matters **EXCEPT:**
    (A) mortgages against the land.
    (B) judgment liens against the land.
    (C) easements that adversely affect the land.
    (D) zoning ordinances that limit the use of the land.

39. One tenant in common attempts to convey the entire fee simple interest in the property to the grantee using a general warranty deed. Which covenant in the deed would be violated?
    (A) Covenant of further assurance
    (B) Covenant of seisin
    (C) Covenant against encumbrances
    (D) Covenant of loyalty

40. The term that **BEST** describes a tenant's interest in the property is:
    (A) a life estate.
    (B) a reversionary interest.
    (C) a remainder interest.
    (D) a leasehold estate.

41. Assume a mortgaged property is leased. Because of default in payment, the mortgagee forecloses on the mortgage. Which of the following statements is true regarding rights under the lease?
    (A) The lessee is automatically released from any further obligation on the lease.
    (B) The lease continues in effect despite the foreclosure.
    (C) The lease is void because the mortgagor has no right to give a lease on mortgaged property.
    (D) The lease may be terminated by the mortgagee but not by the lessee.

42. The sale of a property that is under a long-term lease has which of the following effects?
    (A) Terminates the lease upon 45 days' notice by new owner
    (B) Has no effect upon the term of the lease as far as the tenant is concerned
    (C) Cannot be made unless the present tenant is notified of the intention to sell and given an opportunity to terminate his or her lease
    (D) Terminates the lease and tenant must negotiate new lease with new owner

43. A tenant's rights under a lease are:
    (A) terminated when the property is sold.
    (B) usually terminated when the lessor dies.
    (C) terminated when the property is mortgaged.
    (D) terminated upon a surrender.

44. Which of the following statements about types of leases is true?
    (A) A gross lease is one where the rent is based on an agreed percentage of the gross income.
    (B) A net lease is one where the rent is based on a fixed percentage of the net income.
    (C) A shopping center lease is often a percentage lease.
    (D) An index lease requires constant payments over the term of the lease.

45. When leased premises reach a physical condition whereby the tenant is unable to occupy them for the purpose intended, the situation is legally recognized as:
    (A) a dispossess eviction.
    (B) an actual eviction.
    (C) a constructive eviction.
    (D) a passive eviction.

46. You can be most assured that you are getting fee simple ownership in which of the following cases?
    (A) If the owner will give a general warranty deed
    (B) If the owner can furnish title insurance
    (C) If you retain an attorney
    (D) If you use an escrow company

47. All of the following are required for a valid bill of sale **EXCEPT**:
    (A) signature of the seller.
    (B) description of the items.
    (C) date of transaction.
    (D) name of buyer.

48. Where a person dies testate, his or her real property:
    (A) escheats and is sold at auction by the state.
    (B) goes to the heirs.
    (C) passes by devise.
    (D) goes to the administrator.

49. If an area is rezoned industrial and a commercial establishment is given permission to continue its operation in that area, this is an example of which of the following?
    (A) Variance
    (B) Nonconforming use
    (C) Conditional use permit
    (D) Spot zoning

50. A condominium apartment owner can avoid payment of his or her share of the common expenses by doing which of the following?
    (A) Not using certain common elements
    (B) Abandoning his or her apartment
    (C) Defaulting on mortgage payments
    (D) Payment cannot be avoided

51. The economic life of a building has come to an end when:
    (A) the building ceases to represent the highest and best use of the land.
    (B) the value of the land and the building equals the value of the land only.
    (C) the rent produced is valued at less than a similar amount of money invested elsewhere could produce.
    (D) the reserve for depreciation equals the cost to replace the building.

52. A capitalization rate incorporates:
    (A) return on land and building and recapture of building.
    (B) return on land and building and recapture of land.
    (C) return on land and recapture of land and building.
    (D) return on building and recapture of land and building.

53. If the replacement cost shows a higher value than the appraised value, which of the following most probably has occurred?
    (A) Accrued depreciation
    (B) Excessive appraisal
    (C) Economic obsolescence
    (D) Capitalization

54. Which of the following can be said of real estate appraisers in federally related loan transactions:
    (A) They must have a real estate college degree.
    (B) They usually base their fees on a percentage of the appraised value.
    (C) They must belong to a professional organization.
    (D) They need to be state licensed or certified.

55. All of the following are examples of external obsolescence **EXCEPT**:
    (A) population density.
    (B) direct effect of the elements.
    (C) zoning.
    (D) special assessments.

56. The cost of new construction of the building having utility equivalent to the property under appraisal, but built with modern materials according to current standards, design and layout, is an appropriate definition of:
    (A) reproduction cost.
    (B) replacement cost.
    (C) duplication cost.
    (D) redesign cost.

57. A residence located in an area where there are factories and plants, and where there is much smoke and dust, is suffering from:
    (A) physical depreciation.
    (B) external obsolescence.
    (C) wear and tear.
    (D) functional obsolescence.

58. A house depreciated at 5 percent per year for the past seven years, and the lot has increased 10 percent per year for the same seven years. Originally, the house was worth $6,000 and the lot was worth $10,000. What is the current worth (simple interest)?
    (A) $20,100   (C) $25,100
    (B) $20,900   (D) $42,000

59. A house was assessed for tax purposes at 60 percent of market value and the tax rate was $3.72 per $100 of assessed value. Twelve years later the same ratios were used and the taxes went up by $400. How much did market value go up?
    (A) $10,750   (C) $18,632
    (B) $17,921   (D) $28,671

60. An existing commercial property has an average net monthly income of $600. With an additional $2,000 spent by the owner on repairs, the owner thinks that the net monthly income will rise to $800 after these repairs are made. What is the maximum an investor should pay for this property to earn the equivalent of 8½ percent return?
    (A) $112,941   (C) $142,911
    (B) $121,948   (D) $182,941

61. A building with a net income of $10,000 was appraised at $100,000. What would be the value if the capitalization rate has decreased by one percentage point?
    (A) $90,909   (C) $105,263
    (B) $100,000   (D) $111,111

62. A property sold for $75,000. This was 8 percent above the purchase price. The sales commission was 6 percent. What percentage over the original cost did seller net?
    (A) 1.5 percent   (C) 2.5 percent
    (B) 2 percent   (D) 3.5 percent

63. Which of the following occurs when the mortgagor is declared bankrupt?
    (A) Mortgagor retains equitable title to the property but forfeits legal title.
    (B) Mortgagor no longer owes any money under the mortgage note.
    (C) Mortgagee becomes a general creditor.
    (D) Title passes to court trustee or receiver.

64. Which of the following parties to a real estate sales transaction would have the **MOST** exposure to liability?
    (A) Grantor of quitclaim deed
    (B) Grantor in a loan assumption
    (C) Grantee taking subject to the loan
    (D) Grantor selling subject to the loan

65. A mortgage banker can do all of the following **EXCEPT**:
    (A) service loans for its clients.
    (B) use its own money to make loans.
    (C) loan money and then sell the loan.
    (D) prepare an appraisal for a fee.

66. A veteran seeking a DVA loan to purchase a three-family structure must:
    (A) agree to a loan amortization not to exceed 15 years.
    (B) sign a statement that there will be no negative cash flow.
    (C) occupy one of the units.
    (D) agree to sell with a loan assumption only to another veteran.

67. The DVA:
    (A) regularly makes direct loans up to certain amounts.
    (B) does not apply to women.
    (C) charges interest on its loans.
    (D) guarantees loans to eligible veterans.

68. Where a seller takes back a purchase money second mortgage from the buyer, the seller is responsible for preparing and executing which of the following?
    (A) Deed   (C) Promissory note
    (B) Second mortgage (D) Credit report

69. If a house burns to the ground prior to closing, the buyer may do all of the following **EXCEPT**:
    (A) delay closing until seller rebuilds a replacement.
    (B) close the sale and obtain an assignment of the insurance proceeds.
    (C) rescind the contract.
    (D) renegotiate the price if seller agrees.

70. Which of the following is an element peculiar to the sale and leaseback transaction?
    (A) The seller gets a return on the purchase in the form of rental.
    (B) The property is sold on condition that the new owner lease it back to the seller at the time title passes.
    (C) The buyer keeps capital in inventories, rather than in realty.
    (D) The rental that the seller pays is not income-tax deductible.

71. A buyer wants to take out an FHA loan. The broker should refer the buyer directly to:
    (A) a lending institution such as bank or savings and loan association.
    (B) FHA appraiser in the area.
    (C) Federal Housing Administration office.
    (D) Federal National Mortgage Association.

72. The Federal National Mortgage Association can do all of the following **EXCEPT**:
    (A) purchase conventional loans.
    (B) sell mortgages to institutions.
    (C) buy FHA/DVA loans.
    (C) originate federal loans.

73. The Truth-in-Lending law is designed to do which of the following?
    (A) Limit the amount of interest charged the borrower
    (B) Limit the amount of closing costs
    (C) Disclose whom the lender represents
    (D) Disclose the cost of borrowing

74. If you sell your home and reinvest the proceeds in the purchase of a new and more expensive home, within what period of time must you buy the new home to defer the payment of federal income taxes on any proceeds you realize in the sale of your old home?
    (A) Six months   (C) 24 months
    (B) One year   (D) Five years

75. C purchased a $92,500 home by making a $12,000 down payment, securing a conventional first mortgage and a $15,500 purchase money second mortgage with the seller. What is the approximate loan-to-value ratio of the first mortgage?
    (A) 66⅔ percent   (C) 75 percent
    (B) 70 percent   (D) 80 percent

76. A lending institution will make a 30-year 9½ percent loan for 70 percent of the first $50,000 and 40 percent of the next $45,000 of appraised value. If a house is appraised at $95,000, what will be the first month's interest charge?
    (A) $300.83   (C) $526.46
    (B) $419.58   (D) $752.08

77. A piece of income property has an annual income of $120,000 and monthly expenses of $875. What would be the maximum an investor would pay for the property in order to earn a minimum of 15 percent on the investment?
    (A) $73,000   (C) $730,000
    (B) $109,500   (D) $893,000

78. Real property taxes are $18 per $1,000 of assessed valuation, with the present assessed valuation at 45 percent. The state tax director has promised to increase the assessment ratio of buildings by an additional 15 percent. The property is presently fair market valued at $35,000 for the building and $10,000 for the lot. What is the promised increase in tax?

(A) $45.90   (C) $255.00
(B) $94.50   (D) $364.50

79. In order to purchase a house for $50,000 the lender requires a down payment of four percent of the first $25,000 and eight percent of the next $25,000. In addition, the lender charges four discount points. What is the maximum amount of discount points paid?

(A) $1,880   (C) $1,960
(B) $1,920   (D) $2,000

80. In a 75-acre subdivision, 400 houses were built on 7,500 sq. ft. lots. If each house averaged 50 x 40 ft., what percentage of the subdivision is covered by the houses?

(A) 12.25 percent   (C) 24.5 percent
(B) 20 percent   (D) 49 percent

ANSWERS

1. B It is not necessary that the listing first expire, but the agent must be extremely careful to disclose his or her interest in writing and avoid any possibility of self-dealing or secret profiting.

2. D Failure to disclose material defects in a property for sale could be grounds for misrepresentation by the agent (concealment of material fact) especially in view of the present consumer trend of the courts away from the former caveat emptor doctrine ("let the buyer beware").

3. B The broker would be breaching his or her duty of loyalty and confidentiality to reveal a price to a buyer other than that agreed upon by the owner in the listing or modification thereof. Rather than say, "The property is listed at $100,000 but I know the owner will take $90,000," the broker *should* say, "The property is listed at $100,000 and, if you are going to submit an offer of less than that, I'll take the offer to the seller and see what he or she says."

4. B The broker cannot withdraw money even though he or she has earned his or her commission, unless he or she has the written consent of both seller and buyer.

5. B Most sales contracts involve a short-lived executory transaction and are not recorded. When performed, the deed is recorded.

6. C The recording system neither insures nor corrects title defects, it merely gives constructive notice of the rights of people in certain property.

7. A RESPA is a federal law requiring certain disclosures of closing data to consumers.

8. B Only the agent under an open listing who is the procuring cause will be entitled to the commission. Under a multiple listing, there is only one listing and only one agent; the cooperating brokers would be subagents working with the listing broker.

9. C Under general agency principles, death terminates an executory listing agreement.

10. B The only broker entitled to the commission under an open listing is the one who is the procuring cause of the sale. This is not a requirement under exclusive listings (which might also be net listings).

11. D The broker has a fiduciary duty of obedience and a duty to account for all monies of his or her client. He or she cannot use client monies to set-off or satisfy his or her own claims. A lawsuit may be the only answer.

12. A The deposit money is credited against the total amount of money by which the buyer is indebted to purchase the property.

13. B Mortgage foreclosures would occur when the owner defaults on the mortgage. Title insurance is concerned with title losses.

14. B The abstract would reveal such recorded encumbrances as judgment liens or mortgages.

15. **D** Property managers handle rents, minor repairs and marketing of leases. They are not responsible for making investment decisions, such as handling real estate profits for their clients.

16. **D** The existing second will be paid off so there must be recorded a release or satisfaction piece. Nothing need be recorded concerning the assumption because the obligation to assume will be stated in the deed, which is recorded the instant before the purchase money second mortgage is recorded.

17. **A** The church could be selective on the basis of religion but not race. There is a specific private club exemption under FFH.

18. **C** Panic-peddling is defined as soliciting of sales or rental listings, making written or oral statements creating fear or alarm, transmitting written or oral warnings or threats, soliciting prospective minority renters or buyers or acting in any other manner so as to induce or attempt to induce the sale or lease of residential property, either:

   (a) through representations regarding the present or prospective entry of one or more minority residents into an area, or

   (b) through representations that would convey to a reasonable person under the circumstances, regardless whether overt reference to minority status is made, that one or more minority residents are or may be entering the area.

   Note: The term minority means any group that can be distinguished because of race, sex, handicap, familial status, religion, color or national origin. Vigorous solicitation of sellers in the context of a rapidly changing neighborhood frequently is panic-peddling.

19. **C** An agent must obey the instructions of his or her principal except where there is an illegal intent or act involved. Here, the owner is acting reasonably with no indication of any unlawful bias.

20. **C** For blockbusting to exist, there must be some actual or implied representation about the effect of the entry of minority groups into the area.

21. **D** The property management agreement is a contract so the parties must be named. It is in the best interest of the owner to receive periodic reports.

22. **A** The loan is credited against the purchase price owed by the purchaser and it represents cash the seller will not receive at the time of settlement.

23. **D**

$$\begin{array}{r} 120,000 \\ \times\ \ .55 \\ \hline 66,000 \end{array} \qquad \begin{array}{r} 660 \\ \times\ 3.20 \text{ per } 100 \\ \hline 2,112 \text{ per year} \end{array}$$

$$\frac{2,112}{12} = \$176/\text{month} \qquad \begin{array}{r} \$176 \\ \times\ 6.5 \\ \hline \$1,144 \end{array} \text{ months}$$

Seller has prepaid for the whole year, and there is a 6.5-month unused portion the buyer will benefit from unless some adjustment (proration) is made. In tax prorations, the debit and credit amounts are equal.

24. **A**

$$\begin{array}{r} 73,000 \\ \times\ 75\% \\ \hline 54,750 \text{ loan} \end{array} \quad \begin{array}{r} 54,750 \\ \times\ 5\% \\ \hline 2,737.50 \\ +\ 425.00 \\ -\ 275.00 \\ \hline \$2,887.50 \end{array} \quad \begin{array}{r} 73,000.00 \\ -\ 54,750.00 \\ \hline 18,250.00 \\ +\ 2,887.50 \\ \hline 21,137.50 \end{array}$$

$$\begin{array}{r} 21,137.50 \\ -\ 5,000.00 \\ \hline \$16,137.50 \end{array}$$

25. **A**

$$\begin{array}{r} V\ \ 112,000 \\ R\ \ \times\ \ .94 \\ \hline 105,280 \\ -\ 63,200 \\ \hline 42,080 \\ +\ \ \ 228 \\ \hline 42,308 \end{array} \qquad \text{Proration tax } \tfrac{1}{3} \text{ year}$$

$$\frac{\$684}{3} = \begin{array}{r} \$228 \\ +\ \$42,080 \\ \hline \$42,308 \end{array}$$

26. **D**

$$\begin{array}{r} 1,200 \\ \times\ \ 3 \\ \hline 3,600 \\ 1,500 \\ \hline 5,100 \end{array} \quad \begin{array}{r} 500 \\ \times\ \ 3 \\ \hline 1,500 \end{array} \quad \begin{array}{r} 5,100 \\ \times\ 1.10 \\ \hline 5,610 \end{array}$$

27. **B** $\dfrac{200}{20} = \dfrac{350}{?}$? = (350 × 20) ÷ 200 = 35

28. **D** $48,333

29. **B**   Choice (A) is not correct because the marital unit owns the property as tenancy by the entirety and one spouse cannot seek partition.

30. **C**   Joint tenants hold the property free from claims of dower or curtesy of spouses, as well as free from claims of creditors or heirs of a deceased joint tenant.

31. **D**   Escrow does not take "change orders" from either parties, (i.e., both parties must consent to any change in the original contract or escrow instructions).

32. **A**   If the deed is not recorded, a subsequent purchaser for value (from the original grantor) without notice of the first unrecorded deed could get superior title by recording his or her subsequent deed first. Donees are not protected under the recording law (nor are devisees).

33. **B**   A person who signs a contract without reading it or the fine print does so at his or her own risk. Most contracts of minors are voidable at the election of the minor. In some states, a minor who marries is treated as an adult. Contracts for necessaries are not voidable in some states.

34. **C**   Because an option is a unilateral contract, the optionee is not obliged to perform but, if the optionee does not elect to purchase, then the seller is bound to sell.

35. **B**   The listing is a confidential employment agreement between the seller and the broker and should not be shown to the buyer. There could be inaccurate information on the listing that has not yet been verified.

36. **A**   Assignments by the buyer are valid unless in violation of a clear anti-assignment clause in the contract.

37. **B**   There is no delivery. H did not give up control over the deed as he would have if he had handed it to S or put it in an escrow. To accomplish his purpose, H should have prepared a will.

38. **D**   Zoning ordinances are matters of public knowledge.

39. **B**   Since the grantor does not have the complete estate, i.e., the other tenants in common would have to join in the deed, then he or she would be liable under the covenant of seisin.

40. **D**   It might be noted, however, that a lessor has a reversionary interest in the leased fee.

41. **D**   The mortgagee has the choice of whether to terminate the lease because the lessee acquired the leasehold estate subject to the existing mortgage.

42. **B**   The purchaser takes the property subject to the rights of the lessee under the existing lease (which explains why it is important to inspect the property to discover the rights of parties in possession).

43. **D**   Neither death, mortgage, nor sale of the property will terminate the lease. Surrender involves a release of rights under a lease.

44. **C**   A percentage lease is based on a percentage of gross income.

45. **C**   The tenant is thereafter relieved of rent payments once he moves out.

46. **B**   While no title is certain, title insurance does provide the best assurance of good title.

47. **C**   While the date is frequently given, it is not as essential as these other items.

48. **C**   Testate means to die with a will in which real property is passed by way of a devise.

49. **B**   A variance would be the introduction of a new use that varies from the current zoning; a nonconforming use is the continuation of a use that was permissible prior to the recent zoning change.

50. D If owners were allowed to reduce their monthly maintenance expenses (association dues) by electing not to use the swimming pool, for example, there would be much chaos in managing the condominium. Likewise, until title to the abandoned apartment was transferred, the owner would still be liable for common expenses.

51. B Economic life is the period over which a building can be profitably utilized.

52. A An investor would get a return *on* his or her investment in the land and building (similar to receiving interest) and a return *of* his or her investment in the building through recapture (similar to depreciation rate).

53. A If it costs $100,000 to reproduce a five-year-old building valued at $92,000, there has been an adjustment made for $8,000 of depreciation over the five years.

54. D Appraisers' fees are based upon time and expenses; it would be unethical to have a contingent appraisal fee.

55. B Population changes, changes in zoning or a unusually high assessment might cause external obsolescence of the property. Direct effect of the elements (such as wind, snow) could result in physical deterioration.

56. B Reproduction cost is the present cost of reproducing the improvement with one of an exact replica, not just one with similar utility as in replacement cost.

57. B External obsolescence is loss in value due to conditions of the surrounding neighborhood. The question does not present any facts indicating this house suffered physical damage caused by the dust and smoke.

58. B House =

6,000	300	6,000
× .05	× 7	− 2,100
300	2,100	3,900

Lot =

10,000	1,000	10,000	3,900
× .10	× 7	+ 7,000	+ 17,000
1,000	7,000	17,000	$20,900

59. B

?	?
× 3.72/100	× .60
400	10,753

$$400 \div 3.72 = \quad 107.53$$
$$\times 100$$
$$10,753$$

$$10,753 \div .60 = \$17,921$$

60. A

800/month	V	?
× 12	R	× .085
9,600/yr.	I	9,600

$$9,600 \div .085 = \$112,941$$

61. D

100,000	?
× .10	× .09 = $111,111
10,000	10,000

Income divided by capitalization rate equals value.

62. A

V	?	commission
R	× 1.08	75,000
I	75,000	× .06
		4,500
		to seller

		70,500	V	69,444
		− 69,444	R	× ?
		1,056	I	1,056

$$75,000 \div 1.08 = 69,444$$
$$1056 \div 69,444 = .0152 = 1.5\%$$

63. D The title passes to the receiver. The mortgagor still owes the debt but the lenders most likely rely on the sale of the secured property to obtain reimbursement for the loan. As a secured creditor, the mortgagee would receive a preference in the bankruptcy distribution.

64. D The grantor selling subject to a loan would remain primarily liable for the debt, whereas he or she would be secondarily liable as a surety in a loan assumption. The grantor of a quitclaim deed would have the least exposure.

65. D Mortgage bankers often originate loans and then package them (warehousing) to larger investors and continue to regularly service the loans.

66. **C** Most DVA loans are amortized for longer than 15 years. Frequently, the expenses will exceed the income on the rented units, but there is no prohibition on negative cash flow, just that the veteran occupy one of the units.

67. **D** Direct loans are made in exceptional circumstances with the current limit around $35,000. DVA loans apply to female veterans and certain unremarried widows of veterans.

68. **A** The buyer benefits by having a mortgage loan to purchase the property, so he or she would pay for the cost of preparing the mortgage. Also, the seller does not sign the mortgage. The seller is obligated by contract to convey title to the buyer, so the seller pays for cost of the deed.

69. **A** Seller has the risk of loss until closing so buyer can rescind or accept the deed and insurance proceeds.

70. **B** Rent is tax deductible as a business expense. The buyer is relatively confident the seller will become a triple-A tenant.

71. **A** The FHA does not make the loan.

72. **D** Fannie Mae only operates in the secondary mortgage market.

73. **D** The law does not limit costs or charges, it merely requires their full disclosure. RESPA also regulates disclosure of closing costs.

74. **C** The profit gain tax deferral on a residence applies if the new residence is bought or built within 24 months.

75. **B**

92,500	92,500
− 12,000	× ?% =
80,500	65,000

− 15,000	65,000 = .702 = 70.2%
65,000	92,500

76. **B**

	V	50,000	45,000	35,000
	R	× .70	× .40	+ 18,000
	I	35,000	18,000	53,000 total loan

	V	53,000
	R	× .095
	I	5,035 + 12 = $419.58

77. **C**

875		120,000	V	?
× 12		− 10,500	R	× .15
$10,500 expenses		109,500	I	109,500

109,500 + .15 = $730,000

78. **B** Present tax

45,000	20.25	$459.00
× 45%	× 18	− 364.50
20,250	$364.50	$94.50

Proposed tax

35,000	10,000	25.50
× 60%	× 45%	× 18
21,000	4,500	$459
+ 4,500		
25,500		

79. **A**

50,000
− 3,000 down payment
$47,000 loan × 4% points = $1,880

80. **C** 50 × 40 = 2,000 sq. ft./house
400 × 2,000 = 800,000
75 × 43,560 = 3,267,000

3,267,000
× ?
800,000

800,000 + 3,267,000 = .245 = 24.5%

Appendix V: Review Exams

REVIEW EXAM #1

QUESTIONS

1. Which is true regarding the recording of a deed?
   (A) If the actual deed is lost, the recorded copy will be proof of the grantee's title.
   (B) The deed becomes valid upon recording.
   (C) Recording requires actual notice.
   (D) Deeds from the U.S. government must be recorded in federal court.

2. One may acquire title or ownership in real property by all of the following **EXCEPT**:
   (A) deed.
   (B) inheritance.
   (C) adverse possession.
   (D) lease.

3. At what time is a properly drawn and executed deed first considered to have transferred legal title to the grantee?
   (A) When the grantee's name is filled in
   (B) When it is signed by the grantor
   (C) When it is delivered to the grantee
   (D) When it is found in the possession of the grantee

4. A man whose wife recently died is thinking about moving to his son's home. He is hesitant about renewing his lease after the expiration date, but if he stays on after the expiration date, he would be a:
   (A) tenant at will.
   (B) life tenant.
   (C) tenant in common.
   (D) joint tenant.

5. Which of the following is **NOT** a private restriction on the use of real property?
   (A) Zoning laws
   (B) Condominium bylaws
   (C) Restrictive covenants
   (D) Subdivision restrictions

6. Changing a building use from apartments to condominiums would be accomplished by which of the following?
   (A) Condemnation
   (B) Sale-leaseback
   (C) Conversion
   (D) Rent with option to buy

7. A buyer is interested in purchasing an interest in a resort condominium that would guarantee him or her a specific two-bedroom unit during March of every year. Which of the following forms of ownership might a broker recommend?
   (A) Time-sharing
   (B) Corporate
   (C) Cooperative
   (D) Syndication

8. All of the following violate the Federal Fair Housing Act **EXCEPT**:
   (A) steering.
   (B) blockbusting or panic selling.
   (C) redlining.
   (D) denying a lease to military personnel.

9. Two brokers know of a house that was recently sold to members of a socialist commune. The brokers sense a quick gain and call the other owners in the neighborhood to get them to sell, telling them, "It's becoming a communal neighborhood, and everyone knows members of this commune can't take care of property." This behavior is:
   (A) lawful practice.
   (B) unlawful panic-peddling.
   (C) unlawful discrimination.
   (D) unlawful intimidation.

10. A minority person offered to buy a vacant lot in a residential subdivision for $25,000 in cash. The offer was refused, but two days later the developer accepted an offer from a nonminority buyer for $10,000 in cash. Which is true under the Federal Fair Housing Act?
    (A) This discrimination does not violate the federal act because it involves vacant land.
    (B) The developer is exempt from the law.
    (C) The law only applies to transactions over $50,000.
    (D) The minority person may have a valid claim under the act.

11. A bank's refusal to consider making a real estate loan to which of the following groups **MOST** likely would be a violation of the Federal Fair Housing Act?
    (A) Multiple couples seeking to live in one residence
    (B) Three rock stars taking title as joint tenants
    (C) Military officers
    (D) Several priests buying a condominium apartment

12. Which of the following is racial steering?
    (A) Salesperson introduces minority buyer to minority lender who will give buyer a loan.
    (B) Salesperson shows minority buyer homes only in minority section of town even though buyer wants to see homes in other areas.
    (C) Salesperson directs minority buyer to minority attorney.
    (D) Salesperson directs minority buyer to minority appraiser.

13. In an old area of Baltimore there have been a large number of defaults in multi-family housing loans held by Armbreaker Savings and Loan. Armbreaker decides to hold off making any more loans on multi-family housing projects until it can discover the reason why there are so many delinquent loans. Such a decision would violate:
    (A) Federal Fair Housing Act.
    (B) Equal Credit Opportunity Act.
    (C) Truth-in-Lending Act.
    (D) not a violation.

14. Which practice violates the Federal Fair Housing Act?
    (A) A minority mother owns a fourplex, lives in one unit, and gives preference to having minority mothers rent the other three units.
    (B) A broker takes a listing from a minority mother in which he or she can only sell the single-family home to another minority mother.
    (C) A non-profit retirement home rents to members of one religious denomination only.
    (D) A minority owner refuses to sell to a lawyer.

15. All of the following are important elements to establish a real estate agent as an independent contract **EXCEPT**:
    (A) written contract between agent and broker.
    (B) agent compensation based on performance and not on number of hours worked.
    (C) agent property licensed to sell real estate.
    (D) agent's successfully closing a minimum of two transactions per year.

16. A minority group is moving into an area immediately adjacent to the Devil Estates development. "X" Realty offers to list homes in Devil Estates at a lower than usual rate if the owners list within 45 days. There is no mention of race and the broker acts in good faith. Which of the following is true?
    (A) The broker's license can be revoked.
    (B) This is blockbusting.
    (C) Such practice is legal.
    (D) Brokers cannot lower their standard rate of commission.

17. C obtains an exclusive listing in which the owner instructs him not to sell to anyone who is a certain religion. C shows the property to people of this religion but does not present any of their offers to the owner. Which is true under the Federal Fair Housing Act?
    (A) C is not obliged to show any offer that he feels Owner will reject.
    (B) C must present all offers.
    (C) C must get instructions from Owner about presenting offers from members of the religion.
    (D) C could be punished by HUD if a complaint is filed against him.

18. Which of the following activities is permissible under the Federal Fair Housing Act?
    (A) Taking into consideration the borrower's race in fixing the terms of a loan
    (B) Inquiring into the financial capacity of a prospective purchaser of a dwelling who belongs to a minority group
    (C) Using a form that contains a fill-in section for applicant's religion and national origin
    (D) Refusing to rent to a pregnant woman

19. Which of the following facts is **LEAST** important for an appraiser of a commercial shopping center to discover?
    (A) Person(s) entitled to possession and ownership
    (B) Rents and operating expenses
    (C) Zoning
    (D) Original cost of the center

20. Which is true concerning an agency coupled with an interest?
    (A) It can be revoked by the principal.
    (B) It is terminated by the death of the principal.
    (C) It is illegal.
    (D) It generally is irrevocable.

21. If an agent purchases his client's real property by having his wife secretly act as the buyer, using her maiden name, the agent would **MOST** likely breach which one of these duties?
    (A) Obedience   (C) Loyalty
    (B) Care   (D) Skill

22. Which of the following acts of a broker is **NOT** an example of an agency relationship?
    (A) Signing listings
    (B) Leasing property
    (C) Selling the broker's own property
    (D) Representing the purchaser

23. What type of agency relationship **MOST** likely exists between a property manager and the owner?
    (A) Special   (C) Indirect
    (B) Limited   (D) General

24. A property manager is **LEAST** likely to be concerned with a prospective tenant's:
    (A) physical appearance.
    (B) credit rating.
    (C) profession.
    (D) understanding of the house rules.

25. If there is a break or gap in the chain of title, it is usually necessary to:
    (A) rely on a warranty deed as proof of title.
    (B) establish ownership by a suit to quiet title.
    (C) prepare and record a new abstract of title.
    (D) secure an affidavit from the grantor.

26. Which one of the following expenses is **MOST** likely to be paid outside of closing (POC)?
    (A) Title insurance
    (B) Lender's credit report fee
    (C) Attorney's fees for preparing the closing document
    (D) The conveyance tax

27. All of the following would appear on the RESPA settlement statement required by HUD **EXCEPT**:
    (A) tax prorations.
    (B) escrow fee.
    (C) income tax deductions.
    (D) closing costs.

28. Inspection of the seller's settlement or closing statement (not the HUD-I RESPA form) will indicate which of the following to the seller?
    (A) Amount the seller will receive from the sale
    (B) Amount the buyer will pay at closing
    (C) Interest rate on the buyer's loan
    (D) Buyer's attorney's fee

29. RESPA forms must be used in all of the following loans **EXCEPT**:
    (A) FHA.
    (B) Farmer's Home Administration (FmHA).
    (C) DVA.
    (D) seller financing.

30. Written documents affecting title to real estate are recorded where:
    (A) the titleholder resides.
    (B) the titleholder has legal residence.
    (C) the real estate is located.
    (D) due legal process is to be served.

31. Which of the following is a typical purpose of the closing statement?
    (A) Determine how title is to be held by buyer
    (B) Show how expenses are to be paid
    (C) Show the chain of title
    (D) Show the location of the property

32. A broker obtained a 120-day exclusive-right-to-sell listing but did absolutely nothing to market the property for 60 days. Any of the following is true **EXCEPT:**

(A) The seller can cancel the listing prior to the 120th day.

(B) The seller can withdraw the property from the market.

(C) The broker has earned a commission.

(D) The broker has breached the contract.

33. In which one of the following cases can commission rates be legally set?

(A) At a real estate commission hearing

(B) At an informal meeting of real estate brokers

(C) At a formal meeting of real estate brokers of their firm

(D) At a meeting between the seller and listing broker

34. Which of the following statements about an open listing is true?

(A) An open listing may be terminated by the owner at anytime prior to performance.

(B) An owner may not enter into an open listing contract with more than two brokers at a time.

(C) An open listing must contain a definite termination date.

(D) An open listing is illegal.

35. Automobile expenses of a salesperson accrued in the act of listing a property are typically:

(A) paid by the principal broker whether or not a sale results.

(B) paid by the seller if a sale results.

(C) paid by the buyer.

(D) paid by the salesperson whether or not a sale results.

36. An open listing on residential real estate is generally considered to be which type of contract?

(A) Voidable　　　　(C) Bilateral

(B) Executed　　　　(D) Unilateral

37. A seller wants to list a property with a broker but wants to reserve the right to sell it himself or herself without being obligated to pay a commission. What type of listing would allow what the seller wants?

(A) Exclusive agency

(B) Exclusive right to sell

(C) Multiple listing

(D) Net listing

38. A broker advertises a "Guaranteed Sale" as a means of obtaining listings. This means that if an owner lists the property for sale with the broker for 120 days:

(A) if the property does not sell in 120 days, the listing period is extended for an additional period of time, until the property is sold.

(B) if the property is not sold within the 120-day period, the broker will buy it.

(C) title is guaranteed.

(D) the property is guaranteed against any defects.

39. Which of the following is the **BEST** example of rescission of a contract?

(A) A lease is canceled by mutual agreement of the lessor and lessee.

(B) An offer to purchase is revised by a counter proposal.

(C) An option to purchase is transferred to a new buyer.

(D) A listing results in a commission to a broker.

40. Concerning an option on a parcel of real property, which of the following is true?

(A) It is voidable by the optionor.

(B) It can be made binding on the optionee.

(C) It usually is given by the owner.

(D) It can be enforced by a suit filed by the optionor.

41. *J* has an option to purchase at $120,000 for 180 days. Which is true?

(A) *J* may only assign the option to a third party with the optionor's consent.

(B) *J* may offer a lower price prior to the expiration of the option without losing his right to exercise the option.

(C) Only *J* must sign the option agreement.

(D) *J* can exercise the option within a reasonable time after the 180th day.

42. A buyer makes an offer of $155,000 on a $170,000 listed property. The seller gives the broker a counteroffer of $169,999.99. What should the embarrassed broker do?

(A) Refuse to present the counteroffer

(B) Alter the counteroffer

(C) Follow the seller's instructions

(D) Persuade the buyer to recounter at a middle price

43. In selling a condominium including all fixtures and furnishings, the seller should give the buyer which of the following?
    (A) Inventory of the furnishings
    (B) Affidavit as to the condition of the furnishings
    (C) Truth-in-Lending disclosure
    (D) Promissory note

44. A buyer who has put up $10,000 earnest money on a sales contract for a $200,000 property decides to default. The seller may keep the $10,000 as:
    (A) punitive damages.
    (B) liquidated damages.
    (C) consequential damages.
    (D) special damages.

45. Which one of the following is true about real estate options?
    (A) The optionee must sign the option and have it acknowledged.
    (B) The option money is applied to the purchase price if the option is exercised.
    (C) The optionee must pay the full purchase price before the option expires.
    (D) If the option is not exercised, the option money is forfeited.

46. If the parties to a contract are of legal age and of sound mind, they are said to have:
    (A) consideration.
    (B) legality of object.
    (C) reality of consent.
    (D) legal capacity.

47. *C* rents space to use for a restaurant and installs counters, booths, stoves and other fixtures necessary for business use. These fixtures will become the property of the lessor:
    (A) once they are connected to the real estate.
    (B) if they are not removed by *C* upon the expiration of the lease.
    (C) if the lessee is late with one rent check.
    (D) if the lessor pays for their upkeep.

48. To say that a landlord is bound by an implied covenant of quiet enjoyment to a lessee is to say that the landlord:
    (A) will not allow the lessee to be disturbed by strangers coming upon the property.
    (B) is obligated to make all necessary repairs to the leased premises.
    (C) promises that the lessee will not be evicted by a person who has title superior to that of the landlord.
    (D) undertakes to protect the lessee from loud noises caused by other tenants.

49. Your client wants to purchase land under a ground lease from the lessor-owner. Your client is purchasing a:
    (A) leasehold estate.   (C) leased fee.
    (B) contingent fee.   (D) reverter.

50. The largest source of funds for secondary mortgage money is which of the following?
    (A) Private parties
    (B) FHA
    (C) Mortgage insurance companies
    (D) Federal Home Loan Mortgage Corporation

51. A means by which a business can free money invested in its plant for use as working capital is called:
    (A) a sale and leaseback.
    (B) a land contract of sale.
    (C) a real estate investment trust.
    (D) an assignment of rents.

52. A conventional guaranteed mortgage is a mortgage that is:
    (A) insured by a private mortgage insurance company.
    (B) insured by FHA.
    (C) guaranteed by the seller.
    (D) guaranteed by DVA.

53. As far as the owner of a parcel of real property is concerned, which of the following would MOST likely result in a reduction of equity?
    (A) Liquidation   (C) Exchanging
    (B) Refinancing   (D) Leasing

54. An FHA conditional commitment is an agreement by the FHA to:
    (A) indemnify the lender on a defaulted loan.
    (B) qualify the buyer for a new loan.
    (C) insure a loan made to qualified buyer.
    (D) guarantee the value of the property.

55. Financing real estate through a group of persons who pool their funds to purchase or make a down payment on investment properties is **BEST** described as:
    (A) a syndicate.
    (B) growing equity.
    (C) a participating group.
    (D) an investment trust.

56. The primary function of the Federal Housing Administration is to:
    (A) insure real estate loans.
    (B) build public housing.
    (C) act as a secondary mortgage market.
    (D) establish discount points.

57. Assume you refinanced your home and received $30,000 in cash. Which one is true?
    (A) Your monthly payments are lower than before.
    (B) Your tax depreciation allowance is increased.
    (C) A capital gains tax is due.
    (D) Your debt service is higher than before.

58. A veteran would have to make a down payment to buy a residence using a DVA loan in which of the following cases?
    (A) The veteran owns investment property.
    (B) The sales price exceeds the Certificate of Reasonable Value.
    (C) The veteran is in the National Guard.
    (D) The veteran is unmarried.

59. A veteran who agrees to buy, subject to obtaining an FHA loan, can get his or her money refunded under all of the following circumstances **EXCEPT**:
    (A) He or she cannot qualify for the loan.
    (B) The sales price exceeds the FHA appraisal.
    (C) The property cannot be repaired to meet minimum property requirements.
    (D) The veteran decides the house is too small.

60. Sellers were a married couple when they executed a three-year land contract to sell their house. Upon satisfaction by the buyer, the sellers are divorced and the wife refuses to sign the deed. Which is true?
    (A) The buyer must accept the deed signed only by the husband.
    (B) The buyer can sue the wife for breach of contract.
    (C) The husband must reduce the balance due.
    (D) The husband can rescind the contract.

61. All of the following are true about federal Farmer's Home Administration (FmHA) loans **EXCEPT**:
    (A) They are specifically designed for farmers, rural residents and communities seeking money to finance housing, farms and business opportunities.
    (B) FmHA loans can be made for housing located in open country and in rural communities with small populations, such as under 10,000.
    (C) FmHA loans are typically set at more favorable terms than conventional loans.
    (D) FmHA loans are for veterans only.

62. To be relieved of the primary responsibility of a loan, you must find a buyer:
    (A) willing to subordinate.
    (B) who will purchase subject to the loan.
    (C) who will buy on land contract.
    (D) who will assume the loan.

63. All of the following in a real estate advertisement require full disclosure under the Truth-in-Lending Act, **EXCEPT**:
    (A) monthly payments of $275.
    (B) 360 monthly payments.
    (C) no charge for credit.
    (D) financing by Second Federal Savings & Loan.

64. An ad states that the monthly mortgage payments on an assumed loan are $634. Regulation Z requires further disclosure of all of the following **EXCEPT**:
    (A) terms of repayment.
    (B) amount of down payment.
    (C) simple interest rate.
    (D) annual percentage rate.

65. A real estate broker, who is also a mortgage broker, regularly negotiates the loans for his or her buyer clients. Under the Truth-in-Lending law, the broker would be considered a(n):
    (A) customer.   (C) lender.
    (B) arranger.   (D) borrower.

66. Regulation Z requires the lender to disclose which of the following to a borrower when a first mortgage is made to finance the purchase of a residence?
    (A) Appraised value of the residence
    (B) Total charges required for settlement of a real estate transaction
    (C) Total finance charges
    (D) Cost of a survey

67. After a judicial foreclosure sale, the court would most likely arrange for the purchaser to receive which one of the following?
    (A) Sheriff's deed
    (B) Commissioner's deed
    (C) Quitclaim deed
    (D) Guardian's deed

68. A borrower makes $100 amortized loan payments. This means that:
    (A) each payment has the same amount applying to principal.
    (B) there will be a balloon payment.
    (C) the amount applying to principal increases with each payment.
    (D) there is a lump sum payment.

69. Which is true concerning a real estate mortgage?
    (A) It must be signed by all owners for it to be an effective lien against the entire property.
    (B) Upon the death of one out of two tenants-in-common mortgagors, one-half of the property would pass to the mortgagee.
    (C) It must be signed by each mortgagee.
    (D) Only the promissory note is recorded.

70. A principal difference between a mortgage and a deed of trust concerns which of the following?
    (A) Amortization   (C) Redemption
    (B) Acceleration   (D) Capitalization

71. An amortized mortgage loan is one that is paid in:
    (A) monthly payments with interest in addition.
    (B) monthly payments of interest only.
    (C) monthly payments of principal only.
    (D) monthly payments that include both principal and interest.

72. A lender might require a 100-percent performance bond from a contractor building an addition to your home:
    (A) as added assurance the building will be built.
    (B) to reduce the risk of subordination.
    (C) to eliminate forfeiture.
    (D) as a hedge against inflation.

73. Assume that a property is encumbered by a second deed of trust with a subordination clause. If the owner refinances the first deed of trust with a new lender, which one of the following is true?
    (A) The second deed of trust is now the first lien, since it was recorded first.
    (B) The original first deed of trust is still a lien.
    (C) The second deed of trust is no longer a lien.
    (D) The new deed of trust takes priority over the second deed of trust.

74. The priority of mortgages may be reversed with the execution of a(n):
    (A) partial release agreement.
    (B) assignment agreement.
    (C) subordination agreement.
    (D) release agreement.

75. The legal process of defeating a debtor's interest in property as a result of default on the loan is called:
    (A) defeasance.   (C) redemption.
    (B) defect of title. (D) foreclosure.

76. Which of the following can be said of a mortgage?
    (A) A mortgage creates a lien even if it does not convey title to the holder.
    (B) A mortgage is secured by a promissory note.
    (C) A mortgage is not needed if the loan is under $10,000.
    (D) Only banks use a mortgage.

77. Which of the following is LEAST likely to be present in a wraparound mortgage?
    (A) All-inclusive monthly payments
    (B) An existing underlying mortgage
    (C) Profit from interest override
    (D) Priority of lien by wraparound mortgage

78. The distinguishing feature of an adjustable rate mortgage is that the interest rate:
    (A) changes depending on the borrower's income.
    (B) never varies.
    (C) varies one time each year.
    (D) varies according to an agreed-upon market indicator.

79. A mortgage with a variable interest rate that is determined by economic indicators would be:
    (A) an FHA loan.
    (B) a fixed-rate loan.
    (C) an indexed loan.
    (D) a flexible-payment loan.

80. A seller owns a property and has an $80,000 first mortgage and a $30,000 second mortgage. He or she is willing to sell to your buyer, who has $30,000 ready cash as a down payment to buy the property. The sales price is $130,000, and the seller agrees to take back a wrap-around mortgage for $100,000. What is the proper advice to give the buyer?
    (A) Use the $30,000 as an earnest money deposit
    (B) Have the seller apply at least $10,000 of the down payment to reduce the mortgage balance
    (C) Have the buyer refuse to sign the note
    (D) Put all mortgage payments into a trust account until maturity of the loan

ANSWERS

1. **A** The deed itself is not the title, (it is evidence of title), so there is no loss of title merely because the deed is lost. However, it is to the grantees's advantage to have a copy on record. Even U.S. patent deeds must be recorded in the local record office where the property is located.

2. **D** Under a lease, one acquires a right of exclusive possession—not title or owner-ship, which remain with the lessor.

3. **C** Delivery is the key because the deed could have been signed by the grantor then stolen by the grantee who filled in his own name.

4. **A** Depending on the facts, the tenant also could have been a tenant at sufferance or a holdover tenant. Choices (B), (C) and (D) are concerned with methods of ownership.

5. **A** Zoning laws are public restrictions. Condominium bylaws often restrict the type of uses in the project.

6. **C** Condominium conversion involves the transformation of a rental apartment building under single ownership to a building in which the individual apart-ment units are separately owned as condominium apartments. The building remains basically the same.

7. **A** Under time-sharing, the owners have specific rights of possession in a particu-lar project. In some cases, they have rights to a particular unit for a particular time period; in other cases, both the unit and the time period may vary according to a pre-arranged schedule.

8. **D** While it is not a specified discriminatory act under FFH to refuse to rent to military, it is not a recommended prac-tice and may involve violation of other federal laws.

9. **A** Nothing in the facts indicates discrimina-tion based on sex, color, religion, handi-cap, familial status, race or national origin.

10. **D** The federal law applies to developers and to sales of vacant land that may be used for residential purposes.

11. **D** It is no violation to discriminate against groups of people so long as it is not based on race, sex, color, religion, national origin, familial status or handi-cap (physical or mental).

12. **B** Steering is the practice of directing a prospect into or away from certain areas based on ethnic considerations.

13. **D** Armbreaker's decision is based on sound business judgment rather than discrimi-natory reasons, so there is no violation. Note that ECOA, unlike FFH, also prohibits discrimination based on age.

14. **B** There is a "Mrs. Murphy" exemption, whereby an owner who occupies at least one unit in up to a fourplex can discriminate (except on race) provided he or she does not use the services of a broker.

15. **D** Federal regulations now require only choices (A), (B) and (C).

16. **C** Because there is no apparent connection between the lower commission rates and race, there is no illegal act. If the broker, however, were to emphasize the need to sell due to increased crime caused by the presence of this minority group, then this would be blockbusting.

17. **D** The mere acceptance of a listing with a discriminatory restriction is an illegal act. Not presenting all offers involves licensing law.

18. **B** Race is not a proper factor, but financial capacity is proper regardless of whether the borrower is from a minority group.

19. **D** The appraiser must know, for example, whether he or she is appraising the leasehold estate (lessee) or the leased fee (lessor). Rents and operating expenses are vital in the capitalization or income approach to valuation.

20. **D** An agency coupled with an interest is different from a normal listing in that the agent has some direct interest in the property. Assume a broker owns a parcel that he or she sells to a developer on the condition that the developer give the broker an exclusive listing to sell the completed condominium development. This unique type of agency cannot be revoked nor is it terminated by death.

21. **C** While all the choices are fiduciary duties, this question describes the duty of loyalty. The activity described would violate most licensing laws as well.

22. **C** In selling his or her own property, the broker is acting as a principal, not an agent. Brokers can represent buyers, but they should clearly disclose this representation in the sales contract.

23. **D** The property manager typically has continuing duties to manage and maintain the property, unlike a broker who has limited or special duties to find a ready, willing and able buyer.

24. **A** Too much attention to physical appearance may imply some preference based on discriminatory grounds, and this is a violation of the Federal Fair Housing Law.

25. **B** The best way to clear up the title gap is to get a court opinion rather than just an opinion from the grantor. A new abstract won't be able to show why there was a break in the chain of title.

26. **B** Some lenders collect their own fees and give escrow only the *net* loan amount.

27. **C** The RESPA statement would include choices (A), (B) and (D), but not all tax deductions such as depreciation.

28. **A** The seller's statement reflects only the seller's obligations, not the buyer's.

29. **D** RESPA is mandatory in all federally related loan transactions.

30. **C** If, for example, A and B sign a contract of sale in Florida for property located in Alaska, the deed should be recorded in Alaska.

31. **B** The closing statement is the financial blueprint of the transaction. Choices (A) and (C) concern a title report, and (D) is a tax map.

32. **C** The broker has a duty to use good faith efforts to sell the property. Failure to do so is a breach justifying cancellation or withdrawal.

33. **D** Only broker and seller can negotiate the commission rate. If two or more conspire to fix rates in their community this attempt to fix commission will violate state and federal antitrust laws.

34. **A** Open listings are generally unilateral contracts that can be cancelled prior to substantial performance. A seller can give many open listings but owes a commission only to the broker who is the procuring cause of the sale.

35. D   The salesperson, especially if an independent contractor, pays for most out-of-pocket expenses in connection with a listing, except that the broker often pays for advertising.

36. D   The broker generally is under no obligation to find a buyer. If, however, the broker is the procuring cause of the sale, then the seller owes a commission.

37. A   The seller can reserve the right to sell the property under an exclusive agency (where he or she agrees not to list with other brokers) and under an open listing (in which it can be given to any number of brokers).

38. B   The broker must fully disclose any limitations on his or her obligation to purchase in the event the property is not sold.

39. A   A rescission is a return to the status quo. Choice (A) is also called a surrender; choice (B) is a counteroffer; choice (C) is an assignment.

40. C   The optionor is typically the owner, who receives option money in return for the promise to sell at a specified price to the optionee in the event the optionee decides to buy.

41. B   *J*'s lower offer is an independent act and not relevant. Options are contracts and thus are generally assignable unless restricted.

42. C   It is the broker's duty to follow his or her principal's instructions after explaining all the ramifications of this type of counteroffer.

43. A   It is common practice to itemize the personal property but not to make a sworn statement as to its condition.

44. B   Earnest money is usually a good-faith deposit that can be used by the seller to liquidate the debt in the event the buyer breaches the contract and fails to perform.

45. D   Option money is forfeited if the option is not exercised. If the option money were to be refunded, then the option would not have been enforceable, since there really was no consideration—it was illusory. The optionee is usually given a short period of time to close after the option is exercised, so the full price is often not paid until after the option's expiration date. Choice (B) is a matter of agreement and should be covered in the option.

46. D   Legal capacity refers to competency. Reality of consent refers to genuine consent in an offer and acceptance (no fraud, misrepresentation or duress).

47. B   These fixtures belong to the tenant under the trade fixtures exception, although the tenant must remove them by the time the lease expires.

48. C   This covenant is breached if the lessee is evicted by the true owner other than the landlord. Under choice (A), if the stranger has no valid claim to the property, then the lessee will have to take his or her own protective measures.

49. C   The leased fee is the lessor's interest, which represents the fee simple title subject to the lease. The lessee's interest is called the leasehold estate.

50. A   Private parties include individuals and corporations, and they buy the mortgages, including FHA mortgages that are sold in the secondary mortgage market by organizations like FHLMC. While insurance companies are a good source, mortgage insurance companies insure loans.

51. A   By selling its plant and then renting it back, the seller gains funds yet does not have to relocate; otherwise, the owner would have to refinance its plant to raise the money.

52. A   A popular private insurance program is MGIC, which enables a lender to make a 90-percent loan despite the lender's policy of usually making only 70-percent loans, since the insurance (paid for by the borrower) would insure the lender for that additional 20 percent. FHA has an insurance program for its nonconventional loans.

53. B   In a typical refinancing, the borrower receives cash for part of the equity in the property. For example, assume a property owner has a property worth $100,000 with a $40,000 mortgage. The owner might refinance for a $60,000 loan, thus raising $20,000 in cash (after paying off the $40,000 mortgage) but reducing the equity from $60,000 to $40,000.

54. **C** Under a conditional commitment, the FHA agrees to insure a loan (usually for a certain period such as six months), provided the buyer meets FHA qualification standards.

55. **A** Syndications are usually set up in the form of a limited partnership where the limited partners pool their money and have the real estate venture managed by a general partner.

56. **A** Under the Mutual Mortgage Protection Plan, the FHA insures loans made by approved lenders to qualified borrowers.

57. **D** Your monthly principal and interest payments will increase because you've increased your loan amount by the $30,000 equity you received in cash.

58. **B** While a 100-percent loan is possible under DVA, the loan cannot exceed the appraisal as indicated by the Certificate of Reasonable Value.

59. **D** FHA sales contracts usually contain a contingency provision allowing the buyer to cancel if either the buyer cannot qualify for the loan or the sales price exceeds the FHA appraisal.

60. **B** To get clear title, the buyer needs a deed from both husband and wife and can sue the wife for specific performance. The divorce had no legal effect on the transaction.

61. **D** FmHA is a federal agency under the U.S. Department of Agriculture and makes guaranteed loans and insured loans.

62. **D** In a true assumption, the buyer replaces the seller for primary responsibility on the loan, but the seller remains secondarily liable (unless there is a novation).

63. **D** (D) is such a general statement that it does not trigger the required disclosures that a specific statement such as choice (A), (B) or (C) would trigger.

64. **C** It should also state whether any increase in the annual percentage rate is possible.

65. **B** If deemed an "arranger," the broker is required to make the necessary disclosures concerning credit terms.

66. **C** Regulation Z is concerned with credit disclosure only, not appraisal amount or closing costs (covered by RESPA).

67. **B** The court appoints a commissioner to conduct the public auction and sale, including executing the commissioner's deed transferring legal title to the purchaser.

68. **C** With amortized payments, the monthly amount remains the same, but a portion of that amount is applied each month to reduce principal. In the early years, most of the payment is applied to interest; in the later years most is applied to principal, with no balloon payment due at the end of the loan term.

69. **A** Because all owners must sign, most lenders require a title policy to see who the owners are. Death of a mortgagor does not trigger any survivorship rights in the mortgagee.

70. **C** The equitable redemption period is typically shorter with a deed of trust. Choices (A) and (B) refer to the provisions of note.

71. **D** With an amortized loan there is a zero balance of interest and principal at the end of the loan term.

72. **A** Sometimes contractors get into financial difficulty. The performance bond is designed to provide funds to get the job completed.

73. **D** If it were not for the subordination clause, choice (A) would be correct.

74. **C** With a subordination clause, the lender under a first mortgage may agree to become junior to a subsequent mortgage. This agreement is often used when the holder of raw land sells it by way of a deed and purchase money mortgage to a buyer who will later go out and obtain a construction loan from a lender who requires it be in a first lien position.

75. **D**   The foreclosure process is structured to close off any rights of the mortgagor/debtor to redeem his or her property.

76. **A**   In title theory states, the mortgage actually conveys legal title; most states are lien-theory states in which the mortgage creates a lien even though no legal title is transferred. The mortgage secures the note.

77. **D**   The wraparound mortgage is typically junior to the underlying mortgage that it wraps around.

78. **D**   The rate may, for example, be subject to change according to changes in the U.S. Treasury Bill rate. Such changes may occur several times a year, although there are specified ceilings on the amount of change.

79. **C**   The specific index used, however, differs from lender to lender.

80. **B**   The down payment is $30,000; it is too much for the buyer to put up as a good faith deposit. The first and second mortgage total $100,000, so the buyer should have $10,000 applied to reduce the mortgage balance. The danger in allowing the underlying mortgage balance to exceed the balance owed to the seller is that the buyer could pay off the seller who then leaves town. The buyer is left with the outstanding balance on the property even though he or she has met all his or her obligations to the seller.

REVIEW EXAM #2

QUESTIONS

1. A mortgage clause that gives the mortgagee the right to declare the whole sum due in the event that the borrower sells to another who assumes the loan without the mortgagee's consent is called a(n):
   (A) release clause.
   (B) alienation clause.
   (C) subordination clause.
   (D) prepayment clause.

2. An acceleration clause is BEST defined by which of the following?
   (A) Mortgagor's right to prepay
   (B) Mortgagee's demand for full payment
   (C) Foreclosure
   (D) Promissory note

3. A buyer pays $25,000 as a down payment and agrees to pay the balance of $150,000 at 12 percent interest over ten years to a seller who has a $100,000 first mortgage at 10 percent interest. If the seller gives the buyer a deed, what type of financing device is MOST likely involved?
   (A) Agreement of sale
   (B) Assumption of mortgage
   (C) Wraparound mortgage
   (D) Conventional mortgage

4. An acceleration clause inserted to a benefit a lender in a note covers which of the following?
   (A) A procedure for declaring a debt due and payable upon default
   (B) A penalty for early payment of the note
   (C) A gradually increasing interest rate
   (D) A method of foreclosure

5. All of the following are methods used in estimating replacement costs for a commercial building EXCEPT:
   (A) unit-cost-in-place.
   (B) quantity survey.
   (C) comparative unit.
   (D) engineering breakdown.

6. The term "reproduction cost new," as used in the cost approach to estimating value, means the present cost of reproducing the subject improvement:
   (A) minus depreciation.
   (B) plus land value.
   (C) with one having the same utility.
   (D) with the same or very similar materials.

7. Given the annual income of a property, what is the BEST method to determine its value?
   (A) Capitalization method
   (B) Comparison method
   (C) Replacement cost method
   (D) Summation method

8. All of the following would be considered in the cost approach to appraisal **EXCEPT**:
   (A) operating expenses.
   (B) depreciation.
   (C) land value.
   (D) replacement cost.

9. All of the following should be considered when appraising real property **EXCEPT**:
   (A) owner's rights and interests.
   (B) easements and adequacy of public improvements and utilities.
   (C) zoning.
   (D) foreclosure rights.

10. A building ten years old is being appraised today. It has a useful remaining life of 25 years. The applicable recapture rate is:
    (A) 2.5 percent.   (C) 20 percent.
    (B) 4 percent.   (D) 25 percent.

11. All of the following are examples of physical deterioration as defined by the cost approach to value **EXCEPT**:
    (A) poor condition to floors, ceilings, beams and other structural elements.
    (B) basement damage due to flooding.
    (C) peeled paint on the exterior and siding.
    (D) rundown neighborhood.

12. *S* decides to exchange his rental property with *H*. As an appraiser you would be guided in your evaluation of the appropriate exchange value by which of the following?
    (A) Market data comparables
    (B) *S*'s demands
    (C) *H*'s demands
    (D) Lender's opinion

13. In seeking a listing, the owner tells the broker that the larger house next door recently sold for $135,000. The suggested listing price for the owner's house would be:
    (A) $135,000.
    (B) $135,000 plus commission.
    (C) based upon the square-foot cost of the house next door.
    (D) based on more comparables.

14. An appraiser is interested in all of the following **EXCEPT**:
    (A) zoning of the property.
    (B) a stated definition of value and the purpose of the appraisal.
    (C) a description of the property and type of title.
    (D) the types of financing that are available for the property.

15. The operating practices of a manufacturing business and of the management of rental properties differ in that:
    (A) the real estate manager is not concerned with the economic utilization of capital.
    (B) the manufacturer can curtail supply in a falling market.
    (C) the manufacturer must be licensed.
    (D) there is no difference.

16. Functional obsolescence can be corrected with:
    (A) capitalization.
    (B) modernization.
    (C) depreciation.
    (D) specialization.

17. When determining the net operating income of a property in using the income approach to value, it is proper to:
    (A) omit a management fee if the property is managed by the owner.
    (B) include the owner's income taxes.
    (C) deduct the owner's income taxes.
    (D) deduct typical vacancy and bad debt collection losses.

18. The highest and best use of a site for light industry would have all of the following criteria **EXCEPT**:
    (A) financially feasible use.
    (B) compatibility with surrounding land uses.
    (C) legally permissible use.
    (D) production of highest gross income.

19. Which factor is **LEAST** important in evaluating a property for a manufacturing site?
    (A) Pedestrian traffic
    (B) Ceiling height
    (C) Capacity of water and electrical services
    (D) Capacity of floor load factors

20. Which of the following is the effect of neglect on a building?
    (A) The rate of depreciation is speeded up.
    (B) The rate of obsolescence is speeded up.
    (C) The rate of depreciation is slowed down.
    (D) The rate of obsolescence is slowed down.

21. Which subject would **LEAST** likely be found in a prospectus marketing a time-share condominium?
    (A) Interval ownership
    (B) Floating-use periods
    (C) Prepaid vacations
    (D) Escalating rents

22. In an appraisal using the market comparison approach, you have to take into account special features and make the necessary addition or subtraction adjustments to which property?
    (A) Subject property
    (B) Comparable property
    (C) Both properties
    (D) Neither property

23. The gross-income multiplier is calculated by dividing the sales prices by the:
    (A) monthly net income.
    (B) monthly gross income.
    (C) annual net income.
    (D) annual gross income.

24. The principle of "high leverage" is involved when a buyer can control an expensive property with a:
    (A) small mortgage.   (C) large mortgage.
    (B) 60 percent loan.   (D) no mortgage.

25. Which one is MOST likely treated as an independent contractor?
    (A) Principal broker   (C) Broker in charge
    (B) Salesperson   (D) Secretary

26. The collection of data and the analysis of different approaches to value is known as:
    (A) depreciation.   (C) reconciliation.
    (B) amortization.   (D) accrual.

27. Assume there is a five-year lease at $5,000 per year. The lessor in year three usually cannot:
    (A) mortgage.   (C) raise rent.
    (B) sell.   (D) devise.

28. In a Section 1031 exchange, the basis for the old property becomes the basis for the new property and the capital gains tax is:
    (A) exchanged.   (C) forgiven.
    (B) deferred.   (D) compounded.

29. In appraising investment property, what does the owner deduct to arrive at the net operating income?
    (A) Federal income taxes
    (B) Capital improvements
    (C) Vacancy and debt losses
    (D) All ordinary expenses to the property

30. Which one of the following types of mortgages enables elderly homeowners to borrow against the equity in their homes?
    (A) Sweat equity
    (B) Reverse annuity
    (C) Balloon
    (D) Graduated payment

31. In times of inflation, who suffers most from rent control?
    (A) Tenant   (C) Lessor
    (B) Hotel industry   (D) Optionee

32. Which of the following types of ownership is **LEAST** likely to be subject to regulation by the securities law?
    (A) Limited partnership
    (B) S corporation
    (C) Syndication
    (D) Joint tenancy

33. A sales associate is employed by a listing broker to sell a home. The sales associate is a subagent of:
    (A) seller.   (C) broker.
    (B) buyer.   (D) escrow.

34. In a city's master development plan, all of the following are analyzed and included **EXCEPT**:
    (A) population growth.
    (B) transportation and traffic patterns.
    (C) study of blighted areas.
    (D) state's usury laws.

35. What advantage would the developer/lessee gain if the owner/lessor subordinated his or her fee simple interest?
    (A) Land values would increase.
    (B) Interim construction loan would be on better terms.
    (C) Owner would avoid foreclosure.
    (D) Purchaser could rescind sale.

36. If a person selling real estate securities in the form of a Real Estate Investment Trust (REIT) is guilty of fraud, all of the following could occur **EXCEPT**:
    (A) criminal penalty.
    (B) civil penalty.
    (C) rescission of contract.
    (D) actual damages multiplied by five.

37. Which one of the following types of loans would a borrower want to cover the period between the end of one loan and the beginning of another?
    (A) Filler loan   (C) Subordinate loan
    (B) Bridge loan   (D) Conversion loan

38. All of the following is true about surveys **EXCEPT**:
    (A) They are useful in revealing encroachments.
    (B) They are likely use when lenders are making a loan on real property.
    (C) They may reveal zoning and setback violations.
    (D) They are required in every real estate transaction.

39. All of the following is true about FHA loans **EXCEPT**:
    (A) The interest rate and points are negotiable.
    (B) Points are based on the amount of the mortgage.
    (C) The insurance premium is payable up front or added to the loan balance at 3.8 percent on a maximum loan of $135,000.
    (D) They are restricted to veterans.

40. *A* sees *S*'s ad "FOR SALE BY OWNER." *A* asks *S* if he can show his buyer the property. *S* leaves *A* the key. Which is true?
    (A) *A* is the subagent of *S*.
    (B) *S* is *A*'s principal.
    (C) No agency exists.
    (D) An implied agency exists.

41. A real property tax appraiser would consider all of the following **EXCEPT**:
    (A) years left on the building lease.
    (B) zoning.
    (C) condition of structure.
    (D) location.

42. When determining the highest and best use of a property, an appraiser would consider all of the following **EXCEPT**:
    (A) original purchase price.
    (B) zoning.
    (C) setback requirements.
    (D) restrictions on record.

43. After the buyer visits the property at an open house, the owner decides to leave extra paint cans and firewood. The broker should do which of the following?
    (A) Make a mental note to see if these items are still there at closing.
    (B) Do nothing because they were not on the listing.
    (C) Write them into the offer because they are personal property.
    (D) Do nothing because they are fixtures.

44. Which of the following sales is **MOST** likely used in the market comparison approach to value?
    (A) Probate sale   (C) Foreclosure sale
    (B) Comparable sale   (D) Tax sale

45. A broker examining the seller's conveyance document would likely discover all of the following information **EXCEPT**:
    (A) legal description.
    (B) nonconforming use.
    (C) restrictive covenants.
    (D) estate of ownership.

46. A buyer made a $32,000 down payment on an $80,000 purchase. Payments on a 25-year mortgage were $587 a month. What was the total amount of interest paid over the life of the loan?
    (A) $81,000   (C) $128,100
    (B) $112,000   (D) $144,100

47. When the broker reviews the closing statement, he or she notices that the seller pays the attorney's fee to draw up the purchase money mortgage. The sales contract did not state who is to pay this fee. What should the broker do?

(A) Keep silent
(B) Tell the seller to pay
(C) Tell the buyer to pay
(D) Point out to the closing agent that there may be a problem

48. All of the following are true about nonconventional loans **EXCEPT**:

(A) FHA loans for nonowner occupants are assumable in the first 24 months without lender approval.
(B) The maximum DVA guaranty is set by law.
(C) DVA loans can be assumed and the veteran released from liability if the buyer is proven to be credit worthy.
(D) Under a FHA formal assumption, the original borrower can be released from liability.

49. A ceiling beam in a condo unit is classified as a common element. Who is normally responsible for termite damage?

(A) Unit owner
(B) Management company
(C) Association of owners
(D) Real estate broker

50. An FHA conditional commitment is an agreement by the FHA to:

(A) insure a loan made to a qualified buyer.
(B) guarantee the value of the property.
(C) make a loan subject to a mortgage.
(D) indemnify the lender on a defaulted loan.

51. All of the following owns a future interest in real property **EXCEPT**:

(A) a remainderman.
(B) a holder of a reversion.
(C) a grantor of a life estate.
(D) life tenant.

52. Which of the following is considered a sound office management procedure for the principal broker to adopt?

(A) Bimonthly payroll
(B) Graduated commission scale
(C) Preparation of monthly statements that account for expenses on each listing
(D) Newspaper ads at the discretion of the listing salesperson

53. Mud tunnels at the foundation of a home indicate:

(A) soil settlement.
(B) ground termites.
(C) cracked foundation.
(D) inadequate footing.

54. What is **MOST** likely to occur when salesperson S moves to a new broker?

(A) S takes his listing with him.
(B) His listings are terminated.
(C) His errors and omissions policy is automatically transferred.
(D) His broker can pay him commissions that he earned.

55. Which statement is true concerning the Accelerated Cost Recovery System (ACRS)?

(A) Appraisers favor this method of valuing commercial properties.
(B) Taxpayers can switch from straight line to accelerated depreciation after four years.
(C) Contractors use this system to recoup expenses.
(D) Under the Tax Act the typical method of recovery of depreciation is straight line.

56. Homeowner A refinances his home and takes out $5,000 due to the appreciation in value. Which is true about the $5,000?

(A) It is subject to capital gain tax.
(B) It is tax free to the homeowner.
(C) It reduces the tax basis in the home.
(D) It increases the equity in the home.

57. The seller is usually responsible for which of the following at closing?

(A) Cost to draft note and mortgage
(B) Unpaid charges that accrue on the day of closing
(C) Real estate licensing fees
(D) Cost of appraisal

58. A metal tool shed is set on wooden blocks in the back yard. Nothing is said in the sales contract about the tool shed. Which is true?

(A) A bill of sale is needed to transfer title to it.
(B) It is fixture that belongs to the buyer.
(C) It is personal property that belongs to the seller.
(D) It is an encumbrance that runs with the land.

59. The real estate salesperson has primary fiduciary duty to which one of the following?
    (A) Supervising broker
    (B) Seller
    (C) Buyer
    (D) Sales manager

60. To determine net operating income, all of the following is deducted from gross income **EXCEPT:**
    (A) real property taxes.
    (B) insurance costs.
    (C) debt service.
    (D) utility costs.

61. A salesperson who has listed a seller's house owes a fiduciary duty directly to which one of the following?
    (A) Seller   (C) Buyer
    (B) Broker   (D) Escrow

62. The loan reserve account (customer trust fund) balance is $1,000. Real property taxes are due in December and closing is July 15. The closing statement entry would be which of the following?
    (A) Credit seller $1,000
    (B) Credit buyer $1,000
    (C) Debit seller $1,000 and credit buyer $1,000
    (D) Credit seller $1,000 and debit buyer $1,000

63. The buyer assumes a ten-year sewer assessment in its third year. At closing the correct practice is to prorate:
    (A) annual interest due.
    (B) interest and principal.
    (C) principal only.
    (D) seller to pay balance due.

64. While observing market conditions, a property manager would be aware that an increased demand for rental property would **MOST** likely be caused by which of the following?
    (A) An increase in the mortgage rate
    (B) An increase in disposable income
    (C) A decrease in mortgage rates
    (D) An increase in urban clearance

65. Under a property management agreement, the property manager representing the owners most likely would do all of the following, **EXCEPT:**
    (A) negotiate maintenance service fees.
    (B) rehabilitate and convert property.
    (C) initiate action for recovery of rent.
    (D) file required federal and state reports.

66. If a commercial building is leased on an "absolute" net lease (triple net), for which of the following expenses is the lessor responsible?
    (A) Lease rent
    (B) Insurance
    (C) Maintenance
    (D) Property management fee

67. A house was purchased for $100,000. Improvements of $25,000 were added. The house sold for $250,000 ten months later. How much was the seller's deferred capital gain?
    (A) $25,000   (C) $75,000
    (B) $50,000   (D) $125,000

68. What is a good example of leverage?
    (A) Control of a large asset with a small mortgage
    (B) Ability to change loan terms
    (C) Control of a large asset with little money down
    (D) Purchase of a security

69. Real estate commissions are:
    (A) fixed by law.
    (B) determined by agreement of brokers in the community.
    (C) sometimes set by company policy but could be further negotiated by the seller and broker.
    (D) agreed upon at closing.

70. The government survey system uses which of the following to describe real property?
    (A) Lot and block number
    (B) Ranges, townships and sections
    (C) Plat and parcel
    (D) Metes and bounds

71. In an FHA mortgage, the mortgagee does which of the following?
    (A) Requires the same amount of mutual mortgage insurance for both the first and second mortgages
    (B) Allows unlimited assumptions of the loan
    (C) Collects discount charges from either buyer or seller
    (D) Charges a prepayment penalty

72. Last year a taxpayer paid $800 in real property taxes on his or her home and $5,800 in mortgage payments ($5,100 interest and $700 principal). He or she added a $3,000 room. How much deduction can he or she take on his or her tax return?
    (A) $700   (C) $5,900
    (B) $800   (D) $6,400

73. Two married couples buying an investment property want to retain their inheritance rights in ownership. What type of tenancy might suit their need?
    (A) Joint tenancy
    (B) Tenancy in common
    (C) Tenancy by entirety
    (D) Tenancy in severalty

74. A mortgage tied to an economic indicator is called a(n):
    (A) index mortgage.
    (B) open-end mortgage.
    (C) balloon mortgage.
    (D) escalation mortgage.

75. All of the following is essential for a valid real estate sales contract **EXCEPT**:
    (A) names and signatures of parties to be bound.
    (B) provision for broker's commission.
    (C) consideration.
    (D) description of property.

76. On March 5, *J* agrees to sell his home to *C* with a closing date of April 10. *C* will assume *J*'s 11 percent, 30-year mortgage that has 21 years to go and a balance, after the March 25 amortization date, of $48,500, with principal and interest payments of $525 per month. The loan balance at closing is:
    (A) $46,558.   (C) $47,975.
    (B) $47,652.   (D) $48,500.

77. A seller makes a counteroffer. During the time the buyer is deciding what to do, the broker can do all of the following **EXCEPT**:
    (A) continue to show the property.
    (B) present additional offers.
    (C) answer questions about the property.
    (D) recommend the seller accept another offer.

78. Under the tax laws, *W*, 58 years of age, is married to 53-year-old *M*. They sell their home after living in it four out of the last five years. Which is true if their gain is $120,000?
    (A) *W* is entitled to a $125,000 deduction.
    (B) *W* is entitled to 80 percent of the allowable deduction.
    (C) There is no deduction until *M* reaches the age of 55.
    (D) *W* is entitled to a $120,000 deduction.

79. Which one of the following is true concerning RESPA?
    (A) Seller can require the buyer to use a specific title company.
    (B) It applies to DVA and FHA loans.
    (C) It applies to seller wraparound loans.
    (D) It is the responsibility of the seller.

80. A mortgage with interest only payments for five years and a pay-off in the fifth year is called a(n):
    (A) pay-off mortgage.
    (B) budget mortgage.
    (C) straight mortgage.
    (D) amortized mortgage.

REVIEW EXAM #2

ANSWERS

1. **B** The alienation clause is also called the acceleration or due-on-sale clause. It has been upheld by the U.S. Supreme Court as an enforceable device for the lender to call in the loan if the property is transferred without the lender's consent.

2. **B** The acceleration clause may be triggered by default or by transfer of the property. Choice (A) refers to the privilege of prepayment.

3. **C** The sales price is $175,000 with the seller carrying back a second mortgage from which it will make the payments on the $100,000 first loan at ten percent. (The $150,000 mortgage wraps around the seller's $100,000 first mortgage although the buyer does not assume the first mortgage.)

4. **A** Choice (B) is a prepayment penalty clause; choice (C) may be a variable rate mortgage. Choice (D) could be a power of sale clause in a mortgage.

5. **D** Engineering breakdown refers to a method of estimating accrued depreciation. Choice (C) would covert component costs such as cost per square feet of foundation. Choice (B) involves a more detailed analysis of the cost of each material used in construction, and choice (A) involves estimating the unit cost of each component section in place, including labor and materials.

6. **D** Reproduction cost involves the cost to make an exact replica. Replacement cost involves producing a replacement structure with similar utility. After this cost is determined, the appraiser subtracts a figure for accrued depreciation in arriving at an estimate of value under the cost or summation approach.

7. **A** The capitalization approach converts income into value.

8. **A** Operating income is only relevant when using the income or capitalization approach to value.

9. **D** Foreclosure rights aren't relevant, but choices (A), (B) and (C) all have an impact on value.

10. **B** Recapture rate is designed to give a return of the investment in a building that will be theoretically worth zero at the end of its useful life. Thus each year the building will depreciate four percent.

11. **D** This is an example of external obsolescence.

12. **A** Market value is determined by an analysis of market conditions, not the personal desires of the parties.

13. **D** Listing prices should be based on several comparable sales and not just one, especially where the properties are different sizes.

14. **D** Financing is not relevant to an appraisal, but zoning is because it affects the highest and best use. The appraiser also needs to know whether to look for insurance value, market value, loan value and so on.

15. **B** In falling market, the manager of real estate cannot decrease the supply of unrented units.

16. **B** Certain outdated design problems can be corrected by modernization such as expanding a room or replacing an obsolete plumbing system.

17. **D** Vacancy and bad debt losses must be taken into consideration, whereas personal income tax aspects are not relevant. Under choice (A), even thought the present owner does his or her own management, the next owner might want to hire a manager to perform this function.

18. **D** The highest and best use is concerned with that use which will produce the highest *net* income or yield.

19. **A** Pedestrian traffic patterns are more appropriate for a retail establishment like a shopping center.

20. **A** Neglect will speed up the rate of physical deterioration.

21. **D** There are many forms of time-share ownership—time interval (like tenants in common); license to use; vacation lease; and club members. Often the time periods fluctuate over the years; and they can be exchanged. The concept is attractive to people who vacation frequently in the same resort (and get tired of increased hotel rates).

22. **B** The value of the comparable is adjusted upward or downward depending on whether it has a feature different from the subject property.

23. **D** The gross-income multiplier , used to compare investment property in the market comparison appraisal method, is the ratio between gross income and sales price.

24. **C** The larger the loan amount, the less cash the buyer has invested in the property—the less cash, the greater leverage (or use of other people's money, OPM).

25. **B** The salesperson must not be compensated on a hourly basis. Choices (A) and (C) act in a supervisory capacity. The secretary is also an employee.

26. **C** Reconciliation, formerly called correlation, is more than just averaging the three approaches to value; it weighs many factors.

27. **C** The rent is fixed for five years. If the lessor mortgages, sells or wills the property, it will be taken subject to the lease.

28. **B** Taxes are deferred until the new property is sold.

29. **D** Expenses are deducted to arrive at net operating income. Vacancy and bad debt losses are deducted to reflect the gross effective income.

30. **B** The reverse annuity mortgage allows the homeowner to receive monthly payments to help meet living costs. Thus, the inflow and outflow of funds is the reverse of the standard loan.

31. **C** With inflation, expenses increase while income is frozen by rent control in which the government puts a lid on rent increases.

32. **D** A security often involves stock or an investment contract, as when one invests in a venture with the expectation of making profits through the efforts of the promoter. The sale of an investment condo with a mandatory rental pool arrangement involves the sale of a security and thus requires registration with federal and state securities agencies.

33. **A** The sales associate is the agent of the broker who is the agent of the seller. Thus, the sales associate is subagent of the seller.

34. **D** City planning is not concerned with laws regulating the amount of interest charged on loans.

35. **B** By subordinating the fee, the collateral or security for the loan now includes both the leasehold and the fee simple estates. The owner would only do this after consulting legal counsel. The prime motivation would be to help the project get completed and thus result in a greater sales price to the owner for the property.

36. **D** The antifraud provisions of the *federal* securities laws provide for stiff penalties, but not multiplied by five. The law applies to the seller and the broker.

37. **B** A bridge, or swing loan, is often used to carry the property from the time of acquisition un til it can be improved or developed, so it can qualify for a permanent loan.

38. **D** Many transactions close without a survey being ordered. Most lenders require an extended title insurance policy. The policy covers rights of parties in possession, so a survey is usually ordered.

39. **D** DVA loans are restricted to veterans. FHA loans have a MIP—mortgage insurance premium paid by the borrower to cover the cost of insurance (payable in one lump sum up front or financed).

40. **C** Agency is a consensual relationship. Giving *A* the key is inadequate to evidence an intent to have *A* act on behalf of *S*.

41. **A** The tax assessor is concerned with the value of the fee simple interest.

42. **A** The original purchase price has no effect on present value.

43. **C** The personal property will not pass to the buyer unless included in the sales contract.

44. **B** Involuntary sales are *not* included in the market comparison approach, which stresses sales to ready, willing and able buyers by sellers not compelled to sell.

45. **B** The nonconforming use status is revealed by a comparison of the existing use with the permitted use under the zoning.

46. **C** $128,100

$80,000 - $32,000 = $48,000
25 × 12 × $587 = $176,100
$176,100 - $48,000 = $128,100

47. **D** The problem is that the buyer customarily pays for the cost of drafting the mortgage since the buyer benefits by being able to obtain the loan.

48. **A** FHA loans are no longer automatically assumable. There can be no simple assumption in the first 24 months (one year for owner-occupants), only formal assumptions are allowed. This change is in response to the high number of foreclosures within the first two years of an FHA loan.

49. **C** The association of owners is responsible for repairs to common elements.

50. **A** Provided the borrower is qualified, the FHA commits to insure the loan.

51. **D** A future interest is one that occurs in the future upon the happening of some event such as the default of a life tenant. A life tenant owns a present interest.

52. **C** Brokers need to be careful that expenses don't get out of control or too much money is spent on ads.

53. **B** Subterranean land or ground termites move through mud tunnels.

54. **D** The listings belong to the broker, not the salesperson.

55. **D** The 1986 Tax Reform Act basically limited depreciation to straight line, thus eliminating the ACRS methods developed under the 1981 Tax Act.

56. **B** The $5,000 is not taxable, but it reduces the owner's equity in the home.

57. **B** A question sometimes arises whether the seller or the buyer is responsible for the expenses (like real property taxes, interest, maintenance fees) on the day of closing. Typically, the seller's obligations run up to and *include* the day of closing.

58. **C** The tool shed is easily removable and not permanently attached to the property.

59. **A** The salesperson is the agent of the listing broker who is the agent of the seller.

60. **C** Under the income (capitalization) approach, effective gross income is determined by deducting from potential gross income, an allowance for bad debts and vacancy. To determine net operating income, deduct fixed and operating expenses but not financing costs (debt service).

61. **B** The salesperson is the agent of the listing broker and the subagent of the seller.

62. **D** This is a double entry with the seller being returned the funds he or she had advanced at the start of the loan—funds that the buyer will receive later at loan pay-off.

63. **A** Only interest, not principal, is prorated.

64. **A** Higher interest rates usually mean marginal buyers can't buy and have to rent instead.

65. **B** Clients make the major decisions such as converting a rental building into a condominium.

66. **D** Under the terms of a typical triple net lease, the tenant pays all the carrying charges. The lessor pays for its own property managers.

67. **C** The seller's basis was $100,000 plus $25,000, so the non-recognized gain was $75,000.

68. **C** Leverage involves the use of other people's money to control an asset; e.g., buy real estate with little money down.

69. **C** Price fixing is illegal under antitrust laws. Some firms prefer a certain fee but recognize that the commission is negotiable between buyer and seller.

70. **B** The survey system creates a checkerboard of identical squares covering a given area—also called rectangular survey system.

71. C   Whether buyer or seller pays, the discount charged is up to negotiation. FHA restricts assumption in first 24 months of loan on an investment property.

72. C   He or she can deduct interest and real property taxes.

73. B   They could choose whatever tenancy among themselves; but as to the share of each couple, that should be a tenancy in common. If they were to all be joint tenants, then one could survive the other, thus leaving nothing for the heirs to inherit.

74. A   An example is an index mortgage whose interest rate is tied to the rate of U.S. Treasury bills.

75. B   The broker's fee is often set in the listing agreement. It may also appear in the sales contract but is not necessary.

76. D   Principal is not prorated on a daily basis, only interest.

77. D   Unless instructed otherwise by the seller, the broker should continue to market the property. The seller needs to be careful about accepting additional offers without first revoking the counteroffer.

78. D   The deduction applies if either spouse is 55. It is a once-in-a-lifetime exclusion. Then, they later can't seek $5,000 more.

79. B   RESPA applies to any federally related loan. The *lender* is the party responsible that RESPA disclosures are made.

80. C   A straight mortgage is an interest only mortgage, also called a term mortgage.

REVIEW EXAM #3

QUESTIONS

1. A home was purchased for $100,000 and $10,000 of improvements were added. The home sold for $130,000 with a 6.5 percent commission. What price must be paid for the replacement home in order to defer all gain?
   - (A) $100,000
   - (B) $110,000
   - (C) $120,000
   - (D) $121,500

2. Property taxes for the current year are due on December 31. One property has an assessed value of $42,000 with a tax mill rate of .075. If the house was sold on July 15, what is the proration?
   - (A) Credit the seller $1,444
   - (B) Credit the buyer $1,706
   - (C) Debit the buyer $1,181
   - (D) Debit the seller $1,968

3. *S* bought a house for $130,000. He paid $30,000 down, and took out a $100,000 mortgage at 9½ percent for 30 years. His monthly principal and interest payments were figured at $8.20 per thousand dollars. How much interest had he paid at the end of the 30 years?
   - (A) $127,500
   - (B) $195,200
   - (C) $285,000
   - (D) $310,220

4. A business leases store space for which they pay base rent of $7,200 and 5 percent on sales over $200,000. If last year they paid total rent of $37,465, what was the amount of sales last year?
   - (A) $590,300
   - (B) $605,300
   - (C) $749,300
   - (D) $805,300

5. It is estimated that the reproduction cost of a building 32' by 50' will be $32 per square foot, and that the subject property has depreciated $15,000. What will be the value of the property?
   - (A) $35,200
   - (B) $36,200
   - (C) $41,200
   - (D) $51,200

6. Which of the following proration items is typically paid in arrears?
   - (A) Interest
   - (B) Lease rent
   - (C) FHA points
   - (D) Private mortgage insurance

7. A seller agrees to finance a buyer for $35,000 of the purchase price on an unsecured promissory note. This agreement is entered on the closing statement as which of the following?
   - (A) Debit to buyer; debit to seller
   - (B) Credit to buyer; credit to seller
   - (C) Debit to buyer; credit to seller
   - (D) Credit to buyer; debit to seller

8. Items marked POC (paid outside of closing) may be paid to all **EXCEPT**:
   - (A) seller.
   - (B) lenders.
   - (C) escrow office.
   - (D) appraiser.

9. A buyer offered $140,000 to purchase a house. The buyer offered to pay the seller $15,000 down and $10,000 a year at 12 percent until paid off. What is the appropriate entry on the settlement statement?
   (A) Credit $125,000 to buyer; debit $125,000 to seller
   (B) Debit $125,000 to seller; credit $125,000 to seller
   (C) Credit $140,000 to seller; debit $15,000 to seller
   (D) Debit $140,000 to buyer; credit $10,000 to seller

10. When a buyer is to assume the seller's mortgage balance, escrow is to account for the customer trust account by which entry in the settlement statement?
    (A) Debit buyer
    (B) Credit seller
    (C) Debit buyer; credit seller
    (D) Credit buyer; debit seller

11. The closing statement shows an entry of $64,000 credit to buyer for a loan and a $640 debit for a loan fee. The $64,000 loan is the:
    (A) net loan amount.
    (B) gross loan amount.
    (C) prorated amount.
    (D) adjusted loan amount.

12. All the following expenses are prorated between buyer and seller **EXCEPT**:
    (A) rental income.
    (B) real property tax.
    (C) recording fees.
    (D) assigned insurance policy.

13. In preparing a settlement statement on the sale of a rental property, what is the appropriate entry for any security deposits?
    (A) Debit seller and credit buyer
    (B) Credit seller and debit buyer
    (C) Debit seller only
    (D) Credit buyer only

14. If a house burns to the ground prior to closing, the buyer may do all of the following **EXCEPT**:
    (A) delay closing until seller rebuilds a replacement.
    (B) close the sale and obtain an assignment of the insurance proceeds.
    (C) rescind the contract.
    (D) renegotiate the price if seller agrees.

15. The seller's conveyance document would likely reveal all of the following **EXCEPT**:
    (A) boundaries.
    (B) estate.
    (C) restrictive covenants.
    (D) nonconforming use.

16. If the property already has the maximum improvements permitted under the zoning but the owner wants to add a new structure, the owner would need to first apply for a:
    (A) building permit.
    (B) variance.
    (C) nonconforming use.
    (D) special use permit.

17. All of the following can file a mechanics' lien **EXCEPT**:
    (A) prime contractor.   (C) architect.
    (B) subcontractor.   (D) real estate broker.

18. After a partition of property between two joint tenants in common, the tenancy is:
    (A) entirety.   (C) severalty.
    (B) joint.   (D) common.

19. The principle of "leverage" is involved when a buyer can control an expensive property with a:
    (A) small mortgage.
    (B) 60 percent loan.
    (C) large mortgage.
    (D) no mortgage.

20. Any of the following is protected under the "familial status" provision of the Federal Fair Housing Law **EXCEPT**:
    (A) person who is pregnant.
    (B) person in process of securing legal custody of a child.
    (C) person with a child 19 years old.
    (D) person who has written permission of child's parents to keep temporary custody of child.

21. Which of the following is an acceptable business practice for a real estate agent working with a buyer?
    (A) Filling out a loan application form for the buyer
    (B) Selecting the lender for the borrower
    (C) Advising the buyer about possible loans available in the market
    (D) Co-signing a promissory note in order for the buyer to qualify for a loan

22. Once a licensee has pre-qualified a client, which of the following can the licensee do?
    - (A) Promise the client the availability of a specified loan amount
    - (B) Show the client houses within the probable price range indicated by the pre-qualification
    - (C) Require the client to use a specific lender before the sales contract is drafted and presented to the seller
    - (D) Require the use of the lender who pre-qualified the client

23. *A* owns a duplex building. He occupies one of the units. On what basis may he **NOT** discriminate in renting the other unit?
    - (A) Race
    - (B) Religion
    - (C) National origin
    - (D) Sex

24. Any of the following is required of new multi-family dwellings under the 1988 "handicap" amendments to the Federal Fair Housing Law **EXCEPT**:
    - (A) reasonable modifications at expense of tenant.
    - (B) reasonable accommodations in the rules and policies.
    - (C) premises that are newly designed must meet certain accessibility requirements.
    - (D) lower rent payments charged to handicapped tenants.

25. All of the following supporting documents are normally required by the lender to verify income and employment **EXCEPT**:
    - (A) college transcripts.
    - (B) pay stubs.
    - (C) last two years personal income tax returns.
    - (D) current business financial statements.

26. Which of the following practices is discriminatory under the Federal Fair housing Law?
    - (A) Refusing to make any modifications in a unit that will add to the comfort and safety of a handicapped tenant
    - (B) Refusing permission to a handicapped tenant to make modifications unless the tenant pays the cost
    - (C) Refusing permission to a handicapped tenant to make modifications unless the tenant agrees to restore the premises to approximately the same condition at the end of lease
    - (D) Refusing permission to a tenant who pays the cost and agrees to restore the property to its original condition

27. Which of the following steps can a borrower take to expedite the processing of a loan application?
    - (A) Provide all of the information to the licensee so that the licensee can fill out the application for the borrower
    - (B) Submit all account numbers and branch locations and addresses of banks and lenders with application
    - (C) Provide the lender with a photograph of the borrower
    - (D) Disclose all physical handicaps of borrower

28. A borrower is not obligated to disclose which of the following to a lender when applying for a loan?
    - (A) Receipt of alimony
    - (B) Payment of child support
    - (C) Car loan payments
    - (D) Second mortgage obligations

29. Which type of loan has its interest rate based on some type of index?
    - (A) Adjustable rate mortgage
    - (B) Graduated payment mortgage
    - (C) Rollover mortgage
    - (D) Reverse annuity mortgage

30. Which of the following mortgages has negative amortization?
    - (A) Growing equity mortgage
    - (B) Bi-weekly fixed rate
    - (C) Level payment, fixed rate
    - (D) Reverse annuity mortgage

31. Under RESPA, when escrow is used, how many business days in advance of settlement does the borrower have the right to inspect the HUD-1 Settlement Statement?
    - (A) One day
    - (B) Three days
    - (C) Five days
    - (D) No advance inspection required

32. Under what conditions will a real estate salesperson who drafts a complex original contract for a client be guilty of negligence?
    (A) If the salesperson does not meet the professional standards of a licensed attorney
    (B) If the client fails to make a profit on the deal
    (C) If the salesperson does not have the contract reviewed by his or her employing broker
    (D) If the salesperson fails to get written permission, in advance of drafting the contract, from the Board of REALTORS®

33. A buyer and seller want the agent to draft a purchase money mortgage to include a subordination agreement and a partial release clause. The real estate salesperson should:
    (A) suggest that the parties consult an attorney.
    (B) disclose that this would make the salesperson a mortgage broker.
    (C) fill out a standard purchase money mortgage form.
    (D) obtain the proper language from a bank.

34. If a licensee, who is a buyer's agent, shows an in-house listing, which of the following is true?
    (A) The licensee is a dual agent.
    (B) The buyer is now a "customer."
    (C) The seller is now a "customer."
    (D) The buyer is unrepresented.

35. Which of the following are material facts that must be disclosed by the listing broker?
    (A) The seller is dying of AIDS.
    (B) The building does not conform with tax records.
    (C) The price the seller paid for the property.
    (D) The seller is about to obtain a divorce.

36. All of the following are practical rules in dealing with contingencies EXCEPT:
    (A) make sure the contingency is properly and clearly stated.
    (B) make sure the client diligently adheres to all time provisions.
    (C) obtain all receipts, satisfactions, waivers, approval and failure notices, and other matters in writing.
    (D) require an additional earnest money deposit for each contingency.

37. An "as is" clause is designated to cover:
    (A) disclosed and obvious defects.
    (B) any hidden defects.
    (C) affirmative misrepresentation.
    (D) all property defects.

38. A licensee who is selling an in-house listing and has accepted a power of attorney from the buyer is all of the following EXCEPT:
    (A) a dual agent.
    (B) an attorney-in-fact.
    (C) required to make disclosure of the dual agency to the seller.
    (D) a single agent.

39. Which of the following is the MOST true with respect to the area of fair housing laws?
    (A) Federal law always prevails.
    (B) State law always prevails.
    (C) The law that gives the most protection to the consumer prevails.
    (D) The law that gives the most protection to the home owner prevails.

40. Any of the following can be considered discriminatory advertising EXCEPT:
    (A) ads using words like "private," "integrated" or "traditional."
    (B) a series of ads rising models, but failing to include some representation of other major racial groups.
    (C) advertising limiting housing to people of a particular religion.
    (D) ads for low-income housing.

41. Using several methods of appraisal to arrive at an estimate of value is BEST called:
    (A) reconciliation.
    (B) weighted analysis.
    (C) adjustment.
    (D) assemblage.

42. Changing the zoning from commercial use to single-family residential use is BEST called:
    (A) consolidation.   (C) spot zoning.
    (B) down zoning.   (D) restrictive zoning.

43. The capitalization method is designed to do which of the following?
    (A) Determine net income
    (B) Evaluate commercial joint ventures
    (C) Select the proper capitalization rate
    (D) Convert a property's net income into market value

44. The sublessor is **MOST** likely which one of the following?
    - (A) Tenant
    - (B) Lessee
    - (C) Lessor
    - (D) Owner

45. The lessee would **MOST** likely pay for real property taxes under which type of lease?
    - (A) Percentage
    - (B) Gross
    - (C) Triple net
    - (D) Index

46. The gross rent multiplier is a less reliable measurement of value than the capitalization or cost approach because it does **NOT** consider:
    - (A) location.
    - (B) comparable sales.
    - (C) amenities.
    - (D) extraordinary expenses.

47. What would happen to the value of a fixed-rent property if expenses increased by $8,000, using a capitalization rate of 10 percent?
    - (A) Increases $80,000
    - (B) Decreases $8,000
    - (C) Decreases $80,000
    - (D) No change

48. The Real Estate Settlement Procedures Act requires that the lender do all of the following **EXCEPT**:
    - (A) provide borrower copy of HUD booklet within three business days.
    - (B) allow borrower to inspect HUD settlement statement one business day before settlement.
    - (C) charge a reasonable fee for preparation of RESPA form.
    - (D) provide borrower further estimate of likely settlement charges.

49. Which party benefits most from an assignment of rents provision in a mortgage?
    - (A) Trustee
    - (B) Mortgagee
    - (C) Mortgagor
    - (D) Lessee

50. Any of the following is involved with government's handling of nonconforming uses **EXCEPT**:
    - (A) ban on expanding use.
    - (B) eventual time for use to stop.
    - (C) ban on rebuilding once the structure deteriorates.
    - (D) required to switch to permitted use immediately.

51. Tearing down a corner gas station and convenience store to allow the construction of a shopping center and office building is an example of which appraisal principle?
    - (A) Progression
    - (B) Substitution
    - (C) Highest and best use
    - (D) Regression

52. Compound interest is used in connection with which one of the following types of loans?
    - (A) Partial amortization loan
    - (B) Fully amortized loan
    - (C) Reverse annuity loan
    - (D) Adjustable rate loan

53. The phrase "blind ads" refers to ads that omit:
    - (A) the price of the property.
    - (B) the fact an agent place the ad.
    - (C) the location of the property.
    - (D) the fact the owner is leaving the state.

54. If nothing is stated in a short term apartment lease regarding rent renegotiation, which of the following is true at the end of the lease?
    - (A) Lessor can increase the rent to any amount
    - (B) Mandatory arbitration is required to set the new rent
    - (C) Court appoints a commissioner to set rent
    - (D) Litigation is needed if agreement is not reached within 180 days

55. An elderly retired person is planning his or her estate with the expectation that he or she will live comfortably and then leave all to his or her children. In evaluating the purchase of several properties, this person would be interested most likely in which one of the following appraisal approaches?
    - (A) Capitalization
    - (B) Direct sales comparison
    - (C) Cost
    - (D) Summation

56. A broker purchased one of his or her listings that was on the market for one year. The seller, who was behind in paying taxes and mortgage, carried back a second mortgage at a low rate of interest. The broker paints the house and resells it three months later for a $35,000 profit. How could the broker have reduced the likelihood of a suit by the seller to obtain the $35,000?

(A) Retained an attorney

(B) Used a salesperson to represent him or her

(C) Terminated the listing and advised the seller to retain other counsel

(D) Avoided giving the seller a second mortgage

57. What is the gross rent multiplier if the sales price is $70,000, the gross monthly rent is $525 and the monthly expenses are $125?

(A) .0006   (C) 133.33

(B) .0008   (D) 175

58. In a subdivision with homes in the $140,000 range, a person constructs a home in the $160,000 range. In appraising the new home what appraisal principle would the appraiser need to consider?

(A) Progression   (C) Regression

(B) Reconciliation   (D) Substitution

59. A loan in which the lender agrees not to seek a deficiency judgment against the borrower is best called:

(A) fixed.   (C) adjusted.

(B) non-recourse.   (D) non-monetary.

REVIEW EXAM #3

ANSWERS

1. **D** $130,000 at 6.5 percent = $8,450 = $121,500

2. **B** $42,000
   × .075
   $3,150 + 12 = $262.50/month × 6.5 = $1,706.25

3. **B** 8.20 × 100 = $820/month × 12 = $9,840
   $9,840 × 30 =
   $295,200 − $100,000 = $195,200

4. **D** 37,456
   −7,200
   30,265 + 5% = 605,300 + 200,000 = $805,300

5. **B** 32 × 50 = 1,600 × $32 = 51,200 − $15,000 = $36,200

6. **A** The September mortgage payment, for example, includes the interest for August. FHA points are now paid up front.

7. **D** It is debited to seller because it is money not yet received.

8. **C** The HUD settlement statement is designed to reflect all closing charges, even those that are not paid through the escrow agent.

9. **A** The $125,000 represents the financing carried back by the seller and is used to offset the $140,000 purchase price credited to the seller.

10. **C** The customer trust account (impound or reserve account) is money advanced by the seller to make sure there is enough to pay taxes, condo maintenance fees, insurance and so on. Because the money won't be returned to the seller by the lender until the end of the loan, an adjustment is made at closing and the assuming buyer will be entitled to the refund when the loan is paid off.

11. **B** If the lender deducted the loan fee before depositing the funds into escrow, then the statement would show a credit to buyer of only $63,360.

12. **C** Recording fees are a single-entry expense of either seller or buyer, depending upon custom or agreement.

13. **A** The seller has possession of the tenant's money, which the buyer will have to return to the tenant if the tenant leaves the property in good condition.

14. **A** Seller has the risk of loss until closing so buyer can rescind or accept the deed and insurance proceeds.

15. **D** While the fact a property is nonconforming should be disclosed in the sales contract, it does not appear on the deed.

16. B The owner is looking for an exception to the zoning.

17. D Brokers cannot file a lien for unpaid commission for sales or for rental management.

18. C Each parcel is now held in sole ownership.

19. C The larger the loan amount, the less cash the buyer has invested in the property—the less cash, the greater leverage (or use of other people's money, OPM).

20. C The age of majority under the law is 18.

21. C The agent's role is to give advice, not to make decisions for the buyer.

22. B Because many things can cause a loan to fall through, the agent should caution the buyer not to count on the loan until a final commitment is obtained. Prequalification helps to set the range of properties to preview.

23. A A is exempt under the Federal Fair Housing Law but is still covered by the Civil Rights Act (Racial Discrimination).

24. D The law does not regulate amount of rent.

25. A Lenders are concerned with financial data, not educational background.

26. D The landlord does not have to make modifications to accommodate a handicapped person but does have to agree to modifications paid for by the tenant.

27. B This information is required to obtain a credit history of the borrower.

28. A Payments need to be disclosed, not all sources of income.

29. A The ARM is based on some predetermined index such as the US Treasury Bill rate.

30. D As payments are made, the principal increases. In a GEM the loan is paid off early because principal payments are increased during the term of the loan.

31. A Escrow sends the HUD-1 Settlement Statement, a disclosure document, but no right of rescission exists.

32. A If the salesperson is practicing law without a license, the salesperson is held to the standards of an attorney.

33. A These provisions are too complex for the untrained salesperson and require the use of a legal expert.

34. A As a dual agent, the licensee needs to obtain the written informed consent of both the buyer and seller clients.

35. B This indicates there may be a building code violation. In most states, AIDS is not deemed to be a material fact—disclosure may invade the seller's privacy.

36. D If the buyer fails to meet the contingency despite good faith efforts, the buyer is entitled to return of all the deposit money.

37. A The "as is" clause relates to obvious and disclosed defects. If a seller knows of hidden defects, the "as is" clause won't free the seller of liability for affirmative concealment of such facts.

38. D A single agent represents either a buyer or a seller, never both as in this case.

39. C In some cases state law is more strict than federal law (e.g., federal law doesn't involve "marital status" as a basis for discrimination but state law may).

40. D The fact housing is directed at low-income prospects is not discriminatory. Choice (A) implies that the housing is not open to all.

41. A Different weights are assigned to each method depending on the particular circumstances. Assemblage is the increased value created by consolidating several lots.

42. B Down zoning is a change from a higher use classification to a lower one, often causing a devaluation in property value.

43. **D** This method considers the property's net operating income and the expected return (cap rate) to arrive at an estimate of value.

44. **B** The sublessor is the lessee under the original lease; the tenant occupying the property is the sublessee.

45. **C** Under a net lease the lessee typically pays the carrying charges on the property such as taxes and insurance.

46. **D** If a building incurs large expenses, the gross revenues will bear little relationship to the net.

47. **C** Since rents are fixed, there is an $8,000 loss in income. $8,000 + .10 = $80,000.

48. **C** No fee may be charged by lender for preparing required RESPA forms.

49. **B** The assignment of rents provision allows the mortgagee (lender) to collect rent during the default of the loan.

50. **D** Laws generally permit the nonconforming use to continue until such time as the structure needs to be rebuilt.

51. **C** Highest and best use is that use which at a given time produces the best net return for the property.

52. **C** Under a reverse annuity loan, the lender pays the borrower a certain amount each month. The borrower eventually will pay back principal plus interest on the interest portion of the payments.

53. **B** Licensing laws require that brokers placing ads must identify themselves as licensees; otherwise, a buyer might think this was a "for sale by owner."

54. **A** At the end of the lease the landlord is not required to renegotiate, unless the lease contains specific provisions.

55. **A** The capitalization or income approach analyzes the net operating income and the expected rate of return on the investment.

56. **C** The risk of buying an in-house listing is that the seller will later claim breach of the fiduciary duties of loyalty and full disclosure. While not foolproof, the best technique is to terminate the agency relationship and advise the seller to retain an attorney or another broker.

57. **C** $70,000 + 525 = 133.33.

58. **C** Regression states that as between dissimilar properties, the worth of the better property is adversely affected by the presence of the lesser-quality property. Progression is the opposite.

59. **B** The lender agrees to limit its recovery to the money generated at the foreclosure sale. Some states have antideficiency legislation to curb selling at speculative prices.

Get the Performance Advantage on the job. . .*in the classroom*

Order Number	Real Estate Principles and Exam Prep	Qty.	Price	Total Amount
1. 1510-01	Modern Real Estate Practice, 12th edition	___	$34.95	___
2. 1510-02	Study Guide for Modern Real Estate Practice, 12th edition	___	$13.95	___
3. 1961-01	Language of Real Estate, 3rd edition	___	$28.95	___
4. 1610-07	Real Estate Math, 4th edition	___	$15.95	___
5. 1512-10	Mastering Real Estate Mathematics, 5th edition	___	$25.95	___
6. 1970-04	Questions & Answers To Help You Pass the Real Estate Exam, 4th edition	___	$21.95	___
7. 1970-06	Real Estate Exam Guide: ASI, 3rd edition	___	$21.95	___
8. 1970-09	Guide to Passing the PSI Real Estate Exam	___	$21.95	___

Advanced Study/Specialty Areas

		Qty.	Price	Total Amount
9. 1560-08	Agency Relationships in Real Estate	___	$25.95	___
10. 1978-03	Buyer Agency: Your Competitive Edge Real Estate	___	$25.95	___
11. 1557-10	Essentials of Real Estate Finance, 6th edition	___	$38.95	___
12. 1559-01	Essentials of Real Estate Investment, 4th edition	___	$38.95	___
13. 1556-13	Exam Preparation for the Residential Appraiser Certification	___	$34.95	___
14. 1556-10	Fundamentals of Real Estate Appraisal, 5th edition	___	$38.95	___
15. 1556-14	How to Use the Uniform Residential Appraisal Report	___	$24.95	___
16. 1556-15	Introduction to Income Property Appraisal	___	$34.95	___
17. 1556-11	Language of Real Estate Appraisal	___	$21.95	___
18. 1557-15	Modern Residential Financing Methods, 2nd edition	___	$19.95	___
19. 1556-12	Questions & Answers to Help You Pass the Real Estate Appraisal Exams	___	$26.95	___
20. 1551-10	Property Management, 4th edition	___	$35.95	___
21. 1560-01	Real Estate Law, 3rd edition	___	$38.95	___

Sales & Marketing/Professional Development

		Qty.	Price	Total Amount
22. 1913-04	Close for Success	___	$18.95	___
23. 1927-05	Fast Start in Real Estate	___	$12.95	___
24. 1916-11	Finding & Buying Your Place in the Country	___	$24.95	___
25. 1909-06	New Home Selling Strategies: A Handbook for Success	___	$24.95	___
26. 1913-01	List for Success	___	$18.95	___
27. 1922-06	Negotiating Commercial Real Estate Leases	___	$34.95	___
28. 1913-11	Phone Power	___	$19.95	___
29. 1926-03	Power Real Estate Letters	___	$29.95	___
30. 1907-01	Power Real Estate Listing, 2nd edition	___	$18.95	___
31. 1907-04	Power Real Estate Negotiation	___	$19.95	___
32. 1907-02	Power Real Estate Selling, 2nd edition	___	$18.95	___
33. 1965-01	Real Estate Brokerage: A Success Guide, 3rd edition	___	$35.95	___
34. 1913-13	The Real Estate Sales Survival Kit	___	$24.95	___
35. 1978-02	Recruiting Revolution in Real Estate	___	$34.95	___
36. 1903-31	Sold! The Professional's Guide to Real Estate Auctions	___	$32.95	___
37. 2703-11	Time Out: Time Management Strategies for the Real Estate Professional	___	$19.95	___
38. 1909-04	Winning in Commercial Real Estate Sales	___	$24.95	___

NEW! Audio Tapes

		Qty.	Price	Total Amount
39. 1926-06	Power Real Estate Listings	___	$19.95	___
40. 1926-05	Power Real Estate Selling	___	$19.95	___
41. 1926-04	Staying on Top in Real Estate	___	$14.95	___

Book total ___
Tax ___
Shipping and Handling ___
Less $1.00 off if you fax order ___
Total amount ___

810081

Shipping/Handling Charges:
$0-24.99	$4
$25-49.99	$5
$50-99.99	$6
$100-249.99	$8

Order shipped to the following states must include applicable sales tax:
CA, FL,IL & NY

Real Estate Education Company

Place your order today! **By FAX: 1-312-836-1021**. Or call **1-800-437-9002, ext. 650**
In Illinois, call 1-312-836-4400, ext. 650. Mention code 810081. Or fill out and mail this order form to:
Real Estate Education Company, 520 North Dearborn Street, Chicago, Illinois 60610-4354

Your Satisfaction is Guaranteed!

All books come with a 30 day money-back guarantee. If you are not completely satisfied, simply return your books in saleable condition and your money will be refunded in full.

☐ Please send me the Real Estate Education Company catalog featuring your full list of titles.
Prices are subject to change without notice.

**Fill out form and mail today!
Or Save $1.00 when you order by Fax:
312-836-1021.**

Name _____

Address _____

City/State/Zip _____

Telephone _____

Payment must accompany all orders (check one):

☐ Check or money order (payable to Dearborn Financial Publishing, Inc.)
520 North Dearborn Street, Chicago, Illinois 60610-4354

☐ Charge to my credit card: ☐ VISA   ☐ MasterCard

Account No. _____ Exp. Date _____

Signature _____
(All charge orders must be signed.)   **5-92**

Return Address:

_____

_____

BUSINESS REPLY MAIL

FIRST CLASS   PERMIT NO. 88176   CHICAGO, IL

POSTAGE WILL BE PAID BY ADDRESSEE:

**Real Estate
Education Company**
Order Department
520 North Dearborn Street
Chicago, Illinois 60610-9857

No Postage
Necessary
if Mailed
in the
United States

IMPORTANT · PLEASE FOLD OVER · PLEASE TAPE BEFORE MAILING

NOTE: This page, when folded over and taped, becomes a postage-free envelope, which has been approved by the United States Postal Service. It is provided for your convenience.

IMPORTANT · PLEASE FOLD OVER · PLEASE TAPE BEFORE MAILING